The Foremost Man of the Kingdom

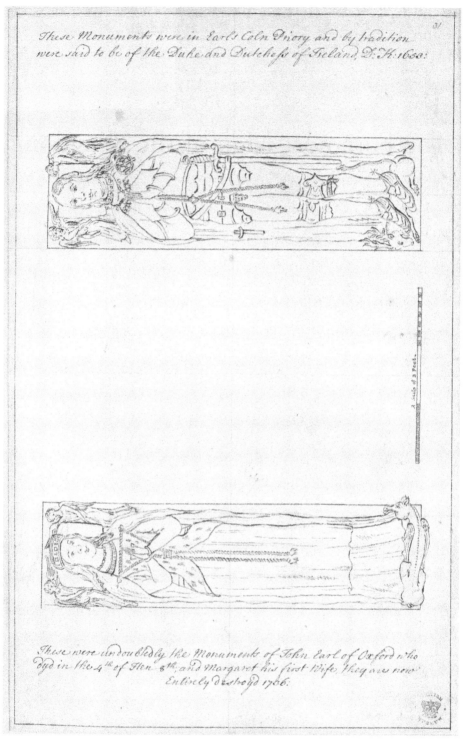

The tomb of John, thirteenth earl of Oxford and his first wife Margaret Neville from a drawing by Daniel King in 1653, now in the British Library, London, Additional MS 27348, p. 31.

The Foremost Man of the Kingdom

John de Vere, Thirteenth Earl of Oxford (1442–1513)

James Ross

THE BOYDELL PRESS

First published as *John de Vere,*
Thirteenth Earl of Oxford (1442–1513) 2011
The Boydell Press, Woodbridge
Paperback edition 2015

ISBN 978 1 84383 614 8 hardback
ISBN 978 1 78327 005 7 paperback

The Boydell Press is an imprint of Boydell & Brewer Ltd
PO Box 9, Woodbridge, Suffolk IP12 3DF, UK
and of Boydell & Brewer Inc.
668 Mt Hope Avenue, Rochester, NY 14620–2731, USA
website: www.boydellandbrewer.com

The publisher has no responsibility for the continued existence or accuracy
of URLs for external or third-party internet websites referred to in this book,
and does not guarantee that any content on such websites is,
or will remain, accurate or appropriate.

A CIP catalogue record for this book is available
from the British Library

Contents

List of Illustrations

FOR C.D.R.

Acknowledgements

This study has been long in the making, firstly working on the de Vere family in the later Middle Ages more generally, and latterly refocusing and substantially expanding that work to focus on the thirteenth earl in particular. One cannot work for so long without incurring a great number of debts, both to friends and family outside the historical field, and to friends and colleagues within it, which it is a great pleasure to acknowledge now. I am very grateful to Merton College, Oxford, and the Richard III society for funding my graduate research, and particular thanks go to Rowena Archer, who supervised my thesis and to whom this work still owes so much.

Access to the private collection at Raynham Hall was kindly permitted by the Marquess Townshend, and I am grateful to the staff there for their help and co-operation. I would like to thank the History of Parliament Trust for allowing me access to as yet unpublished biographies, to Colin Richmond to passing me some of Roger Virgoe's notes on the de Veres and to Carole Rawcliffe for a copy of Susan Flower's introduction to her sadly uncompleted thesis on the de Vere council in the later Middle Ages. I am grateful to Ralph Griffiths and the late Rees Davies for the suggestion of publishing a biography on the thirteenth earl. In addition to those thanked at specific points within this work, for more general advice, suggestions and references in the last few years, my thanks go to Adrian Ailes, Paul Cavill, Linda Clark, Steven Gunn, Samantha Harper, Jonathan Mackman, Stephen O'Connor and Simon Payling.

Particular thanks must go to my mother, Anne Crawford, whose support has been on both the familial and the academic level, to Sean Cunningham for numerous references and freely sharing his expertise on the reign of Henry VII over the last few years, to Ralph Griffiths who read part of this work in draft and offered much support and advice, and to Hannes Kleineke, who, in addition to much help over the years on diverse historical issues, read and commented on an early draft on this book.

Friends and colleagues have supported and helped me during the lengthy process of completing this work. Most of all, I am grateful to Anna, who has lived with the thirteenth earl of Oxford for as long as Margaret Neville did between 1463 and 1471, and who has always encouraged me and never complained at the length of time I spent at my desk.

Abbreviations

All manuscript references are to The National Archives: Public Record Office, London, unless otherwise stated.

BIHR or *HR*	*Bulletin of the Institute of Historical Research*, now *Historical Research*
Bindoff	*History of Parliament: the Commons, 1509–1558*, ed. S.T. Bindoff (4 vols, London, 1982)
BL	British Library, London
Bodleian	Bodleian Library, Oxford
CCR	*Calendar of the Close Rolls*
CChR	*Calendar of the Charter Rolls*
CFR	*Calendar of the Fine Rolls*
CIM	*Calendar of Inquisitions Miscellaneous*
CIPM	*Calendar of Inquisitions Post Mortem*
CIPM Henry VII	*Calendar of Inquisitions Post Mortem for the Reign of Henry VII* (3 vols)
CP	G.E. Cokayne, *The Complete Peerage*, ed. V.H. Gibbs *et al.* (14 vols, in 15, London, 1910–1998)
CPR	*Calendar of the Patent Rolls*
Econ HR	*Economic History Review*
EETS	Early English Text Society
EHR	*English Historical Review*
ERO	Essex Record Office, Chelmsford
Household Books	*Household Books of John, Duke of Norfolk and Thomas, Earl of Surrey* [recte John, earl of Oxford], *temp. 1481–1490*, ed. J.P. Collier (Roxburghe Club, 1844)
'Last Testament'	W.H. StJ. Hope, 'The Last Testament and Inventory of John de Veer, Thirteenth Earl of Oxford', *Archaeologia*, lxvi (1914–15), 310–348
LP	*Letters and Papers, Foreign and Domestic, of the Reign of Henry VIII*
NRO	Norfolk Record Office, Norwich
ODNB	*Oxford Dictionary of National Biography*, general editors C. Matthew, B. Harrison and L. Goldman (online edition, 2004 – present)
Parliament Rolls	*Parliament Rolls of Medieval England, 1275–1504*, general editor C. Given Wilson (16 vols, Woodbridge, 2005)
PL	*The Paston Letters*, ed. J. Gairdner (6 vols, Library ed., London, 1904)

PLP	*Paston Letters and Papers of the Fifteenth Century*, ed. N. Davis (2 vols, Oxford, 1971–6)
PPC	*Proceedings and Ordinances of the Privy Council of England*, ed. N.H. Nicolas (7 vols, London, 1834–7)
RH	Raynham Hall, Norfolk [The archive was briefly catalogued by the Historical Manuscripts Commission, by box and location within the archive, the system that has been followed in this work, but the documents within each box were not numbered]
Roskell	*History of Parliament: The House of Commons, 1386–1421*, ed. J.S. Roskell, L. Clark and C. Rawcliffe (4 vols, Stroud, 1992)
SRO	Suffolk Record Office, Ipswich branch
TEAS	*Transactions of the Essex Archaeological Society*, now *Essex Archaeology and History*
TRHS	*Transactions of the Royal Historical Society*
VCH	*Victoria County History*
WAM	Westminster Abbey Muniments
Wedgwood	J.C. Wedgwood, *The History of Parliament, 1439–1509* (2 vols, London, 1936)

Introduction

John de Vere, thirteenth earl of Oxford, was the last great medieval nobleman. Earl of Oxford for fifty years, subject of no fewer than six kings of England during one of the most turbulent periods of English history, de Vere's career included more changes of fortune than almost any other. His life might be used as an exemplar for the widespread medieval idea of a wheel of fortune: 'Fortune is like a turning wheel – one moment she suddenly lifts a man up, the next she throws him down, and conversely she raises the man who is prostrate and trodden in the dust more generously than he could have hoped.'[1] He suffered personal tragedy as a teenager, with the execution of his father and brother, and a decade in prison in Hammes castle, yet enjoyed twenty-five years as perhaps the 'foremost man of the kingdom'.[2] It is this latter period after 1485 that is perhaps the most important to the historian. None of the salient features of his public career are necessarily associated with the nobility of the reign of Henry VII. Semi-independent ruler of a large region of England, whose regional position was not solely dependent on royal favour, though he maintained good relations with the first Tudor king, he possessed one of the highest incomes in England, which, though boosted by royal patronage, was based mainly on a huge private estate; equally he was a trusted military lieutenant, who put his life at risk for his king at three major battles.

This study is a biography in the sense that it focuses on one man's public career. It cannot be a rounded assessment of an individual. Tony Pollard, writing on Warwick, states that the materials for a biography 'rarely exist for any medieval figure … we thus see the man almost entirely through his actions and public persona'.[3] While something can be said on the earl of Oxford's personality, piety, and interests from the patchy evidence, and on the style in which he lived from household accounts and the inventory of his goods after his death, the best illustrated aspects of his important life are inevitably his involvement in local, regional, national and foreign politics, and it is on these that this study focuses, placed within the context of the English political world of the late fifteenth and early sixteenth centuries. The purpose of this book is threefold: to illuminate the

---

[1] *The Ecclesiastical History of Orderic Vitalis*, ed. M. Chibnall (6 vols, Oxford, 1968–80), vi, 242. For a discussion of the concept of fortune's wheel, see J.S. Bothwell, *Falling from Grace. Reversal of Fortune and the English Nobility, 1075–1485* (Manchester, 2008), chap. 1.
[2] A loose translation of 'le principal personnaige de ce royaulme', a description of Oxford by Flemish ambassadors to England, 7 December 1508: *Letters and Papers Illustrative of the Reigns of Richard III and Henry VII*, ed. J. Gairdner (2 vols, Rolls Series, 1861), i, 371.
[3] A.J. Pollard, *Warwick the Kingmaker* (London, 2007), 6.

career of one of the leading lights of the Wars of the Roses; to reconsider the power and role of the aristocracy in the reign of Henry VII; and to complete the political story of East Anglia in the fifteenth century.

The structure, conditioned by the evidence, is partly chronological and partly thematic. The chronology of the earl's national career is contained within two chapters on the period between 1462 and 1485, and on Henry VII's reign. Rather than repeat certain themes within chronological sections, it seemed best to deal with the topics of the earl's estates and income, his affinity, his role in East Anglia, and what can be gleaned on his interests, home life and personality, within four thematic chapters, though all four of these chapters focus on the period after 1485, so sparse are the sources for such matters before that date.

The first chapter places John de Vere into the context of his family background, and the second covers his eventful career between his accession to the earldom and Bosworth.[4] The contrast of the eventful career of the thirteenth earl of Oxford with those of his predecessors is striking. The twelfth earl was a moderately wealthy, generally apolitical, provincial lord and occasional soldier; the thirteenth was one of the most powerful of late medieval noblemen. This was not simply a result of the peculiar political circumstances of 1461–1485 and after, but also of familial and territorial factors that benefit from greater exploration. Why the twelfth earl, having sat out the battles of 1459–61, became embroiled in a plot for which he was executed in 1462, and the key role that the execution of his father and brother in 1462 played in the thirteenth earl's political decisions, are essential to the understanding of the earl's early political career; equally they allow a fresh assessment of his political affiliations and offer a necessary corrective to often simplistic attributions of loyalty.

The historiography of Henry VII's reign is a problematic area.[5] With certain notable exceptions, many works either treat Henry's reign as a footnote to the Wars of the Roses, or as the preface to Henry VIII's reign, despite recent scholarship stressing the continuities of the period 1471–1529.[6] Two particular historiographical problems emerge in relation to the nobility. Much of the research, important though it is, has focused on the centre – on the increasing power of the fisc, on administrative innovations such as the court of Star Chamber or the changing nature of the privy chamber, on the courtiers and new men around the king, and on Henry VII himself – rather than on the most critical relationship of all for Henry's government, that of the king and his nobility in their regions.[7]

---

[4] Work on his early career includes an accurate factual account by C.L. Scofield, 'The Early Life of John de Vere, Earl of Oxford', *EHR*, xxxix (1914), 228–45. More nuanced is the good summary by S.J. Gunn, 'Vere, John de, thirteenth earl of Oxford (1442–1513)', *ODNB*.

[5] S.J. Gunn, 'Henry VII in Context: Problems and Possibilities', *History*, xcii (2007), 312.

[6] J.L. Watts, 'Introduction: History, the Fifteenth Century and the Renaissance', in *The End of the Middle Ages? England in the Fifteenth and Sixteenth Centuries*, ed. J.L. Watts (Stroud, 1998), 15–17.

[7] This is particularly true of many of the articles in the 2009 special edition of *Historical*

Even the most deservedly influential article on the reign, by Margaret Condon, in discussing the ruling elites focuses only on the nobility at court, and specifically notes that 'nor is more than passing consideration given to the power and status of the nobility at the local level', which is entirely understandable given the size of the topic and her focus on the court.[8] Yet it is precisely their local power that gave most of the nobility their national authority, as Condon acknowledges. When the nobility and the crown are the subject of study, discussion usually focuses around the king's alleged use of bonds and recognizances as a weapon against them.[9] Questions have been recently posited as to the extent to which the nobility were enmeshed in a financial web, but in any case any such mechanistic contacts between king and magnate can only ever have been part of the story, and a thorough overview of the subject of the relationship between crown and nobility is lacking, although the scale of that undertaking 'would make a lengthy book in its own right'.[10] A further problem, which may be part of the reason for the peerage not being the focus of much of the historiography, is that several of the leading noblemen of the reign, such as Jasper Tudor, duke of Bedford, Thomas Stanley, earl of Derby, and, until now, John de Vere, earl of Oxford, await in-depth study in print.[11] This is compounded by a something of a dearth

Research on Henry VII, ed. M.R. Horowitz, and what was until recently the standard biography of the king: S.B. Chrimes, *Henry VII* (London, 1972). Sean Cunningham's recent study, *Henry VII* (Abingdon, 2007) has a far more nuanced view of Henry and his nobility, arguing, p. 192, that 'the extensive connections of the great families … presented a deeply entrenched structure of county government that the Tudor crown had no intention of deconstructing or threatening', but that Henry was 'concerned to achieve crown control over the noble-gentry connections that made local society work well, but also caused most disruption when social links were abused'. For Henry VII and his nobility, see also C. Carpenter, *The Wars of the Roses. Politics and the Constitution in England, c. 1437–1509* (Cambridge, 1997), 221–36.

[8] M.M. Condon, 'Ruling Elites in the Reign of Henry VII', in *Patronage, Pedigree and Power in Later Medieval England*, ed. C.D. Ross (Gloucester, 1979), 110.

[9] For example, J.R. Lander, 'Bonds, Coercion and Fear: Henry VII and the Peerage', in idem, *Crown and Nobility, 1450–1509* (London, 1976), 267–300; T.B. Pugh, 'Henry VII and the English Nobility', in *The Tudor Nobility*, ed. G.W. Bernard (Manchester, 1992), 49–111, largely a refutation of Lander's arguments; M.R. Horowitz, 'Policy and Prosecution in the Reign of Henry VII', *Historical Research*, lxxxii (2009), 412–58.

[10] S. Cunningham, 'Loyalty and the Usurper: Recognizances, the Council and Allegiance under Henry VII', *Historical Research*, lxxxii (2009), 474; Cunningham, *Henry VII*, 173 (quote).

[11] Valuable work has been done on some members of the higher nobility during Henry VII's reign: M.J. Tucker, *The Life of Thomas Howard, Earl of Surrey and Second Duke of Norfolk, 1443–1524* (The Hague, 1964); B.J. Harris, *Edward Stafford, Third Duke of Buckingham, 1478–1521* (Stanford, CA, 1986); R.S. Thomas, 'The Political Career, Estates and Connection of Jasper Tudor, Earl of Pembroke and Duke of Bedford (d. 1495)' (Unpublished PhD thesis, University of Wales, Swansea, 1971) has a brief chapter on Jasper's role after 1485; B. Coward, *The Stanleys, Lord Stanleys and Earls of Derby, 1385–1672* (Manchester, 1983) covers the first earl briskly; and Sean Cunningham has illustrated the royal crackdown on Stanley power after the first earl's death: 'Henry VII, Sir Thomas Butler and the Stanley Family: Regional Politics and the Assertion of Royal Influence in North-West England, 1471–1521', in *Social*

of regional or county studies focusing on the reign of the first Tudor to match those covering the earlier part of the fifteenth century, which have done so much to demonstrate the dialogue between centre and region, rather than just dictation from former to latter.[12] It is worth remembering one of the key tenets of the doyen of late medievalists, K.B. McFarlane, uttered as long ago as 1953, that historians have usually been too much the 'King's Friends' and that the nobility should be assessed on their own terms, rather than viewed through the prism of royal power.[13] The power of the first Tudor king looks rather different when viewed from the perspective of Suffolk, Warwickshire or Cheshire rather than Westminster.

The central portion of this work, therefore, concentrates on de Vere's local power in East Anglia, and on his role at the heart of the Tudor polity – as a battlefield commander, as the man responsible for the political security of East Anglia, and for raising and leading its troops. As a man unaffected by the financial clampdown at the end of the reign it provides a contrast with one or two well known case studies, and also assesses his personal relationship with the king. The case for a substantial delegation of royal power from the king to the earl, leading to regional governance by the king's command, is made. No one case study can provide definitive answers to broad questions on Henry VII and the English nobility, but, at least in the case of John de Vere, Christine Carpenter's view that 'Henry VII's instincts were not to trust them [the nobility], and therefore to exploit their power only as far as he had to' does not hold true.[14]

A study of almost any medieval nobleman is to some extent a study of his locality. John de Vere's powerbase was regional, rather than just restricted to a county (or two), as most other noblemen were. The tendency among historians to focus on single counties rather than regions has tended to hide some of the complexity of noble power, although there are some notable exceptions such as Tony Pollard's work on the north east, particularly with reference to the regional lordship of the duke of Gloucester, but the breadth of de Vere's power

<hr />

Attitudes and Political Structures in the Fifteenth Century, ed. T. Thornton (Stroud, 2000), 220–41. Other good studies of members of the higher nobility include S.J. Gunn, 'Henry Bourgchier, Earl of Essex, 1477–1540', in *The Tudor Nobility*, ed. G.W. Bernard (Manchester, 1992), 134–79; M.E. James, 'A Tudor Magnate and the Tudor State. Henry Fifth Earl of Northumberland', *Borthwick Papers*, xxx (York, 1966). Although the focus is more on the reign of Henry VIII than Henry VII, G.W. Bernard, *The Power of the Early Tudor Nobility: A Study of the Fourth and Fifth Earls of Shrewsbury* (Brighton, 1985) is an important study.

[12] The most influential of those covering (part) of Henry's reign is C. Carpenter, *Locality and Polity. A Study of Warwickshire Landed Society, 1401–99* (Cambridge, 1992). Cunningham's *Henry VII*, chapter 7 contains valuable, if necessarily brief, studies of Kent, the north west and East Anglia.

[13] K.B. McFarlane, *The Nobility of Later Medieval England* (Oxford, 1973), 2–3.

[14] Carpenter, *Wars of the Roses*, 226, though she does acknowledge de Vere's role in East Anglia, 225.

was unusual.[15] This work therefore focuses on a region, labelled throughout as 'East Anglia', embracing not just Norfolk and Suffolk, but also Cambridgeshire, parts of Hertfordshire, and Essex, the heartland of de Vere influence. This is less a revisionist redrawing of regional maps, though broader perspectives than just a county or two offer interesting insights, but more a shorthand for the territorial interest of the de Veres by the late fifteenth century. It also has some basis in the geography, land-owning characteristics and socio-economic structures. southern Essex and southern Hertfordshire, areas in the London hinterland, were somewhat atypical of the region, but northern Essex, Suffolk, Norfolk, much of Cambridgeshire and parts of Hertfordshire form a relatively coherent whole. The region was an unusually prosperous, proto-industrial area, buoyed by the profits of the cloth trade. This trade was the key factor in East Anglia's wealth by the end of the Middle Ages, with leading centres such as Norwich, Lavenham and Colchester providing much of the region's output.[16] This led to a relatively high population density, a relatively high percentage of waged and mobile artisan labourers, compared to agriculturists, and a comparatively highly commercialized economy since a fair percentage of the population were paid in cash, and bought their daily bread, rather than growing it themselves.[17] Yet this was encompassed within a traditional land-owning structure, and the region was crowded with resident lay and temporal lords – dukes of Norfolk and Suffolk, earls of Essex and Oxford, the Lords Fitzwalter and Scales, bishops of Norwich and Ely, mitred abbots of St Albans, Bury St Edmunds and Colchester, and wealthy and powerful gentry, including men like Sir John Fastolf, Sir John Tyrell, and by the end of the period, Sir John Paston III.

However, this diverse, wealthy, and politically advanced region was dominated throughout Henry VII's reign by the thirteenth earl of Oxford. Part of the reason for this was the vast estates the earl owned in East Anglia, and the earl's overall income, from land, royal patronage and profits of office, was much greater than has previously been realized. Further chapters discuss the earl's relationships with the East Anglian towns and with the nobility, especially the Howards, his role in suppressing disorder, and, crucially, the extent of his lordship among the gentry of the region. As the Paston family's 'good lord' for nearly three decades, the book also has new light to cast on many of the Paston letters, and on that famous family.

Lastly, this study looks at the domestic life and familial relationships of the earl. The survival of certain sources, particularly his will and household expense accounts, allow some insight into his daily life, surrounded by a bustling household numbering well over one hundred men, and his interests, including music

---

[15] A.J. Pollard, *North-Eastern England During the Wars of the Roses. Lay Society, War, and Politics, 1450–1500* (Oxford, 1990).

[16] R.H. Britnell, *Growth and Decline in Colchester, 1300–1525* (Cambridge, 1986), 188–9.

[17] L.R. Poos, *A Rural Society after the Black Death: Essex, 1350–1525* (Cambridge, 1991), 21–3; C. Dyer, *Standards of Living in the Later Middle Ages* (Cambridge, 1989), 213.

and entertainment, as well as the outward (financial) manifestations of his piety, such as his patronage to religious institutions and provision for masses to be said for his soul. Evidence from letters, the settlement of his estates, and other business transactions also can demonstrate something of his view of familial relationships and a strong sense of his lineage and dynasty. The inventory of his goods made after his death gives a sense of the magnificent style in which he lived and the clothes and jewels he owned. Nonetheless, his inner thoughts and elements of his character remain opaque to the historian.

Sources

The historian of the Wars of the Roses, and particularly Henry VII's reign is not blessed by many sources that offer much insight into the actions of individuals, nor often into political events that such individuals helped to shape. As Steven Gunn has recently put it: 'the sort of sources medievalists are accustomed to using thin out, while the sort early modernists are accustomed to using are too frail to bear much weight'.[18] The records of one of the two great government departments, the exchequer, are much thinner than earlier in the fifteenth century, as a consequence of the re-routing of much of the royal finances through the King's chamber, which left rather sparse documentation. The great collection of what are now known as the State Papers, which commence around 1509, are within a few years of this date beginning to offer a level of detailed insight into political events that can turn a medieval historian positively green with envy, though such a source has not noticeably led to harmony and agreement among historians of Henry VIII's reign. The chronicles are less informative than for many earlier periods, and they have their own agendas. Even the most detailed near contemporary narrative, the *Anglica Historia* of Polydore Vergil, consciously or unconsciously, seriously underplayed the role of the nobility in political events during Henry VII's reign. The three great noblemen of the first half of the reign, the earls of Derby, Pembroke and Oxford, are mentioned only five times in the manuscript version in total, and nine times in the printed edition.[19]

This study nonetheless makes use of these increasingly frail chronicle and national administrative sources, as all work on later medieval political and social history must do.[20] It also attempts to use the most problematic of governmental

[18] Gunn, 'Henry VII in Context', 302. Similar points are made in Christine Carpenter, 'Henry VII and the English Polity', in *The Reign of Henry VII*, ed. B. Thompson (Stamford, 1995), 11–12.

[19] *The Anglica Historia of Polydore Vergil, A.D. 1485–1537*, ed. D. Hay (Camden Society, third series, lxxiv, 1950), 4, 20, 74–75, 80. The printed version in Hay's edition adds the three men on pages 5, 10–11, 22, 52. All three men are obviously mentioned in the portion of the work dealing with pre-1485 events.

[20] For the general poverty of the fifteenth century chronicles as a political source, see A.

sources, the voluminous records of the Westminster law courts. The use of the legal records is hardly new, and certain county studies and some prosopographical works, most notably the History of Parliament, use the legal records extensively, but not all studies of the nobility could claim the same. Moreover, a certain degree of caution, above and beyond that necessary with source material, must be adopted in the use of such records in studying the nobility. It is often extremely difficult, if not impossible, to ascertain the facts behind contradictory pleadings. Moreover, bringing a case at common law and adhering to the law while pursuing such a case was only one of several possible approaches rather than representing the only way forward. Alternatives included violence, bribery or intimidation of jurors, justices of the peace or sheriffs, or asking for royal interference in the judicial process. The full picture is rarely traceable solely in the records of the courts.

Furthermore, the nobility are under-represented in the legal sources. The nobility, unlike the gentry, were very unlikely to appear as defendants – it took another noble or a very brave knight, esquire or merchant to sue a peer in the plea side of King's Bench or in Common Pleas, nor was the crown usually keen to bring criminal cases against the nobility except in exceptional circumstances. Just occasionally it is possible to see a magnate appearing much more frequently in court: the ability to look for remedies only via the common law was a sign of vulnerability rather than strength, however. The women of the Howard family, the countess of Surrey and the duchess of Norfolk, appear rather more frequently in the legal records between 1485 and 1489, with the first Howard duke dead at Bosworth, and his son, the earl of Surrey, attainted and imprisoned in the Tower, than they do in the period following Surrey's pardon and release.

This would be a thin work based solely on national administrative and legal sources. There are two other types of evidence on which this study draws heavily. The extant documents emanating from the earl's own circle and administration allow some conclusions to be reached regarding the finances and affinity of the earls of Oxford in the fifteenth century. The most useful types of financial documents, both for assessing income, expenditure and the earl's following, are valors, and the annual accounts of the receiver-general and the steward of the household. However, even by the standards of a very poor survival rate of all such types of documents, one receiver-general's account, two household expense accounts, and one damaged valor, represents a below average return for the thirty-five years that the earl was resident in England and in control of his own estates. Other documents provide different types of information. The earl made many enfeoffments over his long career and such business actions provide evidence of association, and in the entrusting of important estates to men who would be responsible for the revenues and the descent of the estates after the

Gransden, *Historical Writing in England: c.1307 to the Early Sixteenth Century* (London, 1982), especially chap. 9, and 466–70; Carpenter, *Wars of the Roses*, 4–5.

earl's death, there is an implication of confidence in the individuals concerned: the enfeoffments might not certify genuine commitment of a feoffee to the earl's interests, but they are certainly suggestive.[21] While a singular pair of documents, the earl's last will and testament provide much practical detail concerning his retaining, his household, and his estates, as well as some hints as to his personal interests and beliefs, even if the will, as with all others, must be treated with caution, as preparations for life after death are not necessarily the most reliable indicators as to how life was lived.

The major source that differentiates this work on John de Vere from other studies of the late medieval nobility is the Paston letters. If not always at the centre of de Vere affinities, the family's connections over fifty years with the de Veres ensure that their correspondence is hugely valuable in understanding the actions of the earls of Oxford in the second half of the fifteenth century. This is particularly true after 1485 when John Paston III was the earl's Norfolk steward, his deputy admiral, and factotum in that corner of the world, and while his brother William was part of the earl's household. Unequivocally, the letters by the earl to the Pastons would have been mirrored in other correspondence with other families in the earl's circle, and in those of other noblemen with gentry families up and down the country. Yet the Paston letters are nearly unique in their survival, and likely to have been dissimilar in their volume, detail, and insightfulness, as a result of the fact that the Paston family themselves were probably atypical of their fellows, because of the rapid rise of the family and their tendency to end up on the wrong side of legal verdicts and local violence. There are fifteen surviving letters from the earl and his countess, and two written to him, in the Paston collection between 1485 and 1503 alone, and the earl is mentioned in many more, as are others in his circle, and national politics events that affected the Pastons' lord produced copious correspondence.[22] While the Paston letters and the Paston family have had much analysis recently, they have not been systematically used to assess the de Veres as East Anglian lords or national political figures. No other nobleman at this period, with the exception

---

[21] M.A. Hicks, *Bastard Feudalism* (Harlow, 1995), 66–8.

[22] I have generally preferred to use Gairdner's edition, for ease of reference in the chronological arrangement, though Davis's modern edition is very valuable in its more scholarly approach: *The Paston Letters*, ed. J. Gairdner (6 vols, London, 1904); *Paston Letters and Papers of the Fifteenth Century*, ed. N. Davis (2 vols, Oxford, 1971–6). A third volume, comprising primarily business papers relating to Sir John Fastolf, has recently been published: *Paston Letters and Papers of the Fifteenth Century: Part III*, ed. R. Beadle and C.F. Richmond (EETS, xxii, 2005).
Recent historical work on the family includes the accessible study by Helen Castor, *Blood and Roses* (London, 2004), and the superbly detailed and insightful trilogy by Colin Richmond: *The Paston Family in the Fifteenth Century: The First Phase* (Cambridge, 1990); *The Paston Family in the Fifteenth Century: Fastolf's Will* (Cambridge, 1996); *The Paston Family in the Fifteenth Century: Endings* (Manchester, 2000).

of the fourth earl of Northumberland, has such a surviving corpus of correspondence from someone in their close circle, and as a source for the thirteenth earl of Oxford the Paston letters add much meat to the bare bones of chronicles, legal records, and financial accounts.[23]

---

[23] There are eighteen surviving letters from Henry Percy to successive heads of the Plumpton family between 1470 and 1489: *The Plumpton Letters and Papers*, ed. J. Kirby (Camden Society, fifth series, viii, 1996), 45–84. However, it would be fair to say that the Paston correspondence is generally more revealing concerning local politics.

PART I

THE DE VERES IN CRISIS, 1450–1485

✦ 1 ✦

The Earl's Familial Inheritance

The noblest subject in England, and indeed as Englishmen loved to say, the noblest subject in Europe, was Aubrey de Vere, twentieth and last of the old Earls of Oxford. He derived his title though an uninterrupted male descent from a time when the families of Howard and Seymour were still obscure, when the Nevills and Percies enjoyed only a provincial celebrity, and when even the great name of Plantagenet had not yet been heard in England. One chief of the house of de Vere had held high command at Hastings; another had marched, with Godfrey and Tancred, over heaps of slaughtered Moslem, to the sepulchre of Christ. The first Earl of Oxford had been minister of Henry Beauclerc. The third earl had been conspicuous among the lords who extorted the Great Charter from John. The seventh Earl had fought bravely at Cressy and Poictiers. The thirteenth Earl had, through many vicissitudes of fortune, been the chief of the party of the Red Rose, and had led the van on the decisive day of Bosworth. The seventeenth Earl had won for himself an honourable place among the early masters of English poetry. The nineteenth Earl had fallen in arms for the Protestant religion, and for the liberties of Europe, under the walls of Maestricht. His son, Aubrey, in whom closed the longest and most illustrious line of nobles that England has seen, a man of loose morals, but of inoffensive temper, and of courtly manners was Lord Lieutenant of Essex and Colonel of the Blues. (Lord Macaulay on the de Vere family)[1]

The de Veres to 1450

Despite its numerous inaccuracies and exaggerations – the presence of a de Vere at either Hastings or the capture of Jerusalem remains unproven, it was the father of the first earl who was one of Henry I's leading ministers, the third earl was not a signatory to Magna Carta, though he was a guarantor – this piece by one of England's more famous and eloquent historians is rather illuminating. What became etched on the consciousness of this historian, as well as others subsequently, about the de Veres were not primarily their achievements, but their longevity. Of the twenty de Vere earls of Oxford, Macaulay could find only seven with (attributed) achievements meritorious enough to mention, as for him it was

---

[1]   T.B. Macaulay, *History of England: From the Accession of James II* (5 vols, London, 1861), ii, 320.

the tenure of an earldom from 1142 to 1703 that was the praiseworthy achievement.

Macaulay's assumption that there was something of import about the longevity of the de Veres was well-founded. Even by the late fifteenth century, they were the oldest of the comital families. This had few practical benefits, but such a distinguished descent did mean something to a society, which, from its middling echelons upwards, was obsessed with lineage, title and descent. Such contemporary reverence can be glimpsed occasionally – John Paston ended a request to the twelfth earl of Oxford for a favour in 1454 with the interesting phrase: 'I besech All myghty God send you asmych joy and wurchep as ever had any of my Lords yowr aunceters.'[2] Such a comment would have been an insult to the de la Poles whose ancestors only four generations before were wealthy merchants from Hull. One of the few contemporary literary works written about the de Veres had lineage and ancient blood as one of its themes: 'Wherefore now of all England he hathe avauntage, / Owte excepte the blode ryall the most trwyste lynage.'[3] 'Trwyste' in the context of this work had wider implications than simple ancestry, also implying loyalty to the Lancastrian dynasty, but pedigree was at the heart of the matter. Nonetheless unimpeachable descent meant little if the actual holder of the dignity was inadequate, especially in the dangerous political world of the second half of the fifteenth century.

Macaulay did have some justification in not mentioning the achievements of many holders of the ancient dignity of the earldom of Oxford. A modern historian has identified the 'evolving tradition of their family', which 'by the end of the Middle Ages, had combined the most distinguished of pedigrees with, in most generations, the most undistinguished of lives.'[4] The de Veres, for all their longevity, were for much of their enduring history neither politically prominent nor particularly wealthy, and this is the primary reason for the comparative lack of historiographical work on the family in the medieval period.[5] That many of the de Veres were unmemorable is not surprising, as no hereditary aristocratic

[2] *PL*, ii, 307.

[3] R. Hanna III and A.S.G. Redworth, 'Rotheley, the de Vere Circle and the Ellesmere Chaucer', *Huntingdon Library Quarterly*, lviii (1996), 33.

[4] J.R. Maddicott, 'Follower, Leader, Pilgrim, Saint: Robert de Vere, Earl of Oxford, at the Shrine of Simon de Montfort, 1273', *EHR*, cix (1994), 641–53.

[5] No serious study of the family over a prolonged chronological period is in print, and with the exception of Edward, seventeenth earl of Oxford, a potential candidate for authorship of Shakespeare's work, little work has been done on individual members of the family. A popular history of the whole family remains the only work covering more than a century: Verily Anderson, *The de Veres of Castle Hedingham* (Lavenham, 1993). Work on medieval earls includes Maddicott, 'Follower, Leader, Pilgrim, Saint'; Robert Halliday 'Robert de Vere, Ninth Earl of Oxford', *Medieval History*, iii (1993), 71–85; Scofield, 'Early Life'. There are biographies of nine of the thirteen medieval earls of Oxford in the new *ODNB* (Aubrey I and X, John VII, XII and XIII, Robert III and IX, Thomas VIII and Richard XI), and one countess, Isabel de Bolebec (d. 1245).

family produced an able incumbent of a dignity in every generation, yet they could, from time to time, provide outstanding figures.

The first known head of the de Vere family, Aubrey, probably originated from Ver in the Norman Côtentin, and may have been the baron who appears in a charter of Conan, count of Brittany between 1056 and 1066.[6] It is not possible to prove that Aubrey did fight at Hastings, as no direct evidence survives for this, but it is highly likely that he did so, not least as, presumably for his service in 1066, he had been granted by 1086 widespread estates in East Anglia. The bulk of these estates had belonged to an important Anglo-Saxon thegn named Wulfwine. The later seat of the earldom, Hedingham, was among those estates recorded as belonging to Aubrey at Domesday, at which time there was already a motte and bailey castle on the site, on whose foundations the extant and impressive twelfth century keep still stands. The Domesday grant of eight manors in Essex, three in Suffolk, six in Cambridgeshire, and one each in the shires of Huntingdonshire and Middlesex, remained the core of the landed wealth of the de Veres throughout the Middle Ages.[7] The Domesday valuation of the estates directly held by the de Veres totalled, including a few smaller holdings, just over £200. This then was a substantial endowment, but very much one of the second rank in terms of power, compared to the vast settlements made to some noblemen. The estates did, however, establish the de Veres as major landholders in Essex, and while later additions to the landed estate were of a wider geographical scope, this county remained the primary focus of the de Vere patrimony throughout the Middle Ages.

Despite a modest landed endowment, the political profile of the family of the de Vere family was high throughout the twelfth century, primarily because of the character and abilities of the two heads of the family between 1112 and 1194. It is clear that Henry I had considerable faith in the abilities of Aubrey II, reflected in his various appointments to the shrievalties of thirteen counties during the 1120s and 1130s, and the grant in fee of the office of great chamberlain of England in 1133.[8] Attention has been mostly been paid to the most high profile and lucrative function of the latter position, namely officiating on state occasions, especially

[6] *Calendar of Documents Preserved in France, Illustrative of the History of Great Britain and Ireland, I: A.D. 918–1206*, ed. J.H. Round (London, 1899), no. 1168. For a discussion of Aubrey's origins, see *CP*, x, appendix J, 110.

[7] *Domesday Book: Essex*, ed. A. Rumble (Chichester, 1983), no. 35; *Domesday Book: Suffolk*, ed. A. Rumble (2 vols, Chichester, 1986), i, no. 35; *Domesday Book: Cambridgeshire*, ed. A. Rumble (Chichester, 1981), no. 29; *Domesday Book: Huntingdonshire*, ed. J. Morris (Chichester, 1975), no. 22; *Domesday Book: Middlesex*, ed. J. Morris (Chichester, 1975), no. 21. He also held the overlordships of eleven more manors in these counties.

[8] *CP*, x, 196. For the chamberlainship, see H.A. Cronne, *The Reign of Stephen, 1135–54* (London, 1970), 201; *CP*, x, appendix F, 54–8; and for the text of the grant, see G.J. Townsend, *History of the Great Chamberlainship of England* (London, 1934), 81.

at the king's coronation,[9] but the functions of the chamberlain, when in attendance on the king, may well have offered more influence than has previously been recognized. His son and heir, Aubrey, during his father's lifetime, made a high profile marriage to Beatrice, heir to Manasses, count of Guines, which allowed him to take the title of count.[10] This increase in status helped, but it was primarily the polarization of civil war and Aubrey's close association with the powerful Geoffrey de Mandeville, earl of Essex, who was the husband of his sister, Rohese, that lay behind the most important event of the twelfth century for the de Veres. The grant of the earldom of Oxford from the Empress Matilda in 1141 was part of the price that de Mandeville and Aubrey III demanded for their support. Aubrey was fortunate, given his fickle loyalties in returning to Stephen's side by 1145, that Henry II confirmed him in his title.[11]

In contrast to these able men who made the most of their abilities and opportunities, the thirteenth century heads of the de Vere family were 'generally obscure men who lived outside the world of affairs'.[12] This was partly a product of the fact that the family was poor for its comital status, and the growth of the de Vere estates was slow. The fourth earl's inquisition *post mortem* of 1263 estimated his total annual income at £504; J.R. Maddicott has stated that 'in comital terms this was a small estate … only Roger de Quincy, earl of Winchester, is likely to have been less wealthy'.[13] At the death of Robert, sixth earl of Oxford, in 1331, the centre of the family holdings was still in Essex, with nine manors there, and there were three more manors in Cambridgeshire and three in Suffolk; these estates were worth perhaps £800–900 per year. Two reasons suggest themselves for such a surprising failure to greatly augment their estates between Domesday and the early fourteenth century. The de Veres often married gentry heiresses whose estates, though by no means neglible, were not extensive, and who brought only limited benefits in terms of lands, as was the case with the marriages made by the third and fifth earls of Oxford to the heiresses of the Bolebec and Sandford families. When they did marry into other noble families, the earls were never important enough to secure the real prize heiresses and through genealogical accident their marriages into families such as Mortimer, Bigod, Roos or de Quincy did not result in the acquisition of their lands. Certainly the de Vere acquisitions and those of the Mowbray family whose inheritance of the vast Brotherton and Segrave estates during the fourteenth century brought them

---

9 J.H. Round, *The King's Serjeants and Officers of State with their Coronation Services* (London, 1911), 112–40.

10 J.H. Round, *Geoffrey de Mandeville: A Study of the Anarchy* (London, 1892), 201n. Aubrey divorced Beatrice at some point around 1144–6: CP, x, 202 & n.

11 *Regesta Regum Anglo-Normannorum*, ed. H.A. Cronne and R.H.C. Davis (4 vols, Oxford, 1913–69), iii, 233–5. For the dating of the grant and the politics of 1139–1154, see Marjorie Chibnall, *The Empress Matilda* (Oxford, 1991), 105–12; Emilie Amt, *The Accession of Henry II in England* (Woodbridge, 1993), 65–72, 77, 79.

12 Maddicott, 'Follower, Leader, Pilgrim, Saint', 641.

13 Ibid., 642.

from a baronial family to the front ranks of the peerage in terms of wealth and title were of an entirely different order of magnitude.[14]

Military service did offer an alternative route to prestige, as well as the chance of profit, and the seventh earl John, who ended the succession of mediocrities holding the earldom, served on an exceptional number of campaigns – in 1333 on the campaign that culminated at Halidon Hill, in Scotland again in 1335 and 1343, at sea in 1339, in Flanders in 1340, in Brittany in 1345, at Crécy and Calais in 1346–7, at Poitiers and in Gascony in 1356–7, and he died at the siege of Rheims in January 1360.[15] In 1357 Edward III granted the earl's son Thomas a £40 annuity during the life of his father, and Thomas also participated on the Rheims campaign; after his accession to the earldom, he served in France in 1369, before his early death in 1371.[16] Such a level of military participation, when combined with increased landed wealth thanks to the seventh earl's marriage to a co-heiress of the Badlesmere family, probably meant that the de Veres had never been wealthier or more respected than at this period. Despite this increase in wealth, much has been made of the supposed poverty of the earls of Oxford in the late fourteenth century. Nigel Saul has commented that by the late fourteenth century the earls 'had difficulty in adequately maintaining their rank'. He argues that 'the mainspring of [Robert, ninth earl of Oxford's] ambition was necessity – financial necessity'.[17] Robert Halliday also commented that his estates 'were small for his rank', though Halliday incorrectly estimated the value of the whole earldom at £750.[18] There is, however, nothing to suggest this even when faced with the inadequate inquisition *post mortem* evidence concerning the estates and income of Earls John and Thomas. Earl John had lands worth perhaps as much as £1300 per year,[19] and Thomas, who in addition to having some £2500 in the hands of his feoffees at his death, had spent £1121 just two years earlier, in buying back the two manors of Laughton and Market Overton, after a deathbed enfeoffment for charitable purposes made by his mother in

---

[14] R.E Archer, 'The Mowbrays, Earls of Nottingham and Dukes of Norfolk, to 1432' (unpublished D.Phil, Oxford University, 1984), 1–82.

[15] *CP*, x, 222–3. His skilful handling of the archers at Poitiers was noted in *Chronicon Galfridi le Baker de Swynebroke*, ed. E.M. Thompson (Oxford, 1881), 143, 148, and see also 76, 79, 124, 127 for the other campaigns.

[16] *CP*, x, 226; *CPR, 1354–8*, 602.

[17] N. Saul, *Richard II* (London, 1997), 121.

[18] Halliday, 'Robert de Vere', 71. He incorrectly states that the income tax of 1436 estimated the earldom at £750, but de Vere was not assessed in that survey, and the estimate comes in fact from H.L. Gray, following tendentious evidence: see below, 25.

[19] The values of twenty manors from Countess Maud's receiver-general account of 1386–7, the only near contemporary account from the de Veres' administration: BL, Harleian Roll N3. The rest are valued from the generally reliable inquisition *post mortem* of Richard eleventh earl of Oxford in 1417 and other sources: *CIPM*, xx, 201–7; *CFR, 1337–47*, 103; *CIM, 1387–93*, 35. The earl's actual inquisition *post mortem*, C135/153, nos 1–30 omits twelve manors, and is otherwise unreliable. Earl John also held the overlordships of well over one hundred knight's fees in nine counties: *CIPM*, x, 518–23.

Figure 1: The de Vere Earls of Oxford, 1331–1540

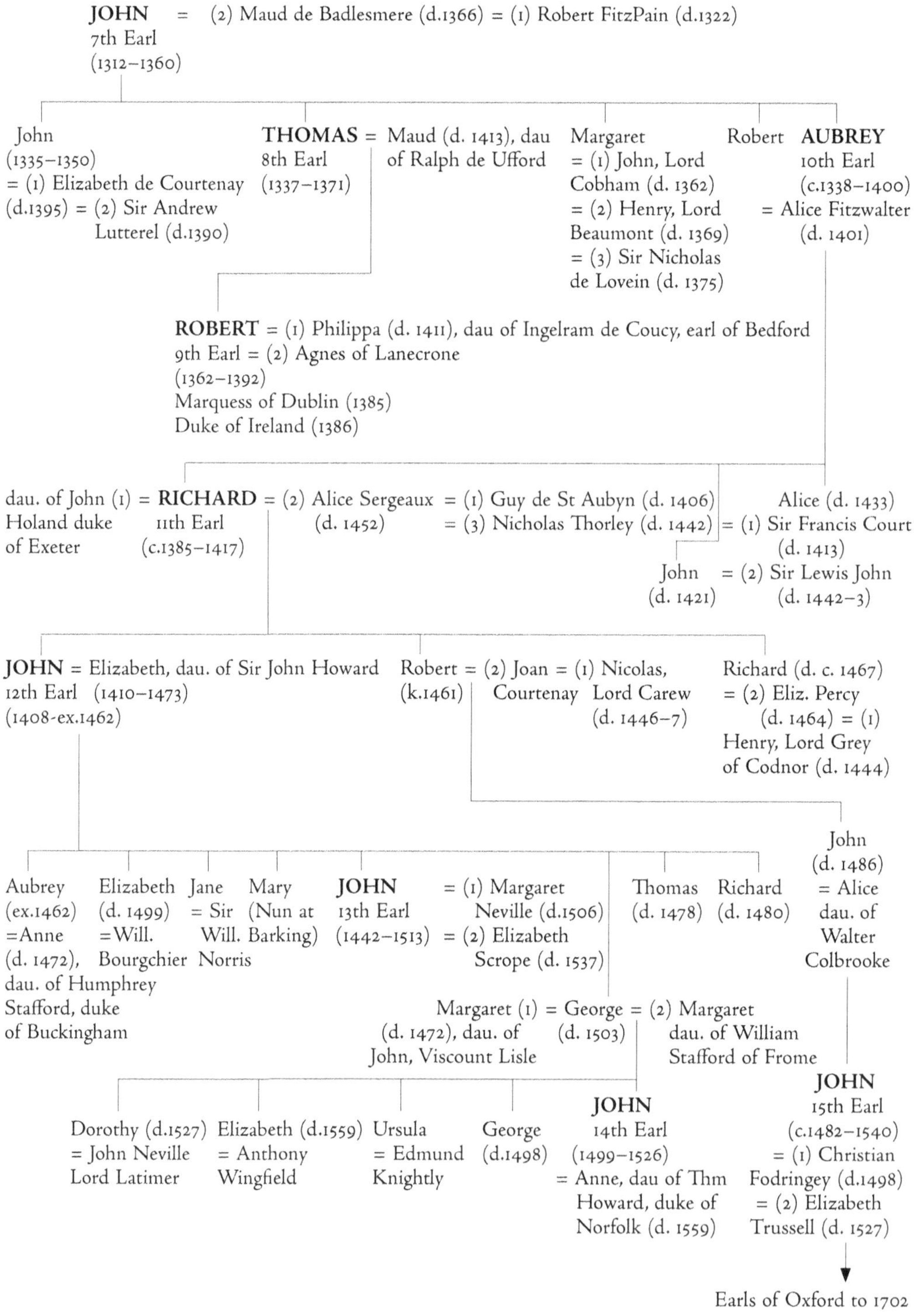

JOHN = (2) Maud de Badlesmere (d.1366) = (1) Robert FitzPain (d.1322)
7th Earl
(1312–1360)

John
(1335–1350)
= (1) Elizabeth de Courtenay
(d.1395) = (2) Sir Andrew
Lutterel (d.1390)

THOMAS = Maud (d. 1413), dau
8th Earl   of Ralph de Ufford
(1337–1371)

Margaret
= (1) John, Lord
Cobham (d. 1362)
= (2) Henry, Lord
Beaumont (d. 1369)
= (3) Sir Nicholas
de Lovein (d. 1375)

Robert   **AUBREY**
10th Earl
(c.1338–1400)
= Alice Fitzwalter
(d. 1401)

ROBERT = (1) Philippa (d. 1411), dau of Ingelram de Coucy, earl of Bedford
9th Earl = (2) Agnes of Lanecrone
(1362–1392)
Marquess of Dublin (1385)
Duke of Ireland (1386)

dau. of John (1) = **RICHARD** = (2) Alice Sergeaux = (1) Guy de St Aubyn (d. 1406)
Holand duke   11th Earl   (d. 1452)   = (3) Nicholas Thorley (d. 1442)
of Exeter   (c.1385–1417)

Alice (d. 1433)
= (1) Sir Francis Court
(d. 1413)

John   = (2) Sir Lewis John
(d. 1421)   (d. 1442–3)

JOHN = Elizabeth, dau. of Sir John Howard
12th Earl   (1410–1473)
(1408-ex.1462)

Robert = (2) Joan = (1) Nicolas,
(k.1461) | Courtenay   Lord Carew
      (d. 1446–7)

Richard (d. c. 1467)
= (2) Eliz. Percy
(d. 1464) = (1)
Henry, Lord Grey
of Codnor (d. 1444)

John
(d. 1486)
= Alice
dau. of
Walter
Colbrooke

Aubrey
(ex.1462)
=Anne
(d. 1472),
dau. of Humphrey
Stafford, duke
of Buckingham

Elizabeth
(d. 1499)
=Will.
Bourgchier

Jane
= Sir
Will.
Norris

Mary
(Nun at
Barking)

JOHN
13th Earl
(1442–1513)

= (1) Margaret
Neville (d.1506)
= (2) Elizabeth
Scrope (d. 1537)

Thomas   Richard
(d. 1478)   (d. 1480)

Margaret (1) = George = (2) Margaret
(d. 1472), dau. of   (d. 1503) | dau. of William
John, Viscount Lisle   Stafford of Frome

JOHN
15th Earl
(c.1482–1540)
= (1) Christian
Fodringey (d.1498)
= (2) Elizabeth
Trussell (d. 1527)

Dorothy (d.1527)
= John Neville
Lord Latimer

Elizabeth (d.1559)
= Anthony
Wingfield

Ursula
= Edmund
Knightly

George
(d.1498)

JOHN
14th Earl
(1499–1526)
= Anne, dau of Thm
Howard, duke of
Norfolk (d. 1559)

Earls of Oxford to 1702

1366.[20] Earl Robert had also married Philippa de Coucy, the English heiress of Ingelram de Coucy, a French hostage who had ended marrying Edward III's daughter in 1365 and reclaiming his ancestral estates in England seized at the start of the Hundred Years War; her estates, confirmed to him in 1382 were worth £300–£400 per year.[21] Therefore Robert had estates worth some £1000 p.a. (including his wife's lands), and was heir to a patrimony worth at least £1000 more, before any patronage had been granted to him, so was hardly poor.[22] What problems there were for the de Veres at this date sprang from the burden on the estates from 1371 to 1453 of a succession of long-lived dowager countesses – Maud, widow of Thomas, eighth earl of Oxford, dowager from 1371 to 1413, Philippa, widow of Robert, ninth earl of Oxford, dowager from 1388 to 1411, and Alice, widow of Richard, eleventh earl of Oxford, a dowager from 1417 to 1453. Not only did each legitimately hold a third of her husband's estates for life, but Maud also held nearly another third in jointure.[23]

After over a century of comparative obscurity and the avoidance of serious political entanglements, the meteoric rise of Robert, ninth earl of Oxford, marquess of Dublin, and duke of Ireland, ended in a spectacular fall, and provided a salutary lesson for his descendants. Earl Thomas married Maud, daughter of Ralph de Ufford, chief justice of Ireland and brother to Robert de Ufford, earl of Suffolk. Their only child Robert was born in 1362, and Thomas died in 1371. No formal guardian was appointed for Robert, though a few months after his father's death his marriage was granted to Ingelram de Coucy, earl of Bedford and Isabel his wife, daughter of Edward III, who married Robert to their younger daughter Philippa.[24] Robert continued his family's recent good service in England's foreign wars, serving in France under Thomas of Woodstock, later duke of Gloucester, in 1380, and under the king in a royal expedition against Scotland in 1385, with the substantial retinue of two knights, 118 men-at-arms and 200 archers.[25] At an

---

[20] *Registrum Simonis de Sudburia*, ed. R.C. Fowler (2 vols, Canterbury and York Society, xxxiv, xxxviii, 1927–38), i, 6; and see G.A. Holmes, *The Estates of the Higher Nobility in Four-teenth Century England* (Cambridge, 1957), 31. From eighteen of the thirty-nine manors that Earl Thomas held at his death, his wife Maud had an income of £586 in 1386–7: BL, Harleian Roll N3.

[21] Confirmation (*CPR, 1381–5*, 177; SC8/7223) was necessary as Ingelram had returned to his French allegiance in 1377, but Phillippa, granddaughter of Edward III, was always intended to be heir to his English estates, her elder sister to his French lands. For the valuation of the estates: *CPR, 1361–4*, 427; *CIPM*, xiv, 107–9; Ross, 'De Vere Earls', 21–2.

[22] For this estimate, see Ross, 'De Vere Earls', 20–2.

[23] For Maud's career after the death of her son, and her dispersal or loss of many de Vere estates see the author's 'Seditious Activities: the Conspiracy of Maud de Vere, Countess of Oxford, 1403–4', in *The Fifteenth Century III: Authority and Subversion*, ed. Linda Clark (Woodbridge, 2003), 25–41.

[24] *CPR, 1370–4*, 137.

[25] For the French campaign, see *CCR, 1377–81*, 402; E403/478, m. 21; *Oeuvres de Froissart*, ed. K. de Lettenhove (26 vols, Brussels, 1867–77), ix, 245, 276, 277; A. Goodman, *The Loyal Conspiracy. The Lords Appellant under Richard II* (London, 1971), 124, 127. For the Scottish

early stage he formed a close friendship with the young Richard II, and it was
the injudicious level of patronage granted to him by the king that was to prove
his undoing. Robert was generously supplied with land and wardships, and then
most spectacularly in 1385 with the grant of the rule of the whole of Ireland for
life, with all royal rights in the lordship, excepting only liege homage. He was to
hold in fee any lands that he conquered, and to maintain a force of 500 men-at-
arms and 1000 archers in Ireland for two years, during which time he was to pay
no rent, and after that date 5000 marks per annum. He was also granted a new
title in 1385, marquess of Dublin, upgraded to duke of Ireland in the following
year.[26] Arguably these were not just the 'the shadows and trappings of power
without its substance',[27] as at least 766 troops were sent to Ireland, and de Vere
played at least some role in the administration,[28] nor is there anything in Richard
II's record either before or after this grant to suggest that he would treat one of
the dominions of his crown in anything other than a serious manner. Nonetheless, the political implications of the grant to a young and relatively inconse-
quential earl can only have infuriated many of the nobility. To make matters
worse, during 1386 or 1387 he repudiated his wife Philippa de Coucy, who, in the
words of the chronicler Thomas Walsingham, 'was young, beautiful and noble,
being of the line of the illustrious King Edward by his daughter, Isabella, and
afterwards took to wife a certain Bohemian saddler's daughter in the household
of the Queen called Lanecrone, who was, in short, ignoble and hideous'.[29] In
fact, Lanecrone was a damsel of the Queen's chamber, and was almost certainly
of noble birth.[30] Reconstructing the relations between Robert and Philippa is
now impossible, but the lack of children after eleven years of marriage may well
have been a factor in Robert's severance of the union. However, his repudiation
of Philippa enraged many of the nobility, especially her uncle, Thomas of Woodstock, duke of Gloucester. The king's patronage to, and trust in, de Vere and
his other intimates, such as Michael de la Pole and Simon Burley, brought the
country to the brink of civil war by November 1387. The Appellant lords, led by
the duke of Gloucester, accused the court circle of treason. De Vere, the only one
to offer military resistance, made his way to Chester, where he was chief justice,

retinue and expedition: E403/508 m. 19; N.B. Lewis, 'The Last Medieval Summons of the
English Feudal Levy', *EHR*, lxxiii (1958), 19; BL, Harleian MS 1309, fol. 39v; 369, fol. 92v;
Ashmole MS 865; *Oeuvres de Froissart*, x, 395–6; *The Westminster Chronicle, 1381–94*, ed. L.C.
Hector and B.F. Harvey (Oxford, 1982), 128–30; Saul, *Richard II*, 143–5.

[26] *Parliament Rolls*, vii, ed. C. Given-Wilson, 17–19; *CP*, x, 229.

[27] A. Tuck, *Richard II and the English Nobility* (London, 1973), 8.

[28] Protections for the leaders and musters of retinues for the force can be seen in *CPR*,
1385–9, 91, 125–6, 128, 130, 156–8, 163, 189. A number of grants under Robert's signet concerning
Ireland can be seen in *Rotulorum Patentium et Clausorum Cancellarie Hiberniae Calendarium*,
ed. E. Tresham (Irish Record Commission, 1828), i, part i, 131–7, esp. nos 9, 35, 39, 46, 47, 60,
61, 121, 144, 233, 234.

[29] *Historia Anglicana*, ed. H.T. Riley (2 vols, Rolls Series, 1863–4), ii, 160.

[30] See *CP*, x, 231–2n and the discussion there of her origins.

and raised an army of some 4000 Cheshiremen. He led them south to join the king but was intercepted by the Appellants at Radcot Bridge in Oxfordshire, where, after a brief skirmish and betrayed by his levies, de Vere took flight.[31] He evaded the Appellants' forces, and took the only option left to him – exile. Attainted in the Merciless Parliament of 1388, de Vere had a brief sojourn at the French court, but settled in Brabant, where he died in 1392, aged only 30.[32]

Robert's heir was his uncle Aubrey, who, after beginning his career as a prominent retainer of the Black Prince and then playing an influential role at court in the first few years of Richard II's reign, had avoided becoming too closely associated with his nephew's rapid rise, and even more precipitous downfall. His short career after being restored in 1393 to the earldom was primarily an exercise in retrenchment, and an attempt to salvage as many of the family estates as he could from the chaos of Robert's forfeiture, an exercise in which he was only partially successful.[33] Aubrey's comital career also saw the loss of the great chamberlainship, when in 1398, after legally recovering the office as a result of the reversal of Robert's attainder the previous year, he quitclaimed the office to the king, possibly under duress.[34] Comparatively elderly, and in ill-health, Aubrey played no role in the revolution of 1399, but after the rebellion in favour of Richard II in 1400 the earl of Huntingdon fled to him at Hadleigh castle, after which Hadleigh was temporarily seized by the king.[35]

The impact of Robert's ruination on later generations of de Vere earls is difficult to gauge. Certainly his two immediate successors, Aubrey and Richard, had low-key political careers, and stayed clear of the problems over the succession of the Lancastrian dynasty in 1399, and its unsettled first two decades. It may also have had a longer-term impact on the twelfth earl, who would be the next de Vere to suffer political disaster, but in a very different way. It cannot be supposed that the nine-year-old future earl John was called to his father's deathbed in 1417, told the story of great-uncle Robert, and advised to 'flee the company and councel of proude men, of coveitowse men, and of flateryng men', as the duke of

---

[31] R.G. Davies, 'Some Notes from the Register of Henry de Wakefield, Bishop of Worcester on the Political Crisis of 1386–8', *EHR*, lxxxvi (1971), 556; J.N.L. Myers, 'The Campaign of Radcot Bridge in December 1387', *EHR*, xlii (1927), 20–33; *Knighton's Chronicle, 1337–96*, ed. G.H. Martin (Oxford, 1995), 420–3; Goodman, *Loyal Conspiracy*, 16–55.

[32] *Westminster Chronicle*, 222–5; *Oeuvres de Froissart*, xiii, 98–9; xiv, 32–4; G.S. Haslop, 'Two Entries from the Register of John de Shirburn, Abbot of Selby 1369–1408', *Yorkshire Archaeological Journal*, xli (1964), 291; *Chronique du Religieux de Saint-Denys*, ed. M.L. Bellagut (Paris, 1839), 331, 408, 494; 'The Kirkstall Abbey Chronicles', ed. J. Taylor (Thoresby Society, xlii, 1952), 70.

[33] Ross, 'De Vere Earls', 25–9.

[34] *CPR, 1391–6*, 312; *1396–9*, 290; *CP*, x, appendix F, 60; *Parliament Rolls*, viii, ed. C. Given Wilson, 67–8; Townsend, *History of the Great Chamberlainship*, 90.

[35] M. Bennett, *Richard II and the Revolution of 1399* (Stroud, 1999), 189–91; *CCR, 1399–1402*, 43.

Suffolk advised his son when he departed for exile in 1450.[36] Yet as the repercussions of Robert's downfall were still rumbling as late as the 1460s,[37] the twelfth earl's avoidance of political conflict until the last months of his life may owe something to lessons the family learnt the hard way.

A survey of the eleventh earl's career is effectively a survey of English military activity in the early fifteenth century, as the only public activities in which he participated with any form of enthusiasm were martial, demonstrated by his involvement in three campaigns in five years. He fought under the command of the duke of Clarence in 1412–13, with Henry V at Agincourt in 1415, and with the duke of Bedford at the naval battle of Harfleur in 1416. The Agincourt campaign of 1415 is, for almost all who took part in it, very well documented and Richard de Vere's indenture and retinue roll survive. He indented on 29 April to take a retinue of forty men-at-arms and one hundred archers across the sea in the king's service.[38] Richard evaded the sickness that laid low many men during the siege of Harfleur, and fought at the battle of Agincourt itself, where a London chronicle stated that:

> Huntyngdon and Oxforde bothe,
> Were wonder fierce all in that fight,
> That first was laid they made full wroth;
> Through them many onto death were sent;
> The Erles foughten with main and might
> Rich hauberk they tore and rent
> Our king to help they were full light.[39]

The reward for his presence at the battle was admission to the order of the Garter.[40] Richard died, of unknown causes, in February 1417 at the early age of 32.

John de Vere, eldest child of Earl Richard, was born on 23 April 1408.[41] Three months after his father's death, John's wardship was granted to the king's uncle, Thomas Beaufort, duke of Exeter, who held it until his death on 31 December 1426, after which his custody was granted to the duke of Bedford for the two years before John attained his majority.[42] In a petition of 1437 John claimed that 'he was married by the advice of the said late duke of Exeter' to Elizabeth Howard, the wealthy granddaughter and heir of Sir John Howard. This was a

---

[36] *PL*, ii, 143.

[37] See below, 53–4.

[38] E101/46/36, mm.1–2; J.H. Wylie, 'Notes on the Agincourt Roll', *TRHS*, third series, v (1911), 129. The magnate retinues were small because the crown indented with an unusually large number of captains: *The Battle of Agincourt. Sources and Interpretations*, ed. A. Curry (Woodbridge, 2000), 420; H. Nicolas, *History of the Battle of Agincourt* (London, 1832), 373.

[39] Curry, *Agincourt: Sources and Interpretations*, 291.

[40] H. Collins, *The Order of the Garter, 1348–1461: Chivalry and Politics in Later Medieval England* (Oxford, 2000), 74, 125.

[41] *CIPM*, xxiii, 163–4 (proof of age).

[42] E28/32 (25 May 1417); *CPR, 1416–22*, 110; *1422–9*, 395.

very good match, and the couple were married between May and August 1425. However, the king's council on 1 March 1425 had granted John's marriage to several persons who had lent the king money.[43] The grant of the wardship to Exeter did not include John's marriage; it is possible that Exeter was not aware of this, but it is more likely that the young earl and Exeter felt that the value of the marriage was such that it was worth risking the council's displeasure.[44] This proved to be considerable, since for marrying without royal licence the earl was fined £2000 on 26 June 1429, some eight days before he was given livery of his inheritance. The amount was, complained de Vere, 'having regard to the value of his lands, greater than has been inflicted in the like case'.[45] It was a price worth paying eventually, because Elizabeth's lands were worth so much, but it was still a heavy fine.[46]

Despite the fine, and a consequent piqued refusal to attend the king's coronation expedition to France in 1430, his union with Elizabeth Howard in 1425, at the respective ages of seventeen and fourteen,[47] gave him financial security. Elizabeth brought a very substantial number of estates to the family, as she was the sole heiress to her grandparents Sir John Howard and his first wife Margaret Plaiz, through her father, John Howard's eldest son, another John, who died in 1410. Elizabeth's mother, Joan Walton, was also an heiress, to her mother's Sutton estates, and her father's Walton lands. These four inheritances of Howard, Plaiz, Sutton and Walton, were extensive, totalling twenty-eight manors, worth a little under £700 p.a. Moreover, they were all in East Anglia, with fifteen in Essex, three in Suffolk, eight in Norfolk and two in Cambridgeshire, so that they further enhanced the local influence of the de Veres. Elizabeth's contribution to the prosperity of the de Veres was not just territorial. The marriage proved fruitful, with eight children reaching adulthood. Aubrey was the eldest son, and it is likely that all three daughters, Elizabeth, Jane and Mary, were born before the second son, the future thirteenth earl, in 1442, if only because his mother was already thirty-three at this date, and she had subsequently three more sons. Such a fertile wife gave the twelfth earl apparent dynastic security, although he was not to know that only one of his five sons would produce male grandchildren, and there were to be no great-grandchildren in the male line.

Assessing the earl's total income is problematic, despite the survival of several important accounts, both because his extant estate records are all clustered in the period 1431–1443 when not all the estates which were to descend to him were in

[43] CPR, 1422–29, 271; 1436–41, 71–2; CCR, 1422–9, 172
[44] CPR, 1416–22, 110.
[45] CPR, 1422–9, 543; 1436–41, 71–2; CCR, 1422–9, 440. £1700 was paid over the next eight years, and although the earl petitioned to be reprieved of the last £300, the request was rejected, though he was offered 'compensation in wards or other casualties up the value of £200', though there is no record of any such being granted.
[46] CPR, 1422–9, 543; 1436–41, 71–2.
[47] On 22 May 1425 Elizabeth was of full age, i.e. 14: CCR, 1422–9, 172; C139/15/19, nos 2, 4, 6–7; C139/88/56, nos 2, 4, 6–8.

Figure 2. The Inheritance of Elizabeth Howard
(Howard, Plaiz, Sutton, Walton and Scales)[48]

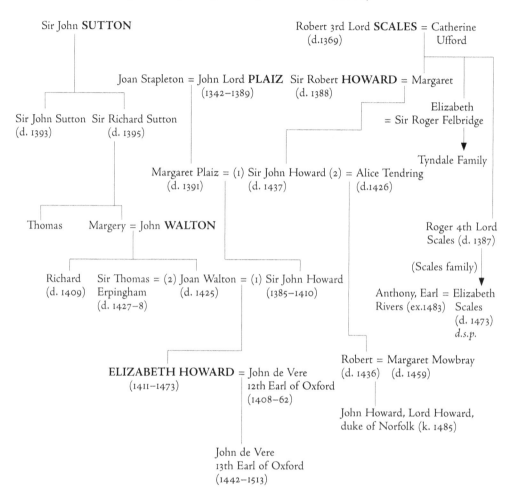

[48] Adapted from A. Crawford, 'Victims of Attainder; The Howard and de Vere Women in the Late Fifteenth Century', in *Medieval Women in Southern England*, ed. K. Bate and M. Barber (Reading Medieval Studies, xv, 1989), 59–60. On the death of Elizabeth Scales, her husband, Anthony, Earl Rivers and Lord Scales, held for term of his life until his execution in 1483. The heirs were the descendants of the two daughters of Robert, third Lord Scales, Margaret and Elizabeth, who were in 1485 John de Vere, earl of Oxford, and Sir William Tyndale: *CIPM Henry VII*, i, 14–17.

his hands, and as there was a dual accounting system in place whereby two officials, the steward of the household and the receiver-general, were responsible for
both receiving and spending manorial income. Where manorial accounts survive,
this dual accounting system can be seen in action; the problem lies in that in
no year are there extant accounts for the two officials in question, so estimates
of income can only be conjecture.[49] The steward of the household had receipts
of £340 in 1431–2, and four years later the receiver-general received £404 from
estate officials.[50] Combining these two accounts would leave a figure of total
income at around £750, which is what would be expected at this stage of the
earl's career, before the death of his wife's grandfather and his own mother. The
earl avoided paying the 1436 income tax which might also have given an estimate of his wealth at this period.[51] Between 1437, when the earl had acquired
control of the entire Howard inheritance, and the death of his mother in 1452,
the twelfth earl was holding lands inherited from his father which were valued
by the latter's inquisition *post mortem* at £458 a year, though certainly worth
somewhat more, as well as lands in right of his marriage which were valued by
a reliable source at £683 p.a.[52] Thus his annual income was a minimum of £1144.
After 1452 the earl's acquisition of his mother's dower estates and her own inheritance would have added another £350 p.a., according to inquisition *post mortem*
values, making a minimum total income of £1491 a year. If one takes into account
the undervaluation, his income towards the end of his career might have been
in the region of £1700. This estimate is supported by evidence from his son's
administration in the 1490s.[53] The twelfth earl was thus a considerably richer
man than his father, and his marriage meant that Oxford was not among the
poorest of English earls. By 1452, the earldom of Oxford may have been richer
in terms of landed revenue than those of Devon, Arundel, Worcester, Shrews-

[49] See Ross, 'De Vere Earls of Oxford', 39–46 for a more detailed analysis of the account
system.

[50] ERO, D/DPr 137, printed in *Household Accounts from Medieval England*, ed. C.M. Woolgar
(2 vols, Oxford, 1992), ii, 522–48, total at 525; RH, Attic box marked 'Miscellaneous'. There
are also receiver-general's accounts surviving from 1437–8 and 1442–3: BL, Add. Ch. 40009,
a, b; ERO, D/DPr 138.

[51] H.L. Gray, 'Incomes from Land in England in 1436', *EHR*, xlix (1934), 617–8, followed
the evidence of the petition by Oxford in 1437 in which de Vere states that the value of his
lands was £500 p.a. Demonstrably this petition should not be taken as reliable evidence for
the value of the de Vere lands, given that he was pleading poverty to reduce a large fine. Gray
estimated Alice's dower at £250, but was not aware of further evidence relating to the income
tax in the memoranda rolls, where Alice's dower was valued at £340: E159/212, Recorda,
Hilary term, rot. 14d.

[52] *CIPM*, xx, 201–7; RH, Box 24. The latter contains an account of 1436–7 of the Howard
estates, covering not only the lands that were in the earl's hands at the time, namely Elizabeth's maternal inheritance of the Sutton and Walton estates, but also valuing those manors
of Elizabeth's paternal inheritance of Howard and Plaiz, which was still in the hands of her
grandfather until his death in 1437.

[53] See below, 107–8.

bury, Pembroke and even the dukedoms of Somerset and Exeter.[54] In no way could he be compared to the richest earls, such as Warwick, Northumberland or Salisbury or the more affluent dukes like York, Buckingham or Norfolk, but he was a very wealthy landowner with an unusually compact group of estates in East Anglia.

The earl had no estates in Normandy, since his father had died before the conquest of Normandy had started, and had therefore missed out on the landed endowments that many of the higher nobility had gained between 1417 and 1436 and to a lesser extent after that date. Nevertheless he was active in the defence of the duchy and the English claim to the throne of France. Oxford's first expedition was to the relief of Calais in 1436, under the command of Humphrey, duke of Gloucester.[55] In the event there was little fighting since the divisions among the Burgundians meant that they failed to mount an effective siege and the threat of an English relief army was enough to disperse them.[56] The earl was also a member of the major embassy which met with the French at Calais on 29 June 1439 to negotiate a peace settlement.[57] Beyond adding prestige, the lay lords seem to have played only a minor role in the unsuccessful negotiations, although, ironically, during the peace talks two ships of Oxford's were reported to be in hot pursuit of four large ships heading north.[58] Following the failure of

[54] The earl of Devon was assessed in 1436 at £733 annually, though his mother held lands probably worth as much again, the Fitzalan estates were worth perhaps some £1400 p.a. at this date, and Lord Tiptoft in 1436 was assessed at an annual income of £1098: Gray, 'Incomes from Land', 617–8; C.D. Ross and T.B. Pugh, 'The English Baronage and the Income Tax of 1436', BIHR, xxvi (1953), 23. For Shrewsbury (c. £1500 p.a.): A.J. Pollard, 'The Family of Talbot, Lords Talbot and Earls of Shrewsbury in the Fifteenth Century' (unpublished PhD thesis, Bristol University, 1968), 314–6. The Beaufort dukes of Somerset had English estates estimated to be worth approximately £1300 p.a. in the 1420s, and as little as £700 annually in 1451: M.K. Jones, 'The Beaufort Family and the Wars in France, 1421–1450' (unpublished PhD thesis, Bristol University, 1982), 3–19. For the earl of Huntingdon, later duke of Exeter (£1002 in 1436): M.M.N. Stansfield, 'The Holland Family, Dukes of Exeter, Earls of Kent and Huntingdon, 1352–1475' (unpublished D.Phil, Oxford University, 1987), 218–22. Pembroke had an income of £1500 by 1457: Thomas, 'Political Career ... of Jasper Tudor', 140.

[55] CPR, 1429–36, 602, 611. No indenture survives for the earl, but it seems likely he indented with Gloucester, who certainly had two earls in his retinue: E403/724, m.4; Griffiths, Henry VI, 447.

[56] A Chronicle of London from 1089–1483, ed. N.H. Nicolas (London, 1827), 122; The Brut or the Chronicles of England, ed. F.W.D. Brie (EETS, 1908), ii, 469–70, 574–84; Griffiths, Henry VI, 203–5; J.A. Doig, 'Propaganda, Public Opinion and the Siege of Calais in 1436', in Crown, Government and People in the Fifteenth Century, ed. R.E. Archer (Stroud, 1995), 79–106; J.A. Doig, 'A New Source for the Siege of Calais in 1436', EHR, xc (1995), 404–16.

[57] PPC, v, 334; The Chronicles of London, ed. C.L. Kingsford (Oxford, 1905), 146; C.T. Allmand, 'The Anglo-French Negotiations of 1439', BIHR, xl (1967), 1–33; idem, 'Documents relating to the Anglo-French Negotiations of 1439', in Camden Miscellany XXIV (Camden Society, fourth series, ix, 1972), 79–149.

[58] PPC, v, 386. This was not necessarily irresponsible piracy, and may have been an act of war

these peace negotiations the English government made an effort to improve the defences of Normandy and to involve the nobility in the war. Richard, duke of York, was appointed Lieutenant General of France in 1440 for five years. When he arrived in Rouen on 25 June 1441, John de Vere and his countess, and several other magnates including Henry Bourgchier and James, earl of Ormond, were in his retinue.[59] Oxford's retinue was of an impressive size, comprising sixty men-at-arms and 210 archers.[60] The substantial numbers in the retinue were undoubtedly a consequence of the fact that of the few noblemen going on the campaign, Oxford was second only to York in wealth and status, and this would have attracted those wishing to serve from beyond his normal recruitment area.[61] The earl's second son, the future thirteenth earl, was conceived while the earl and his wife were in Normandy, probably in December 1441, although, unlike Edward IV, conceived in Rouen a few months earlier, there were no subsequent rumours that this was a result of an dubious liaison between his mother and an archer in the English garrison there.[62] The twelfth earl had probably returned from France by the time of his son's birth on 8 September 1442.[63]

Despite Oxford's loyal service in France, he was not much of a courtier and this is reflected by a very limited amount of royal patronage granted to him, despite the king's excessive largesse in the 1440s and the early 1450s, which led to two parliamentary resumptions in the early 1450s. There were only two grants to Oxford – the more important being the profits of the river Colne, from the north Bridge of Colchester to a place called 'le Westnasse', which led immediately to a law suit with the burgesses of Colchester who claimed that the stretch of river in question had been granted to the town by Richard I. Oxford lost the case by 1457.[64] In 1452 he was also granted the restitution of the keeping of the park and houses at Havering atte Bower, Essex, which 'premises have pertained time

---

if the vessels were French, as hostilities had not ceased.

[59] *The Historical Collections of a London Citizen*, ed. J. Gairdner (Camden Society, n.s., xvii, 1876), 183; *Chronicles of London*, 147–8; *The Brut*, ed. Brie, ii, 477.

[60] E101/53/33, m.1; a partial muster of the retinue in May 1441 is in E101/54/9.

[61] For York's lieutenancy, and the Pontoise campaign, see P.A. Johnson, *Duke Richard of York, 1411–60* (Oxford, 1988), 36–41; A.J. Pollard, *John Talbot and the War in France* (London 1983), 54–8.

[62] For the story about Edward see M.K. Jones, *Bosworth, 1485. Psychology of a Battle* (Stroud, 2002), 65–71.

[63] The earl, not appointed to governmental business in England after June 1441, was appointed to a loan commission in March 1442, and to the peace commission in May and August: *CPR, 1441–6*, 61, 470–1.

[64] *CPR, 1446–52*, 33; C44/29/15, date illegible, but probably 1448; KB27/750, rot. 92; C254/145; C245/40, no. 8; KB27/752, fines rot. Evidence of how seriously the earl took the case can be seen in his appearance in person in King's Bench to plead his side of the dispute: KB27/748, rot. 35. For a fuller description of the dispute and its legal proceedings, see Morant, 'The History of Colchester', in idem, *Essex*, i, 90–1, and History of Parliament Trust, London, unpublished article on 'Colchester' by C.E. Moreton for 1422–1504 section. I am grateful to the History of Parliament Trust for allowing me to see this article in draft.

out of mind' to his ancestors.[65] Oxford did also receive confirmation of a number of grants to his ancestors of markets, fairs and free warrens in June 1442.[66] The twelfth earl kept clear of serious problems in East Anglia as well, there being only one example of Oxford being in dispute with someone of equivalent status, the bishop of Norwich.[67]

The thirteenth earl of Oxford was heir to a long-established family, but one that for all its longevity had enjoyed little power and influence during much of its history. While his father was probably, by the end of his life, the wealthiest of all the de Veres in terms of landed revenue, this was a consequence of a recent marriage, and the failure of the family to seriously augment their estates over the preceding three centuries is surprising. The lack of landed wealth and power, did, however, keep the family from serious political disaster at most periods; Robert, duke of Ireland's short and disastrous career provided a salutary lesson in why it was extremely dangerous being powerful and prominent at court. The tenth, eleventh and twelfth earls' careers were unspectacular between 1392 and 1450, and certainly the last was in many ways typical of most magnates at this period. Almost all served in France at one time or another and the twelfth earl conscientiously performed these duties. Like many among the second rank of the nobility, in terms of status and wealth, he avoided being drawn into the factional disputes in high politics in the 1430s and 1440s. He seems to have been content to remain a country rather than a court magnate, but also managed to generally steer clear of the local disorder that was such a feature of the mid-fifteenth century. It was only after 1450 that this resolve to avoid local or national conflict was to be seriously tested, as the country descended into faction and ultimately civil war.

John, twelfth earl of Oxford, 1450–61

It might have felt in the spring of 1450 that the 1440s had been traumatic for England in general and East Anglia in particular, and that the 1450s would surely be much easier after the fall of the King's principal minister, and East Anglia's leading figure, the duke of Suffolk. While much has been written about Suffolk's regional hegemony in East Anglia, both criticizing his power, and arguing its legitimacy,[68] there is no doubt that some felt hard done by; when, as Margaret Paston put it, 'there xal no man ben so hardy to don nether seyn azens my Lord

---

[65] CPR, 1446–52, 522.

[66] CPR, 1441–6, 88–9.

[67] For this interesting quarrel, see Ross, 'De Vere Earls', 110–15.

[68] For the defence, see particularly H. Castor, *The King, the Crown and the Duchy of Lancaster: Public Authority and Private Power, 1399–1461* (Oxford, 2000), chapter 4, and J.L. Watts, *Henry VI and the Politics of Kingship* (Cambridge, 1996), chapter 6; for the prosecution, R.L. Storey, *The End of the House of Lancaster* (London 1966), chapter 2, and Colin Richmond, most recently, 'East Anglian Politics and Society in the Fifteenth Century', in *Medieval East Anglia*, ed. C. Harper-Bill (Woodbridge, 2005), 183–208.

of Sowthfolk', something had gone wrong.[69] What, of course, no one was to know was that the 1450s would see a breakdown of law and order that had not happened for well over a century, and eventually a descent into civil war.

Oxford had stayed out of the major power struggle in East Anglia between the dukes of Suffolk and Norfolk, although the bishop of Norwich, with whom he had fallen out, was one of Suffolk's circle.[70] De Vere had not suffered because of Suffolk's local dominance, though it appears that he had little sympathy with de la Pole's national regime as he was apparently not present at any meetings of the council between 1445 and 1449, nor did he witness a charter at court between 1444 and June 1450.[71] He was present in the first session of the parliament in spring 1449, but was not at the second session at Winchester in the summer.[72] He was, however, present in the parliament that condemned Suffolk, since he signed the declaration by the Lords that Suffolk's impeachment and exile without trial by his peers would not harm the nobility's right to that trial.[73]

This general aversion to Suffolk's regime meant that Oxford seems initially to have been sympathetic towards Richard, duke of York when the latter returned from Ireland in 1450. The earl was prepared to accept York's recommendations for Norfolk's MPs, relating to John Paston on 18 October 1450 that 'my Lord of Norfolk met with my Lord of York at Bury on Thursday' and 'a gentilman of my Lord of York toke unto a yeman of myn ... a tokene and a sedell of my Lords entent, whom he wold have knyghtes of the shyre'. Enclosing the names, he merely noted 'me thynkith wel do to performe my Lords entent'.[74] The earl's association with York at this period is evident in his participation in the duke's procession through London on 3 December 1450, a demonstration that implicitly underlined York's commitment to public order, and de Vere was in attendance at court, witnessing charters on 30 January and 24 March 1451, while York's position as a potential leading minister still hung in the balance.[75] However, between the adjournment of the parliament on 18 December 1450, and the delayed resumption of business on 29 April support switched to the duke of Somerset as the new leading minister.[76] Oxford seems to have had little desire to participate in government under Somerset after the latter's ascendancy became clear. He attended only one council meeting between May 1451 and December 1452, though he did not completely absent himself from court as he is recorded as

[69] *PL*, ii, 86.

[70] Griffiths, *Henry VI*, 285, 348; R.J. Schoeck, 'Lyhert, Walter (d. 1472)', *ODNB*.

[71] Watts, *Henry VI*, 211, fig. 3; C53/188, m. 32; 190, m.28; *CChR*, vi, 44, 114. He was a witness to a confirmation of the king's foundation grants to Eton in 1445–6: BL, Cott. Ch. XIII. 14.

[72] Watts, *Henry VI*, 244n.

[73] *Parliament Rolls*, xii, ed. A. Curry and R. Horrox, 105–6.

[74] *PL*, ii, 184–5.

[75] 'John Benet's Chronicle', ed. G.L. Harriss and M.A. Harriss in *Camden Miscellany XXIV* (Camden Society, fourth series, ix, 1972), 203; C53/190, m. 27.

[76] Griffiths, *Henry VI*, 684–92; Watts, *Henry VI*, 266–86.

a charter witness on 30 October 1451, 17 March and 20 May 1452.[77] Oxford made no move to support York, however, when the latter raised what was in effect a loyalist rebellion in February 1452, presumably as he could not justify taking up arms against his king. However, no source mentions his presence among the king's force at Dartford, nor, in common with ten other lords, did Oxford take part in a general commission of oyer and terminer to which he was appointed on 28 September 1452 for thirteen eastern and central counties, implicitly aimed at the suppression of York's supporters.[78]

If he was not prepared to commit himself nationally, the same cannot be said of the earl's actions locally. The primary theme of the Paston letters in the early 1450s is the attempt to bring Suffolk's East Anglian affinity to justice, at least as John Paston and his circle viewed it, and in particular Sir Thomas Tuddenham and John Heydon. Helen Castor has argued that Tuddenham, Heydon and others were members of a legitimate and established local political network, based on the duchy of Lancaster estates in East Anglia, and that this network had been assimilated into the duke of Suffolk's lordship.[79] Nevertheless, as Castor admits, the drawback of this link, 'when the public authority of the crown was compromised by too close an association with private interests', was demonstrated by the reaction of certain sections of county society which had suffered from these private interests in the more favourable circumstances after Suffolk's fall.[80] A general commission of oyer and terminer was issued on 1 August 1450, touching all trespasses, misdeeds, and other criminal acts committed in Norfolk and Suffolk, and was headed by the duke of Norfolk, the earl of Oxford, Lord Scales, the royal justice, William Yelverton, and several other East Anglian gentry. The commission was partly in response to the complaints of Cade's rebels about bad government, and also in answer to a request for such a commission from the leading men of the two counties, including Oxford himself.[81] It was not long before this general commission turned into a specific attack on Tuddenham and Heydon, the leading members of Suffolk's affinity, primarily because of the hostility of many local gentry, as well as elements of the political society of the city of Norwich. Not long after the first session on 17 September, discussion of the indictment of Tuddenham, Heydon and others began to fill the Pastons' correspondence.

Oxford's personal contribution to this political and judicial process was striking. William Worcester noted the earl's attendance at all four sessions that the commission held between November 1450 and March 1451, during which

[77] C81/1546, no. 56; *PPC*, vi, 167–353; C53/190, mm. 25, 26; *CChR*, vi, 114–5; Watts, *Henry VI*, 288.
[78] Watts, *Henry VI*, 297n; *CPR, 1452–61*, 54.
[79] Castor, *King, Crown and the Duchy*, chap. 4.
[80] Ibid., 126.
[81] *CPR, 1446–52*, 388; Watts, *Henry VI*, 67n; and see *PLP*, i, 57; ii, 42–3, where it is clear Oxford was working to a populist agenda.

time he also attended at least four sessions at Colchester of two further commissions.[82] It was only on 29 April and 3 May 1451 that he missed two sessions of the Norfolk oyer and terminer, owing to the resumption of parliament on 29 April. By contrast the duke of Norfolk, who had certainly suffered more from Suffolk's affinity than had Oxford, attended only one of the six sessions noted by Worcester.[83] Aside from the formal sessions of the commission, Oxford's presence at, or correspondence relating to, several meetings and arbitrations are noted in the Paston letters.[84]

Why did Oxford become so involved in these judicial proceedings? He did not appear to have had substantive issues with Tuddenham and Heydon regarding his personal affairs. The earl, instead, gave an explicitly altruistic explanation for his stance. In a letter of 2 January 1451, making his priorities clear to the sheriff of Norfolk and Suffolk, the earl stated that he would not attend parliament for the 'pupplyk wele of all the shire' demanded he participate in the commission and he 'wist that the commons shuld be easid as Goddis law wold'.[85] Beyond this stated aim, there may have been other reasons. It is clear that Oxford was also acting with an interest group in the shire, which included the Pastons. Oxford's territorial stake in Norfolk was too small (eight manors) for him to control the shire but a successful end to the oyer and terminer commission would have been a considerable boost to Oxford's lordship and enabled him to increase his well-wishers and associates.

How successful was the earl both in respect of the commission and his lordship? Tuddenham and Heydon were indicted in the autumn of 1450. Given the weight of evidence Tuddenham's guilt was self-evident and on 16 November 1450 he was fined for over 300 separate offences, which totalled the enormous sum of £1396.[86] Heydon's punishment is unknown. By the following July, when the duke of Somerset was fully in control, Tuddenham was pardoned all but £200 of this fine.[87] Moreover at a session of the oyer and terminer in Walsingham on 4 May 1451, attended by Lord Scales, but not by Oxford, Norfolk or Yelverton,

---

[82] *PL*, ii, 145 (at Norwich starting on 16 November and 15 December, totalling seven days; at Lynn on 13 January; at Norwich again on 2 March 1451). KB9/267, no. 42 notes his presence at a session at Beccles, 6 December 1450. Oxford appeared in person on 1, 3 and 26 February 1451 at Colchester at proceedings of a commission to inquire into all treasons and felonies in that town (C81/763, no. 9343; KB9/268, nos 41a, 43), and at a session at Colchester on 4 March 1451 under force of a commission to investigate heretics and Lollards in Essex (*PL*, ii, 226; *CPR*, 1446–52, 440).

[83] *PL*, ii, 145, on 2 March 1451.

[84] Ibid., 163–5, 211; *PLP*, ii, 528–30, and see Richmond, *Paston Family: First Phase*, 41n; Castor, *King, Crown and the Duchy*, 163–5.

[85] *PL*, ii, 203–4.

[86] E199/30/23; *PL*, ii, 145. See also KB9/267, no. 25; KB29/83, rot. 39; E372/296, Norfolk and Suffolk rot. 2d.; Griffiths, *Henry VI*, 589.

[87] *CPR*, 1446–52, 455.

many of the charges against Heydon and his allies were dismissed.[88] However, neither man was re-appointed to the commission of the peace in Norfolk until March 1455, and some sort of justice had been served upon both Tuddenham and Heydon; their political influence never again reached the same heights as it had done in the 1440s, although this was in part a result of the reduced power of their aristocratic connections in East Anglia.[89] Oxford was placed in a difficult position by the fact that Suffolk's old affinity had better connections at court than he did with which to influence both the king and the other lords. The duke of Somerset's support was in part based on the royal household and other elements of Suffolk's old regime, which, of course, gave Tuddenham and Heydon a natural ally at the heart of government once Somerset became the leading minister of Henry VI. With this support at court, there was little likelihood that Oxford and Norfolk could achieve great success. However, if, as Colin Richmond says, 'By Easter 1451 it was becoming clear that in the battle of county against court the county's victory was to be limited', any sort of victory at all was primarily a result of the efforts of Oxford and to a lesser extent Norfolk.[90]

The years immediately following the commission saw a great reduction in the references to Oxford by the Paston circle. This may, at least in part, be attributable to a change of local political stance. The first evidence for this is from the returns of an oyer and terminer commission of 1453, where Norfolk, John Howard and other Mowbray servants were forced to find security for their good behaviour towards the duchess of Suffolk, but also to the earl of Oxford, the Lords Roos and Scales, Sir Richard de Vere, the earl's brother, and many others. Towards the earl, Norfolk pledged to keep the peace under pain of £2000.[91] While Oxford had not been directly attacked, his presence on what might be termed the opposite side to Norfolk is significant, given their apparently close association and common interests in the commission of 1450–1. Had Oxford realized that local peace was not to be found in the overbearing duke, and decided to shift his stance to offer support to the duchess? This certainly seems to be the case, especially when his rapprochement with two de la Pole retainers, and former opponents, Tuddenham and Heydon, is considered. The earliest evidence for this is from 1456, in John Heydon's case, when he was among the earl's feoffees in what seems likely to have been a major settlement of his estates, and in Tuddenham's by 1457–8, by which date he was in receipt of a life annuity of £10 from Oxford, but in both cases the establishment of concord could well have happened earlier.[92]

[88] Castor, *Blood and Roses*, 76–8, though Castor surprisingly omits any mention of Tuddenham's fine late the previous year.

[89] *CPR, 1446–52*, 592; *1452–61*, 672.

[90] Richmond, *Paston Family: First Phase*, 60.

[91] KB9/118/2, part 1, nos 16–17, 21, 25, 57.

[92] For the enfeoffment, see C140/10/23 and below, 37; Tuddenham's annuity is mentioned in

What was de Vere trying to achieve? Such a policy shift might be a genuine dislike of local disorder, and disgust with Norfolk's actions, but could also be a desire to be on the winning side. Certainly his actions in Norfolk and Suffolk over two decades suggest that he attempted to be either associated with, or certainly not hostile to, the faction in local politics which had the greatest backing from Westminster. Inaction during Suffolk's ascendancy, involvement with the commission attacking the former de la Pole power structures while the reforming York looked as if he might take over, followed by a switch, after York's failure, back to a certain accomodation with the de la Poles, while their ally Somerset dominated government: all these tactical choices show de Vere unwilling to be on the opposite side locally to the most powerful faction at court. This strategy was prudent and shrewd in two counties where he was not territorially dominant (Norfolk and Suffolk) and needed allies. After 1455, as high politics polarized and civil war loomed, Oxford's strategy became even more necessary. The earl pursued a studied neutrality while the result of the power struggle at the centre hung in the balance until Towton, manifested in a very balanced set of feoffees in a major settlement of his estates in 1456. Such a policy safeguarded his own interests in East Anglia, but also illustrates the interconnection between national and local politics, and the earl's need to keep the bigger picture in view.

The extent of John de Vere's lordship in Essex is also crucial, although compared to Norfolk and Suffolk the evidence is much less illuminating. It is to the credit of John de Vere that he accepted with no apparent problems the arrival of a potential rival to his family's traditional lordship in Essex in the 1430s, and to both him and to Henry Bourgchier that they co-operated so amicably during the 1440s and 1450s. The Bourgchiers were no more than prominent Essex gentry in 1400, and their rise in the fifteenth century was rapid, thanks largely to the marriage of Sir William Bourgchier in 1405 to Anne, widow of Edmund, earl of Stafford and daughter of Thomas, duke of Gloucester. Anne was also co-heiress to the estates of the Bohun earls of Hereford and Essex, and some of these estates she settled on her son by her second marriage, Henry Bourgchier, who was created Viscount Bourgchier in 1446, and earl of Essex in 1461. Given the close proximity of their seats at Halstead and Hedingham – only five miles separate the two – and the fact that both held most of their estates in the north and northeast of the county, there was an enormous potential for rivalry in terms of influence and competitive retaining. The arrival of a new magnate on a county scene where the other magnate felt his family had a right to 'rule' the county led at least twice to serious friction in the 1440s and 1450s, in the cases of Courtenay and Bonville in the West Country, and the intrusion of the Neville family into parts of the north that the Percy family thought their sphere of influence. This did not occur in Essex. Many men had good connections with both de

RH, Attic, box marked 'Comes Oxonie'. For Heydon, see also Appendix I, in Richmond, 'East Anglian Politics and Society', in *Medieval East Anglia*, ed. Harper-Bill, 201.

Vere and Bourgchier, with no sense of split loyalties.[93] Both were moderates in the 1450s and their close association in governmental business and to a lesser extent in politics is demonstrated by Oxford's enfeoffment of both Henry and his brother Thomas, archbishop of Canterbury, in 1456.[94] There is no evidence of any disputes between them, and indeed order was reasonably well kept in Essex during the disturbed 1450s.[95] They regularly served in person on commissions and often together.[96] Oxford was the senior partner in terms of rank, until 1461, and wealth, a point only partly countered by Bourgchier's better connections with Stafford and York.[97] Relations with the other Essex noble family, the Lords Fitzwalter, were also amicable, helped by the fact that Earl Aubrey, had married Alice, daughter of Walter, fifth Lord Fitzwalter, and there was, therefore, a fairly close blood relationship.

The duke of Somerset's regime suffered a severe setback in August 1453 when the king had a mental breakdown, and his authority, which had implicitly supported Somerset, was removed. During the autumn the duke of York gradually gained power – Somerset was placed in the Tower in December 1453 and in March 1454 York was appointed Protector during Henry's incapacity, and constituted a formal council.[98] Oxford was involved in the establishment of the council, since he was present at a meeting on 30 November 1453, and signed two warrants on 13 February 1454.[99] On 3 April 1454 at the meeting of the 'king's council' when York asked who would attend the protectorate council, Oxford, like most others nobles, replied that he would do that which was in his power 'as farr as his sikness would suffer hym with the wyche as he sayd he was many tyemes full sore vexed with'.[100] Since he did serve, as did many of the nobles, it seems unlikely that this was anything more than a disclaimer. Oxford had offered no active support to either York or Somerset, but his age and experience meant his might well have been a respected voice, and he would have been welcomed on the Protectorate council, to give it a wider, non-partisan, scope.

During the Protectorate Oxford made a determined effort in the business of royal council and government for the first time. He attended council eight times

---

93 See Ross, 'De Vere Earls', 219, 222–4.

94 C140/10/23.

95 KB9/268–292. Essex saw very few major violent incidents in the 1450s, although there were a slightly greater number in the last few years of the decade, but no evidence of problems between the Essex magnates.

96 For example, in the somewhat disturbed period of 1450–1, they both sat on commissions at Colchester in February 1451: see above, 31, n. 82.

97 Bourgchier's income was around £850 in 1436, compared to Oxford's £1150 by 1437, and c. £1000 in 1461, compared to Oxford's c. £1700: Woodger, 'Henry Bourgchier', 204, and see above, 25.

98 PPC, vi, 167, 171; Parliament Rolls, xii, 257–9.

99 Johnson, Duke Richard of York, 128.

100 R.A. Griffiths, 'The King's Council and the First Protectorate of the Duke of York, 1453–4', EHR, xcix (1984), 80.

between 13 February and 29 June 1454 during the first protectorate and twice more on 5 and 11 December 1455, after the establishment of the second.[101] This was a level of attendance quite out of character for Oxford and suggests that the earl had some sympathy for York and for what he was trying to achieve. This impression is strengthened by Oxford's personal involvement in a specific aspect of government business during 1454, namely his appointment to the keeping of the sea, alongside the earls of Salisbury, Shrewsbury, Worcester and Wiltshire, the Lords Fitzwarin and Stourton, and his brother, Sir Robert Vere. This was an experienced group, but Oxford would seem to have been well-suited to the appointment, since he had several ships of his own, and he himself was active in pursuance of this commission.[102]

With the recovery of Henry VI early in 1455 Somerset rapidly regained his former position as leading minister. The resulting tension between York and Somerset erupted at what is normally described as the first battle of the Wars of the Roses at St Albans on 22 May 1455. According to the account in the Paston letters: 'The duke of Norfolke come a day aftyr the jurney was done with [6000] men. And the Erle of Oxinford also.'[103] That Norfolk, who was more closely associated with York than Oxford, was late, led at least one historian to assume that Norfolk's support was half-hearted and that he was late on purpose.[104] The same is likely to be true of Oxford, who had offered little active support to either faction between 1450 and 1455, and who would have had very little to gain by fighting, and certainly not against his anointed king. He did not have the anxiety of York or the Nevilles, who feared exclusion from government or worse, but given that he appears to have had little sympathy for Somerset, it cannot be assumed, as Lander states, that the earl 'would certainly have been on the royalist side' had he arrived in time, and it seems likely that he had no wish to be anyone's partisan.[105]

Despite his victory at St Albans, York was unable to establish a lasting control over government, and his brief second protectorate was ended in February 1456. An uneasy peace was broken at the battle of Blore Heath in September 1459 and a series of engagements was only terminated by the victory of York's son,

---

[101] C81/1546, nos 74, 75, 79, 80, 82; E28/84, nos 15, 17, 22, 23, 58; E28/87, nos 8, 9, 14; R. Virgoe, 'The Composition of the King's Council, 1437–61', *BIHR*, xliii (1970), 159.

[102] E28/74, no. 66; *PPC*, v, 384, 386; C.F. Richmond, 'Royal Administration and the Keeping of the Seas, 1422–85' (unpublished D.Phil, Oxford University Press, 1963), 254. His involvement can be traced in *PL*, iii, 2; C76/138, m. 31; 141, m. 9. For the problems he had in trying to secure payment of his salary, A. Steel, *The Receipt of the Exchequer, 1377–1485* (Cambridge, 1954), 276, 341; E401/839, mm. 8, 9, 12–14; E13/151 m. 82d.; *Letters and Papers Illustrative of the Wars of the English in France During the Reign of Henry VI*, ed. J. Stevenson (2 vols, in 3, Rolls Series, 1864), ii, 493–4. For his brother Robert, see the unpublished biography by Hannes Kleineke for the History of Parliament Trust, 1422–1504 section.

[103] *PL*, iii, 30.

[104] C.A.J. Armstrong, 'Politics and the Battle of St. Albans, 1455', *BIHR*, xxxiii (1960), 18.

[105] J.R. Lander, *Crown and Nobility* (London, 1976), 301.

Edward IV, at Towton on 29 March 1461. The sources for the battles do, as a rule, record the principal noblemen who were with the king at any moment of political crisis. In an assessment of the numbers of noblemen who fought in the sequence of battles and stand-offs in these two years, Colin Richmond established that both viscounts, ten of the fourteen earls and all the dukes fought on at least one occasion and mostly on more.[106] Of the four earls who did not fight, Worcester was abroad, Warenne, the heir of the duke of Norfolk, aged only fifteen in 1459, was too young to participate and the earl of Westmorland was possibly simple, as William Worcester calls him 'innocens'.[107] All but one member of the higher nobility was either recorded as fighting, or there is a reason for his non-participation. The one exception to this was Oxford, who is not mentioned by any chronicles after 1455 until 1462, nor is he connected to any battle by the Paston letters. Several men were probably not eager to participate – the earl of Arundel fought only once, at the second battle of St Albans, and Lord Stanley was more of an interested observer than a participant on several battlefields. Yet Oxford, in avoiding the battlefield altogether, was unique.

The earl also evaded commitment to either cause by an appearance at a partisan parliament or council. He was summoned to a council at Coventry in August 1458, but there is no record that he actually attended.[108] He was summoned, but did not attend, the Lancastrian parliament of 1459 since he did not sign the oath of allegiance to Henry VI, which he would surely have had to do, had he been present.[109] During the Yorkist parliament of 1460, he was licensed to be absent from all parliaments and councils on grounds of ill health on 12 November.[110] This ill-health may have been genuine, but fits a pattern of avoidance of politically sensitive councils and parliaments during the later 1450s. He was, however, at court in June 1461, when he witnessed the creation of Henry Bourgchier as Earl of Essex, and was present in Edward IV's first parliament in November 1461 on six of the eight days recorded in the fragmentary sources of attendance for this parliament.[111] The earl presumably felt that he had to make an acknowledgement of the newly victorious king.

Oxford's position was seemingly accepted by both sides. The earl was appointed to governmental business by whoever was in control, including all forty-nine commissions of the peace in Cambridgeshire, Norfolk, Suffolk and

---

[106]   C.F. Richmond, 'The Nobility and the Wars of the Roses, 1459–61', *Nottingham Medieval Studies*, xxi (1977), 83.

[107]   Ibid., 82.

[108]   Watts, *Henry VI*, 347n.

[109]   J. E. Powell and K. Wallis, *The House of Lords in the Middle Ages* (London, 1968), 503, and for this parliament see more generally Griffiths, *Henry VI*, 822–9; Watts, *Henry VI*, 352–4.

[110]   *CPR, 1452–61*, 645.

[111]   C53/192, m. 2; *The Fane Fragment of the 1461 Lords' Journal*, ed. W.H. Dunham (New Haven, CT, 1935), 4, 7, 10, 13, 17; R. Virgoe, 'A New Fragment of the Lords' Journal of 1461', *BIHR*, xxxii (1959), 86–7.

Essex from 1454–1460, and to all seven in the same counties in the new king's reign until February 1462.[112] He was also appointed to partisan business, specifically two commissions of array to resist the Yorkists in Essex on 21 December 1459 and 28 April 1460,[113] although there is no evidence that he acted on either. Helen Castor asserts that the earl's appointment to these two commissions was evidence that 'he had committed himself to the queen against York', but this seems unlikely, as the same commissions included Henry, Viscount Bourgchier, who was to fight for the Yorkists shortly afterwards, and the commissions issued for Norfolk and Suffolk at the same time included another committed Yorkist, the duke of Norfolk.[114] The enfeoffment that Oxford made in 1456 of all the lands in the three counties for which returns from his inquisition *post mortem* survive suggests a man making preparations to sit out the political strife.[115] It is an interesting balance of men comprising those with Yorkist connections such as Henry, Viscount Bourgchier, and his brother Thomas, archbishop of Canterbury; an East Anglian, John Heydon, with good links to the court; neutrals such as William Booth, archbishop of York and John, Lord Stourton; family such as his brother Sir Richard Vere and his cousin Sir John Marney; and servants like Thomas Gournay, esquire, Thomas Denys, William Robson and his receiver-general John Keche. The lack of a high profile supporter of the court faction in the enfeoffment was perhaps compensated for by the long-standing marriage of Oxford's son and heir Aubrey with the duke of Buckingham's daughter, Anne.[116]

Thus, there is no sound evidence to show John de Vere committing himself to either cause between York's first protectorate in 1454 and November 1461, on the battlefield, in council or parliament, or apparently on government business. Moreover, a document surviving probably from January or February 1461, lists lords according to their supposed political affiliations of either Yorkist or neutral. Oxford is cited among the latter, and he is in fact the only earl in that column, although other lords like Rivers and Stourton appear.[117] This was drawn up by

---

[112] *CPR, 1452–61*, 661, 665, 672, 678; *1461–7*, 560, 564, 568, 573.

[113] *CPR, 1452–61*, 558, 603.

[114] Ibid., 560, 603; H. Castor, 'Vere, John de, twelfth earl of Oxford (1408–1462)', *ODNB*.

[115] C140/10/23. The returns are from Cornwall, Oxfordshire and Buckinghamshire, but the presence of several East Anglian landowners makes it probable that estates in those counties were also enfeoffed.

[116] The couple were married by January 1443, when Anne's father paid Oxford £20 for the sustenance of Anne, 'consort' of Aubrey: National Library of Wales, Peniarth MS 280, fol. 24; C. Rawcliffe, *The Staffords, Earls of Stafford and Dukes of Buckingham* (Cambridge, 1978), 21, 120. The unusual use of 'consors' rather than 'uxor' might imply that both parties were under the canonical age of marriage. This is certainly possible in Aubrey's case (see below, 43 n. 145), though it is hard to be precise about Anne's age. *PL*, iii, 218 should be read as a comment on the existing marriage and the effect it might have on Aubrey's incipient Lancastrianism.

[117] E163/28/5; see Griffiths, *Henry VI*, 880, n.82 and Watts, *Henry VI*, 361n for the date and form, and C.F. Richmond, 'The Nobility and the Wars of the Roses: the Parliamentary Session of January 1461', *Parliamentary History*, xviii (1999), 261–9 for a full discussion of the document.

or for the leading Yorkist lords and is an important contemporary comment on Oxford's position, confirming that he had successfully avoided commitment to either side during the struggle of the last few years of the 1450s.

Historians discussing the participation of the nobility in the early stages of the Wars of the Roses have agreed that, as Richmond states, the higher nobility 'above all others could not evade responsibility', and as McFarlane put it 'it was difficult for any members of the class, however constitutionally wary, to hold aloof. Their position involved them. To opt out meant the sacrifice of their inherited responsibilities as patrons of a territorial clientèle, the local expression of their lordly status.'[118] So why did Oxford remain above the fray? Practically, he had much to lose and little to gain by becoming involved. He was a much richer man than his father, and his lordship extended much further. While he might lose some of his local following by staying aloof, if he ended up on the losing side he would put much more, such as his life and his family, in jeopardy. If he were to choose the winning side he would gain little as he was not powerful enough, unlike the Nevilles, to make a great difference on his own: it is unlikely that he would have been showered with offices and wealth as Warwick was in 1461, or indeed as his son was in 1485, when the circumstances were very different. Oxford had no close familial or martial links with the most powerful protagonists, nor had been closely associated with any before the civil strife. He was content to give York a passive support throughout the first half of the 1450s, and especially during the Protectorate, whilst never really committing himself in his cause. Perhaps he sympathized with the politically reforming stance that York was taking, but could not, however, justify York's actions against the anointed king. The most plausible explanation is that he made a decision to avoid the dangers of civil war, and to protect his own lands and interests by staying at home. However, this leaves some explaining to do as to why, having been conspicuous by his absence at the battles of Northampton, second St Albans and Towton, the earl was executed for treason just eleven months into Edward IV's reign.

The conspiracy of 1462

John de Vere's involvement in a plot to kill Edward IV in February 1462 is the most perplexing aspect of his political career. It came after at least seven years of an absence of commitment to either side in the violent political and dynastic struggle. The bare outline of the conspiracy was repeated in virtually every major

---

[118] Richmond, 'Nobility and the Wars of the Roses', *Nottingham Medieval Studies*, 83; K.B. McFarlane, 'The Wars of the Roses' in idem, *England in the Fifteenth Century* (London, 1981), 245. McFarlane goes on to add that a surprising number of the nobility did stand aloof, but that was a feature more typical of 1469–71, and especially 1483–7 than 1459–61.

chronicle of the time,[119] of which this extract from a London chronicle is a typical example:

> And the xii day of ffebruary therle of Oxenford and ther Lord Aubrey Vere, his sone, sir Thomas Tuddenham, William Tyrell and other were brought into the Tower of London. And upon the xx day of the said moneth the said Lord Aubrey was drawn from Westmynster to the Tower Hill and there beheded. And the xxiii day of the said moneth of ffebruary sir Thomas Tuddenham, William Tyrell, and John Montgomery were behedid at said Tower Hill. And upon the ffriday next folowyng, which was the xxvi day of ffebruary, therle of Oxenford was led upon ffot from Westmynster unto the Tower Hill, and there beheded; and after the corps was had unto the ffrere Augustynes, and there buried in the Quer.[120]

John and Aubrey were in fact tried at some point between 12 and 20 February by the newly appointed constable, the earl of Worcester, found guilty and condemned to death.[121] The trial was done by 'law Padua', according to Warkworth's chronicle, or by Roman rather than by English law.[122] Upon these facts the chronicles seem agreed. Unfortunately, they agree on little else, and it is not easy to establish a coherent account of the episode, what form the conspiracy took, how it was betrayed, and above all, by what was it motivated.

Edward IV had only been king for a year by March 1462, and there was widespread residual support for Henry VI. Rumours were rife of a large-scale invasion of England from France in favour of Queen Margaret, from Scotland by the Lancastrians in exile there and from troops raised by the duke of Somerset.[123] A letter from the earl of Warwick and Antonio della Torre, envoy of King Edward, to Francesco di Coppini, the Papal legate, explicitly states that Oxford's plot

[119] 'A Shorter English Chronicle', in *Three Fifteenth Century Chronicles*, ed. J. Gairdner (Camden Society, n. s., xxviii, 1880), 78; *Six Town Chronicles*, ed. R. Flenley (Oxford, 1911), 163; *Great Chronicle of London*, 198–9; *The New Chronicles of England and France*, ed. H. Ellis (London 1811), 652; 'Benet's Chronicle', 232; *A Chronicle of the First Thirteen Years of the Reign of King Edward IV, by John Warkworth*, ed. J.O. Halliwell (Camden Society, o.s., x, 1834), 5; *Historical Collections of a London Citizen*, 218; E. Hall, *The Union of the Two Noble Families of Lancaster and York* (Scolar Press, 1970), A.i. The 'Brief Notes' says that Aubrey was hung and disembowelled, '*suspensus et tractus*', rather than beheaded, in *Three Fifteenth Century Chronicles*, ed. Gairdner, 162.

[120] *Chronicles of London*, 177.

[121] No records survive of the trial. For the court and what remains of its records, see G.O. Squibb, *The High Court of Chivalry* (Oxford, 1981), 27; L.W. Vernon-Harcourt, *His Grace the Steward and the Trial of Peers* (1907), 391; and see more generally M.H. Keen, 'The Jurisdiction and Origins of the Constable's Court', in *War and Government in the Middle Ages: Essays in Honour of J.O. Prestwich*, ed. J. Gillingham and J.C. Holt (Woodbridge, 1984), 159–69; idem, 'Treason Trials under the Law of Arms', *TRHS*, fifth series, xii (1962), 98–9.

[122] *Warkworth's Chronicle*, 5. He adds that 'most people were sorry' that they were executed, a comment in keeping with his 'mildly' Lancastrian views; Gransden, *Historical Writing*, 259, and more generally on Warkworth, 257–61.

[123] As described in 'Brief Notes' in *Three Fifteenth Century Chronicles*, ed. Gairdner, 158, and for the authorship, method, and his positive verdict on the reliability of this source, see xv–xix.

was to go with Edward's army as it set out to subdue the north of England and then to fall upon the king's army from the rear as soon as Lancastrian forces came within striking distance. In addition, the duke of Somerset was to descend on England from Bruges, the earl of Pembroke from Brittany, and King Henry from the north with the king of Scots.[124] Sir John Fastolf's former chaplain, Thomas Howes, wrote to John Paston around February 1462 reciting that 'hit was leten me wete in ryght secrete wyse that a pyssaunce is redy to aryve in thre parties of this londe, by the meane of Kyng Herry and the Quene that was, and by the Dewk Somercete and others' totalling the absurd number of 120,000 men, one force landing by the River Trent, another in Wales and the third from the Channel Islands.[125] It is tempting to think that Howes had heard something from someone in the de Vere circle, but there is no evidence of this, and it may just have been wild rumours. A more plausible story, from which wilder rumours could have sprung, is given in a 'Brief Latin Chronicle' which proposes that Oxford was conspiring with Somerset to use Essex as a landing site for an seaborne invasion: '*Facta est conspiratio contra dictum regem Edwardum per Comitem Oxon. et filium ejus … ut in parte Esexie introducerent ducem Somersetie per navigium cum hostili exercitu.*'[126] This seems more likely, given the involvement in the conspiracy of a number of East Anglian men, but the exact details cannot be easily ascertained.

Two sources give almost totally opposing accounts of how the king discovered the plan. Hearne's fragment of an old English chronicle states that 'Harry Vere lorde Aubrey accusid his owne fadir erle of Oxforde of treason, wherupon they were bothe taken … and brought to the toure.'[127] The account itself records that it was written by someone in the household of Thomas Howard, duke of Norfolk, and may well have drawn on the duke's own knowledge, although most especially for the period after 1468.[128] Despite this potentially knowledgeable authorship, there are significant problems with this account. Aside from the lack of reliability suggested by the naming of Aubrey de Vere, the fact that it places the events in February 1460, and that it was probably written some fifty years after the events it describes,[129] there are two more important reasons for not accepting this account. One will be dealt with shortly when the problem

---

[124] *Calendar of State Paper Milan, 1385–1618* (hereafter *CSP Milan*), 107. For the roles of della Torre and Coppini over the previous two years, see C. Head, 'Pius II and the Wars of the Roses', *Archivum Historiae Pontificae*, viii (1979), 139–78.

[125] *PL*, iv, 32.

[126] 'A Brief Latin Chronicle', in *Three Fifteenth Century Chronicles*, 175. The chronicle is contemporary, and provides factual detail not found elsewhere: ibid., xx–xxviii.

[127] *Chronicles of the White Rose of York*, ed. J.A. Giles (London, 1845), 11–12.

[128] Ibid, 22–3. For a full discussion of the authorship, see D.A.L. Morgan, 'Hearne's "Fragment" and the Long Prehistory of English Memoirs', *EHR*, cxxiv (2009), 811–32, especially 814–8.

[129] C.L. Kingsford, *English Historical Literature in the Fifteenth Century* (Oxford, 1913), 176–7. It must date from between 1516 and 1522.

of motivation is considered. The other reason is the timing. As Cora Scofield notes, John de Vere was appointed to a commission of the peace for Norfolk on 12 February, the day he and his son were arrested in Essex.[130] Therefore, the conspiracy was discovered very suddenly. It seems rather unlikely that Aubrey went to London, told the King that he and his father were traitors, and then trotted back to his family home in northern Essex, where he was arrested. Nor is it likely, although it cannot be proved, that he would have written a letter to the king detailing the conspiracy, since he surely would have wanted to speak to the king face to face to exonerate himself. Moreover, if it had been Aubrey who betrayed them, it would seem strange that he too was executed, given Edward's general policy of clemency early in his reign. As R.J. Mitchell states, this 'account may be disregarded'.[131] A slightly more plausible, if still rather elaborate, account survives in the letter by Warwick and della Torre to Coppini.[132] According to this a messenger, carrying letters from the earl and the other conspirators to the Queen in Scotland, had a crisis of conscience in a church near York, and took the letters to the King in London. Edward had copies made of them and then sent the messenger to King Henry, making him promise to return with the reply, which the messenger did. This letter seems to be an official report, especially as Warwick's name appears on it, and King Edward comes out of it well. However, there is no reason not to believe it, and indeed a very similar account is contained in the 'Brief Notes' penned by a monk in the monastery of Ely.[133] According to this version, the messenger got as far as Northampton before being struck by his conscience. It is hard to be certain whether the accounts are independent, though the Ely version contains more detail. Another account, erroneously ascribed to William Worcester, is that the conspirators, all of whom are listed, were suspected of correspondence with Queen Margaret: '*arrestantur, ob suspicionem litterarum receptarum dominae Margaretae*'.[134] Whether these letters were in reply to correspondence from Oxford is unknown, but seems plausible. Taken all together the evidence suggests that the conspiracy was betrayed by a messenger or by discovered letters, and not by Aubrey betraying his father.

All of the executed co-conspirators were East Anglian, and most were already connected to the earl. Sir Thomas Tuddenham's career is well known. He was present at the coronation of Edward IV in 1461, and was associated with Alice, duchess of Suffolk, who had made a timely switch to the House of York before

---

[130] C.L. Scofield, *The Life and Reign of Edward IV* (2 vols, London, 1923), i, 231; *CPR, 1461–1467*, 564. Only 'Benet's Chronicle', 232, states that they were arrested in Essex and by whom (the earl of Worcester, Lord Ferrers and Lord Herbert).

[131] R.J. Mitchell, *John Tiptoft* (London, 1938), 87.

[132] *CSP Milan*, 106.

[133] 'Brief Notes', 162.

[134] 'Annales Rerum Anglicarum' in *Wars of the English in France*, ed. Stevenson, ii, 779. It is ascribed to Worcester here, but see K.B. McFarlane, 'William Worcester: A Preliminary Survey', in *England in the Fifteenth Century*, 209–10, for the argument that Worcester was not the author.

1460. However, his sympathies seem ultimately to have been Lancastrian, and an order for his arrest went out as early as April 1461, his estates having been seized.[135] William Tyrell the elder, of Gipping in Suffolk, seems to have been a reasonably committed Lancastrian, enjoying various offices under Henry VI, and being elected to the partisan parliament of 1459.[136] John Montgomery, of Great Tey in Essex, is a more shadowy figure, who having been active in the late 1440s, an MP for Lyme in 1449–50, and a Sergeant-at-Arms in the royal household between 1446 and 1462, seems to have been little involved in local political life in the 1450s, though his sympathies again appear to have been Lancastrian, in contrast to his father, Sir John, who was well connected with York, and his brother, Thomas.[137] 'William Worcester' mentions another man, John Clopton, who was arrested but not executed. Clopton certainly had a general pardon from the king on 27 February 1462, the day after the earl was executed, which would suggest involvement in the conspiracy.[138] The pardon should not be taken as evidence of a reward for betrayal. Clopton was among those who had been enfeoffed by the twelfth earl in 1456, and although this is the only known connection between the two, he did go on to serve the thirteenth earl, which makes it unlikely that he betrayed the conspiracy.[139] His devotion to the family was demonstrated by his commissioning of a stained glass image of Elizabeth, countess of Oxford, in the nave of his parochial church at Long Melford, Suffolk, along with images of John Montgomery and William Tyrell. Tuddenham, Tyrell and others were described as the earl's 'ffeed men' by one of the London chronicles.[140] Tuddenham certainly was, and it is not unlikely that Tyrell and Clopton were also the earl's annuitants. Colin Richmond has noted that Montgomery, Tyrell and Clopton all married daughters of Robert Darcy of Maldon, which would link these three, but it may have been the connection with the de Vere family that brought them all together into treason.[141] The names of Sir William Kennedy, who was executed on 1 March, and the abbot of Bury St Edmunds and three of his monks are added by other sources.[142] William Kennedy is obscure; he might have been the Scottish Sir William Kanete who committed acts of

---

[135] Richmond, *Paston Family: Endings*, 137.

[136] Unpublished article on 'William Tyrell I' by C.E. Moreton, History of Parliament Trust, 1422–1504 section; Wedgwood, ii, 893. Other members of the prolific Tyrell family had close links with Oxford, but the elder William was not obviously among them. However, Tyrell was quite closely associated with John Clopton: *CPR, 1452–61*, 528, 606; *CFR, 1452–61*, 259.

[137] Unpublished article on 'John Montgomery' by C.E. Moreton, History of Parliament Trust, 1422–1504 section; Wedgwood, ii, 604–5.

[138] *CPR, 1461–7*, 113; 'Annales Rerum Anglicarum', in *Wars of the English in France*, ed. Stevenson, ii, 779.

[139] C140/10/23, no. 4; 'William Tyrell I'.

[140] *Great Chronicle of London*, 198.

[141] Richmond, *Paston Family: Endings*, 136.

[142] 'Annales Rerum Anglicarum' in *Wars of the English in France*, ed. Stevenson, ii, 779; 'A Short English Chronicle', in *Three Fifteenth Century Chronicles*, 78; 'Brief Notes', 162.

piracy in the 1450s, and who may or may not have been the same man who stole goods worth over £300 from the abbot of Westminster on the day after the battle of second St Albans.[143] If he was a Scot, then the story of correspondence with Queen Margaret in Scotland is more plausible. General pardons were also issued to the abbot of Bury on 16 March 1462, and to John Heydon on 23 April, which may or may not indicate involvement in the conspiracy, though they are suggestive.[144] No source elaborates on their role within the conspiracy.

There is a possible explanation for the conspiracy, which seems so out of character for this neutral earl. The only member of the family who appears to have had any Lancastrian sympathies was Aubrey, the earl's eldest son and heir. Aubrey was in his late twenties or early thirties, already financially independent of his father, and therefore free to act on his own account.[145] He appears to have been pursuing his own policy in local affairs, and indeed may have been casting a covetous eye over the Fastolf inheritance, which the Pastons were claiming. William Paston, writing to his brother, warned him that 'it is full nesessary to mak zow strong be lord chep ... [as Aubrey] was lathe with master Fastolff be fore he dyed'.[146] If this reading of this letter is correct Aubrey was pursuing a policy that would have been not only damaging to the Pastons, but also at variance with his father's attitude to the Pastons in particular and Norfolk politics in general.

In the same letter on 2 May 1460, William Paston stated that 'myn Lord Awbry hathe weddit the Duke of Bokyngham dowter ... and he is gret with the Qwene',[147] suggesting clearly that Aubrey's political sympathies were Lancastrian. Other scraps of evidence hint that Aubrey was deeply involved and that those around him knew something of the conspiracy. The 'Brief Notes' state that Aubrey was arrested and taken to London, but do not mention his father who was taken into custody at the same time. In fact the only reference to the earl in this source

---

[143] *Calendar of Early Chancery Proceedings Relating to West Country Shipping*, ed. D.M. Gardiner (Devon and Cornwall Record Society, n.s. xxi, 1976), nos 67a–e; KB27/803, rex rot 6d.; C.L. Kingsford, *Prejudice and Promise in Fifteenth Century England* (Oxford, 1925), 53, 89, 90.

[144] C81/1490, nos 38, 41.

[145] Knighted in 1441 (BL, Lansdowne Ch., 156), his age is uncertain. He must have been a minimum of twenty-five in 1462 as he was appointed for the first and only time to a commission of the peace in 1458 for Suffolk, and to a commission of array in the same county: *CPR*, 1452–61, 490, 678. Evidence for an earlier birth comes from the fact that he appears as a feoffee in 1456, along with, among others, Tuddenham and Heydon, for Sir Miles Stapilton: KB27/774, rex rot. 8v; CP25/1/293/73/412. A number of manors had been settled in jointure on Aubrey and his wife Anne at the time of their marriage in 1443; these were Wigston Magna in Leicestershire, Calverton and Whitchurch in Buckinghamshire, Badlesmere in Kent, Bures, Hedingham Vaux and Downham in Essex and Kensington and Notting Barns in Middlesex, together worth in excess of £200 p.a. For other estates he may have held, which provide evidence of a slightly earlier birth, see Ross, 'De Vere Earls', 48–9.

[146] *PL*, iii, 218.

[147] Ibid., 218.

is the bald statement: 'decapitatus erat comes Oxonie'.[148] One of the Paston letters indirectly implies uncertainty about Oxford's involvement, in the admission of a connection of Aubrey's, John Fermour, that John Gylys, a privy secretary to the earl, might have had knowledge of this conspiracy: 'and if any wrytyng were made by the seyd Erle, the seyd Gylys knew ther of in this gret matyeres'.[149] Another letter by John Wykes on 25 March describes John Fermour's arrest because 'he dwellid with the Erle of Oxonfords son, and purposid to have passid the see withou[t] lycence'.[150] Thus those associated with Aubrey were under great suspicion. It is not possible to say with any certainty whether Aubrey hazarded his life on Henry VI's behalf at any of the battles between 1459 and 1461, though it is unlikely, as there is no record of him being present at any, nor was he attainted in parliament, or pardoned. It is probable that Oxford restrained his son from such action, since his influence was unlikely to be strong enough to protect him from the consequences of being on the losing side.

One alternative explanation for the conspiracy can be discounted. In a letter, dated 31 May, which both Gairdner and Davis attribute to 1461, the earl wrote to John Paston, and asked 'if ye or any of yowre men here that Howard purposith hym to make any aray at owre manor of Wynche' he should inform John Keche, the keeper of the manor, who could then hold out until Oxford arrived.[151] Sir John Howard had just been appointed sheriff of Norfolk, and Gairdner states that he 'appears to have had very great influence just after the accession of Edward IV, which he used in a very overbearing manner'.[152] Sir John was Countess Elizabeth's cousin, descended from a younger son of Sir John Howard the elder. Winch was the ancestral seat of the Howards, which had come to John de Vere with his marriage to Elizabeth. Howard seems to have had designs on Winch, and in fact was in possession of three old Howard manors in Norfolk, including Winch, by May 1462.[153] It has been suggested that it was fear of Howard's designs on Oxford's manors in Norfolk that caused John de Vere to seek some security in removing Howard's source of influence, Edward IV. Colin Richmond has speculated that 'Because Sir John Howard's covetous eye was on East Winch before the earl was executed, one wonders whether it might not have had a part to play in his downfall.' J.S. Roskell surmised that de Vere's inheritance of Winch and other Howard manors led 'to bitter feuds between the earl of Oxford and Lord Howard, which influenced their fateful alignment in the civil wars'.[154]

---

[148] 'Brief Notes', 162.

[149] PL, iv, 35–6 (my italics); PLP, i, 105–6. Probably written in March, this comes from a rough draft of a report to perhaps the Sheriff of Norfolk, in several hands, including John Paston's.

[150] PL, iv, 37. John Fermour was part of the earl's household in 1449, when he was described as a gentleman of East Winch (the earl's Norfolk residence): KB27/754, rots. 53, 111d.

[151] PL, iii, 275; PLP, ii, 235.

[152] PL, iii, 275.

[153] PL, iv, 39.

[154] Richmond, Paston Family: Endings, 135; Roskell, iii, 433.

This is, however, an unsatisfactory explanation. Despite the fact that Oxford's letter was written in May 1461, and Howard was in possession by May 1462, there is no record of him actually entering Winch and the two other manors until after the conspiracy. If he had, one might have expected perhaps a written protest, the start of legal proceedings, or even a report in the Paston letters of fighting at Winch.[155] In any case had Howard illegally entered Winch, Oxford's most obvious solution was surely to take it back by force, rather than to wait ten months and try to dethrone Edward IV. The entry to these manors seems more likely to have been after the earl's execution, when Countess Elizabeth was not really able to protect her inheritance. She was under suspicion herself, and was closely watched until the end of May.[156] This timing is supported by an entry in the records of the court of Common Pleas in the Michaelmas term of 1466, where the countess sued Howard and thirteen others for her manors of Fersfield, East Winch and Brokehall. Her attorney rehearsed the descent of the manors, and claimed that they should be in her hands. The defendants accepted her claim and she recovered seisin.[157] This seems to be collusive action, and was probably a way of formally re-establishing her possession of the manor. The presence of her son-in-law, William Norris, among Howard's associates, hints that some accommodation had been made, probably in March 1462, whereby Howard would take or lease the three manors for a fixed term, and then return them. It may well have been against the countess's wishes, but she had little room for manoeuvre. Howard did also have the grace to return them, unlike the rather worse fate of Elizabeth's estate in 1473.

However great his influence was, it seems unlikely that Howard could have seriously considered seizing by force some of the earl's estates while the earl was still alive, even if Oxford had heard rumours to this effect. Oxford had also shown no signs of disloyalty to the young king by May 1461, nor had he stirred himself to aid Henry VI during the previous years of civil war, and the king would not want a potential magnate supporter alienated, when his regime had comparatively little, non-Neville, noble support. Indeed the earl was attempting to increase his influence with the Yorkist regime, granting a life annuity to a rising star at the court, Sir Thomas Montgomery, in June 1461.[158] Perhaps the most convincing evidence is that relations between the de Veres and the Howards were amicable during the 1460s, which hints that some sort of arrangement had been made after the conspiracy, and friendly relations would have been much

---

[155] None of the legal records contain any reference to any trouble actually occurring: KB27/800–4, KB9/295–300. A valor of Howard's estates from Michaelmas 1463 to 1464 included the three manors, when they provided him with profits of just over £86: *The Household Books of John Howard, Duke of Norfolk, 1462–1471, 1481–1483*, ed. A. Crawford (Stroud, 1992), xlvi.

[156] Scofield, *Edward IV*, i, 233.

[157] CP40/821, rots. 436, 543.

[158] DL29/430/6910.

less likely if Howard had seized these manors by force, especially if this had led directly to the death of the thirteenth earl's father in the conspiracy.[159] Nor is there any sense of an accumulation of local problems driving the earl into rebellion, of which Howard was the last. The rather bitter dispute between the earl and the bishop of Norwich had ended a decade earlier, an argument over the manor of Wenham with the Debenham family had seemingly quietened somewhat since a court case seven years before 1462,[160] and the earl's relations with the Bourgchier family were amicable enough to survive the head of that family becoming considerably more influential with the elevation to the throne of a relative and his subsequent promotion to being de Vere's social equal.[161]

For a man whose concerns and commitment seem only to have been to preserve himself and his interests intact, and who seems to have given no support to either side in the dynastic struggle, the conspiracy appears to be totally out of character, with the risks too great to serve his own interests, and showing an ideological commitment to the cause of Henry VI not even remotely evident from his behaviour over the previous ten years. It may therefore have been Aubrey, his eldest son and heir, in great favour at the Lancastrian court, who had the ideological commitment to the Lancastrian cause, perhaps through his wife, and who was the prime mover in a conspiracy which sought a Lancastrian restoration and that the increasingly elderly earl was inexorably drawn into his son's rash venture. It may be that in this case, it was the sins of the son that were visited upon the father.

Conclusion

The twelfth earl conscientiously fulfilled his duties to the crown throughout his career, both in East Anglia and abroad in France. But his participation in high politics was infrequent; he does seem to have had a poor attendance record at councils, he appears to have been rarely at court no matter who was in power, and he was conspicuous by his absence during the military struggles between the

---

[159] Howard made two hunting trips with the thirteenth earl that lasted for several days and one other visit, in 1465–6, and his youngest daughter Jane was part of the dowager countess's household: see *Household Books of John Howard*, ed. Crawford, 301, 338, 339–40, 355. For the de Vere estates in Howard's hands, see ibid., 474.

[160] Ross, 'De Vere Earls', 134–6.

[161] The earl had several ongoing legal cases in the later 1450s, but almost all were of the minor kind that most landowners faced on a regular basis: e.g. CP40/779, rot. 407; 781, rot. 368d. (v. William Menwynnek, his Cornish receiver, concerning a debt of £63, the earl claiming damages of £100); CP40/780, rots 206d. (v. Charles Nedwell and John Juy, debt of £20), 275 (v. Thomas Michell of Stapleford and William Springfield of Thaxted respectively for damaging his property), 365 (v. John and Thomas Cutte debt of £13, and Aubrey had a case v. Thomas Lee of Ipswich for theft of horses), 411 (three debts cases v. Hugh Bekenham, 10 marks, v. John Waynflete and Robert Pyrne, £8, v. John Bury £10).

king and the Yorkists. It was this total refusal to commit himself to either side that made John de Vere's career unusual. As was true of some of the nobility, he had no pressing motivation deriving from the defence of his own interests or lordship forcing him to take up arms; there was no dispute or conflict for influence or 'rule' in Essex or elsewhere which seems to have been the primary motivation for some of the combatants such as Bonville, Courtenay, Percy and Neville, and which explains, to some extent, their political alignments. On the level below the foremost participants, there was a general reluctance to be drawn into the conflict. It may be that the ideological aspects of the war did not matter enough to some men for them to want to risk lands and life by fighting for either side, or, as is possible in Oxford's case, that a moderate support for York's attempt at reform was not enough to force him to take up arms against his anointed king. However, while many nobles were very reluctantly drawn into the dynastic struggle, virtually all of the higher nobility were forced to become involved. In the successful avoidance of the conflict between 1459 and 1461, John de Vere was unique; it is in the light of this that the conspiracy of 1462 seems so out of place. No action in John de Vere's career even hints that such a conspiracy either would have been likely or had any ideological appeal for him.

John de Vere, soon to become the thirteenth earl of Oxford, thus received a mixed legacy from his family. There were some underlying strengths to his position. The ancient descent of the family increased his 'worship' in a society deeply concerned with lineage, and generated an unchallengeable tenure of many of his manors. The twelfth earl, by a good marriage, had substantially increased the family's estates, and brought them to a position amongst the middle earners of the higher nobility. The twelfth earl was the first of the family to exercise a genuinely regional influence; acquisition of land and frequent residence in Norfolk allowed him to play a real role in that county's politics, and to make connections with local gentry that his successors could build on, as well as enjoy the traditional de Vere social and political leadership in northern Essex and southern Suffolk. Yet, the events of 1462 put all this in jeopardy. Aside from the difficulties of recovering the earldom, the Yorkist dynasty would look with suspicion upon the family thereafter. Nor could the psychological impact of the executions of a father and elder brother upon the second son be anything other than devastating, and would affect his personal outlook for a long time to come.

The Thirteenth Earl: Sedition, the Readeption, and Imprisonment, 1462–85

> *Oxford Call him my king by whose injurious doom*
> *My elder brother, the Lord Aubrey Vere,*
> *Was done to death? and more than so, my father,*
> *Even in the downfall of his mellow'd years,*
> *When Nature brought him to the door of Death?*
> *No, Warwick, no; while life upholds this arm,*
> *This arm upholds the house of Lancaster*
> (William Shakespeare, *King Henry VI, Part III*,
> Act III, Scene III, lines 101–107)

Regaining the earldom and the early years, 1462–9

For all that the executions of 1462 were a tragedy for the young John de Vere, the irony was that it was this event that was the making of the man. Prior to the shocking death of his father and brother, John had been destined for a career as a second son, a member of the gentry. Born on 8 September 1442, and nineteen years old in February 1462, his father would presumably have been looking for a gentry heiress for his second son to marry, and although Aubrey had not yet had any children, his position as second in line to the comital title was precarious.[1] Doubtless he would have given loyal service to his older brother, as his younger siblings were later to give to him, but his horizons would have been limited.

We know very little of John's upbringing, education or family relationships while his father was still alive. There is later evidence that he could read in at least three languages, English, French and Latin. While some of these skills, particularly the French, may have been acquired later, it seems likely that he had

---

[1] Date of birth from his father's inquisition *post mortem*: C140/10/23. S.J. Payling, 'The Economics of Marriage in Late Medieval England: The Marriage of Heiresses', *Econ HR*, liv (2001), 413–29. Payling argues, 424–6, that younger sons tended to marry heiresses, though rarely the prize noble heiresses, while the elder son often did not, as was the case with Aubrey's marriage to the noble, but landless, Anne Stafford.

basic schooling in reading and writing in English and Latin before he became earl.[2] While two of his younger brothers were to be destined for the priesthood before the catastrophe of 1462, John de Vere was second in line to the comital dignity, and would presumably have received the same education as his older brother. Such learning would not have been wasted even had his brother become earl, if John went on to marry an heiress or acquired land of his own, as Nicholas Orme has noted the necessity for noble and gentle proprietors to become acquainted with the documentation of their estates, administration and legal affairs, in order to have oversight of their officials and prevent fraud.[3] As the twelfth earl had four sons, including John, close in age, it is likely that he would have retained the services of a tutor in his household, and that John's early education would have been at home. Whether he then went to one of the grammar schools near to Hedingham, such as Bury St Edmund's or Colchester, or indeed one of the Cambridge colleges, where his younger brother George was by 1462, is not known.[4]

It is therefore not clear where John de Vere was when his father and brother were seized at Hedingham, nor is his location during the pivotal period between their arrest and execution known. Was he with his mother, in what is likely to have been a close watch, if not actual custody? Was he taken with his father and brother and questioned at the same time? How much did he know of the conspiracy, and was he indeed directly involved? Was he forced to watch the executions as a salutary lesson? None of these questions can be answered. At the time, a further question must have been preying on John de Vere's mind – what was going to happen to him, and the earldom to which he was now heir?

Edward IV has been deservedly praised for 'his record of mercy to his enemies [which was] quite remarkable for a ruthless age'.[5] The execution of the earl and his eldest son was thus to some extent out of character for the king, but is to be explained by the fact that John and Aubrey were the first noblemen to betray the king, having, de facto, accepted Edward's kingship between Towton and February 1462, during which period the twelfth earl had been present in parliament and at court. After the executions, the king was able then to exercise his customary clemency towards the earl's second son, if he so chose. Yet, while no attainder was posthumously passed on the twelfth earl of Oxford after his execution, for some considerable time the future of the earldom was still in doubt. Admittedly John and William Grene, associates of the twelfth earl, were named as stewards of all the manors he had held in Essex, Suffolk or Cambridge for life on 1 March 1462, and John Keche, the late earl's receiver-general was granted that

---

[2]   See below, 218.
[3]   N. Orme, *English Schools in the Middle Ages* (London, 1973), 31.
[4]   For the schools, see ibid., 298, 300.
[5]   C.D. Ross, *Edward IV* (London, 1974), 65 and more generally 64–8; H. Kleineke, *Edward IV* (London, 2009), 53, 71.

office for most of the earl's lands in April.[6] On 1 June Henry Bourgchier, earl of Essex was granted fifteen de Vere manors as long as they remained in the king's hands, but on 12 August this grant was surrendered and almost all the de Vere manors were granted to Richard, duke of Gloucester in tail, a crushing blow to the prospects of the young John de Vere.[7] Within a year, however, Edward had changed his mind concerning the future of the earldom. In July 1463, some of these estates were granted to George Neville, bishop of Exeter, during the minority of John de Vere, indicating that the king had decided not to endow his younger brother with the de Vere estates permanently. Even so, it was not until 18 January 1464, some five months after his twenty-first birthday, that John was allowed to succeed to his father's estates, with all the profits since the preceding Michaelmas.[8] While Cora Scofield has argued that de Vere succeeded to the earldom without question, the grant to Gloucester, however short-lived, must have indicated otherwise to the earl. It appears that Edward IV came very close to not exercising clemency in the case of John de Vere.

The factor that probably convinced Edward to change his mind, and aided de Vere's political restoration, was John's marriage to Margaret Neville, sister of the earl of Warwick. The union cannot be dated firmly any earlier than 1471, but it is most probable that the marriage took place during the earl's rehabilitation process between 1462 and 1464. Certainly Michael Hicks has argued that the earl's marriage to Warwick's sister 'probably helped [him] to recover his family earldom of Oxford', a statement with which the most recent biographer of the Kingmaker, Tony Pollard, agrees, dating it to about 1463.[9] The balance of probability is that the marriage took place either between August 1462 when the estates were granted in tail to Gloucester and a grant in July 1463 of some of the

---

[6] *CPR, 1461–7*, 139; *PL*, iv, 39. John Grene was a feudal tenant of the earl: *CIPM*, xx, 240. William Grene, his brother, was a farmer of the de Vere manor of Garboldisham (Norfolk) in 1442–3, and an auditor of Countess Alice's estates in 1445: ERO, D/DPr 138; CP40/759, rot. 128. Both were, however, more closely connected with Henry Bourgchier: unpublished article on 'John Green III' by C.E. Moreton, History of Parliament Trust, 1422–1504 section; Woodger, 'Henry Bourgchier', 271–2. Keche had been enfeoffed by the earl in 1456, is known to have served as his receiver-general in 1457–8, and was keeper of Winch in 1461: C140/10/23; RH Attic, box marked 'Comes Oxonie'; *PL*, iii, 275. An order to the keeper of the privy seal was made on 14 April to make letters patent appointing Keche as receiver for all the lands of the earl and his wife, except sixteen specified manors, either seized by John Howard, or which had already been granted out by the king, though no enrolment was made on the Patent Rolls of Keche's appointment: PSO 1/22, no. 1169. The appointment was known by May in Norfolk: *PL*, v, 39.

[7] *CPR, 1461–7*, 142, 193, 197, 229. A number of smaller grants were made by Edward IV of de Vere lands and offices during pleasure, or as long as they were in the king's hands, the first, rather callously, within a day of the earl's execution: *CPR, 1461–7*, 179, 184, 187, 188, 189, 193; C81/790, nos 858, 877, 878, 882, 898; 791, nos 930, 937; PSO 1/21, no. 1117; 22, nos 1160, 1181.

[8] *CPR, 1461–7*, 298; Scofield, 'Early Life', 229.

[9] M.A. Hicks, *Warwick the Kingmaker* (Oxford, 1998), 234; Pollard, *Warwick the Kingmaker*, 16, 63. Neither Scofield, 'Early Life' nor Ross, *Edward IV*, put any date on the marriage.

same estates to George Neville, during the minority of de Vere, or during the five months after his twenty-first birthday before he was granted livery of his inheritance, perhaps with the estates being withheld until the knot had been tied. The marriage is almost certain to have occurred by 1465, when at the enthronement of George Neville as archbishop of York, Oxford was seated in a place of honour at the high table, and a countess of Oxford was seated in the second chamber. It could have been the dowager countess Elizabeth, but the probability is that it was the new countess Margaret, seated next to her sister and sister-in-law, Lady Hastings and the countess of Warwick.[10] In addition to the considerable advantage of political restoration in marrying Margaret Neville, there was at least one other benefit to John de Vere: Margaret had had a sum of 1000 marks settled on her by the terms of her father's will in 1460 to provide her with a dowry.[11] In circumstances other than those in which John de Vere found himself between 1462 and 1464, an adult, or nearly adult, earl would have been worth rather more as a husband for a noble daughter, and Warwick certainly had the financial resources to add to that sum, but financial considerations must have been secondary in the marriage if it took place before January 1464.[12]

The earl's mother, Elizabeth, had also been under suspicion, though she was pardoned in all but name on 28 May 1462; the king accepted her 'good and faithful' disposition, and she was freed from custody, and allowed to hold all manors, lands and tenements that had come to her by right of inheritance, gift or purchase.[13] However, no dower was ever assigned to her, contrary to the 'law and custom of England'. Legally, she was in a position to claim dower, as her husband was never attainted, and indeed her daughter-in-law, Aubrey's wife, successfully petitioned for her jointure (comprising all Aubrey's lands), but Elizabeth does not appear to have done so.[14] It seems likely that it was a condition of her 'pardon' in May 1462 that she would not ask for dower, especially as Edward initially had the whole de Vere estate earmarked for his younger brother, Gloucester, granting it to him a couple of months later. If so, this was a further example of a hard-nosed practicality underlying Edward's clemency. In practice, the countess was financially comfortable even without a dower, as her own inheritance was worth

[10] *Johannis Lelandi's Antiquarii de Rebu Britannicis Collectanea*, ed. T. Hearne (6 vols, London, 1770), vi, 3–4; Pollard, *Warwick the Kingmaker*, 64.

[11] *Testamenta Eboracensia*, ed. J. Raine (Surtees Society, xxx, 1855), 244.

[12] The marriage of his daughter Elizabeth to the young John, duke of Suffolk, cost Richard, duke of York just over £1500 in 1458: J.A.F. Thomson, 'John de la Pole, Duke of Suffolk', *Speculum*, liv (1979), 529. Viscount Beaumont's heir was worth 2300 marks to the duke of Buckingham in 1452 and the marriage of the Earl Marshal fetched 3000 marks in 1411: see McFarlane, *Nobility of Later Medieval England*, 85–7.

[13] The pardon is C81/791, no. 957. It was reported on 4 May that provision would be made for her – she would receive 500 marks a year in two instalments from her own lands and those of the earl by the hands of John Keche, the receiver-general: *PL*, iv, 39.

[14] See C.D. Ross, 'Forfeitures for Treason in the Reign of Richard II', *EHR*, lxxi (1956), 561. The earl's estates were regarded as forfeited by rebellion.

in the region of £700 a year. She maintained a low profile over the next few years, and it is not impossible that she was in poor health, as her pardon in 1462, when she was 52, mentioned her 'age, weakness and continued infirmity of body', and she was certainly physically frail by 1472.

Tellingly John de Vere's first recorded action as earl may have been a reburial of his father. The twelfth earl was interred in the Austin Friars after his execution: 'the corps was had unto the ffrere Augustynes, and there buried in the Quer'.[15] However, Sir John Howard's household book records an entry on 9 March 1464, less than two months after the thirteenth earl was given licence to enter into his inheritance, of an 'offeryng at my lord of Oxynfordys terment'.[16] The original editor of the household books, Collier, read 'terment' as tomb, but the sense usually associated with 'terment', or 'terement', is that of burial, funeral or interment. Assuming the entry in the household books did relate to a reburial, it might have been in a more appropriate and expensive tomb. This is supported by a later description of the earl and his son as being 'sumptuously interred'.[17] The other possibility is rather more grisly – it is likely, though not mentioned in any source, that the earl's head was exhibited, perhaps on London bridge, as a example of the dreadful punishment meted out to traitors. If so, the new earl in 1464 would have wanted licence to remove it as quickly as possible, and the 'terment' therefore was the placing of the severed head into the tomb. With either possibility, it is surprising that de Vere did not take the opportunity to move his father and brother to the family mausoleum at Earls Colne, as indeed he was later to do in 1492, but perhaps such a move would have been too politically charged at this date to contemplate. Nonetheless, the reburial of his father, undertaken so soon after his accession to the earldom, is a clear sign of the earl's priorities and the motives underlying his political actions in the next decade.

The estates to which John de Vere succeeded in January 1464 were those of his father's inheritance, less nine manors worth £200 annually which Anne Stafford, widow of his brother Aubrey, held in jointure until she died in 1472, but not the extensive Howard estates which remained in the hands of his mother until her death in December 1473.[18] Some provision had been made for one of his three younger brothers, with the manor of Dullingham enfeoffed for the use of Thomas.[19] George, destined for the priesthood until his father's execution,

[15] Chronicles of London, 177.
[16] Household Books of John Howard, ed. Crawford, 245.
[17] J. Weever, Ancient Funeral Monuments within the United Monarchy . . . (London, 1631), 418.
[18] For the jointure see CPR, 1461–7, 76. The estates he held were estimated in an inquisition in 1475 after the earl's attainder, at some £659 5s 3d p.a., a considerable underestimation: C145/327/28 (transferred from C140/52/28); CIM, 1422–85, 230–4. The valuations for three small manors, Hedingham Vaux, Saxton and Belchamp are either not given or are illegible. It includes the lands held until 1472 by Anne Stafford, worth some £200. ERO, D/DPr 128 is a receiver's account for five of the earl's manors in 1466–7.
[19] C145/327/28, no. 4; CIM, 1422–85, 233–4. In 1489, after Thomas's death, his older brother

and Richard, probably in his teens, had no such endowment and both may well have remained within the earl's household or that of his mother for the next few years. The earl's income from land is likely to have been around £800 a year at this stage, and he was therefore in somewhat straitened financial circumstances.

Nonetheless, in local politics, the earl, in contrast to his father's last years, proved active and vigorous in the defence of his rights and the acquisition of new estates. With a Yorkist king on the throne, he was able to secure in the parliament of 1464 the repeal of the act of 1399 by the Lancastrian Henry IV, which revived the attainder of 1388 of his ancestor, Robert de Vere, duke of Ireland.[20] It is another early indication of a concern with his family honour and history, and was clearly something the earl felt strongly about: when the de Vere cartulary, now Bodleian Rawlinson B 248, was put together for the earl between twenty and forty years after 1464, it was still felt important to devote six folios to copying the most relevant parliamentary proceedings against the duke.[21] The 1464 repeal was passed with a number of provisos, protecting the rights of those who had acquired Robert de Vere's estates, but at least one manor was arguably not covered by these provisos, and Earl John attempted to recover the wealthy Sussex estate of Laughton and the associated hundred of Shiplake. Laughton and the manor of West Dean had been acquired as part of the inheritance of Margaret Badlesmere, wife to John, seventh earl of Oxford, but had been settled on Maud, wife of the eighth earl in jointure in 1371.[22] After the duke of Ireland's forfeiture, the reversions of these and other estates were granted to the duke of Gloucester, who intended them to form part of the endowment of his newly founded college of Pleshey. In 1401 Laughton was held by Sir John Pelham for life, at the annual rent of £60 paid to Countess Maud, with reversion to Thomas, archbishop of Canterbury, and others, as feoffees for the duke of Gloucester.[23] Laughton, however, was retained by the Pelham family, rather than being conveyed to Pleshey. It might have been argued that this manor was still covered by one of the provisos in the act of 1464 – that manors destined for Pleshey were exempt – but it was on this point that the earl fought. A legal process was started against the owner, Sir John Pelham, bastard son of the previous Sir John, and 'dyvers debates and contravercies' ensued. Oxford, on 16 July 1466, settled for a payment of 1000 marks from Pelham in return for quitclaiming his

George was holding the manors of Dullingham, Preston and Langdon; ERO, D/DPr 139, m.1.

[20] *Parliament Rolls*, xiii, ed. R. Horrox, 204–7; Scofield, 'Early Life', 229–30; Lander, *Crown and Nobility*, 140.

[21] Bodleian Library, Oxford, Rawlinson B 248, fols 8v–14r, including articles i, ii, x, xv, xvii, xxii, xxix–xxxii, xxxviii, xxxix in the parliamentary accusations by the Appellants; *Parliament Rolls*, vii, ed. C. Given-Wilson, 84–98.

[22] *CCR, 1369–74*, 271–2; *Sussex Feet of Fines, 1307–1509*, ed. L.F. Salzmann (Sussex Record Society, xxiii, 1916), 173; *CPR, 1391–6*, 512; BL, Add.Ch. 31577(10)

[23] BL, Add. Ch. 30362; *Calendar of Feudal Aids*, vi, 521.

title, and allowing the latter to keep the manor.[24] Whether or not this was the original intention, such a substantial payment was not a bad return for a claim to a manor that had been lost to the family for over fifty years.[25] Oxford was also involved in a *quo warranto* proceeding initiated by the crown over his possession of the office of master forester of Essex. In a plea held before Henry Bourgchier, earl of Essex, on 14 January 1465, he traced the possession of the office back to his ancestor Thomas de Clare, who he claimed held the office in his demesne as of fee, which the crown disputed. A jury, however, found in his favour, and the earl retained the office.[26]

So vigorous was the new earl's lordship that in one case that he was reprimanded by the Queen for his partisan handling of a dispute between John Paston and a certain Simon Blyant over the manor of Cotton in Suffolk. The Queen wrote to the earl on 25 June 1467, concerning the fact that despite the dispute being under the arbitration of two 'learned men' appointed by Oxford, the earl had made an award by his own authority. Despite Blyant 'sufficiently provyng hys ryght in the same maner', the Queen complained that 'ze have not restored the same Symon unto hys possession of the seid maner but contynuelly kepe hym owt of the same, wich, yf it so be, is not only to hys right grete hurt and hinderaunce, but also oure mervaile'.[27]

A complicated property transaction led to the earl becoming embroiled in a dispute with his father's old adversary, Gilbert Debenham, esquire, over the manor of Tattingstone in Suffolk. The manor, which had been in the possession of the Holbrook family in the fourteenth century, had been acquired by the royal

[24] BL, Add. Ch. 30421. There were quite elaborate arrangements for surety of the payment, and Pelham also made an obligation for £1000 in case of non-payment, to be placed in the hands of the bishop of London. Pelham also agreed to cover all legal expenses. For the actual payments made see BL, Add. Ch. 30422–3, and for the case in chancery that de Vere initiated and then agreed to drop see C254/148, nos 13, 15.

[25] Likewise, the reversal of the attainder allowed the earl to claim the estate of West Dean in Sussex: *CPR, 1391–6*, 98, 347; *Sussex Feet of Fines 1307–1509*, ed. Salzmann, 202. It is unclear whether Oxford attempted to regain possession in the 1460s, but on 20 November 1488 Oxford granted the manor to Henry Halle of Ore, esquire, in a deed made at West Dean itself, and in a separate document on the same date quitclaimed the manor to Halle: East Sussex Record Office, SAS/M406–7. As the Halle family had probably acquired the manor by 1436, it is not clear whether the earl was simply releasing any residual claim to Halle, presumably again in return for a handsome payment, or whether he had actually seized possession of the estate in 1485, and subsequently decided to sell it back to its previous owner: unpublished article on 'William Halle', History of Parliament Trust, 1422–1504 section, citing a dispute in 1436 (CP40/700, rot. 127) and Halle's will in c. 1449 (PROB11/1, fol. 103). I am indebted to Dr Linda Clark for her draft biography of Halle and a number of other references on this subject. See also *Abstracts of Sussex Deeds and Documents*, ed. W. Budgen (Sussex Record Society, xxix, 1924), 92.

[26] BL, Add. Ch. 28620.

[27] *PLP*, ii, 611, and see also 382–4. For the earlier history of the dispute, the circumstances of the letter and its factual inaccuracies, and Oxford's attempted good lordship, see Richmond, *Paston Family: Fastolf's Will*, 118–121; *Endings*, 135–6, 199–200n.

justice, Thomas Fulthorp, by the 1440s. Gilbert Debenham, however, married to Elizabeth Holbrook, had other ideas, and at some point in the early 1460s seems to have occupied the manor, and sued Fulthorp's son, another Thomas, and many others for re-entering Tattingstone in November 1464, a case that he won.[28] During the Easter term of 1467, the earl acquired Fulthorp's claim to the manor through collusive action in the court of Common Pleas.[29] His will notes that he purchased the property, and probably the adjoining manor of Crepping Hall in Stutton also held by Fulthorp,[30] but it is not clear how much cash changed hands. Despite Debenham's claim to the Tattingstone estate, the earl must have thought that he would be able to defend the manor from the depredations of the Debenhams where Fulthorp could not, and he was, in the short term, correct, especially when circumstances during the Readeption allowed him to arrest and imprison Debenham.[31]

At the same time as this purchase Oxford was ceding his interest in three manors in the hands of his childless uncle Richard, who died probably in 1467. Richard had enfeoffed the same Thomas Fulthorp and one John Bernard, gentleman, of the manors of Langley and Bradley in Berkshire by 1467, and probably did the same with the manor of Market Overton in Rutland.[32] Fulthorp, by a deed dated 24 March 1467, released his rights to the manor of Market Overton to John Bernard, and just over a month later confirmed this grant by a quitclaim enrolled in Chancery. On 9 May Fulthorp also released his rights to the manors of Langley and Bradley to Bernard.[33] Bernard then enfeoffed Sir

---

[28] CP25/1/224/118, no. 6; KB27/816, rots. 26, 29, 52; Coppinger, *Manors of Suffolk*, vi, 105; Wedgwood, ii, 264.

[29] CP40/823, rot. 334. The earl was at Tattingstone on 7 January 1469, when he wrote a letter to Sir John Paston from the manor: *PL*, v, 5. Tattingstone produced a net £21 4s 4d in 1473–4: SRO, HB8/1/784.

[30] Crepping and Tattingstone tended to change ownership together – both manors had been the subject of a fine of 1433, when they were in the hands of Thomas Fulthorp and Beatrice his wife. However, the purchase of Tattingstone in 1467 simply specifies the estate as the manor of Tattingstone and appurtenances. The earliest certain evidence of possession of de Vere's possession of Crepping is 1475: CP25/1/224/118, no. 27; C145/327/28, no. 11; *CIM*, *1422–85*, 231, 234; Coppinger, *Suffolk*, vi, 101, 104–5.

[31] Tattingstone was among his estates granted to Richard, duke of Gloucester in 1471, then, ironically, it was granted by the king to Debenham in 1476: *CPR, 1467–77*, 297, 590; *CIM*, *1422–85*, 230–1. The Fulthorp claim was taken up against Debenham as late as 1484, but must have lapsed after the earl's restoration of 1485; CP40/890, rot. 152. For the arrest, see C1/71/2 (undated); Wedgwood, ii, 264–5; W.I. Haward, 'Gilbert Debenham: A Medieval Rascal in Real Life', *History*, xiii (1928–9), 311–2.

[32] The enfeoffment of Langley and Bradley is mentioned in a later conveyance of the manor in 1469, though no date is given for Richard's grant: Lincolnshire Archives, 1ANC2/A/18/33. It is not known under what terms Richard held the estate and whether there was a reversion to the main line of the de Veres if he died childless, although reversions could be broken by a common recovery.

[33] E210/2655 (Bernard to Montgomery and others, 30 March 1469, but noting earlier deed of 24 March 1467); *CCR, 1461–8*, 435 (Fulthorp to Bernard, April and May 1467).

Thomas Montgomery and others, and in June 1469 Oxford and Piers Baxter, clerk, demised and confirmed the manor of Market Overton in Rutland, with its advowson, which they jointly held with George, archbishop of York, John Walter, clerk and William Staveley, esquire, to Sir John Say and Thomas Prowet.[34] This was confirmed by a collusive action in Common Pleas in Trinity term 1469, comprising two separate suits against Say and Prowet, which the earl 'lost' at a hearing on 30 October, three months after his demise of the property to them.[35] Bernard sold the manors of Langley and Bradley to Alice, duchess of Suffolk, in August 1469.[36] The most likely explanation for this complicated series of transactions is that Fulthorp and Bernard were acting as feoffees for Richard de Vere, and disposing of the three manors for charitable purposes, a sale in which the earl acquiesced, possibly with a payment for any reversionary rights, while the earl was purchasing Tattingstone and Crepping from Fulthorp at the same time. It is possible, however, that there was a more complicated exchange of property between the earl and Fulthorp for which documentation has not survived. From the earl's point of view the acquisition of two Suffolk manors at the expense of whatever reversionary claim he had to three more remote holdings made territorial sense.

De Vere appears to have continued his father's policy of maintaining amicable relations with other East Anglian magnates, particularly with the now influential Henry Bourgchier, earl of Essex: on 1 July 1466 Bourgchier, Sir Thomas Tyrell and Sir Thomas Montgomery witnessed the earl's enfeoffment of two trusted servants, James Arblaster and John Power, with eight manors.[37] While Oxford may have had issues with Gilbert Debenham, he seems to have had none with Debenham's patron, John Mowbray, duke of Norfolk, and while he is unlikely to have approved of Mowbray's aggressive and divisive siege of the Pastons' castle of Caister in August and September 1469, he chose not to intervene directly. Another East Anglian, growing increasing influential, was de Vere's cousin, Sir John Howard. Some insight into de Vere's personal life can be gained from Howard's household account. Howard may have endeared himself to the young earl by attending the twelfth earl's reburial.[38] The two spent a week hunting together between 21 and 28 August 1465 at Lavenham in Suffolk, and again between 29 March and 10 April 1466. Howard 'paid for costes at my lord

[34] Bodleian, Dodsworth MSS lxxvi, 67; *Calendar of Charters and Rolls preserved in the Bodleian Library*, ed. W.H. Turner (Oxford, 1978), 685; *VCH Rutland* (2 vols, London, 1908–35), ii, 142.

[35] CP40/832, rots. 345, 347.

[36] Lincolnshire Archives, 1ANC2/A/18/33, grant by Bernard to the duchess on 14 August, though no sum is mentioned in this document.

[37] BL, Harl. Ch. 57 C14. The manors were Lavenham, Preston (Suffolk), Langdon (Essex), Chesham, Aston Sandford (Bucks.), Chipping Norton (Oxon.), Great Abington and Swaffham (Cambs.). It is in the form of a straight conveyance to Arblaster and Power, without reference to any use. Might it have been setting up a jointure for Countess Margaret?

[38] *Household Books of John Howard*, ed. Crawford, 245 (9 March 1464).

of Oxfordes' on 2 May 1465, and they dined together at a tavern in Ludgate on 6 February 1467.[39] Yet these were not just social occasions. The earlier meetings between the two probably had business at the heart of them, since Howard was still occupying Countess Elizabeth's manors until Michaelmas term 1466, and negotiations for their return may have occupied some of their time together.[40]

The Readeption, 1469–71

During Oxford's first four years as earl he had proved vigorous and reasonably successful on a local level. Given the circumstances in which he inherited it was not an insignificant achievement to have steered a course which had not provoked royal suspicion, helped recover for his mother the estates Howard had snatched in 1462, defended his own interests when necessary, and maintained good relations with the other East Anglian magnates. While the national scene was superficially calm between 1464 and 1468, the earl occupied himself with local business, but this state of affairs was to change.[41] What started as a firm and successful partnership between the house of York and the Neville family gradually disintegrated during the 1460s, and, as the partnership weakened, so did Edward IV's hold on the throne. What caused the split between the two was a complex amalgam of factors. On Warwick's behalf, Edward IV's secret marriage to Elizabeth Woodville in May 1464, while Warwick was in France treating for a French bride, was a humiliation, but perhaps more worrying was Edward's obvious predilection for a Burgundian alliance against France, rather than the reverse, which was Warwick's earnest desire. Certainly for the well informed second Crowland continuator Warwick's hatred of the duke of Burgundy, and Edward's Burgundian leanings, were 'the real cause of dissension between the king and the earl rather than the marriage between the king and Queen Elizabeth'.[42] Domestic politics played their part as well. The acquisitive tendencies of the new queen's family made them unpopular, and Warwick clearly disliked some of Edward's new nobility, especially William Herbert, earl of Pembroke, and Humphrey Stafford, earl of Devon. All these issues were symptoms of the underlying cause of Warwick's discontent, that the earl was increasingly failing to achieve his grandiose ambition of ruling England through a pliable Edward IV. By 1467 it was clear to many that the signs were ominous; the Milanese ambassador commentated that 'nor are matters adjusted between

[39] Ibid., 301, 385, 511.
[40] See above, 44–6.
[41] For a detailed analysis of the 1460s, see among others Ross, *Edward IV*, 64–181; Hicks, *Warwick the Kingmaker*, 255–79; Pollard, *Warwick the Kingmaker*, 43–77; Kleineke, *Edward IV*, 48–93.
[42] *The Crowland Chronicle Continuations, 1459–1486*, ed. N. Pronay and J. Cox (Gloucester, 1986), 115.

the king of England, who seems very adverse to France, and Warwick; they are constantly at strife.'[43] Warwick, enormously powerful though he was, did not operate alone. His brothers, John Neville, successively earl of Northumberland, then Marquess Montagu, and George Neville, archbishop of York, were able supporters; others fell under his influence, surprisingly in the case of Edward IV's brother, George, duke of Clarence, who married Warwick's daughter in 1469. To this coterie of ambitious men, another of Warwick's relations by marriage and a further potential rebel could be added – John de Vere, earl of Oxford.

Despite the background of the executions of 1462, the first two years of John's career as earl had been marked by an attempt to bring him into the Yorkist establishment. After being restored to all his estates, he was first appointed to the Essex bench in November 1464, to those of Suffolk and Norfolk in March and April 1465, and to that of Cambridgeshire in February 1466.[44] More importantly, he was made a knight of the Bath at the coronation of Elizabeth Woodville in May 1465, and in the absence abroad of the earl of Warwick, who held the position, he officiated as great chamberlain on the same occasion, which was perhaps a recognition of his family's claim to the office.[45] He also officiated as queen's chamberlain, an office he held by virtue of his possession of the manor of Fingrith in Essex by 'graund serjauntie to be chamberlaine to the Quene of England on the day of her coronation hir chambre and the doore therof to kepe as the auncestrees of [Oxford] have be seased of the said office of tyme that ne mynde is'. In lieu of the traditional fee of the queen's bed and other perquisites he was paid 20 marks.[46]

None of these royal favours, however, had reconciled John de Vere to the new regime, and the earl was not much at court – he did not witness a royal charter in the 1460s, nor does he appear as a royal councillor.[47] Between 1464 and 1468 de Vere seems to have kept a low profile on the national stage while Edward IV appeared to be relatively secure, but as soon as the opportunity arose in the disagreement between the king and Warwick, Oxford proved that his feelings were deeply hostile to Edward IV. This was first apparent by July 1468 when Oxford was one of the first to avail himself of the offer of a general pardon after an uneasy couple of years for the king.[48] What Oxford had been doing to make him take up such an offer is unknown, but given his actions in the next year, it could well have been because he was plotting serious treason. One wonders if there was a connection with the Lancastrian agent Cornelius, who had been captured bringing diverse letters from Queen Margaret into England, and under torture

---

43 *CSP Milan*, 121.

44 *CPR, 1461–7*, 560, 564, 568, 572–3.

45 'Annales Rerum Anglicarum', in *Wars of the English in France*, ed. Stevenson, ii, 783; G. Smith, *The Coronation of Elizabeth Wydeville* (London, 1935), 10, 18, 22, 23, 56, 61.

46 E404/73/1/122 (25 February 1466).

47 C53/191–5; C81/1547; E28/89, 90.

48 C67/46, m.36; Scofield, 'Early Life', 230.

had 'confessed many things' in June 1468, a month before Oxford's pardon.[49] In any event the pardon gave the earl little protection, as in November he was arrested and placed in the Tower, as Godfrey Greene described to Sir William Plumpton:

> My lord of Oxford is commit to the Tower, and it is said, kept in irons, and that he has confessed myche things; and on Munday before St. Andrew Day [28 November] one Alford and one Poiner, gentleman to my [lord] of Northfolk, and one Sir Piers Skinner of London were beheaded, and on the morne after was Sir Thomas Tresham arest and is commit to the Tower, and it is said he was arrested upon confession of my lo[rd] of Oxford, and they say his liuelhood and Sir John Marneys liuelhood and divers other liuelhuds is given … away by the King.[50]

One letter written by a German in London on 30 December 1468 erroneously stated that Oxford had been beheaded with two gentlemen of the king's household.[51] Oxford appears to have been released by 7 January 1469, as he wrote to John Paston on that day from Tattingstone in Suffolk. He received another general pardon in April 1469, and on 10 May 1469 Thomas Heigham, David Mortymer, William Godmanston, John Fermour, Thomas Bendish and Robert Skern, esquires, mainprised for the earl's future good behaviour.[52] Sir John Marney, his cousin, was also pardoned in April, while Tresham remained in jail, probably until the summer of 1470.[53] Given no suspicion attached at this time to the man with whom the earl would shortly work in concert, the earl of Warwick, it seems most likely that Oxford, like his brother and father before him, had been in contact with Margaret of Anjou. It would also explain the ease with which Oxford was received by Margaret a year later at Angers, when she remarked that Oxford and his friends 'had suffered much thing for King Henry's quarrels'.[54] While this remark denoted sympathy for the executions of 1462, it could also refer to the earl's recent incarceration and possible harsh treatment.

The political crisis between June 1469 and May 1471, when Warwick first attempted to rule through Edward IV, then turned his support to the cause of Henry VI, only to be defeated by Edward IV's whirlwind campaign to recover his kingdom, has been thoroughly studied.[55] Yet Oxford's role during the Readeption is sometimes understated. He was not only one of the leading players, but

---

[49] 'Annales Rerum Anglicarum', in *Wars of the English in France*, ed. Stevenson, ii, 789.

[50] *Plumpton Letters*, ed. Kirby, 40; Scofield, 'Early Life', 230–1; Ross, *Edward IV*, 122–3; Scofield, *Edward IV*, i, 481.

[51] Letter of Hermann Wanmate to Mayor Heinrich Kastorp at Lubeck, in *Hanserecesse, 1431–1476*, ed. G. von der Ropp, vi (Lubeck, 1890), 94–5. I am indebted to Dr Hannes Kleineke for this reference and for a translation.

[52] C237/46; *PL*, v, 5; *CPR, 1467–77*, 155.

[53] Unpublished article on 'Thomas Tresham' by C.E. Moreton, History of Parliament Trust, 1422–1504 section; Ross, *Edward IV*, 123.

[54] *Chronicles of the White Rose of York*, ed. Giles, 232.

[55] See for example Ross, *Edward IV*, 126–77; Hicks, *Warwick the Kingmaker*, 271–311; Scofield, 'Early Life', 231–7.

also the only man acceptable to both sides in the uneasy Neville–Lancastrian alliance that underpinned Henry VI's Readeption. He was connected to Warwick by marriage, and indeed acted with him throughout, but he was not simply a rebellious Yorkist, like Warwick or Clarence. Whatever the truth behind the conspiracy of 1462, his father and brother had been executed for King Henry's cause, and he may have been in contact with Margaret of Anjou in 1468. One might also speculate about whether it was therefore Oxford who advocated Warwick's dramatic volte-face in switching his allegiance from Edward IV to Henry VI in 1470. Oxford was the only man among those who fled to France in that year who had old Lancastrian family allegiances. Might it have been Oxford who advised Warwick to accept Henry's cause – to switch from trying to rule through the strong-willed Edward IV to trying to rule through the weak-willed Henry VI?

Being a member of the Neville 'party' was crucial at a national and local level for the earl. While Edward IV had made some effort to tie Oxford into the fledgling Yorkist establishment, de Vere could hardly have felt truly welcome, and was never likely to exercise much influence or power as the son of a traitor. The Neville marriage connection therefore was crucial to any influence at court. Oxford was in a good position to observe the beginning of Warwick's marginalization from the decision-making process, which raised for de Vere the prospect of isolation from any real power at Westminster, which in turn would have raised questions about Oxford's influence and authority in Essex. While he personally had good relations with Henry Bourgchier, the latter was now a more powerful figure than the twelfth earl had ever faced.[56] Promoted to earl of Essex, connected by blood to the new king, and increasingly well endowed with land, Bourgchier was Oxford's equal in his heartland of Essex, and it might be that, in a way that the twelfth earl had not, Oxford could have foreseen a diminution in his family's local position, unless he had access to a powerful faction at court.

Yet beneath all this – a lingering allegiance to the Lancastrian dynasty, a pragmatic loyalty to the Neville party which gave him the influence to recover his estates and survive as a member of the peerage, and concern for his local influence – was the fact that underpinned all Oxford's dealings with Edward IV: the latter had authorized the deaths of Oxford's father and brother. Oxford's concern with his family honour in general, seen in his reversal of Robert's attainder and in numerous example after 1485, and for his father in particular, given the fact he had him reburied in 1464, and in 1492 moved him again from the Austin Friars to the family mausoleum at Earls Colne, means that the executions of 1462 were surely the primary motivation for his opposition to Edward IV, as soon as that became a viable option rather than political suicide. Had the Yorkist regime not fallen apart in the late 1460s, perhaps Oxford would have eventually made an accommodation in his own mind with the new dynasty, but when the crisis

---

[56] See Woodger, 'Henry Bourgchier', especially chapters 2 and 4.

came in 1469, just seven years after his father was beheaded, Oxford probably did not give the alternatives to allying with Warwick and opposing Edward IV much consideration.

Warwick's initial strategy was secretly to promote disorder in the north, while achieving political ends in the south. Pointedly ignoring Edward IV's progress through East Anglia, Oxford joined Warwick and Clarence by 4 July 1469 at Sandwich, as Robin of Redesdale's rebellion took hold in the north. He probably did not accompany them to Calais to witness the marriage between Clarence and Warwick's daughter, Isabel, on 11 July as he did not sign the manifesto issued from Calais in the names of Warwick, Clarence and the archbishop of York against the Woodvilles and the king's closest friends. However, he had rejoined them by Sunday 18 July at Canterbury, from whence he wrote to John Paston, asking him to procure three horse harnesses for him.[57] On 26 July royalist forces, commanded by William Herbert, earl of Pembroke, were defeated at Edge-cote, and the king passed into Warwick's control. Oxford was appointed on 4 September as one of the auditors of the duchy of Cornwall, an indication of an increased profile, but Warwick's control was brief, and by the time Edward arrived in London in mid-October, he was, to all intents and purposes, his own master again. When Oxford and the archbishop of York proposed to join Edward in London, they received the ominous message from the king that 'they scholde com when that he sent for them'. While marking the end of Warwick's control over the king, Edward was not in a position to take revenge for his humiliation, and according to a letter by Sir John Paston to his mother in October 1469, 'the kyng hymselffe hathe good langage of the Lords of Clarance, Warwyk, and of my Lords of York [and] of Oxenford, seyng they be hys best frendys; but hys howselde men have other langage'.[58] Oxford continued to be appointed to local business by the crown, heading two commissions of array for Essex and Hert-fordshire on 29 October 1469 and a commission *de wallis et fossatis* in Norfolk and Cambridgeshire on 1 March 1470.[59]

Events took a more dramatic turn in March 1470 when another rebellion in the north, secretly sponsored by Warwick, failed, and Warwick and Clarence fled to France. Precisely when Oxford joined them is not known; there is only a brief statement from a London chronicler that 'abowte thys tyme therle of Oxenforde, heryng of the Duke of Claraunce and therle of Warwyk being in Fraunce, gate ovir to them'.[60] The implication of 'abowte thys tyme' is a period around Easter, which in 1470 fell on 22 April. This would certainly fit, as Warwick and Clarence

[57] *PL*, iv, 300.
[58] *PL*, v, 62–3.
[59] *CPR, 1467–77*, 170, 195.
[60] *Chronicles of London*, 181; Ross, *Edward IV*, 145. Edward's letter to Thomas Stonor on 3 April mentions just Clarence and Warwick as his rebels, not Oxford: *The Stonor Letters and Papers, 1290–1483*, ed. C.L. Kingsford (2 vols, Camden Society, third series, xxix, xxx, 1919), i, 116–7.

appear to have fled by 14 April, when King Edward reached Exeter in pursuit of them, and Oxford was unlikely to have delayed long, as he would surely have been arrested had he dallied in England. By the early summer Warwick made the crucial decision to agree to King Louis's plan to seek a Lancastrian restoration, perhaps influenced, and probably encouraged, by Oxford to do so, and went to Angers to meet Queen Margaret on 22 June. The Kingmaker's reception was chilly, but Oxford received a warmer welcome: 'And after that they pardoned the Earl of Oxford being with the earl of Warwick; to whom the Queen said that his pardon was easy to purchase, for she knew well that he and his friends had suffered much thing for King Henry's quarrels.'[61] The Lancastrian Prince of Wales was betrothed to Warwick's younger daughter Anne, and plans were laid for an invasion of England with French aid. This came to fruition when Warwick, Clarence and Oxford landed in Devon on 13 September, issuing a proclamation that they had authority to deliver their sovereign lord, Henry VI, from prison.[62] Edward was in the north to put down yet another rebellion, but Warwick's advance, and the defection of Marquess Montagu left the king in an untenable position, and he took flight to Holland.[63] The deeply uninspiring Henry VI was released from prison on 6 October and restored to the throne. One of the London chronicles stated that Oxford rode in three days later 'with a fair company', but this is contradicted by a royal warrant which notes Henry was released 'by the favour and trewe aquitaille of oure Right entirely welbeloued Cousins, Duc of Clarence, Erles of Warrewik and Oxenford', and states that these three noblemen, 'accompaigned w[it]h other lordes, knightes, squires and gentlilmen … departed from oure Towre of London towards the Bisshops Palais by Paul's Churche …'[64] It is quite specific about the movement of those in London at the time. Oxford may have left subsequently to raise troops, and returned three days later.

Oxford bore the sword of state at the re-crowning of Henry VI at St Paul's on 15 October,[65] and he received a temporary appointment as constable of England for the trial of the earl of Worcester, who as constable had condemned his father and brother in 1462. One rather suspects that Oxford would have asked for this appointment, and it was presumably with great satisfaction that Oxford condemned Worcester to death. Tiptoft was executed on 18 October, with Warkworth's Chronicle commenting that 'the Erle of Worcester was juged be suche lawe as he dyde to other menne', a reference to the opprobrium that the 'Butcher

[61] *Chronicles of the White Rose*, ed. Giles, 232. Polydore Vergil has 'John earle of Oxfoord, who a lytle before had passed over to quene Margarete' there before Warwick's arrival: *Three Books of Polydore Vergil's English History Comprising the Reigns of Henry VI, Edward IV and Richard III*, ed. H. Ellis (Camden Society, o.s., xxix, 1844), 131.

[62] *Great Chronicle of London*, 211.

[63] Ross, *Edward IV*, 151–3.

[64] *Chronicle of London*, 182; E404/71/6/36.

[65] *Annales or a Generall Chronicle of England*, ed. J. Stow (London, 1615), 423.

of England' had gained in the first decade of Edward IV's reign.[66] By 9 January 1471, Oxford had also been appointed steward of the royal household.[67] This was an important post, and again shows the earl's prominence during the Readeption.

It was, however, at the local level that Oxford's role was most important. Since John Mowbray, duke of Norfolk, John de la Pole, duke of Suffolk, and Henry Bourgchier, earl of Essex, were all Yorkists, East Anglia was potentially a major headache for the Readeption regime. Oxford, as the only prominent noble from the region who was a supporter of the Readeption, was the one man who could represent the new order there.[68] Oxford was backed by what authority the Readeption government could muster, and his name appears on every royal commission appointed for the area.[69] On 18 February, Henry VI granted 100 marks to Oxford 'for his costes and charges that he hath and shal bere and susteyne for our sake in the countees of Norffolk, Suffolk, and Essex for the restful rule of the same'.[70] It was well earned as the earl used his new authority as well as his existing power rather effectively. He began to reward his supporters, including John Paston II: 'as for my lord of Oxynforthe, he is bettyr Lord to me, by my trowthe, than I can wyshe hym in many maters; for he sent to my Lady of Norff . . . only for my mater, and for non othyr cause, my onweting, or wythout eny preyer of me'. He went on to add 'but I tryst we shall sped of othyr ofyseys metly for us, for my mastyr the Erle of Oxenforthe bydeth me axe and have'.[71] In the case of the Pastons this policy of rewarding supporters was successful as both Sir John and his brother fought with Oxford at Barnet.[72] Backing from Westminster, allied to his own estates and following, allowed the earl to enjoy temporarily an extraordinary local ascendancy. A gleeful John Paston, having suffered the duke of Norfolk's seizure of Caister a year earlier, commented: 'The Dwk and the Dwchess swe to hym [Oxford] as humbylly as evyr I dyd to them; in so myche that my lord of Oxynforth shall have the rwyll of them and thers'.[73] Further evidence of his power can be seen in the frantic manoeuvring in November 1470, as the earl prepared to visit Norwich, and John Paston, John Heydon, and others

[66] *Warkworth's Chronicle*, 13; Scofield, 'Early Life', 234; Ross, *Edward IV*, 155; Mitchell, *Tiptoft*, 140. Maurice Keen has noted, however, that all Tiptoft's executions were done legally, whatever the justice of the case. Oxford's execution of Tiptoft was more 'problematic': 'Treason Trials under the Law of Arms', *TRHS*, fifth series, xii (1962), 98–9.

[67] As is evident in an indictment held before de Vere as steward and the duke of Norfolk as marshal for a murder within the verge of the household: KB9/1052, no. 2; KB27/839, rex rot 6.

[68] Suffolk, married to Edward's sister, received commissions during the Readeption, but cannot have been fully trusted: *CPR, 1467–77*, 245–9; *Stonor Letters*, ed. Kingsford, i, 116–17; Thomson, 'John de la Pole', 533–4.

[69] *CPR, 1467–77*, 245–50, 252, 609, 613, 617, 622, 630.

[70] E404/71/6/42; E401/901, m. 1.

[71] *PL*, v, 84; see also Richmond, *Paston Family: Fastolf's Will*, 224–5; *Paston Family: Endings*, 139–40.

[72] Richmond, *Paston Family: Endings*, 141–3.

[73] *PL*, v, 84–5; see also Ross, *Edward IV*, 158.

competed to show that 'the love of the contre and syte [city] restyth on owr syde', and that their faction was the key to the rule of the area.[74] Oxford succeeded in securing East Anglia for the Lancastrian cause: when Edward landed at Cromer in Norfolk on 12 March 1471, the earl's brother, Thomas, forced him to re-embark. As the Yorkist narrative account of Edward's return, *The Arrivall*, laconically stated 'those parties wer right sore beset by th'Erle of Warwyke and his adherents, and in especial by th'Erle of Oxenforde, in such wyse that, of lykly-hood, it might not be for his wele to land in that contrye'.[75] Obviously helped by the arrest and imprisonment in London of the eastern Yorkist lords on the eve of Edward's landing, he nonetheless secured a wide region, primarily Yorkist in sympathy, against the Yorkist king, which was no small achievement in the circumstances.[76]

It took some time for the news of Edward's attempted landing in Norfolk to reach de Vere as two days after it occurred the earl wrote from Hedingham to his brother in Norfolk, saying he understood 'the faithfull gwydyng and disposicion of the cuntre, to my gret cumforte and pleaser'. Five days later, Oxford wrote a more formal letter to Henry Spilman, Thomas Seyve, John Seyve, James Radcliff and John Brampton, senior, informing them of Edward's landing in the north, and citing his commission of array, commanded the recipients to join him at Bishop's Lynn, with their retinues, where he intended 'fro thence to goo forth with the help of God, you and my fryndes, to the recountr of the said enemyes'.[77] Those to whom the letter was addressed were not of Oxford's own circle, but could and were able to be summoned to support a 'royal' campaign.

Oxford's political dominance, and ability to recruit unhampered by other nobles,[78] did enable him to tap the manpower resources of East Anglia, though it is difficult to know how many men he brought to the Barnet campaign. He was certainly recruiting before Edward's landing: 'I have disposed me with all the power that I can make in Essex and Suffolk, Cambrygeshire and other places' mustering at Bury on 18 March, while his brother was presumably raising men in Norfolk at the same time.[79] He was described as being at Newark with the duke of Exeter and Viscount Beaumont with a 'great felowshipe, which th'Erle and

---

[74] *PL*, v, 89.

[75] 'Historie of the Arrivall of King Edward IV A.D. 1471', ed. J. Bruce in *Three Chronicles of the Reign of Edward IV*, ed. K. Dockray (Gloucester, 1988), 2; see also Ross, *Edward IV*, 161.

[76] H. Kleineke, 'Gerhard von Wesel's Newsletter from England', *The Ricardian*, xvi (2006), 69.

[77] *PL*, v, 95–6.

[78] As soon as Oxford had left East Anglia, John Howard, who had taken sanctuary in Colchester, and Mowbray, released from the Tower, were able to return to Suffolk and recruit there, though it may have been too late to raise substantial support: A. Crawford, *Yorkist Lord. John Howard, Duke of Norfolk, c. 1425–1485* (London, 2010), 62–3; Ross, *Edward IV*, 158, 166; M.A. Hicks, *False, Fleeting, Perjur'd Clarence* (Gloucester, 1980), 104, 106–7.

[79] *PL*, v, 94–5.

they had gatheyd in Essex, Norfolk, Suffolk, Cambridgeshire, Huntingdonshire and Lincolnshire, to the number of 4000 men'.[80]

Two sources suggest that Oxford had a deep commitment to the cause of defeating Edward IV during the Barnet campaign. According to *The Arrivall*, after Edward had offered a pardon to Warwick at Newark, 'certayne persons beinge with hym [Warwick] in companye, as th'Erle of Oxenforde, and other, beinge desposed in extrem malice agaynst the kynge, woulde not suffre hym t'accepte any mannar of appoynment'. Fabyan stated that after Clarence's defection 'Wherwith the other lords were sumdale abasshed; the whiche notwithstandynge, the sayd lordes by the specyall comforte and exortacion of the erle of Oxenforde, as it was sayde, helde on theyr iournay towarde Barnet, the sayde erle of Oxenforde beinge in the vanwarde'.[81] These two sources, independent of each other, provide compelling evidence for Oxford's commitment to defeating Edward.

Oxford needed such zeal to sustain him as he was dogged with ill luck throughout the campaign that culminated at Barnet. *The Arrivall* noted that when Edward learnt that Exeter and Oxford were at Newark with 'great felowshipe' he immediately advanced towards them, only to find that the lords had, according to this partisan source, 'determyned shortly within themselfe that [they] might not abide his comynge, wherefore, erly, aboute two of the cloke in the mornynge, they flede out of the towne, and ther they lost parte of the people that they had gatheryd and browght with them'.[82] Two foreign sources suggest that there was a second skirmish when Oxford and his companions attempted to link up with Warwick, who, confronted by Edward, had shut himself in Coventry and refused to fight. According to these sources Edward sent forces to intercept Oxford, Exeter and Beaumont, and somewhere near Leicester on 3 April, Oxford's troops were put to flight. Gerhard von Wesel, a Hanseatic merchant in London, writing a few days after Barnet, describes how Edward 'had cut off and slain many of the Earl of Oxford's followers on the way there [Coventry]'.[83] Commynes is more precise about the date, but also just adds that some of Edward's troops put the duke of Exeter, Beaumont and others to flight.[84] No English source mentions

---

[80] 'Arrivall', 8; *Chronicles of London*, 182; *Recueil des Chroniques et Anchiennes Histories de la Grand Bretagne a Present Nomme Engleterre par Jehan de Waurin*, ed. W. Hardy (5 vols, Rolls series 1864–91), v, 649. For those known to have fought with the earl at Barnet see below, 180–1.

[81] R. Fabyan, *The New Chronicles of England and France*, ed. H. Ellis (London, 1911), 661.

[82] 'Arrivall', 7–8; J.A.F. Thomson, '"The Arrival of Edward IV" – The Development of the Text', *Speculum*, xlvi (1971), 86–92; Scofield, *Edward IV*, i, 573.

[83] Kleineke, 'Gerhard von Wesel's Newsletter', 66–83, quote from 77.

[84] *Memoires de Philippe de Commynes*, ed. M. Dupont (3 vols, Paris, 1840–7), iii, 283. Scofield, *Edward IV*, i, 571, 573 has reference to two skirmishes, citing Commynes, Wesel, and Waurin, though the latter does not mention it, referring only to the incident at Newark: *Recueil des Chroniques... par Jehan de Waurin*, v, 649–50. P.W. Hammond also has two skirmishes: *The Battles of Barnet and Tewkesbury* (Stroud, 1990), 64.

this skirmish, which, had it occurred, would have had a thousand or more men on both sides; its absence from the *Arrivall* is striking, especially if Edward's troops had won a substantial encounter, so its occurrence must be open to doubt. Oxford certainly managed to link up with Warwick, as he was with Neville when the latter left Coventry for London a few days later.

The battle of Barnet on 14 April 1471 was probably the lowest point in de Vere's career.[85] Not only was the battle lost, but Oxford was the agent by which defeat was snatched from the jaws of Lancastrian victory. Although the accounts of the battle differ in the detail, what is clear is that Oxford's force, misaligned in the fog that shrouded the battlefield, overlapped the opposing division, commanded by Lord Hastings. The Great Chronicle of London described what followed:

> It happid therle of Oxynfford to sett upon the wyng or end of the duke of Glowce-tir's [recte Hastings's] people and afftyr sharp ffygth slew a certayn of theym and put the revenant to flygth and anon as they had a whyle chacid such as ffled som retournyd and fyll to ryfelyng and soom of them wenyng that all had been wone, rood in alle haast to London and there told them that Kyng Edward had lost the ffeeld.[86]

Warkworth's chronicle recounts that Oxford, realizing that there was much fighting left to do, regrouped some of his scattered force, and came back to the foggy battlefield, whereupon disaster struck:

> But it hapenede so that the Erle of Oxenfordes men hade upon them ther lordes livery bothe before and behynde, which was a sterre with stremys; and the myste was so thycke, that a manne myghte not profytely juge one thynge from anot-hore; so that the Erle of Warwickes menne schott and faughte ayens the Erle of Oxenfordes menne wetynge and supposynge that thei hade bene Kynge Edwardes menne; and anone the Erle of Oxenforde and his menne cryed 'treasoune! trea-soune!' and fledde awaye from the felde with 800 menne.[87]

However, this story of the mistaken badges derives only from Warkworth, and a number of other chronicle sources do not mention the episode. Fabyan's chronicle argues that 'if his men hadde kept theyr arraye and nat fallen to ryfflynge, lykely it hadde ben … that victory hadde fallen to that partye'. The Great Chronicle of London also mentions the 'ryfelyng' while Gerhard von Wesel's newsletter simply states that '3000 of Edward's followers fled to the rear, which, however, neither side was able to detect because of the fog'.[88] *The Arrivall* does not mention the incident with the similar badges, simply saying that Oxford's troops 'fell in the

---

[85] For the battle, see Ross, *Edward IV*, 168; Scofield, 'Early Life', 236–7; A.H. Burne, *Battle-fields of England* (London, 1950), 112; P. McGill, *The Battle of Barnet* (Lincoln, 1996), 18, 37; Hammond, *The Battles of Barnet and Tewkesbury*, 64, 77.

[86] *Great Chronicle of London*, 216.

[87] *Warkworth's Chronicle*, 16.

[88] Fabyan, *New Chronicles*, 661; *Great Chronicle of London*, 216; Kleineke, 'Gerhard von Wesel's Newsletter', 81. For the developing situation at Barnet, see C.D. Ross, *The Wars of the Roses. A Concise History* (London, 1976), 123–4.

chace of them and dyd moche harme' without mentioning their return to the battlefield.[89] Moreover, the 'star with streams' is an unknown de Vere badge. If his men were not wearing the full de Vere coat of arms, quarterly gules and or, in the first quarter a mullet argent, a mullet (or five pointed star) would be the obvious badge, not a mullet with streams. There should also have been the main de Vere standard with the earl. The confusion was surely a group of men in the fog returning to a battlefield which had swung nearly ninety degrees and coming up on their own men by mistake. This was the decisive moment in the battle, and it ensured a Yorkist victory. Oxford and his men fled, after further fighting lasting half an hour according to one account,[90] and Warwick's division was overwhelmed by the combined troops of the divisions of Edward and Gloucester. Warwick and his brother Montagu were killed, and the duke of Exeter wounded, captured and imprisoned. Worse news for de Vere was to follow three weeks later: at the battle of Tewkesbury, the Lancastrians suffered a final defeat and the duke of Somerset, the earl of Devon, and most importantly Edward, the Lancastrian Prince of Wales, were killed or executed after the battle.

One of the more interesting letters in the Paston collection is one which was probably penned by Oxford to his wife at some point during the Barnet campaign. The letter is signed with a series of flourishes, which Fenn supposed began with an O and ended with a D, and attributed to Oxford, an attribution for various different reasons that Gairdner and Davis have agreed with:

> Ryght reverent and wyrchpfull Lady, I recomande me to yow, lettyng you wete that I am in gret hevynes at the makyng of thys letter; but thankyd be God, I am eschapyd my selfe, and sodenly departyd fro my men; for I understanyd my chapleyn wold have detrayed me; and if he com in to the cuntre, let hym be mad seuer &c. Also ye shall gyff credence to the brynger of thys letter, and I beseke yow to reward hym to hys costs; for I was not in power at the makyng of thys letter to gyff hym, but as I wass put in trest by favar of strange pepyll, &c
>
> Also ye shall send me in all hast all the redi money that ye can make, and asse mone of my men asse can com well horsyd; and that they cum in dyverse parcellys. Also that my horse be sent with my stele sadelles; and byd the yoman of the horse cover theym with ledder. Also ye shall send to my moder, and let hyr wete of thys letter, and pray hyr of hyr blessing …
>
> Also lete Pastun, Fylbryg, Brews come to me. Also ye shall delyver the brynger of thys letter an horsse, sadell and brydell. Also ye schallbe of gud cher, and take no thowght, for I schall byrnge my purpose abowte now by the Grace of God, Qwhome have yow in kepyng.[91]

Aside from the signature, that this letter is from Oxford is very likely, especially given the reference to Paston, Felbrigg and Brews.[92] The mixture of practicality

---

[89] *Arrivall*, 19.

[90] *Great Chronicle of London*, 217.

[91] *PL*, v, 101–2; *PLP*, ii, 591. The letter is a copy, in John Paston III's hand. The original was presumably showed to him and his brother by the countess.

[92] Sir Thomas Brewes (1406–82) was a correspondent of the twelfth earl in 1450: *PL*, ii, 163–4; it is probable that this was Thomas's son, Robert (1441–1513).

(leather covered steel saddles), barely covered desperation and despondency make for a revealing letter, although the bearer of the letter clearly had a verbal message as well. The dating is, however, problematic. Colin Richmond has suggested that it might date from the skirmish at Leicester before Barnet, an encounter that is suggested above to be doubtful, but also pointed out that 'but thankyd be God, I am eschapyd my selfe, and sodenly departyd fro my men; for I understanyd my chapleyn wold have detrayed me' sounds rather more like the aftermath of Barnet than the supposed skirmish, when Oxford and his men were meant to have retreated to Coventry.[93] It would also be likely that both John Pastons would have been with the earl at this stage of the campaign. The absence of his retinue, referred to in the phrase 'favar of strange pepyll', a lack of money and the reference in the last sentence to future success (referring to Queen Margaret's invasion force) might suggest that the letter was penned after Barnet. Certainly *The Arrivall* notes that in the aftermath of the defeat, 'The Erle of Oxenford fled and toke into the contrie, and in his flyenge, fell into company with certayne northern men, that also fled from that same filde, and so went he, in theyr company northwards, and, after that, into Scotland.'[94] Could the northern men of this account be the 'strange pepyll' of Oxford's letter?

What must have made the defeat at Barnet even more agonizing for Oxford was, as Tony Pollard has put it, 'The Readeption of Henry VI could well have succeeded. It was supported by a majority of the political nation and commanded considerable popular backing. Its failure was ultimately military.'[95] Although there was an uneasy mix of Lancastrians, Yorkists and neutrals among the political strata of Readeption England, this forced a policy of conciliation and clemency: 'moderation was imposed on the new government by necessity'.[96] It seems likely that only Edward and Gloucester were attainted by the Readeption parliament, and such a policy of leniency might well have begun to heal old wounds had it survived the military challenge. This is not to say that there were not substantial problems, both in accommodating the interests of those on different sides of the political divide, and on a whole tranche of other issues, most especially a pro-French foreign policy that Warwick had committed himself to which ran counter to England's commercial interests, but there was popular support for Henry VI, and these issues were not insurmountable. Had the verdict of Barnet gone the other way, Oxford would have been extremely well placed to benefit, likely to have been showered with rewards and with the ear of both Margaret of Anjou and Warwick the Kingmaker. As it was, he was left in a desperate situation after Barnet and Tewkesbury, and it would be another fourteen years before the wheel of fortune was to swing full circle for him once more.

---

93 Richmond, *Paston Family: Endings*, 141n.
94 *Arrivall*, 20.
95 Pollard, *Warwick the Kingmaker*, 74.
96 Ross, *Edward IV*, 155.

Resistance, imprisonment and Bosworth, 1471–85

If any period in John de Vere's life showed his commitment to unseating Edward IV, it was the three years after Barnet. The Lancastrian cause was finished after the battles of Barnet and Tewkesbury, with Henry VI and his son Edward dead, no major magnate support in England left at large, and Edward IV's reputation and authority higher than it had ever been – yet de Vere tried to fight on. The problem, both in establishing de Vere's actions between 1471 and 1474, and assessing his motivation, is the lack of evidence. For obvious reasons secret attempts to lure Englishmen into treason from abroad were likely to leave little trace, and his landings, unaccompanied by popular manifestos, also produced few documents, although some diplomatic sources, most notably the correspondence of the Milanese ambassador at the French court, do shed some light on his actions.

The earl's first resort after the defeat at Barnet was Scotland, where on 28 April, two weeks exactly after the battle, a safe conduct valid for six months was issued to Oxford and forty Englishmen by King James III.[97] It is unknown how long he stayed there, as the first reliable reports of his activities are from April 1472, a year later, when he was involved in attacks on Calais. An uninformative account of payments to the deputy warden of Calais, John, Lord Howard, details these as 'diverse assaults by diverse enemies of the lord king called "Esterlynges" and others in the company of John, recently earl of Oxford, landing both on the shore of the port of Calais as well as in diverse places within the march', and which were described by Scofield as 'of a more or less serious character'.[98] At the same time, in England on 26 April George Neville, archbishop of York, 'was arested and apeched of hye tresone, that he schuld helpe the Erle of Oxenforde', and was sent to Hammes.[99] The indictment of Neville does not actually mention Oxford, simply stating that the archbishop received one John Bank, a Yorkshire yeoman, read letters from other obscure Yorkshiremen, and discussed an uprising aimed at deposing the king, expressing his support.[100] This is a fairly insubstantial story, and although enough to be arrested for, it seems more likely, as Warkworth indicated, that contact with Oxford, attacking Calais at this time, was the reason for Neville's detention.

It may be that Neville's arrest hindered Oxford's plans, and another entire year elapses before there is any more information of his activities. It is likely that he spent most or all of it in France, as in May 1473 the Milanese ambassador reported that the duke of Burgundy, as a condition of prolonging a truce with France, 'wants the king of France to promise not to keep the earl of Oxford in

---

97   *Register of the Great Seal of Scotland* (11 vols, Edinburgh, 1882–1914), ii, 210.
98   E364/107, m. 10; Scofield, 'Early Life', 238.
99   *Warkworth's Chronicle*, 25; PL, v, 137.
100   KB9/41, no. 41; Michael Hicks, 'Neville, George, 1432–76', *ODNB*.

his kingdom any longer or harbour anyone of the earl of Warwick'.[101] However, Oxford was useful to King Louis, being happy to act as a diplomatic pawn for him. Disturbed by the English preparations for an invasion of France, Louis was seeking to stir up trouble for Edward, something that Oxford was happy to acquiesce in, meaning there was, for the time being, a similarity of purpose. On 12 May, the Milanese ambassador relayed the news that 'the ambassadors of the King of Scotland have been here some time, with offers to wage active war on the King of England'.[102] There may have been a connection with Oxford's actions a few weeks earlier; on 16 April 1473, Sir John Paston wrote to his brother and relayed the news that 'the Erle of Oxenfford was on Saterdaye at Depe [Dieppe], and is purposyd into Skotland with xii schyppys. I mystrust that werke'.[103] He certainly arrived in Scotland, as English emissaries complained to the Scottish council of the breaking of the truce by receiving the 'rebell and tratour', the earl of Oxford, and many ships. In response the Scots argued that he had 'a sauf conduct grantit to him quhen he was liege man and in the gude grace of his soverane lord, for twa yers, and unwornen oute to this Michaelmas day'. This presumably refers to the safe conduct granted after Barnet, although this was for six months not two years, and while he had been in the good graces of Henry VI, he was certainly not in those of Edward IV. However, the Scottish council went on to say that they refused to extend Oxford's safe-conduct for another year 'for the quhilk he departit richt evill content'.[104]

Whether this denial of any help to Oxford was true or just diplomatic sophistry, Oxford did not stay long in Scotland, and was probably disappointed by his reception there. On 28 May he made an obvious move, which was a landing in Essex, near St Osyth, only a few miles from his favoured residence at Wivenhoe, and in an area where he and his mother had been the greatest landowners by some margin. However, his coming cannot have been a great surprise, since Paston wrote on 16 April concerning rumours circulating that a man had been questioned concerning Oxford and that he had accused one hundred 'gentylmen in Norffolk and Suffolk that have agreyd to assyst the seyd Erle at hys comynge thyder, whyche as itt is seyd, sholde be within viij dayes after Seynt Donston, iff wynde and weddyr serffe hym – fflyeng tales'. Despite Paston's scoffing Oxford did land nine days after the feast of St Dunstan (19 May), and he must have had some prospect of support, both having been in contact with some of the gentry there beforehand, and in the expectation of raising his own tenantry. Presumably, however, the earl of Essex had heard the same tales as Paston and was prepared, since in the event Oxford 'teryed nott longe, ffor iff he had, the Erle

---

[101] *CSP Milan*, 175–6.
[102] Ibid., 174.
[103] *PL*, v, 184.
[104] *Calendar of Documents Relating to Scotland*, ed. J. Bain (5 vols, Edinburgh, 1888–1986), iv, 409, dated to c. 1475, but referring to events of 1473.

of Essexe rod to hym wardys, and the Lords Denham and Durasse'.[105] That the element of surprise was lacking is confirmed by a letter from William Dengayne to Sir William Calthorpe written on 1 June which stated that 'this londing of hym that is cleped the Erle of Oxenforth itt shold have take effecte uppon the Saterday or the Sonday next before this my writing byfore which tyme my maister harecourte hadde commaundement by the lordes to aiourney with them in to the countie of Essex to the resisting and subduyng' of the landing.[106] The forewarning was one problem but the proximity of London also counted against him, since to raise the county in rebellion would have been very difficult, given the speed with which royal forces could have been put into the field against him, even if Bourgchier had not been prepared. It was reported shortly afterwards by Sir John Paston that 'the Erle of Oxenfford is abowt the Ilde of Tenett [Thanet, Kent] hoveryng, som seye wyth grett companye, and som seye with ffewe'.[107]

At this crucial juncture, Oxford was hamstrung by the withdrawal of French support. This abandonment would have been all the more galling as it was made for the wrong reason. King Louis had sent French ships with Oxford to Scotland a few weeks earlier, and on the day before he landed in Essex, the Milanese ambassador to France reported that Louis had 'sent to England the earl of Oxford ... to become the leader of the earl [of Warwick]'s party and to do what he can against King Edward'.[108] However, by July, Louis's views had begun to change. The Milanese ambassador reported on 6 July that Oxford had sent to King Louis 'twenty-four original seals of knights and one duke, who have promised and pledged their troth to make war on King Edward'. He then requested 'a good sum of money to begin this war. His Majesty has not yet made up his mind about this because he fears art and fraud in the earl, and that the seals may be counterfeit'.[109] News of Oxford's subsequent seizure of St Michael's Mount in Cornwall inexplicably took until February to reach the French court, and in the intervening period suspicion of the earl deepened. By 9 December, the French believed that Oxford had 'come in and taken his place at the court of King Edward. When a brother of this earl arrived in Normandy, he was stopped, their treachery being recognised', and that King Louis 'complained bitterly about the English earl of Oxford, because he was told how the earl had deceived and defrauded him, giving him to understand that he was an enemy of King Edward, but that he afterwards kept his feet in two shoes, practising a double treachery'.[110] Louis's unfounded suspicions and eventual complete misreading of Oxford's

---

[105] *PL*, v, 186, 188. The earl of Essex was paid £20 for his expenses in the 'resisting and repressing of John, recently called earl of Oxford and others, the king's rebels' after their landing near Colchester: E405/56, m.3.

[106] NRO, Le Strange P20 (8); Richmond, *Paston Family: Endings*, 151n.

[107] *PL*, v, 189.

[108] *CSP Milan*, 175.

[109] Ibid., 176.

[110] Ibid., 176–7.

intentions appear to have sprung both from the lack of communication in the autumn of 1473 and from the fact that Oxford had overstated the ripeness of a potential rebellion in England: the December letter notes that 'the affairs of England are at peace without war or other internal dissension, and that the earl of Oxford ... reported the exact opposite'. Oxford obviously had to persuade Louis that he had a good chance of success of exploiting existing tensions and fomenting rebellion in order to receive French support, but apparently overstated the case.

There was no war in England, but Oxford was also right that there was general uneasiness at this time: 'the whole kingdom appeared to be in a state of apprehension and nervous irritability'.[111] Much of this was centred on the duke of Clarence. The Milanese ambassador reported that Oxford had sent to King Louis the seal of a duke who had promised to rebel against Edward. Historians have been divided over whether this duke might have been Henry Holland, duke of Exeter, or George, duke of Clarence.[112] The more convincing case seems to be that it was Oxford's old associate Clarence, already in dispute with his brother Richard over the Neville inheritance, and always ready to change sides, who may have been intriguing with Oxford. Clarence also had great estates and influence in the southwest, having been granted the estates of the Courtenay earls of Devon in 1471, and had important connections with the cadet branches of the Courtenay family; this makes the otherwise unlikely seizure of St Michael's Mount in September 1473 more explicable.[113] It certainly makes more sense to assess Oxford's actions during these years in the light of an association with Clarence. Oxford was enough of a politician to realize that he could not dethrone Edward himself, and support in England would have had to come from Clarence rather than the powerless Exeter, who indeed was in prison from May 1471 until May 1475.

After his failed landing in Essex, de Vere spent several weeks privateering in the channel, getting 'grete good and rychesse', including the plundering of a ship of one Hugh Reynson sailing for Holland,[114] before descending on St Michael's Mount in Cornwall on 30 September 1473, with his brothers George, Thomas, and Richard, Viscount Beaumont and, according to two sources, eighty men, and seizing the castle 'with a sotule poynte of werre'.[115] It was an intelligent choice of

[111]   Scofield, *Edward IV*, ii, 57 (quote) and 57–62 captures the mood at this time very well.

[112]   See the case for Clarence in Ross, *Edward IV*, 191–2 and Scofield, *Edward IV*, ii, 29, 58–63, 85–90, 190; and the counter-argument in Hicks, *Clarence*, 118–20.

[113]   Hicks, *Clarence*, 71–2, 206–10.

[114]   C1/48/270.

[115]   *Warkworth's Chronicle*, 26; *William Worcestre: Itineraries*, ed. J.H. Harvey (Oxford, 1969), 103. Warkworth's chronicle is by far the most comprehensive source for the events at St Michael's Mount. However, the most recent historian to consider authorship has suggested that the author was not John Warkworth, master of Peterhouse College, and a feoffee of Countess Elizabeth at this date, but an unknown east midlander, possibly connected to St Albans abbey, so it is hard to know where the extremely detailed account of the siege originated from:

castle, since as Warkworth commented it was 'a stronge place and a mygty, and can not be geett yf it be wele vytaled withe a fewe menne to kepe hit; for xx ti menne may kepe it ageyne alle the world'.[116] Oxford was a Cornish landowner, and of a Cornish line through his grandmother, Alice Sergeaux, and there may have been hopes of stirring up a Cornish rebellion. Indeed, after the seizure of the castle, the earl 'and his menne came doune into cuntre of Cornwale and hade riyhte good chere of the comons'.[117] However, the occupation of the Mount was still a hopeless act unless he could attract major support in England, but there is indeed evidence that this was precisely what he hoped to do throughout his campaign of 1473, and it is no coincidence that it was in the southwest, where Clarence was a regional power, that Oxford landed. However, he also needed foreign aid, and an effort to persuade Louis that his intentions were genuine may have been partly behind his seizure of the Mount. What Oxford did not count on was the time that the news of his actions took to reach France. It was as late as February when one of the earl's brothers and another Englishman 'reported several days ago to his majesty how the Earl of Oxford, by the greatest ingenuity, had captured and held an impregnable fortress in England'. In response one French ship was sent to the Mount to victual Oxford but encountered such stormy weather it turned back.[118] A further six ships were sent by 22 March to succour the fortress, but such was the delay in communication, Oxford had surrendered more than a month before their departure was reported by the Milanese ambassador in France.[119]

Oxford's descent on Cornwall had been rumoured since shortly after his failed landing in Essex, as on 5 June from Shrewsbury, King Edward wrote to the sheriff of Devon of 'the grete rumor of the landing of oure rebel and tratour John late Erl of Oxenford' in that county; despite the inaccuracy of the rumour the sheriff was commanded not to suffer any assembly of common people and that 'ye sit stil and be quiet'.[120] When it did actually occur, King Edward appointed a number of Cornish knights and esquires to besiege the castle, of whom Sir John Arundell of Trerice and Henry Bodrugan were the most senior.[121] Arundell was killed in a skirmish on the sands before the Mount soon after, and command of the siege devolved to Bodrugan. For reasons of his own, however, Bodrugan was not anxious to prosecute the siege with any great vigour. According to Wark-

---

J.A.F Thomson, '"Warkworth's Chronicle" Reconsidered', *EHR*, cxvi (2001), 657–64; and also L.M. Matheson, *Death and Dissent: Two Fifteenth Century Chronicles* (Woodbridge, 1999), 61–93.

[116] *Warkworth's Chronicle*, 26.

[117] Ibid., 26.

[118] *CSP Milan*, 176–9. The Milanese ambassador suspected that these ships were to stop English troops crossing to Flanders, rather than to supply or relieve the castle.

[119] Ibid., 178–9.

[120] BL, Add. Ch. 56425; D.A.L. Morgan, 'The King's Affinity in the Polity of Yorkist England', *TRHS*, fifth series, xxiii (1973), 17.

[121] *CPR, 1467–77*, 399–400.

worth's chronicle 'every day the Erle of Oxenfordes menne came doune underis trewis, spake with Bodryngham and his menne; and at the laste the seid Erle lacked vytaile, and the said Bodrygan suffryd hyme to be vytailed'.[122] It was the opportunities offered for gain that made Bodrugan in no haste to end the siege. A later parliamentary proceeding against Bodrugan alleged that on the strength of royal commissions to resist the earl in Cornwall he 'assessed the people of the said county for large and impressive sums, and extortionately levied those sums from them by oppression and imprisonment, and converted and took the same to his own use and profit, to the universal harm of the same county'.[123] It was not until a fresh commission was issued in December 1473 to Bodrugan but also to John Fortescue, esquire of the body, and sheriff of Cornwall, that the siege became a serious undertaking, with the forces opposing de Vere numbering 300 soldiers, four ships and some ordnance.[124] There was fighting 'and for the most party every day eche of theme faughte with othere, and the seide Erles menne kylled diverse of Fortescu menne', and Oxford himself was wounded in the face with an arrow. In the end the siege was ended by the public offer of a pardon to all who would submit and take an oath of fealty, except Oxford, his three brothers and Beaumont.[125] Earl John discovered that by January 'only viii or ix menne that wolde holde withe hym; the whiche was the undoynge of the earl', and in the end he surrendered on 15 February: 'if he hade not do so, his owne menne wulde have brought hym oute'. This disillusionment among his men may have been as much a result of the failure to provoke an uprising and the lack of French assistance as the temptation of a pardon.[126] Oxford, George and Thomas Vere, and Beaumont were brought before the king, and while their lives had been spared as a condition of their surrender, as a result of Edward IV's desire to end the siege quickly, no other conditions were made, and Oxford was sent to Hammes castle to remain a prisoner for life.[127] Only two of Oxford's brothers

[122] *Warkworth's Chronicle*, 26.
[123] *Parliament Rolls*, xiv, ed. R. Horrox, 288. See A.L Rowse, 'The Turbulent Career of Sir Henry Bodrugan', *History*, xxix (1944), 17–26.
[124] *CPR, 1467–77*, 418. For the royal forces, see BL, Stowe 440, fol. 69; E405/57, mm. 5, 7; E405/58, m. 5. Payments for the forces, which also included 260 mariners, totalled over £400. For the siege see *Warkworth's Chronicle*, 26–7; *CPR, 1467–77*, 399–400; *Parliament Rolls*, xiv, 287–8; Rowse, 'Turbulent Career of Sir Henry Bodrugan', 17–19; T. Taylor, *St Michael's Mount* (Cambridge, 1932), 127, 132; Scofield, 'Early Life', 239–41; Ross, *Edward IV*, 192. An indication of medieval writers' tendency to exaggerate numbers of men can be seen in William Worcester's estimate of the besieging forces at 11000, some twenty times the actual force: *Worcestre: Itineraries*, ed. Harvey, 103.
[125] *Warkworth's Chronicle*, 27; *PL*, v, 201; *CPR, 1467–77*, 418.
[126] *Warkworth's Chronicle*, 27; Scofield 'Early Life', 241. C81/1507, no. 49 records a list of pardons to fourteen men for all treasons committed before 21 February 1474 (a week after the castle surrendered). These may well have been in the Mount with Oxford, as several were his tenants at Hedingham, Colne, Oakley and Downham.
[127] *Warkworth's Chronicle*, 27; C81/1507, no. 2.

were captured at the Mount – one, probably Richard, was in France around 7 February, and appears to have remained at liberty.[128]

Michael Hicks has described Oxford's efforts in 1472–4 as 'puny' and an 'irritant' to Edward. In practice, they may have turned out to deliver little, but given that he had been at the courts of Scotland and France, and was likely to have been in contact with Clarence and George Neville, they deserve to be regarded as a more serious threat.[129] There was no guarantee that help would not materialize and Edward's anxiety to end the siege, offering life pardons to those involved, indicates a nervousness about these possible consequences – 'the Kynge and his counselle sawe that therof myche harme myght growe'.[130] Had King Louis not misjudged his motives, and failed to support the earl when in great need, the threat might have been much greater.

What lay behind Oxford's actions in 1471–4? Oxford is generally described as a committed, 'diehard', Lancastrian. However, as McFarlane pointed out over forty years ago Oxford's 'acceptance of a Yorkist king before 1468 and his betrayal of some of his Lancastrian fellow conspirators in that year make it impossible to regard him as an unwavering supporter of Henry VI'.[131] Moreover, in 1464 Oxford had, in parliament, the most public place possible, gone onto record as describing Bolingbroke's seizure of the throne in 1399 as 'ayenst the lawe of God and of the land, his feith and his liegeaunce', and described him as 'in dede and not of right kyng of England'.[132] Admittedly, he was petitioning to have the attainder of Robert de Vere, reimposed by Henry IV, annulled, and stating such rhetoric need not necessarily indicate that he believed it. Indeed, admitting Lancastrian sympathies in the mid-1460s was to invite prison, exile, or execution, and while Oxford may have been kept his political convictions to himself for a time, there is little to criticize there. While the Lancastrian cause was a viable one between 1469 and 1471, he probably was a genuine adherent of Henry VI, whatever he had said in 1464. What, however, the period 1471–4 suggests is that his deepest commitment was not to the Lancastrian cause *per se* but to a personal vendetta against Edward IV for the executions of 1462. He continued to intrigue against Edward after the deaths of Henry VI and his son. This does not appear to have been to replace Edward with other Lancastrian claimants – the obscure exile, Henry of Richmond, did not appear to have entered the reckoning at this stage, nor given his imprisonment from the aftermath of Barnet to his death, did Henry Holland, duke of Exeter. Oxford may have been looking at trying to replace the king with the only other realistic candidate, George, duke of Clarence.[133] If it was

[128] *CSP Milan*, 177–8; see below, 77–8.
[129] Hicks, *Warwick the Kingmaker*, 288.
[130] *Warkworth's Chronicle*, 26.
[131] McFarlane, 'Wars of the Roses', in *England in the Fifteenth Century*, 245.
[132] *Parliament Rolls*, xiii, 205.
[133] For an argument that George was at this point the eldest surviving son of Richard, duke of York, and therefore ought to have been the Yorkist king, see Jones, *Bosworth*, 63–82.

Clarence who was the duke pledging to make war on Edward in 1473, it would not have been for the first time, given Clarence's betrayal of his brother in 1469–70, and Oxford, married to a Neville, closely associated with George Neville, arrested in 1472 for treason, could have dangled enticing prospects, such as the throne, before the duke, formerly so closely associated with Warwick. Scofield argues that 'if Oxford was acting in the interest of any one but himself that person was, or was at least suspected to be, the husband of his wife's niece and Warwick's former colleague, the duke of Clarence'.[134] It is obvious what Oxford would gain from a change of king – restoration to his lands, and revenge against Edward IV. Such an attitude would show a personal, rather than an idealistic, motivation for his political stance during this period, comprising revenge against the man ultimately responsible for the deaths of his father and brother, rather than unseating the Yorkist dynasty, though if this were to have been achieved in 1471 it would presumably have been welcome. He is arguably more accurately described as anti-Edward than pro-Lancastrian in the 1460s and 1470s.

A second, and to some extent complimentary, motivation was Oxford's continuing attachment to the Neville party. Oxford was more of his own man than some adherents, such as Clarence, who was brought up at Middleham for some time in the 1460s, and de Vere certainly had a different political inheritance. However, most of the earl's political associations were with the Nevilles before 1471, and this continued after Barnet, as he intrigued with George Neville, and, probably, Clarence. King Louis appointed Oxford 'to become the leader of the earl [of Warwick]'s party to do what he can against King Edward' and Oxford may have seen himself as the inheritor of Warwick's mantle of opposition. However, as became apparent after Barnet, the Neville party, always more interested in personal and familial aggrandizement than a coherent programme of opposition and reform, had lost its popular appeal with the death of its star attraction, the earl of Warwick himself.[135] Oxford chose to act secretly rather than issuing the type of popular manifestos that had been such a feature of English political life since Cade's rebellion, but lacking the boost of publicity and without the same personal glamour as the Kingmaker, de Vere was unable to imitate Warwick's success. This is not to say Oxford did not have a certain renown; he was still enough of a political 'name' to make the idea of impersonating him attractive for a rebel. On 20 November 1477, William Alington, sheriff of Cambridgeshire and Huntingdonshire, was paid £6 in reward for apprehending 'oon persone callyng hym self Erle of Oxon, as other great felons in the said Cuntre'.[136] It proved little enough danger for the government and illustrates the difference in status between Oxford and Warwick.

---

[134] Scofield, 'Early Life', 242.
[135] As late as 1486, Warwick's name and the badge of the ragged staff were being used to incite popular rebellion: C.H. Williams, 'The Rebellion of Humphrey Stafford in 1486', *EHR*, xliii (1928), 181–9.
[136] E404/76/3/24, cited in Scofield, 'Early Life', 243.

The victorious Edward IV made full use of the forfeited lands of Henry VI's Lancastrian supporters after Barnet. On 4 December 1471 all of the earl's lands were granted to Richard, duke of Gloucester, and in early 1475 he and his brothers George and Thomas were attainted in parliament.[137] As this demonstrated, the earl's actions had consequences for his family as well as himself, and all suffered some hardship during the 1470s. Perhaps most affected were his three brothers, loyal supporters during the Readeption. The eldest, George, had been destined for the priesthood and in 1459, when he was just sixteen, George's father appointed him to the wealthy benefice of Lavenham, Suffolk. However, he gave up this career in the aftermath of the double execution in 1462, when he became his brother's heir.[138] He married, probably during the Readeption, Margaret (died 1472), sister and co-heir of Thomas Talbot, viscount Lisle (died March 1470), who was a good catch for a younger son. Her lands in Somerset, Worcestershire, and Staffordshire were worth £68 p.a., with the reversion of another £23 p.a. on the death of her grandmother.[139] George was never pardoned, and in 1479 Peter Curteys, keeper of the great wardrobe was paid £7 5s for the clothing and victuals of a George Vere and his others of his household for twenty-five weeks. This was probably the earl's brother, and it is not clear whether this was a formal imprisonment, or more likely a house arrest, and it may well explain why George was rather surprisingly reported as being present at Richard III's coronation in 1483 – that his 'keeper' was present as well.[140]

The youngest brother, Richard, took up George's intended role in the priesthood, taking a degree at Cambridge, and during the Readeption the earl secured for him a grant of the free chapels of Eaton Bray and Thorn in Houghton Regis, Bedfordshire. Family loyalties proved stronger than this career. Although Richard, duke of Gloucester, promised his mother early in 1473 that he would find 'competent benefices' for him, despite Richard's then current participation in rebellion against Edward IV, Richard was with his brothers in the landings of the summer of 1473. He was probably the one at the French court in February 1474 trying to procure relief for St Michael's Mount – perhaps for practical reasons as a clergyman (or an aspirant clergyman) would have passed more freely through France. He was neither attainted nor pardoned for his involvement with his brothers in treason, and indeed it is unknown whether he ever submitted

---

[137] CPR, 1467–77, 297; Parliament Rolls, xiv, 299–309; Ross, Edward IV, 186–7.

[138] Biographical Register of the University of Cambridge to 1500, ed. A.B. Emden (Cambridge, 1963), 608; Calendar of Papal Letters (London, 1921), xi, 546; Claude Morley, 'Catalogue of the Beneficed Clergy of Suffolk, 1086–1550', Proceedings of the Suffolk Institute of Archaeology, xxii (1934–6), 81. On 18 July 1462, the king presented one John Walter to the parish church of Lavenham, void by the resignation of George Vere: CPR, 1461–7, 193.

[139] Margaret died in December 1472, according to her inquisition post mortem and a Paston Letter: C140/41/40; PL, iii, 176; CP, viii, 57–9.

[140] E403/850, m.3; BL, Harl. MS 2115, fol. 152, cited in Excerpta Historia, ed. S. Bentley (London, 1831), 384. For another possibility as to identity, see below, 79.

to Edward IV, or remained in France.[141] His absence from the parliamentary attainder, made between June 1474 and March 1475 might indicate an early death; equally as a clergyman, he may just have been ignored in the parliamentary proceedings. Very little is known about the life of the middle brother, Thomas. Both he and his brother George were knighted during the Readeption or earlier, as both are described as knights in the parliamentary attainder. Thomas was the only de Vere to seek and secure a full pardon from Edward IV in 1478.[142] It is not known whether he married, and though two sources record his early death, they disagree slightly, one stating 11 September 1478, and a more contemporary inquisition 9 September 1479.[143] He was buried at Earls Colne priory.[144]

Oxford's resistance left his wife and mother as vulnerable as his brothers, and neither countess of Oxford had any allies left. His wife, Margaret Neville, who had seen two of her powerful brothers, Warwick and Montagu, killed at Barnet, and the third, George, archbishop of York, imprisoned in 1472, as well as her husband fled into exile, had no lands of her own, and had no dower granted out of John's forfeited lands. She was thus left without income. Fabyan's story that she had to exist on charity is possible – in 1478 the London mercer, John Sutton, bequeathed to her a primer with two clasps and £10 in his will, and 50s each to her priest and her two gentlewomen – and certainly her financial position was precarious until she was granted a pension of £100 p.a. in 1482.[145] She received a general pardon in 1475, and was incorrectly reported dead in 1476, but it is only in 1477 that there is any real discussion of her predicament in the Paston letters.[146] Sir John Paston wrote to his brother saying that 'my lady of Oxenfforth lokyth after yow and Arblaster bothe. My lord off Oxenfford is nott comen in to Inglonde that I can perceive, and so the goode lady hathe need off helpe and cowncell howe that she shall doo.'[147] Paston was correct in that it must have been increasingly clear that Edward IV meant Oxford to remain in incarceration in Hammes until his death, and that she was therefore in need of help and council. She did not keep the title of countess after her husband's attainder, being referred to as 'Margaret, wife of John Veer, recently earl of Oxford' in government documents. It is not known where she resided after April 1472, when she was

---

[141] Emden, *Biographical Register of Cambridge*, 608; *CPR, 1467–77*, 235, 418; C1/1/145; M.A. Hicks, 'The Last Days of Elizabeth, Countess of Oxford', in his *Richard III and his Rivals* (London, 1991), 305.

[142] *Parliament Rolls*, xiv, 368–9.

[143] BL, Cott. Vesp B xv, fol. 75v; C145/327/1, no. 11.

[144] BL, Cott. Vesp B xv, fol. 75v, notes an inscription on his tomb there: 'Here lieth the noble knight Syr Tho de Veer, sonne of John de Veer, late erle of Oxenford and of the good and virtuous lady Elizabeth his wyfe.'

[145] *CPR, 1467–77*, 507; *1476–1485*, 254, 450; Fabyan, *New Chronicles*, 663; Crawford 'Victims of Attainder', 65–6; C.D. Ross, *Richard III* (London, 1981), 130. I am grateful to Dr Anne Sutton for the reference to the mercer: PROB 11/6, fol. 288v.

[146] *CPR, 1467–77*, 507; *PL*, v, 251.

[147] *PL*, v, 289.

reported by Sir John Paston to be still in St. Martins in London, where she had presumably been in sanctuary since Barnet.[148]

There is one source, though somewhat problematic, that suggests that the earl and Margaret had a son, George, who died before his father's restoration. A record of the fraternity of Our Lady's Assumption, connected to the London Company of the Skinners, noted as being admitted to the fraternity in 1478: 'Syr John Veer, Erle of Oxenford, My Lady Dame Margarete his wyff, My Lord George Veer, ther son.'[149] The register covers several centuries, but the hand in which the entries for 1478 are written occurs only for a couple of years, suggesting that the register was amended annually or fairly regularly. It was a prestigious fraternity, with other high status members, but obviously someone would have had to pay for the admissions of the earl, Margaret and George as the earl was in prison the whole year, and Margaret, impoverished as she was, was unlikely to have expended the necessary cash, nor is it likely that any member of the family would have been present at any induction ceremony.[150] There are other entries in the register of high status members admitted while not at liberty, most notably Margaret of Anjou in 1475.[151] The primary question is whether the clerk writing the register simply erred in noting down the family relationship, and George, the earl's brother, was meant. If not, this entry allows the possibility of two other sources mentioning a George as referring to the earl's son not his brother. As mentioned above, there are payments in 1479 to Peter Curteys, the keeper of the great wardrobe, for the food and clothing of 'Georgii Veer filii nuper comitis Oxon[ie]' and other of his 'familia' or household for the space of half a year.[152] Clearly, this could be read as George being the son of the attainted thirteenth earl, but George, the earl's brother, was also the son of a 'recent' earl of Oxford and was certainly in captivity or house arrest at this time. No source specifies where George was imprisoned, but separating him from his brother would have been probably a wise precaution. A 'Sir Geo. Verre' was recorded as being present at Richard III's coronation, though again this is more likely to be the thirteenth earl's brother, not his son.[153] A seventeenth-century historian picked up on the story: Ralph Brooke alleges that the earl had a son, though called John here, who

[148] *PL*, v, 137.

[149] Guildhall Library, London, MS 31692, fol. 35v, printed in *Records of the Skinners of London, Edward I to James I*, ed. J.J. Lambert (London, 1933), 81. Immediately after the entry, a piece of parchment was sewn on top of what was previously there. It would be intriguing to know whether entries had been covered up, or whether it was simply a slip of the clerical pen, but it would require very delicate conservation work to remove the addition.

[150] E.M. Veale, *The English Fur Trade in the Later Middle Ages* (London Record Society, xxxviii, 2003), 113–14; C. Barron, *London in the Later Middle Ages* (Oxford, 2004), 213–14. The financial obligations for members are set out in J.F. Wadmore, *Some Account of the Worshipful Company of the Skinners of London* (London, 1902), 33–42.

[151] Guildhall MS 31692, fol. 34v; *Records of the Skinners*, ed. Lambert, 83.

[152] E403/850, m. 3; for Curteys (or Curtis), see Wedgwood, ii, 244–5.

[153] Bentley, *Excerpta Historia*, 384.

'died in the Tower of London young, in the time of his father's banishment'.[154]
The entry in the Skinners' register makes the existence of a son of the earl and
Margaret possible, though the provable existence of a brother of the same name
makes it unlikely, as does the dearth of references in de Vere or other contemporary sources.

The dowager Countess Elizabeth was as vulnerable as Countess Margaret;
her husband and eldest son had been executed as traitors a decade earlier, three
of her four surviving sons were attainted, and, in her seventh decade, she was
increasingly frail. To predatory eyes, she was also a landowner without legal
male heirs.[155] In July 1472 Countess Elizabeth enfeoffed her estates, worth in
the region of £700 p.a., to a number of feoffees.[156] The immediate benefit of
this was to allow the income from these estates to be used for the performance
of her will, but would allow the estates to be diverted to a third party as a
beneficiary. As three of her sons were likely to be attainted when the next parliament met, and the fourth was a clergyman, the enfeoffment was most likely to
have been for the benefit of her daughters Elizabeth or Jane, if her sons could
not find political restoration. At Christmas 1472, according to later depositions
organized by Oxford in 1495, the countess was visited at the nunnery of Stratford le Bow in Essex, where she was then living, by the duke of Gloucester.
He informed her that 'the kyng his brother had gevyn unto the seid dewke the
kepyng and rewle of the seid lady and of her londes. Whereuppon this deponent
[Sir James Tyrell] sawe the seid lady wepe and make grette lamentacion'.[157] Two
of the deponents testify to the fact that the countess was fearful of being sent to
the north of England, a threat that was meant to make her surrender her lands.
Many of Elizabeth's feoffees believed that her ensuing surrender of her lands
was thus made under duress. The duke of Gloucester did carry out a similar
threat a few months later in June 1473 when the widowed countess of Warwick
was taken to Middleham castle, and shortly after deprived of her lands, with the
king's connivance.[158] In relation to the countess of Oxford, however, Gloucester
recorded a different story; that Elizabeth agreed to surrender her lands to him
in return for an annuity of 500 marks for life, payment of her debts totalling
£240, and the promotion of her youngest son to a benefice. Michael Hicks has
pointed out that this was very uneven agreement; Elizabeth's lands were worth
about £700 p.a., so an annuity of 500 marks a year was a little under half the

---

[154] R. Brooke, *A Catalogue and Succession of the Kings, Princes, Dukes, Marquesses, Earles and Viscounts of this Realm of England* (London, 1622), 265; CP, x, 243.
[155] For a full account of the following episode, see Hicks 'Last Days', passim; Crawford, 'Victims of Attainder', 67–9; Ross, *Richard III*, 31, 130.
[156] There appear to have been several separate enfeoffments, one being of the manors of East Bergholt, Suffolk, and Little Oakley, Essex, on 12 July 1472: RH, Box 38.
[157] C263/2/1/6, printed in Hicks, 'Last Days', 310.
[158] Ross, *Richard III*, 29.

annual value.[159] Had Gloucester bought these estates on the open market, at the standard twenty years purchase price, they would have cost him £14000. In the event, as Elizabeth died within a year, he can only have paid a maximum of £333 in an annuity and £240 in debts. Gloucester demanded that the countess' feoffees seal the deed of release, but only six had done so by 9 January 1473, with seven initially refusing. This led Gloucester, along with the countess (in name only), to bring a chancery suit against those who had refused.[160] They resisted for over a year, indicating how sordid they found the duke's actions. The last recorded response by the recalcitrant feoffees was as late as January 1474, and is a good illustration of the delaying tactics used:

> The seyd Bysshop [of Ely], Thomas Montgomery, John Warkeworth, William Paston, James Arblaster and Roger Touneshend saye that … beforn this tyme att their instaunce upon this seyd bille the seyd countesse was examnyed in this courte be the reverent fader in god the Bysshop of Bathe and Welles thane chauncellor of Englond and other of the Kyngs iuges upon the seyd bille. It is fathermore that the seyd countesse is now decessed and it is seyd that she hath made a wyll and maister Piers Baxter heir executour which was att the making of the seyd wyll and with the seyd countesse att heir decesse and what covenanunt was made between the seid duk and countesse or what was the seyd confession of the same countesse upon heir seyd examinacion or what was heir late wyll nor what thei aught of right to doo thei knowe nought. Wherefore for ther trought and declaration thei prayn that such persones, examinacions and matters as be … in this behalfe may be harde and examydd and thei wylberedy to doo as this court wyll award sauyng to them such annuiyties and interst as thei or any of them haue in the same accordyng unto goode reson and conscience.[161]

It was not until Chancellor Booth shortly after made a decision in favour of the duke that the remaining feoffees were compelled to sign the deed, and by which time the countess had been dead some weeks.

To the powerless earl, it must have been agonizing to hear of his family's misfortunes. Physically, his incarceration in Hammes castle was comfortable enough; 50 marks, payable at Easter and Michaelmas from the treasurer of Calais to the lieutenant of Hammes, was allowed for his upkeep between 1474 and 1477, afterwards upped to 50 Flemish pounds, which was approximately the same amount in sterling.[162] This does not appear to have made prison bearable, according to the one source that remains to illustrate Oxford's state of mind

---

[159] Hicks, 'Last Days', 305. Nonetheless, she received a rather better deal than the countess of Warwick, who was regarded as if she were legally dead.

[160] She died 28 December 1473: BL, Cott. Vesp. B xv, fol. 75v. What survives of the hearings in chancery are mainly in C1/1/145, printed in *Calendars of the Proceedings in Chancery in the Reign of Queen Elizabeth to which are prefixed Examples of Earlier Proceedings in that Court* (3 vols, London, 1827–32), i, xc–xci.

[161] C4/2/51 (not printed before).

[162] PSO1/43/2204 (12 October 1476); E364/111, m. 13, upped as a result of a letter of privy seal dated 14 November 1477, and see also E364/115, m 2d.; Schofield, 'Early Life', 241–2. The Flemish and English pounds were a very similar amount in 1475, though by 1482 £1 sterling

during his incarceration. John Paston, repeating old hearsay on 25 August 1478, said that Oxford had 'lyepe the wallys and wente to the dyke to the chynne; to whatt entent I can nott telle; some sey, to stele awey, and some thynke he wolde have drowned hymselffe, and so it is demyd'.[163] Given the timing, which was after the duke of Clarence's death in February of that year, and which must have seemed to mark the end of any possible chance that Oxford had of ending his imprisonment, the option of suicide is perhaps believable.[164]

The event that changed Oxford's prospects was, of course, the usurpation of Richard III, and his probable murder of Edward IV's two sons in 1483. This changed the political landscape of England, and alienated many previously committed Yorkists, thereby suddenly bringing Henry Tudor, as a potential alternative or replacement for Richard III, into prominence. One such disillusioned Yorkist was Sir James Blount, who had been Oxford's custodian at Hammes since 1476.[165] It is tempting to suggest that Oxford had a hand in alienating Blount from Richard, and certainly if Oxford spoke with Blount, it would have been to urge him to transfer his allegiance. A different hint comes from the Burgundian chronicler, Jean Molinet, who alleges that it was Thomas, Lord Stanley who persuaded Blount to release Oxford, thereby making Stanley's key role at Bosworth more explicable, but this story is not recorded in any other source.[166] Molinet also implies that Oxford had been in communication with Henry before his release, as discussing Oxford and Stanley he writes '*Deux grands seigneurs d'Angleterre entre les aultres ... excitèrent le comte de Richmemont de aspirer à la couronne*.'[167] Blount left Hammes with Oxford and both of them went to Henry Tudor in France in late October or early November 1484, just before the arrival of William Bolton, who had been sent by Richard III on 28 October to transfer the earl to England.[168]

Back in England there were seditious activities by some men connected with Oxford. On 2 November 1484, treasonous words were uttered at Colchester by Sir John Risley, his servant William Coke of Lavenham, Sir William Brandon, William and Thomas Brandon, esquires, Sir William Stonor and John Sterling of Castle Hedingham, weaver, who, it was alleged in a later indictment, were conspiring with Henry Tudor and the earl of Oxford.[169] William Coke had

---

was 28s in Flemish: W.H. Prior, *Notes of the Weights and Measures of Medieval England* (Paris, 1924), 44.

[163] *PL*, vi, 2–3.

[164] Scofield, 'Early Life', 243.

[165] *CPR, 1467–77*, 591; Wedgwood, ii, 84.

[166] *Chronique de Jean Molinet*, ed. J.A. Buchon (5 vols, Paris, 1827–8), ii, 406.

[167] Ibid., 406.

[168] Fabyan, *New Chronicles*, 672; *Great Chronicle of London*, 237; *Chronicle of Hardyng with Grafton's Continuation*, ed. H. Ellis (1812), 535; Scofield, 'Early Life', 245; R.A. Griffiths and R.S. Thomas, *The Making of the Tudor Dynasty* (Stroud, 1985), 122–4.

[169] KB27/908, rex rot. 8; Roger Virgoe, 'Sir John Risley (1443–1512), Courtier and Councillor', *Norfolk Archaeology*, xxxviii (1981–3), 143; C.S.L. Davies, 'Bishop John Morton, the Holy

been the earl's servant in 1471, and had suffered for his lord, so he claimed, at the hands of the ever-ruffianly Gilbert Debenham.[170] The conspirators, it was alleged, plotted the destruction of the king, and then took a boat at East Mersea, Essex, and made their way to Henry Tudor.[171] This must have been around the time of the earl's escape, and does raise questions over whether, as Roger Virgoe argues, 'the incentive came from the earl of Oxford's escape' or whether Oxford had been in correspondence with these men while still in prison.[172] If Oxford was still assumed to be in prison on 28 October by the king, it seems unlikely that news could have reached Essex by 2 November of his escape, so it may be that there had been some kind of correspondence, through the obvious intermediaries of Coke or Sterling. There is one other hint that Oxford had active connections in England before 1485: seeking a reward of an office in the Exchequer for a certain William Page in 1486, Oxford wrote that 'of truth it is he right truly before the kings comyng into this realm demeanyd hym aswell to his grace as unto his frends and was right loving to me and myne'.[173] It may have been in connection with the activities of Risley in 1484, or perhaps while a servant of Margaret, countess of Oxford, that Page had earned the earl's gratitude, but the implication that Page had been acting for Henry Tudor is clear in the letter.

It is clear why Henry Tudor, obscure, friendless and of no use to Oxford in 1471–3, was a very different prospect in 1484. He was already the focus of opposition to Richard III, had a small court in exile, and as such offered to Oxford the only possible route for the restoration of his estates, and a return to his wife. For the earl, while he would have known that Tudor's claim to the throne was weak, Richard III stood in the way of the earl's return home, and after fourteen years away that would have been enough. The earl was an important addition to Henry Tudor's cause and Polydore Vergil describes the reaction of Tudor to Oxford's arrival:

> Whan Henry saw therle he was ravisshed with joy incredible that a man of so great nobilytie and knowledge in the warres, and of most perfyte and sownd fyde-lytie, most earnestly bent to his syde, was at the last by Gods assisstance delyvered owt of ward, and in so fyt tyme coommyd to help him, in whome he might repose his hope, and settle himself more safely than in any other; for he was not ignorant that others who had holden on king Edward syde yealdid unto him by reason of the evell state of time, but this man who had so oft foughte for king Henry was he thowght delyveryd from that ward by the hevenly help, that he might have one of his owne faction to whom he might safely commyt all thinges; and therfor

See and the Accession of Henry VII', *EHR*, cii (1987), 7–8. Morton can also be connected to many of the conspirators.

[170] C1/66/218; Haward, 'Gilbert Debenham', 313. He acted as an attorney in the earl's grant to Earls Colne in 1492: C54/354, m. 20d.

[171] KB27/908, rex rot. 8.

[172] Virgoe, 'Risley', 143.

[173] WAM, 16039.

rejoysing above all measure for therle of Oxfoorthis cooming, he began to hope better of his affaires.[174]

Nor was Vergil the only commentator to emphasize Oxford's nobility and chiv-alric qualities – the Crowland chronicle continuations describes him as 'next in rank after him [Henry Tudor] in the whole company and a very valiant knight'.[175]

Fidelity was one quality Tudor would have welcomed, but military and diplo-matic experience was another. A fair proportion of Oxford's martial history was negative – his flight with Exeter and Beaumont from Newark, the second half of the battle of Barnet, the abortive landing in Essex – so much would depend on whether he could learn from the failures. His experience was immediately put to the test, as he quickly returned to Hammes to relieve the garrison there, commanded by James Blount's wife, which had been besieged by the loyalist garrison of Calais. According to Polydore Vergil, while Thomas Brandon slipped into Hammes with thirty men to bolster the garrison, Oxford sniped at the rear of the besieging force, forcing the Calais garrison to settle for an agreement, whereby the Hammes garrison was allowed to leave unharmed, and Oxford brought them all back to Paris and Henry Tudor.[176] However, as two histo-rians have pointed out, the offer of a pardon to the Hammes garrison in general and Thomas Brandon in particular makes it difficult to accept the fact that all the garrison left with Oxford.[177] De Vere's diplomatic experience may also have greatly aided Tudor. It is difficult to know precisely what role Oxford played in persuading the French to support Tudor at this time, given the paucity of sources, and Henry, who Oxford had never met before, was always his own man. However, speculatively, the earl's advent might have carried some weight with the regency administration of Charles VIII. His previous stays in France in 1471 and 1473 must have given him some contacts at, and experience of, the French court; his occupation of St Michael's Mount, where French ships came too late to aid him, and a comparative wealth of experience in English politics, might have helped sway the French into backing Tudor. Such diplomatic nous might also partly explain the latter's delighted reaction to his arrival.

There was one reason that Oxford's arrival created problems for Henry. Most of the men around Henry in exile were alienated Yorkists, such as Thomas Grey, marquess of Dorset, Sir Edward Woodville and Giles Daubeney. Oxford, with a history of resistance to Edward IV, arriving suddenly and immediately moving to the heart of Tudor's circle, might have caused friction. As Sean Cunningham has put it 'Oxford's steadfast refusal to accept Edward IV's kingship might have

[174] *Three Books of Polydore Vergil's English History*, 208–9; see also the derivative passage in the *Chronicle of Hardyng with Grafton's Continuation*, 535.
[175] *Crowland Chronicle*, 181.
[176] *Anglica Historia of Polydore Vergil*, 212–3; *Chronicle of Hardyng with Grafton's Continua-tion*, 538–9; Griffiths and Thomas, *Making of the Tudor Dynasty*, 123; Chrimes, *Henry VII*, 37.
[177] Ross, *Richard III*, 202; P. Murray Kendall, *Richard III* (London, 1955), 486; *CPR, 1476–1485*, 526.

caused some difficulty for the senior Yorkists among Henry's supporters.'[178] This might have been one reason why the marquess of Dorset tried to return to England at this time. Yet Jasper Tudor was also one of Henry's circle who had long fought Edward IV, and if there was an element of a marriage of convenience about the disparate group begging the French king for backing for an invasion of England in the winter of 1484 and the spring of 1485, their ultimate goal was enough to unite most of them. Finally, the French did decide to back Henry Tudor as king of England, and then gave him enough money to recruit and equip a small military expedition.[179] Yet, when Henry's force of perhaps 2000 men left the mouth of the Seine on 1 August 1485, it must have seemed like a fairly hopeless expedition. De Vere, however, would have been conscious, from bitter experience, that Edward IV had invaded England with a small force in 1471 and had managed to reclaim his crown. Moreover, the earl had very little to lose, and everything to gain – revenge, recovery of his estates, and a reunion with his wife.

It was at Bosworth that Oxford finally laid the ghosts of Barnet to rest.[180] Granted the bulk of the troops under his command, with Henry Tudor holding only a small force in reserve, Oxford's task was to resist the Yorkist vanguard for as long as he could, hopefully to allow Stanley self-interest to overcome their dislike of actually undertaking any fighting and intervene on Tudor's side. Even with the bulk of Henry's troops, Oxford's division was outnumbered by the opposing Yorkist force commanded by his old friend, opponent and current occupier of many of his family estates, John Howard, now duke of Norfolk. This numerical disadvantage, in addition to the fact that the earl commanded a multinational and probably rather rag-tag force, meant that Oxford 'fearing lest hys men in fyghting might be envyroned of the multitude, commandyd in every rang that no soldiers should go above tenfoote from the standerds'.[181] This has been described as his 'tactical genius'[182] and it meant that his division was not overwhelmed by the superior numbers of the Yorkist vanguard. It may have been 'tactical genius' but it must surely have also been a response to his only other experience of full scale battle, at Barnet, where he lost control of his men after

---

[178] Cunningham, *Henry VII*, 27, and see also M.K. Jones, 'The Myth of 1485: Did France Really Put Henry Tudor on the English Throne?', in *The English Experience in France, c. 1450–1558*, ed. D. Grummitt (London, 2002), 85–105, esp. 96–7.

[179] A.V. Antonovics, 'Henry VII, King of England, "By the Grace of Charles VIII of France", in *Kings and Nobles in the Later Middle Ages. A Tribute to Charles Ross*, ed. R.A. Griffiths and J. Sherborne (Gloucester, 1986), 169–84.

[180] For the battle generally, see Ross, *Richard III*, 210–27; Chrimes, *Henry VII*, 40–50; M. Bennett, *The Battle of Bosworth* (Gloucester, 1985), passim; Jones, *Bosworth*, 141–70.

[181] *Three Books of Polydore Vergil's English History*, 223; *Chronicle of Hardyng with Grafton's Continuation*, 545–6; *Crowland Chronicle Continuations*, 181, where Oxford's force is described as a mixture of French as well as English troops; 'The Ballad of Bosworth Field', in *Bishop Percy's Folio Manuscript*, ed. J.W. Hales and F.J. Furnivall (London, 1868), 253–5.

[182] M. Bennett, *Lambert Simnel and the Battle of Stoke* (Stroud, 1997), 3.

the rout of the enemy, and was thus a painful lesson well learnt. As Bennett argued, 'The earl of Oxford's adroit leadership and the valour of the troops under his command prevented an early rout.'[183] At some stage in this conflict between the vanguards Howard was killed, and the Yorkist force began to fall back before Oxford's tightly grouped infantry assault: 'with the bandes of men closse one to an other, [the earl] gave freshe charge uppon thenemy, and in array tryangle [a wedge formation] vehmently renewyd the conflict'.[184] Oxford's advance was probably one of the major factors that induced Richard III to decide on his charge on Henry Tudor.[185] The outcome – the failure of the king's brave charge, the Stanleys' treacherous intervention, and Richard's death – is well known. The battle of Bosworth decided the fate of a kingdom, but it also changed the fate of John de Vere. It turned him from a landless exile into one of the most important men of the kingdom, and his key role in the battle meant he was rewarded with lands, offices and influence, though one senses that his role in bringing down the Yorkist dynasty and assuaging the memories of Barnet, might have been nearly reward enough.

---

[183]   Bennett, *The Battle of Bosworth*, 110; Chrimes, *Henry VII*, 48; Jones, *Bosworth*, 163–4; Cunningham, *Henry VII*, 36–42.
[184]   *Three Books of Polydore Vergil's English History*, 224.
[185]   One chronicle erroneously states that Oxford executed Norfolk and Surrey after the battle: *Chronique de Jean Molinet*, ii, 408.

PART II

'THE PRINCIPAL PERSONAGE IN THE KINGDOM', 1485–

1513

✦ 3 ✦

Estates and Wealth

all which castells, honours, manours, londs and tenenements be of the olde enheritance of myn Erldom / all which manours, londs and tenements I lately purchased. (Will of the earl, 1512)[1]

Ownership of land was the basis of political power in the later Middle Ages. It was possible for those without much land to wield power through office-holding, manipulation of the law, and perceived power and influence at court, but such rule was usually temporary, difficult to pass on to an heir, and often resented by those under its sway. There were obviously exceptions, when such power did not lead to opposition: William, Lord Hastings, whose mediocre territorial endowment was greatly supplemented by royal grants of land and office, dominated much of the midlands during the second half of Edward IV's reign, without much local hostility. Normally, however, ownership of land in a county or region, provided the owner was no fool, was the basis of local influence and power. As well as producing cash for the conspicuous consumption that was the hallmark of the higher nobility, ownership of estates drew neighbours and tenants into the orbit of the owner, and fostered patterns of service among them. Social bonds were generated amongst the gentry serving a lord and between the lord and knight or esquire, through feasting, hunting, hospitality and shared experience on campaign, though these are more difficult for the historian to trace. Cash additionally allowed the payment of that still controversial expense, the bastard feudal retaining fee.

Great estates tended to be more fluid in their composition than is often acknowledged. While in 1513 the thirteenth earl held ten (of nineteen) manors granted to his distant ancestor Aubrey de Vere by Domesday, only 44 per cent of his manors had been held by his grandfather, Earl Richard in 1417. Inheritance through marriage, royal grant and purchase accounted for all these increases. Likewise, only thirty-six of fifty-one manors (70 per cent) held at the accession of Earl Robert in 1371 made it into the thirteenth earl's hands in 1464, with

---

[1]   PROB 11/17, fols 88v, 89r.

two forfeitures accounting for the bulk of the losses, along with a few sales or exchanges. Thus the acquisition and retention of estates was a time-consuming business, often involving considerable cash outlay, effective legal advice and royal favour. Once a secure title to an estate was achieved, there was then the question of making the estate as productive as the lord wished it to be.

Forfeiture was a disaster for many reasons, not the least of which was the likely dispersal of the estates, and the history of the de Vere estates between 1471 and 1485 is complicated. In 1471 the earl's estates were granted nearly in their entirety to Richard, duke of Gloucester, and the latter acquired the estates of the Dowager Countess Elizabeth in 1473.[2] At some point this initial gift was surrendered, for a re-grant to Gloucester in 1475, on the same terms of tail male, included thirty-one of the thirty-eight of the de Vere estates previously granted in 1471.[3] The estates that the king had recovered and some of those not initially distributed were soon disposed of in 1475 – Hedingham and five others to Queen Elizabeth, the bishop of Salisbury and William Dudley, dean of the chapel of the household, five more in Suffolk and Cambridgeshire to John, Lord Howard in tail male, Wigston in Leicestershire to Walter Devereux, Lord Ferrers, and Tilbury-juxta-Clare in Essex to Sir Thomas Grey of Cambridgeshire, knight of the body. In 1476 the manor of Tattingstone, Suffolk, was granted to Gilbert Debenham, and in 1480 the king assigned Downham and Bures Giffard, Essex, to the Queen's sister Anne, wife of Sir William Bourgchier.[4] Gloucester, as duke and then king, also dispersed most of his newly acquired de Vere estates. In 1477, various of Gloucester's feoffees had granted the manor of Fowlmere in Cambridgeshire to Queens' College, Cambridge, in frank almoin, to pray for the good estate of the king, the queen, Gloucester, his wife and son, and tellingly for the souls of John, twelfth earl of Oxford and Elizabeth his consort.[5] Might this have been a twinge of conscience for the manner in which he had extracted the manor of Fowlmere and the rest of the Howard estates from Countess Elizabeth? In 1480 the duke granted the manors of Bentfield Bury in Essex, Chelsworth in Suffolk and Knapton, Norfolk to St George's chapel, Windsor.[6] After Richard became king the former de Vere estates were nearly all used to reward his followers. In 1483 Richard granted twenty manors to John,

[2] CPR, 1467–77, 297; and for these estates in Gloucester's hands see DL29/41/803; 295/4848; 430/6909–10; 637/10360A. For a more detailed description of the dispersal of the de Vere estates at this time see the author's 'Richard, Duke of Gloucester and the de Vere Estates', *The Ricardian*, xv (2005), 20–32.

[3] CPR, 1467–77, 560.

[4] CPR, 1467–77, 538, 543, 563–7, 569, 590–1; CPR, 1476–85, 179. For Grey see Wedgwood, ii, 398–9.

[5] CPR, 1476–85, 34. For the probable dispersal of the other former Howard manors, see M. Hicks, 'Richard III as Duke of Gloucester' in his *Richard III and his Rivals*, 267.

[6] St George's Chapel, Windsor, MS XI Pɪɪ, 12.

duke of Norfolk, in tail male, which the latter held until his death at Bosworth.[7] In 1484 nine more manors were granted to Sir Robert Percy, controller of the royal household, in tail male; seven more, including Hedingham, were assigned to Sir Thomas Montgomery for life; Hauxton in Cambridgeshire was alienated to a yeoman of the crown, John Abell, and Calverton in Buckinghamshire went to Thomas Bryan, chief justice.[8]

With the earl's estates so scattered it is no wonder that arriving in London after the battle of Bosworth John de Vere was importuned with 'grete suyt and labour … for matyers concernyng hym sylf … ffor than such personys as had occupyed his landys by gyfft of kyng Edward or by purchas were ffayn to restore it wyth alle such proffytis, as they hadd parceyvyed of the said landys by alle the tyme of his absence'.[9] This must have been gratifying, and the situation was clarified during Henry VII's first parliament when the earl's attainder was reversed and he was restored to all the estates that he had held in 1471, together with those of his mother, who had died in 1473.[10] The earl was fortunate that he was closely associated with a new regime, and the Tudor broom meant that all the grants made of his estates by the vanquished dynasty could be easily swept aside. His great-grandfather, Aubrey, when he was restored to the dignity of the earldom in 1393 after the death of the forfeited duke of Ireland, had no such advantage and had been unable to recover many estates granted away by Richard II.

A further inheritance swelled the earl's landed holdings. In 1473 his mother had become co-heiress to the estates of the Scales family on the death of the childless Elizabeth, daughter of the last Lord Scales, though her husband Anthony, Earl Rivers, held the lands until his execution in 1483. Countess Elizabeth was descended through her father from one of the two daughters of Robert, Lord Scales (died 1369), and in 1485 the two heirs of the Scales' estates were John de Vere and William Tyndale.[11] Neither was in any hurry to divide up the estates, as Edmund Paston was appointed in April 1486 to take all the profits from the Scales' lands until 'a reasonable particion may laufully be made in that behalf', and three years later he was claiming certain expenses, though the estates had certainly been divided by that stage.[12] Whenever the lands were partitioned, Oxford took seisin of the manors of Barkway, Rokey and Newsells

[7] CPR, 1476–85, 359, 497; Ross, Richard III, 165. For an account of most of these manors and other Howard estates see BL, Add. Ch. 16559, published in Household Books of John Howard, ed. Crawford, xlviii–lv.

[8] CPR, 1476–85, 430, 434, 452, 514.

[9] Great Chronicle of London, 239.

[10] Parliament Rolls, xv, ed. R. Horrox, 119–22.

[11] See Genealogy 2, above, 00. For a legal case relating to Tyndale's share of the estates and a detailed descent see CP40/965, rots. 46–9.

[12] PL, vi, 124–5. The letter of appointment is dated 7 April, and although no year is mentioned, 1486 is much the most likely. It is clear the estates had been divided some time before Michaelmas 1488, as the receiver-general's account details the profits from the earl's portion of the estates, received from various farmers and bailiffs: ERO, D/DPr 139, m.2.

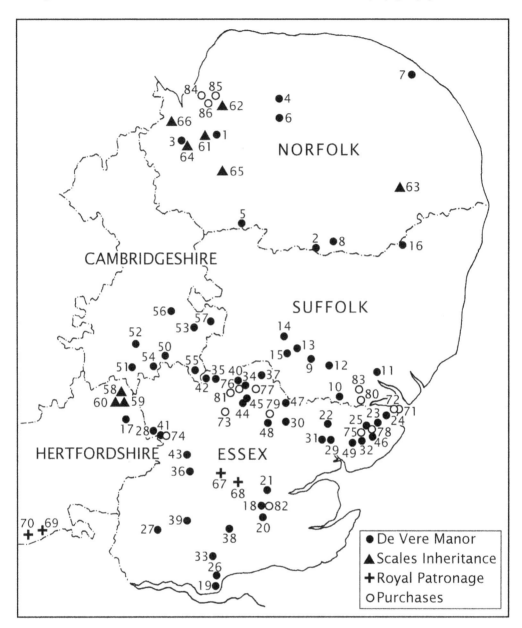

NORFOLK

CAMBRIDGESHIRE

SUFFOLK

HERTFORDSHIRE   ESSEX

- De Vere Manor
▲ Scales Inheritance
+ Royal Patronage
○ Purchases

The de Vere Estates in East Anglia, 1485–1509[a]

[a] This map is of the earl's own estates, either inherited, purchased or granted by the king in tail. It does not include any estates of Viscount Beaumont, nor the dower of his widow, Elizabeth, when she married the earl in 1508–9, nor any of the many stewardships, wardships or other temporary acquisitions.

Key to Map

De Vere Manors:
1: East Winch
2: Garboldisham
3: Wiggenhall (St. Germans)
4: Toftrees
5: Weeting
6: Tittleshall
7: Knapton
8: Fersfield
9: Chelsworth
10: East Bergholt
11: Brokehall
12: Aldham
13: Preston
14: Cockfield
15: Lavenham
16: Mendham
17: Great Hormead
18: Purleigh (Waltons, Barons, Flanerswick, Mundon and Jakelottis)
19: East Tilbury (Gobins)
20: Stow Maries (Hayes)
21: Maldon
22: Mose
23: Great Oakley
24: Little Oakley
25: Skighaugh
26: Mucking (Waltons)
27: Stapleford Abbotts
28: Bentfield Bury and Bury Lodge
29: Wivenhoe
30: Crepping
31: West Donyland (Battleswick)
32: Cruswiche in Weeley
33: Langdon
34: Little Yeldham
35: Steeple Bumpstead
36: Fingrith
37: Easton Hall
38: Downham
39: Doddinghurst
40: Tilbury-juxta-Clare (Tilbury, Skayes, Brays and Northtoft)
41: Stansted Mountfichet
42: Helions Bumpstead
43: Great Canfield
44: Sible Hedingham (Prayors/Bourehall, Pevers and Greys)
45: Castle Hedingham

46: Beaumont
47: Bures Giffard
48: Earls Colne
49: Great Bentley
50: Great Abington
51: Fowlmere
52: Hauxton
53: Dullingham
54: Hinxton
55: Castle Camps
56: Swaffham
57: Saxton

The Scales Inheritance:
58: Newsells
59: Barkway
60: Rokey
61: Middleton
62: Hillington
63: Howe (Scales)
64: Wiggenhall (Fittons)
65: Barton Bendish
66: Terrington Hall

Royal Patronage:
67: Little Waltham (Walkefare & Powers)
68: Le More (Moor park)
69: Bushey
70: Boreham & Boreham Calwattes

Purchases:
71: Harwich
72: Dovercourt
73: Wethersfield
74: Burnells in Stansted
75: Garnons in Tendring and Tendring (reversion)
76: Great Yeldham
77: Gestingthorpe (Netherhall)
78: Beaumont Berners
79: Colne Engaine (Sherriffs)
80: Tattingstone (and Holbroke Park)
81: Berwick, Scotneys and Toppesfield (reversions)
82: Gibbecrake in Purleigh
83: Crepping
84: Wolferton
85: Sandringham
86: Babingley

in Hertfordshire, Middleton, Hillington, 'Scaleshoo' (in Howe), Barton Bendish, Terrington Hall, and probably Wiggenhall in Norfolk.[13] Together, these estates were valued in a valor of 1485–97 at a total of £193 p.a.[14] In 1496 the earl purchased from Tyndale three more Norfolk manors of the Scales inheritance, Wolferton, Babingley and Sandringham, though it is not known at what cost. They were worth, according to his inquisition *post mortem*, £26 13s 4d p.a.[15]

Oxford purchased a considerable number of other estates. In a collusive action in the court of Common Pleas in the Hilary term of 1488, he acquired the manors of Harwich and Dovercourt (Essex) from William Berkeley, earl of Nottingham, though it is unclear what cash changed hands.[16] These manors produced £28 according to a receiver-general's account of 1488–9, though they were valued at £38 11s 6d p.a. in 1513.[17] The manor of Netherhall in Gestingthorpe, worth between £5 and £10 a year, was also acquired by the earl by 1488, when it appears in his receiver-general's account. This may have been acquired either from John de la Pole, earl of Lincoln, before his rebellion in 1487, or bought from the crown shortly afterwards, since the earl's will of 1512 notes in passing that the manor was purchased. Oddly, however, a grant of the manor by the king in 1497, in tail after the forfeiture of the earl of Lincoln, does not mention either that he was in possession or that any sum had been paid.[18] Additionally, the manor of Beaumont Berners in Essex, worth £18 3s 5d p.a., was bought from John Bourgchier, Lord Berners, in 1502 for perhaps 400 marks,[19] and the manor of Sheriffs in

---

[13] C142/28/68, 88; *CIPM Henry VII*, i, 15–17; F. Blomefield, *An Essay towards a Topographical History of Norfolk* (11 vols, London, 1805–1810), ix, 184.

[14] NRO, Towns. 196, MS 1615, except for Terrington, taken from *CIPM Henry VII*, i, 16. The earl already held land in Wiggenhall but no distinction is made in the valor between the estates. For Barkway see also, BL, Add. Ch. 16572. The earl's inquisition *post mortem* valued the estates at £205: C142/28/68, 88.

[15] PROB11/17, fol. 89; C142/28/88; The will of 1512 states they were purchased, and the date can be fixed to 1496 by the presentation to the rectory of Wolferton: Blomefield, *Norfolk*, ix, 195–6.

[16] CP40/903, rots. 152d., 343d. (Harwich), 159d., 345d. (Dovercourt). An act of parliament in 1504 ratifying an agreement of the division of Berkeley's lands, reserved the rights of Oxford to these two manors: *Parliament Rolls*, xvi, ed. R. Horrox, 338–44; E150/299/8. Having formed part of Aubrey de Vere's lands at Domesday, the earl had been feudal overlord of the manors: *Domesday Book: Essex*, no. 35; Morant, *Essex*, i, 496.

[17] D/DPr 139, m.1; E150/299/8.

[18] PROB11/17, fol. 89; *CPR, 1494–1509*, 109. To add to the confusion a copy of a royal grant to Oxford survives, dated 1494: ERO, D/DCw/T40. Valuation at £5 p.a. in the receiver's account, £10 in his inquisition *post mortem*: D/DPr 139, m.1; E150/299/8.

[19] Valuation from de Vere's inquisition *post mortem*: E150/299/8. In 1501 de Vere paid the king £4 for a licence to purchase Beaumont Berners and 360 acres of arable, fifty-two acres of meadow, 180 acres of pasture, sixty acres of wood and £7 13s 4d rent in Beaumont and adjacent parishes, and one quarter of the manor of Springfield. The acquisition occurred, strangely, both as a collusive action in Common Pleas, and as a final concord in the same court: CP40/959, rot. 415; 961, rot. 21; *Feet of Fine for Essex*, iv, 106. Lord Berners's quitclaim on 19 November 1502 to the earl and ten feoffees was enrolled two days later in King's Bench:

Colne Engaine in the same county was purchased in 1508 from one John Skyllyng for a sum in the region of £100.[20] He also purchased land in Purleigh and elsewhere in Essex comprising one messuage, 1290 acres of land and 40s rent from Edward, Lord Grey of Wilton, for apparently just £50 in 1502, the annual revenue of which was estimated in the earl's inquisition *post mortem* to be £8.[21] The earl's will of 1512 also noted the purchases of the manors of Wethersfield and Burnells in Stansted. Wethersfield was worth, following his inquisition *post mortem*, £3 9s 4d p.a., though when this property was purchased is unknown.[22] Burnells appears to have been purchased from the Hungerford family, though it is not known when. It was worth in the region of 10 marks a year.[23]

A further business arrangement, designed initially to benefit a member of his family, ended with the earl purchasing the reversions of a further five Essex estates. By an arrangement with John Doreward in 1493, the latter's niece and co-heir Christine Fodringhay was to marry the earl's cousin John de Vere; after the death of Doreward and his wife Margaret, the newly-weds were to have the manors of Great Yeldham, Toppesfield, Berwick, Scotneys and the reversion of Tendring settled on them and their heirs of their bodies, and in default of such heirs, the reversion was to the earl, who paid an undisclosed sum for the whole transaction. Christine died childless in 1498, meaning that, in default of heirs of their bodies, the reversions came to Oxford, as no life interest had been reserved for the earl's cousin, John. As Margaret, widow of Doreward, and later wife of Sir James Hobart did not die until four years after the earl, Oxford only ever held the reversions of the estates; in 1512 these were in the hands of his feoffees seised to use for the performance of his will, and after twenty years were to descend to his nephew and heir male John, rather than to his cousin.[24] Cousin John was amply compensated when the earl acquired for him the wardship and marriage of the wealthy heiress Elizabeth Trussell in 1507. Yeldham was esti-

---

KB 27/965, rot. 20d. The 'fictitious' consideration of 400 marks noted in the fine represented twenty times the sworn annual value of the property (matched by the valuation from the earl's inquisition *post mortem*), and is a guide to a purchase price on the open market. It does not tell us what money actually changed hands: see *Abstracts of Surrey Feet of Fines, 1509–1558*, ed. C.A.F. Meekings (Surrey Record Society, xix, 1946), xxii–iii for a discussion of considerations in fines.

[20] *Feet of Fine for Essex*, iv, 116. For the consideration of £100 see preceding footnote. C1/368/94 is an undated plea before the chancellor to ensure that various deeds relating to the manor of Sheriffs, which were being withheld from him, were handed over.

[21] *Feet of Fine for Essex*, iv, 105; E150/299/8. The fine states that £40 was the consideration, but a memoranda of acknowledgement by Lord Grey, enrolled on the Close Rolls, states that he had received £50 in full payment of all sums due from the earl: C54/364, m. 15d.; *CCR, 1500–9*, 206. This property was sometimes called 'Gibbecrake' in Purleigh.

[22] PROB11/17, fol. 89; E150/299/8.

[23] The manor passed from the deceased Margaret, wife of John Heveningham, to her heir Nicholas Hungerford in February 1496: *CIPM Henry VII*, i, 554.

[24] PROB11/17, fol. 89; *CIPM Henry VII*, i, 494–5; *CP*, x, 247; Morant, *Essex*, 300.

mated to be worth £12 annually, though no de Vere source estimates the annual value of Toppesfield, Berwick, Scotneys and Tendring.[25]

To purchase land on such a scale – eleven manors and five reversions – was rather unusual for a member of the higher nobility, and was in fact rather more reminiscent of a courtier building up a landed estate. McFarlane noted a couple of examples of baronial families purchasing estates – William, Lord Latimer (d. 1381) and Ralph, Lord Cromwell (d. 1456) – but argued that noble families were generally slow to add to their estates by purchase, though occasionally estates were acquired as endowments for younger sons.[26] The Staffords, for example, purchased only three manors (in 1383) between 1383 and 1521.[27] De Vere's purchases indicate considerable cash resources as there is no evidence of any borrowing.

The geographical situation of these purchases is also interesting. All were adjacent to other de Vere manors: Great Yeldham and Gestingthorpe border Castle Hedingham, with Toppesfield (including Berwick and Scotneys) and Wethersfield only a couple of miles further away. Tendring was located between the de Vere manors of Beaumont and Great Bentley; Harwich and Dovercourt border Little Oakley; Burnells was in the parish of Stansted, as were the de Vere manors of Stansted Mountfichet and Bentfield Bury; Beaumont Berners and Colne Engaine lay adjacent to the earl's manors of Beaumont and Earls Colne; and the earl already held two manors in Purleigh when he acquired land there from Lord Grey of Wilton. The ex-Scales manors that he purchased, aside from offering a secure title to the co-heir, also consolidated the de Vere holdings in Norfolk, lying no more than ten miles from his manors of East Winch, Middleton, Wiggenhall, Hillington and Terrington. Such proximity hints at a policy of territorial consolidation. There are other examples of such a policy, especially in the mid-sixteenth century when monastic land was on the market, but it was more unusual at the turn of the century, and shows either a more fluid land market than is normally supposed or a surprising coincidence that so many manors should be conveniently available.[28]

A further factor which increased Oxford's income was royal patronage. The single biggest grant related to Viscount Beaumont. By 1487, de Vere's old comrade William Beaumont, had, as the parliament roll put it neither 'sadnes and discretion to rule and kepe' his estates, and on 7 March 1488 Oxford was granted the 'rule, disposition and keeping of all his lands … and of all interest which the king has in said lands … to hold during the life of said Viscount'.[29] Beaumont never formerly came out of Oxford's care before his death in 1507,

[25] E150/299/8.
[26] McFarlane, *Nobility of Later Medieval England*, 84.
[27] Rawcliffe, *Staffords*, 191–4.
[28] Bernard, *Power of the Early Tudor Nobility*, 141–3.
[29] *CP*, ii, 62–4; *CPR, 1485–94*, 222. The king's control of Beaumont's estates was enshrined by a parliamentary act in 1487, clarified in 1495: *Parliament Rolls*, xv, 345–6; xvi, 190–1.

and Oxford retained control of his person and estates for nearly twenty years.[30] While there must have been expenses involved in this grant, such as the care of the viscount, provision for his wife and her household, and the expenses of running the estates, given that Beaumont's lands were worth in 1514–5 just under £1500 p.a., it seems likely that there was considerable profit to be made from this, as no source mentions any rent to be paid to the king.[31] Allowing 50 per cent for administrative expenses, a residual household, and any annuities assigned on manors, Oxford might have expected to make £750 annually from this grant. Beaumont died in December 1507, a year after the earl's wife Margaret, but in late 1508 or early 1509 Oxford married Beaumont's widow Elizabeth. She was assigned dower on 6 December 1509, which comprised three manors in Lincolnshire, three in Leicestershire, two in Norfolk, five in Suffolk, one in Hertfordshire, six in Sussex, one in Hampshire, two in Middlesex, lands in Westminster and St Giles called 'Beaumontes landes', and six advowsons in four counties.[32] These twenty-four manors in nine counties were estimated to be worth £464 7s 10d in Beaumont's inquisition *post mortem* in 1509, and the earl and Elizabeth received £519 p.a. from these estates according to a minister's account of 1514–5.[33]

The keeping of Beaumont's estates was by no means the only grant to de Vere, as he received a considerable amount of further royal patronage that took the form of grants of land, both in tail male and for life. The first grant on 13 January 1486 was the manor of the More (Moor Park), in Hertfordshire, which had been a favoured residence of Oxford's old associate George Neville, archbishop of York.[34] This was followed by a grant on 29 July 1486 in tail male of the manors of Framlingham, Kelsale, Hacheston, Peasenhall, Walton and the hundred of Loes, Suffolk, and Willington in Bedfordshire, all previously held by John Howard, duke of Norfolk, worth on earlier evidence about £250 p.a.;[35] the manors of

---

[30] Two sources suggest Beaumont's mental incapacity may not have been constant. He was with Oxford at Hedingham on 20 January 1488, when he was named as being present at the taking of a bond. Since the effect was to make him a witness to it, the implication was that he was not necessarily permanently incapacitated at this point: C255/8/4, no. 144. Bodleian, Rawl. Lit. f. 37 is a small illuminated volume and was in Beaumont's possession, as on fol. 105v. is a mutilated inscription made on 5 March 1498 which reads: 'Memorandum that I Willyam viscount Beaumount … geve unto Elisabeth my wife this psalter boke / She toccupie the same during her life / And if it happen me the said viscount to over live my said wife than this boke to remayne unto me to dispose it after my myende and wille.' By this date Beaumont been in care for eleven years, but his phrase 'my myende and wille' hardly suggests self-knowledge of any mental condition.

[31] SC6/HenVIII/345, mm. 51–3.

[32] *LP*, I, i, no. 289 (13).

[33] SC6/HenVIII/345, mm. 51–3; C142/24, nos 29, 34, 43, 62 (1), 67, 79, 85, 86. The figure for the Lincolnshire manors from C145/318 (an inquisition of his lands taken in 1463 after his attainder).

[34] *CPR, 1485–1494*, 63; C82/6, no. 21; C66/562, m. 19.

[35] In an account of John, duke of Norfolk in 1483–4, Framlingham produced £37 11s 5d, Kelsale £60 12s 2d, Hacheston £8 18s, Peasenhall £22 16s 6d, Walton £6 13s 4d, and the

Boreham,[36] and Walkefare and Powers in Little Waltham, Essex, together with the manor of Bushey, Hertfordshire, all late of Francis, Viscount Lovell; 'Botesworth' in Northamptonshire, late of William Catesby; and a great inn and five messuages in London, previously held by George, duke of Clarence.[37] When Thomas Howard, earl of Surrey, was restored to his lands in 1489 the proviso was added that the restoration should not affect any grants of Howard lands to Oxford and others, and Howard was forced in effect to buy these manors back, Oxford surrendering them for an annuity of 100 marks though this was much less than they were worth.[38] This was a substantial haul of patronage: the More produced a gross revenue of £78 4s 2d in 1528–9, Bushey yielded £110 in 1516–7, the lands in Boreham and Little Waltham generated £45 in 1488–9, in addition to the annuity of 100 marks from Thomas Howard.[39] This would suggest a figure of perhaps £300 p.a. by 1490, not including Botesworth or the London messuages. Oxford also continued to enjoy, jointly with his wife, the pension of £100 p.a. that had been granted to Margaret for the duration of the earl's life by Edward IV.[40] This was not the only royal pension he received; from the treaty of Étaples in November 1492, the earl received an annual pension of 1050 livres

hundred 30s 6d. The account does not include Willington which produced £123 in 1420–1, when Framlingham produced over £127: *Household Books of John Howard*, ed. Crawford, liii; R.E. Archer, 'The Mowbrays; Earls of Nottingham and Dukes of Norfolk, to 1432' (unpublished DPhil thesis, Oxford University, 1984), table vi, following 149.

[36] Boreham and Boreham 'Calfox' (D/DPr 139, m.2) or 'Calwattes' (Morant, *Essex*, ii, 13).

[37] *CPR, 1485–1494*, 121. Bushey is described in the patent roll grant as previously being held by Clarence, but see *VCH Hertfordshire*, ii, 181. Bushey was held at a rent of £41 13s 5½d according to a 'commitment' and a warrant for the great seal in February 1486, though since it is not mentioned in the later Patent Roll grant, the rent may have been dropped: *CFR, 1485–1509*, 34; C82/7, no. 27. This is supported by the fact that the rent appears once in the pipe rolls, in 2 Henry VII, but not later: E372/332, dorse of Essex and Herts. rot. The manor was farmed out at some point to Thomas Thrale (*VCH Hertfordshire*, ii, 181), and the reversion was granted to Sir Thomas Boleyn in 1511: *LP*, I, i, no. 833 (14). I cannot trace the manor of 'Botesworth' at all; it does not appear either among Catesby's lands, Oxford's accounts or indeed in the *VCH* for Northamptonshire.

[38] *Parliament Rolls*, xvi, 11–12, 49–53, 108–114. The lands of Thomas Howard provided the rather small sum of £56 9s 4d in the receiver-general's account of 1488–9: ERO, D/DPr 139 m. 3. One can only assume that this was a result of the steward of the household receiving some of the cash or that the estates were very heavily burdened with annuities or expenses. For Howard's annuity to Oxford, see R. Virgoe, 'The Recovery of the Howards in East Anglia, 1485–1529', in *Wealth and Power in Tudor England*, ed. E.W. Ives, R.J. Knecht and J.J. Scarisbrick (London, 1978), 13. The parliamentary proceedings directed that 'all other agreements had or made by the said earl of Surrey to John, earl of Oxford, Ralph Shelton, knight, and William Okeley, yeoman...since the feast of Christmas in the said fourth year (1488) be good and effectual', presumably refering to the annuity to Oxford, and perhaps compensation for Shelton and Okeley whom Oxford may have appointed to manorial or estate offices on the Howard lands: *Parliament Rolls*, xvi, 52.

[39] SC6/HenVIII/1594; 1598; ERO, D/DPr 139, m. 2; Virgoe, 'Recovery of the Howards', 13.

[40] For the grant, see above, 78. Payments of the pension can be seen in the pipe rolls, e.g. E372/332, rot. Essex res.; E372/333, rot. Essex res. d.

tournois (approximately £140) from Charles VIII of France, which, with the brief exception of 1495, was paid until Oxford's death in 1513.[41]

Yet more income derived from the wages for, and profits of, the considerable number of royal offices that were granted to Oxford. The office of admiral of England was granted on 21 September 1485, followed the next day with the appointment of the earl as constable of the Tower of London with the wages of £100 p.a., as well as keeper of the lions and leopards in the Tower, at 12d per day (£18 5s p.a.), with expenses of 6d per day for each animal.[42] The earl was also granted the office of chief steward of the duchy of Lancaster south of Trent, with wages of £100 p.a.,[43] besides a number of lesser grants such as steward and constable of Castle Rising, Norfolk, and steward of the honour of Clare after the death of Cecily, duchess of York, at the annual fee of 20 marks.[44] On 5 November 1496 he received the keepership of Colchester castle and the king's lordship there.[45] One month later he was granted the reversion of the stewardship of the honour of Rayleigh and bailiff of the hundred of Rochford, with total fees of over £20.[46] He also held the hereditary post of steward of the forest of Essex, at an annuity of £9 2s, with expenses for his officials being paid by the crown.[47] The fees for these posts were not of course pure profit, as Oxford usually had to pay for officials and some expenses, but there is little doubt that the earl would have made a substantial profit from this accumulation of offices, and perhaps especially as admiral with its wide ranging opportunities for gain.[48] One minor example of the latter can be seen in a legal case early in Henry VIII's reign. The earl sued John Lympany, merchant, and recently mayor of Exeter in 1508–9, for debt, the latter having allegedly reneged on an agreement that he would pay the earl just over £5, in two instalments, in return for being appointed

---

[41] C. Giry-Deloison, 'Money and Early Tudor Diplomacy. The English Pensioners of the French Kings (1475–1547)', *Medieval History*, iii (1993), 140.

[42] *CPR, 1485–94*, 22, 23 bis, 42, 119. For his fee as constable see for example E101/55/19; E404/79, nos 106, 214, 322; E407/192, fol. 18a; E405/85, m.4. He was paid £36 on 1 December 1485 for the keeping of the lions and leopards: E404/79, no. 323 and see also nos 56, 105, 110, 279; E404/80, nos 176, 237; E405/85, m.4d.

[43] R. Somerville, *History of the Duchy of Lancaster* (2 vols, London, 1953), i, 263; ERO, D/DPr 139, m. 3; DL42/21, fol. 1v; DL37/62, mm.1, 7d (grant of sixty oaks to the earl from the manor of Wethersfield, 3 February 1489).

[44] *CPR, 1485–94*, 75, 142; SC6/HenVII/1081, m. 3.

[45] *CPR, 1494–1509*, 73; E36/182, p. 44 (confirmation of the grant).

[46] *CPR, 1485–1494*, 455.

[47] *LP*, I, ii, 2422 (9). See the successful plea concerning the rights of the steward, before Lord Fitzwalter and Sir Reginald Bray on 16 August 1489: DL39/2/25; *CPR, 1485–94*, 296.

[48] See *The Black Book of the Admiralty*, ed. T. Twiss (4 vols., Rolls Series, 1871–6), i, 7–9, 21–3, 41–87, and esp. 397–409, for the rights in waifs, flotsams, ligan and deodands, a share in every prize taken, fees such as 4d in every pound paid in mariners wages, the jurisdiction and customary profits of the court of the admiralty, which included 20d in every pound of money recovered between parties in the court, and other customary fees for the moving of the admiral's seal.

to the office of deputy admiral of Devon for the term of a year.[49] Such selling of office was to be expected, and the profits of such sales are likely to have been lucrative, given all maritime counties had such offices.

The earl was also appointed to offices within the administration of several private individuals and institutions. He became steward of all the estates in Essex of the deanery of St Paul's, after the dean became involved in treasonable activity in connection with Perkin Warbeck in 1494, which could have been an attempt by the threatened dean to curry favour with the influential earl, or may have been ordered by the king, given the security issues.[50] De Vere was also appointed steward of the Essex estates of Katherine, duchess of Bedford, in 1496–7, after the death of the previous steward, Oxford's retainer Sir Thomas Montgomery, at the fee of 10 marks a year,[51] and steward of the liberty of the abbey of Bury St Edmunds, at the fee of 20 marks a year.[52]

There were a number of grants of wardships which, given a lively trade in such patronage, can only have resulted in profit for the earl, though the sources are somewhat patchy on this subject. The earl was not alone exploiting such a lucrative market, as royal income from such sources rose from £350 p.a. in 1491 to £6000 p.a. by 1507, but actually anticipated it, as most of the wardships he was granted were before the great expansion of this royal business of the 1490s.[53] He was granted the wardship of Giles, son and heir of William Alington, and custody of his lands, without rent, on 9 April 1486, for a payment of £260;[54] the

---

[49] CP40/996, rot. 339d.; CP40/997, rot. 325d. The office granted was literally 'half-admiral'. The earl claimed a debt of £4 (what he was owed for three-quarters of the year), and damages of a further £5. The case does not appear to have reached a verdict, and was probably settled out of court.

[50] *The Estate and Household Accounts of William Worsley, Dean of St. Paul's Cathedral, 1479–1497*, ed. H.W. Kleineke and S. R. Hovland (Donnington, 2004), 12–17, 101. John Ayloff actually carried out the duties, as Oxford's deputy, receiving the small fee of £1 6s 8d. The dean's Essex estates were substantial, generating around £400 in 1495–6: ibid., 97–9.

[51] SC6/HenVII/1842, m. 8d.

[52] The fee noted later in Henry VIII's reign was twenty marks, and these tended not to fluctuate: SC6/3481/70, 71. His appointment is known through his occasional business in the royal courts as steward, for which see below, 169 n. 90.

[53] Cunningham, *Henry VII*, 136.

[54] *CPR, 1485–94*, 100; *CIPM Henry VII*, i, 13–14; Bennett, *Battle of Bosworth*, 129. The actual sum agreed was 800 marks, but de Vere had paid royal debts to a creditor, Richard Gardiner, alderman of London, of £100 and 100 marks, and along with an initial payment of 140 marks towards the 800, these sums were taken as full satisfaction of the sum of 800 marks: *Material for a History of the Reign of Henry VII*, ed. W. Campbell (2 vols, Rolls Series, 1873–7), i, 213–5. A fictitious entry on the receipt rolls stating Oxford had paid £533 6s. 8d. (the 800 marks) on 18 February 1486 was added for his discharge from this debt: E401/956, m. 7. The payments to Gardiner were obviously part of some complicated arrangement, as Oxford granted the wardship, marriage and keeping of Giles' lands to Gardiner on 4 May 1486, though a provisional grant on 8 December 1485 was arranged before the letters patent had been drawn up: *Historical Manuscripts Commission, Fifty-Fifth Report, Various Collections* (8 vols, London, 1901–13), ii, 296–7. Giles was only three at this date so the wardship would have

lands of John Griffon, without rent, in June 1486;[55] the wardship and marriage of the heir of Ralph, Lord Greystoke, without rent, in December 1487;[56] the wardship and marriage of John, son and heir of Sir Richard Enderby, for a payment of 500 marks on 31 May 1488;[57] the wardship and marriage of Geoffrey, son and heir of Thomas Radcliffe, esquire, without rent on 2 July 1488;[58] the manor of Churchill, Oxfordshire in November 1488 for as long as it was in the king's hands as a result of a minority;[59] and the wardship and marriage of Elizabeth, sister and heir of John Trussell, was granted to him and his cousin, John de Vere, for a payment of 1000 marks, and an annual rent of £387 18s, less £20 for Elizabeth's maintenance, on 29 April 1507.[60] His cousin, John, later fifteenth earl of Oxford, married Elizabeth Trussell between 1507 and 1509.[61] He purchased from Sir Richard Empson the custody and wardship of Jane, daughter of Robert Ingleton,

run until 1504. The lands, excluding the substantial jointure of William's wife, were worth £29 p.a. The connection endured despite the wardship passing out of his hands, as Giles was paid an annuity of £3 6s 8d p.a. by Oxford in 1509: 'Last Testament', 319.

[55] CPR, 1485–94, 117; CIPM Henry VII, i, 17; Nicholas Griffon, his son and heir, was aged nine at his father's death in September 1485. The lands, again excluding a jointure, were worth about £27 p.a.

[56] CPR, 1485–94, 178, 197; CIPM Henry VII, i, 102, 107–9, 133, 182–3. His granddaughter and heir, Elizabeth was thirteen at his death in 1487. Lord Greystoke's lands were worth, excluding one manor held by his daughter-in-law, £287 14s 6d p.a. Oxford appears to have sold the wardship and custody on, though for what price is unknown, to Henry, Lord Clifford, from whose custody Elizabeth was stolen and married by Thomas, Lord Dacre in 1487–8: 'A narrative written by Lord William Howard', in Selections from the Household Books of Lord William Howard of Naworth Castle, ed. G. Ornsby (Surtees Society, lxviii, 1878), 391.

[57] CPR, 1485–94, 228; CIPM Henry VII, i, 124–7, 150. John Enderby came of age on 26 June 1496. His lands were worth £105 p.a. His proof of age states that 'his lands were in custody of Edmund [surname lost] esquire, by assignment from John, earl of Oxford, whom the king had given the same'. He presumably at least recovered his investment of 500 marks.

[58] CPR, 1485–94, 228; CIPM Henry VII, i, 118. Geoffrey was aged nine or more in 1488. His lands, excluding one manor held in jointure, were worth £32 13s 4d p.a.

[59] CPR, 1485–94, 260. The manor was in the king's hands because of an unlicensed alienation, and would remain there until the end of the minority of William Barantyne, who was eight in 1488. Oxford granted it at some point before William's majority in 1503 to Sir Robert Reed, though when and at what price is unknown: CIPM Henry VII, ii, 425–6; Bindoff, i, 378. The manor was worth either 40 marks or £20 according to two different inquisitions: CIPM Henry VII, i, 82, 187.

[60] CPR, 1494–1509, 542; CP, x, 247. Elizabeth Trussell was ten or more in 1507. Her lands were estimated by her brother's inquisition post mortem at £271 12s 8d p.a., but were thought to be worth 500–600 marks p.a. in one of Henry VII's chamber books, and an account of the fifteenth earl of his manors in the right of his wife in 1527–8 recorded a net income of about £328: E101/414/16, fol. 125r; NRO, NRS 11066. The payment of 1000 marks is not mentioned in the patent roll grant, but in a book of payments early in Henry VIII's reign, the earl, Robert Tyrell, Robert Lovell, William Waldegrave, Henry Tey and others were bound in five obligations to pay 1000 marks on 1 June 1510 if Elizabeth Trussell was then alive, and this is also mentioned in Edmund Dudley's notebook: E36/215, fol. 324v; BL, Lansdowne 127, fol. 41r.

[61] CP, x, 247.

and at some stage he had also held the wardship of Gilbert Pinchbeke,[62] which he sold to Elizabeth, duchess of Norfolk, that of Clement Harleston which he had purchased for some 800 marks,[63] and that of John Cressener.[64] This considerable amount of patronage demonstrates Oxford's favour with the king, particularly early in the reign, when a number of grants were made without rent, and whether the earl retained the wardship or sold it on, he undoubtedly made substantial profits from this source. It may have been this trade in wardships, along with cash wages and profits from office-holding, which provided some of the disposable income for purchasing several manors and undertaking a major rebuilding programme at Castle Hedingham in the early years after Bosworth. Later in the reign, as Henry VII systematically exploited the feudal system for his own enrichment, Oxford began to pay more substantial sums for wardships, but nonetheless was able to get those he wanted by virtue of his good relationship with Henry and one or two were bought at less than the asking price. The Trussell wardship, while expensive, was designed to be for the advancement of his family, and Oxford would not have balked at the sum to be expended. Generosity is not a trait normally associated with Henry VII, but early in his reign he was generous in his grants of land and wardships to the earl. While Henry may later have become at best less open-handed, at worst mean and avaricious, this earlier munificence is worth emphasizing as one of Henry's political tools as he sought to establish his dynasty.

The earl also exploited his own position in the feudal hierarchy for profit. He may be more typical of his class in this respect than is often imagined at this date, as it is an under-studied aspect of noble finance and of noble–gentry relations, although McFarlane noted that 'the great lords continued to find their feudal rights remunerative'.[65] For each estate held of him by knight's service, the earl was

---

[62] This led to a plea to the chancellor around 1504–5 (C1/174/58) that Oxford was being defrauded of his rights, as Anne, wife of Robert Ingleton, had unlawfully been assigned dower despite Robert dying under age: *CPR, 1494–1509*, 344, 345, 395; *CCR, 1500–9*, no. 184; *CIPM Henry VII*, ii, 415–6, 426–7. For Pinchbeke, see *Testamenta Vetusta*, ed. N.H. Nicolas (2 vols, London, 1826), ii, 483.

[63] E101/415/3, fols 192v, 284v; BL, Add. MS. 21480, fols 66v, 172v, where it was noted that the earl 'must bynd hym by obligacions and fynd sureties the nexte terme in 800 marks for the warde of Harleston'. Oxford appeared to get the wardship slightly cheaply – it was offered to Bray for 1000 marks: E101/414/16, fols 124v, 125r. See also *CPR, 1494–1509*, 596. Clement was the son and heir of John Harleston and, aged five at his father's death, he was co-heir to estates in Essex, Kent and Lincolnshire: *CIPM Henry VII*, ii, 237–8, 284, 329.

[64] E101/414/16, fol. 124v (10 August 1497) – 'the ward of Cressener that my lord of Oxon sueth fore and now hath bought'. John Cressener, cousin and heir of Alexander Cressener, esquire, who died in 1496, was heir to estates in Essex and Suffolk worth a little over £20 a year: *CIPM Henry VII*, ii, 25, 58–9.

[65] McFarlane also commented on the incomplete nature of the surviving records, while noting some examples of extant feodary's accounts: *Nobility of Later Medieval England*, 215–6. Pollard noted that right of wardship [and relief] of his subtenants was clearly of significant financial value to Lord Fitzhugh: *North-Eastern England*, 98; M.E. James also mentioned

entitled to a payment, or relief, when an heir over twenty-one inherited from his parents, as well as a formal act of homage, and he was also entitled to the wardship of any heir under twenty-one who held land of him, providing that the heir was not also holding land of the king directly. However, it is clear that Oxford did not start systematically exploiting such forms of revenue until the winter of 1497. An account and survey of 1597 of the honour of Castle Hedingham in Essex, Suffolk and Cambridgeshire survives, made by an unnamed feodary of William Cecil, Lord Burghley, who was then the owner of the estate.[66] The feodary had access to a number of surveys, accounts and books for the period when the honour was in de Vere hands, dating as far back as Henry III's reign, but which are now lost. The primary source for the thirteenth earl is a book referenced in the 1597 account as 'Liber 2 homagium'. This records all homages made to the earl from the holders of the hundred or so knights' fees of the honour of Hedingham from 1498 onwards.

The book of homages records that between February 1498 and approximately 1509 at least fifty-four men made homage to the earl in person, and of those who did so, the book records that thirty-six paid a relief on a standard scale of 100 shillings for a whole knight's fee, and proportionally less for a fraction of a fee.[67] These sums totalled £120 for that period. For those that did not pay a relief, there are a number of explanations. First, the 1597 feodary was not careful in his notation of his original source and there is no guarantee that he noted down the relief paid in every instance. Second, five of the homages made to the earl were by heirs who were under age, and of whom it is specifically noted that the relief was remitted, or at least respited, as they were, or had been, in the wardship of the earl, and presumably he had had his due from the profits of the ward's lands.[68] In one instance, a relief from William Ford was remitted 'because he came to the said lands by purchase and not by inheritance'.[69] Lastly, it was obviously a matter of policy occasionally to waive the relief. Sir Roger Wentworth,

the continuing profitability of such rights in connection to the Clifford family in the mid-sixteenth century: 'The First Earl of Cumberland and the Decline of Northern Feudalism', *Northern History*, i (1966), 48–51. There are some comparative sums for the duke of Buckingham in the early years of the sixteenth century: Harris, *Edward Stafford*, 125–6.

[66] Bodleian, Rawlinson B 319. ERO, D/DPr 145 is a similar fee book of the honour of Hedingham, dating from 1596. However, the latter is incomplete (only 55 folios compared to the 150 of Rawlinson B 319), not covering all the fees in Essex, nor any other county, nor is it as comprehensive where it does cover the same knights' fees as the Rawlinson MS. The ERO manuscript is probably a draft which was either never completed or part of which is now missing.

[67] Bodleian, Rawlinson B 319. Those that made homage and paid a relief are fols 2r, 3r, 9r, 11r, 12r, 13r, 14r, 15r, 17v, 21r, 30r, 33r, 39v, 42r (3), 43v, 46r, 47, 55r, 62v, 65v, 66v, 67v, 79r, 81v, 92v, 98r, 100r, 102v, 111r, 112r, 119r (2), 123r. Those who made homage but paid no relief are 5v, 26r, 27r, 31r, 34r, 43v (2), 52r, 63v, 84r, 85r, 86r, 118r. For those in wardship when making homage, see following note.

[68] Ibid., fols 20r, 41r, 56v, 88r, 118r.

[69] Ibid., fol. 46v.

one of the earl's retainers, did not appear to pay the £10 owed for two knights' fees he held of the earl in Belchamp Walter, Essex, when he did homage, nor did the earl's Suffolk steward, Thomas Heigham, for two and a half knights' fees in Denham and Downham.[70]

The earl occasionally passed on a wardship for cash or as a reward. The book of homages records that in 1504 or 1505 he sold the keeping of the lands and the marriage of Lawrence, son and heir of Richard Foster to Isabel Foster, presumably Lawrence's mother, for the sum of £20.[71] Another source records that the wardship of Richard Bendish was granted by the earl to Sir Robert Tyrell and another man in 1502, though whether for cash or as an exercise in patronage is not stated.[72] In November 1485 the earl granted the wardship and the custody of the estates of the son and heir of James Lynde, of Stoke Lisle, Oxfordshire, who held of him by knight service, to the abbey of Notley.[73]

While it was occasionally a matter of policy to waive such dues, that was the earl's prerogative to exercise; an undated letter to the abbot of St Mary Graces, next to the Tower of London, not only supports the evidence from the feodary's book, but also demonstrates the earl's insistence on his rights:

> Reverend and right welbelovid in god, I commaund me to you and where you owe unto me homage for your lands lying in Meseden in the county of Hertf' holden of me by the servyce of a hoole knights fee and also owe to pay me Cs for the relief of the same, where I of long tyme have forborn, I now pray you without further delay to be with me at my castell of Hedingham at this Easter next comyng for the same entent, or ells at that tyme to shew bifore me and my councell a sufficient discharge in that bihalve. Wher if ye fail to do I assure you I shall for my remedy therof take such advauntage agenyst you as shalbe suffred w[i]t[hin?] the law, and God kepe you. Written at my seid Castell the xiiii day of February.
> [Signed] Yowre Oxynford[74]

No further evidence shows whether the abbot complied with the earl's demands, but the latter was well within his rights.

The book of homages also shows that it was not until late in 1497 or early in 1498 that the earl began to systematically exploit this source of income and influence, which 'I of long tyme have forborn'. The book quite clearly starts around that

---

[70] Ibid., fols 5v, 84r, 86r.

[71] Ibid., fol. 102v.

[72] Bodleian, Rawlinson B 257, p. 2. An early seventeenth-century book recording the knight's fees and yearly fines for respite of suit of court of the honour of Castle Hedingham, using many of the same sources as Rawlinson B 319.

[73] BL, Harl. Ch. 83 C1; *VCH Oxfordshire* (15 vols, London, 1907–2006), vi, 316, though this has a Thomas Lynde dying in 1485.

[74] SP 1/7, fol. 92, summarized in *LP*, I, i, no. 1626 and printed in J.E. Cussans, 'Edwinstree Hundred', 131, in volume one of his *History of Hertfordshire* (3 vols, London, 1870–81); *VCH Hertfordshire*, iv, 89 (manor of Meesden). The letter is not dated by year, but from the date in February, may well be from 1498, when the earl was systematically enforcing his feudal overlordship.

date, but of the thirty-four men who paid a relief between 1498 and 1509, a very high number, twenty-four, did so in 1498 and 1499. There was no mass extinction of the Essex gentry in those years, as it is clear that many men were summoned to do homage and pay a relief for lands that they had held for many years. For example, Hugh Nailinghurst, esquire, died in 1492, possessed of lands in Great Rayne, held of the earl. His heir, Clement, aged thirty at his father's death, did not do homage for this estate until 3 January 1498.[75] A more extreme example, concerns Thomas Cotton, whose father died on 2 August 1455 possessed of land in Landwade in Cambridgeshire, which was held of the de Vere family, but who did not make homage or pay his 100 shillings relief until 1498–9.[76]

What is not clear is why there was a change of policy in 1497–8, and whether there was a financial or a political imperative behind it. The earl was clearly aware of his feudal rights – there are several references in the 1597 feodary's survey to an extent of the knights fees of the honour of Castle Hedingham that was made in the first year of Henry VII's reign – but he appears not to have exploited this systematically as a source of revenue for the first twelve years after Bosworth. The threat of Perkin Warbeck had just been extinguished in 1497, but given the uncertainty of the times, it could be argued that this was an attempt to emphasize Oxford's lordship in East Anglia, by enforcing the symbolic act of homage. However, so many of the men who held land of him were in his circle already that this would have had little impact on county society. It seems more likely to have stemmed from financial motives, with the earl copying his sovereign's attempts to maximize his income from feudal rights. A similar motivation can be discerned in a flurry of activity in the Michaelmas term of 1499, when the earl initiated a string of legal cases in the court of Common Pleas to recover unpaid debts.[77] At least £120 over ten years was raised from the exploitation of his feudal rights and the wardship of a number of minor landowners; this would have been a reasonable return for the administrative effort. This sum was of course from the honour of Castle Hedingham alone – the earl held other honours and overlordships, and occasional evidence shows his exploitation of these as a source of revenue as well.[78] None of these methods seems to have caused the earl significant unpopularity, as there was no apparent contemporary reaction during his lifetime or after his death, unlike Henry Clifford, first earl

---

[75] Bodleian, Rawlinson B 319, fol. 52v; *CIPM Hen VII*, i, 321–2, though this gives the feudal overlord as Richard, bishop of London.

[76] Bodleian, Rawlinson B 319, fol. 119v; Wedgwood, ii, 228; *CIPM Hen VII*, ii, 291–2, though this gives the overlord as Margaret, countess of Richmond.

[77] See below, 169–70.

[78] In 1498 Robert Plummer made his homage 'in the councell hous' at Castle Hedingham to Oxford as Lord Scales for the manor of Sandon and paid 100s relief for the service of a whole knight's fee: ERO, D/DAyT1/45. Morant, *Essex*, i, 494, states that John Reydon did homage in person at Castle Hedingham in 1498; BL, Harl. Ch. 57 C15 is an acknowledgement of 100s relief paid by John Reydon for the manor of Reydon Hall in Ramsey, though it is dated October 1487. C1/130/42 relates to 100s relief due from the abbot of Missenden to the earl.

of Cumberland whose inability to control the Pilgrimage of Grace was partly due to the fact he had alienated both his mesne tenants and the peasantry by raising rents and trying to enforce feudal dues, nor did Oxford need to resort to suing his own servants and tenants as the duke of Buckingham did on a regular basis (forty-nine cases during his lifetime) to enforce his feudal rights and other profits.[79]

The major problem in trying to assess John de Vere's total income is that none of the major sources, a receiver-general's account of 1488–9, a valor of c.1485–97, and his inquisition *post mortem* in 1513, were intended to do such a task. Inquisitions *post mortem* by this date almost invariably gave either net annual values or a full extent for each manor held by the dead tenant in chief, but the problems of undervaluing estates in this type of document are well known, nor do they include the profit of offices or wardship.[80] Receiver-generals' accounts do give a total of revenue received into the hands of this official, but not all the revenue from the estates came into his hands, and in Rees Davies' words the receiver-general's account 'is concerned with his own personal liability, not with the problem of determining how much of the estate's income had been realised in any particular year'.[81] Valors, while giving a clearer idea of landed income, and concerned in part with 'the desire of landlords to determine the amount of profit and loss they made or expected to make from their estates', again focus on land rather than profits of office, wardship or other casualties.[82]

Perhaps the most interesting document among these accounts is the valor.[83] While the last membrane and probably the first two membranes are lost, leaving the document without an overall heading or a final *summa*, the internal structure of the document mitigates this to some extent, and some five and a half membranes are still extant. However, the date no longer survives, and although it must have been created between 1485 and 1497, and probably between 1486 and 1488, the internal evidence is contradictory.[84] It is divided into two sections,

[79] Harris, *Edward Stafford*, chapter 5, and for some of the legal cases, 96–100, 143; James, 'First Earl of Cumberland', 53–7.

[80] See C.D. Ross and T.B. Pugh, 'Materials for the Study of Baronial Incomes in Fifteenth Century England', *Econ HR*, vi (1953), 186–8, for a wider discussion of this problem.

[81] R.R. Davies, 'Baronial Accounts, Incomes and Arrears in the Later Middle Ages', *Econ HR*, xxi (1968), 213.

[82] Ibid., 214.

[83] NRO, Towns. 196, MS 1615.

[84] The heading of the second section, 'D[omi]nia et man[er]ia subsequenta de hereditam[ento] *Elizabeth nuper comitisse Oxonie m[at]ris d[omi]ni n[u]nc*', means it cannot date from before Bosworth. It cannot date from later than Blackheath in 1497, where Robert Tyrell and Robert Drury were knighted, as both are titled as esquires in the document. The document must, therefore, date from between 1485 and 1497. The most likely possibility within this period is 1486–8, from the following pieces of evidence:

    i.   It must date from later than April 1486, when Edmund Paston was appointed receiver of Scales land until a 'reasonable partition be made'. The Scales estates were divided by the time the valor was drawn up, with the earl in possession of his share of the estates.

the first covering the earl's paternal estates, from which at least two membranes are missing, which means that, being arranged by county, all but one or two of the entries for the Essex estates have been lost. However, this section has its own gross and net totals, so it is clear what the valuations of the missing manors were. The second section covers the estates of the earl's mother, including the Scales estates acquired on his restoration in 1485. The last membrane is no longer extant, so that the manors of Bentfield Bury, Stapleford Abbotts, Barons in Purleigh, Mundon, Jakelottis and Mose (all Essex) are missing, as is the *summa* for this section. The valor does not include any manor that was either purchased after 1485 or was granted for life or in tail male by the king, though possibly these might have been found in a missing third section. Each manorial entry in both sections notes the total income from the fee farm and/or assize rent, profits of court, etc. It then deducts annuities assigned, fees of estate officials, and repairs and expenses made in that year. The final entry for each manor gives a net income '*valet clare hoc anno*'. While this is more detailed than some valors, it can be classed as such, as it does not enter into the more complicated matters of arrearage, nor the actual sums paid from the manorial officials to the central administrators, as for example any receiver-general's account does.

While the valor does give a clear statement of the expected revenue from the earl's lands, the sums do need to be treated with a certain amount of caution. De Vere's paternal estates are estimated to have produced £1213 2s 6d gross, and a net profit of £1023 6s 1d. This total does not include the £60 estimated to be the value of the three manors granted to the earl's brother George. There is no surviving *summa* for the second section covering the earl's maternal estates. The net total for the manors covered is £655 12s 9d net, but there are at least six missing, and the total, not including the Scales inheritance, had been estimated at £683 in a valor of 1436–7. Before accepting an estimate of clear value of £1678 15s 5d, plus the revenue from six missing manors, the annuities assigned

ii. The manor of Wigston in Leicestershire is included in the valor. The manor was granted to Sir James Blount (d. 1492) by 1488. The grant is likely to have been fairly soon after Bosworth however.

iii. Hinxton and Crepping in Suffolk granted to Earls Colne priory in 1492. Hinxton accounted for in the valor and Crepping (annual value £10 p.a.), although not mentioned, may well be included with its neighbour Tattingstone, as the latter's revenue is £10 higher than in other accounts.

This does leave a problem. An annuity of £10 assigned to the manor of Tendring is noted in the valor to a knight with the surname of Fynas, but whose first name is omitted. A £10 annuity from Tendring was paid to a Thomas Fynas, esquire, in the receiver-general's account of 1488–9 (ERO, D/DPr 139, m.4). Thomas Fynas, esquire, in 1488–9 could be either Thomas Fiennes, knighted at the creation of Prince Henry as duke of York on 31 October 1494, and summoned to parliament as Thomas Fiennes, Lord Dacre (of the South) from October 1495, or his uncle, Thomas, of Claverham, Sussex, knighted at Prince Arthur's marriage in 1501: Dugdale, *Baronage of England*, ii, 244; *The Knights of England*, ed. W.A. Shaw (2 vols, London, 1906), i, 145. Who the '– Fynas, knight' in the valor would be if the document it dates from 1486–8 is unclear.

on particular manors should be added to the total. Payment to manorial officials was ordinary expenditure, but retaining annuities, assigned to particular manors, should be classified as extraordinary expenditure. There are a total of £45 5s 4d of such annuities included in the account. There are additional annual payments of over £50 to ecclesiastical institutions and figures, all assigned to particular manors, but these had been granted in perpetuity long before, and therefore can be discounted. To the clear value of £1678 then, one needs to add the profits of the missing manors and £45 of annuities, to have a more accurate idea of total landed income from his inherited estates.

As a comparison, the estates he inherited from his parents are estimated by his inquisition *post mortem* as being worth annually £1548, which, while something of an underestimate, was not wildly inaccurate.[85] The earl's inquisition *post mortem* is a guide to his landholding in 1513, which was rather greater than in 1485 as a result of purchases and royal patronage, but does not give a full record of his income, as it excludes any profits from office or wardship. Total landed income, as recorded in the inquisitions, was £1782 14s 3d, though sixteen manors are not included in the valuation.[86] The combination of the missing manors and undervaluation, means that the total landed income in 1513 was more likely to be over £2000 than under £1800, though even this does not include Countess Elizabeth's dower lands from her first marriage.

The major problem in using these documents to assess income is that within a few years of 1485 the lands he inherited from his parents produced less than half of his annual income. The valor does not include any of the manors later purchased, any of the royal patronage in land, and neither valor nor inquisition detail his control of the Beaumont estates, nor any profits of office or wardship. The receiver-general's account, which does include some non-manorial receipts, is, however, more problematic. Rather like the twelfth earl's accounts of the 1430s, the receiver-general's account does not record the complete income of each manor in the year; it simply records the receiver's liabilities. This is the only explanation for the fact that the account in 1488–9 records a landed income for the earl in that year lower than that for the same manors in the earl's inquisition *post mortem*, namely £1352 compared to £1548.

---

[85] C142/28, nos 2, 51, 53, 56, 63, 68, 83, 88, 118, 123, 130; E150/299/8. The latter is a better copy of the partly illegible Essex inquisition (C142/28/83), though it is not quite complete, missing valuations for Langdon and Cruswhiche recorded in no. 83.

[86] The manors missing from the inquisition are Bushey and the More (Herts.), Chipping Norton (Oxfordshire), Holbroke Park (Suffolk), Terrington Hall (Norfolk), 'Botesworth' (Northants.), Doddinghurst, the two manors in Little Waltham, the two manors in Boreham, Burnells in Stansted (though possibly included in the figure for Stansted Mountfichet), Helions Bumpstead (though possibly included in the figure for Steeple Bumpstead) and Sheriffs in Colne Engaine (all Essex), and Chesham and Cheshambury (Bucks.). Additionally, the reversions of Toppesfield and Tendring are omitted, while that of Berwick and Scotneys is included, but without a valuation.

Comparison of Selected Manorial Income, 1485–1513[87]

Manor	Receiver-General 1488–9	Valor, 1485–97 (net)	IPM, 1513
Castle Hedingham	£12 10d	Missing	£23 16s 6d
Tilbury (Essex)	Nil	Missing	£36 3s 4d
Lavenham (Suffolk)	£20	£57 7s 2d	£61 19s 7d
Castle Camps (Cambs.)	£36	£41 8s	£37 19s
East Winch (Norfolk)	Nil	£20 8s 10d	£24 19s
Great Oakley (Essex)	£8 19s 2d	£35 5s 2d	£27
Wivenhoe (Essex)	£14 5s 2d	£29 8s 7d (does not include 40s in annuities)	£38 11s 9d[88]
Maldon (Essex)	£28 12s 4d	£40 2s 2d	£43 9s 8d[89]

As is clear from the table, and the same was true of the twelfth earl's accounts of the 1430s and 1440s, lower revenues appear particularly on manors where the earl was regularly resident, or manors neighbouring them; the contrast with the more distant Castle Camps is noticeable. A considerable proportion of the receipts from many estates did not go to the receiver, being either immediately reimbursed without appearing on his account, or were paid to another member of the central administration by the local official. Some of the receipts were immediately taken by the controller of the household to pay for food and wages. This is clear from an account of several de Vere manors in 1499–1500, comprising a miscelleanous collection of bailiffs' and farmers' accounts of various manors, without much obvious to unite them – they were too geographically diverse to be a receivership, comprising manors in north and north-east Essex (Wivenhoe, Bures Giffard) central and south-eastern Essex (Maldon, Downham, Waltons in Purleigh, Hayes-in-Stowe), and four manors in eastern Hertfordshire (Great Hormead, Barkway, Rokey and Newsells). What groups all but one of them (Newsells) in this account, is that all the cash receipts from these manors went directly to the hands of Robert Rochester, controller of the household. The income received into his hands totalled £166 17s, with some of the cash generated paying for purchases of stock at a manorial level, and some paying for administrative expenses of various officials drawing up new rentals on the manors of Bures Giffard, Great Hormead and Barkway. Only at Newsells was the cash profit from the manor, £16 13s 4d, paid to the receiver-general, Clement Heigham.[90] It would seem likely that the profits of certain manors had been set aside for the controller of the household to receive directly: it might be that the cash from

[87] ERO, D/DPr 139 (1488–9), NRO, Towns. 196, MS 1615 (1485–97), C142/28/2, 83, 88, 123; E150/299/8 (1513).
[88] With the little manor of Battleswick and the small holding of Cokyns.
[89] With the holdings of Mundon, Jakelottis, Flaxland, Warehill and Flannerswick.
[90] ERO, D/DBm M501.

Newsells, which was unusually noted to have been paid to the receiver-general by the hands of the senior retainer, Robert Tyrell, was an anomaly.

Such a system, whereby the controller of the household received substantial sums directly from some manorial officials, would also explain the fact that the receiver-general in 1488–9 granted £889 to Henry Smith, controller of the household, yet in 1507–8 the earl's total household expenditure was £1498.[91] Without a full household account showing how the household was funded, it is difficult to be certain, but this seems much the most likely explanation. This was not untypical: Kate Mertes has argued 'profits of home manors seldom went to the receiver, being absorbed immediately by the household'.[92] An additional factor behind the low income in the receiver-general's account was that most annuities were tied to particular estates, and would have been deducted at source, so that neither the receiver-general nor the household official would have received the revenue. Annuities paid to retainers amounted to £198 p.a. in 1513.[93]

One further aspect of expenditure concerns the household of the countess. It was the general practice for married noblewomen to have a separate household, funded by an assignment of rent or land, or by a jointure – the Percy household officials in 1512 only paid wages to every gentlewoman or 'chambere' attending upon the countess of Northumberland who was 'nott at my ladys fyndynge'.[94] Elizabeth Howard certainly had a separate administration during the lifetime of the twelfth earl – a set sum of £40 was paid from the profits of East Bergholt in Suffolk in 1443–6 to the cofferer of the countess, and it is likely that revenue from other manors was set aside for her.[95] However, it is uncertain how Countess Margaret's household was funded, as there is no extant evidence for assignment of cash or of land set aside for her, and she was dead by the date of the 1507–8 household account, when the number of household servants – regardless of which official paid for them – was likely to be substantially diminished.

Although income from the earl's own lands can be estimated relatively accurately from the three sources of the valor, the inquisition *post mortem* and the receiver-general's account, there is no full record of the huge amount of revenue generated from other sources. Occasionally proceeds are noted – the receiver general's account records receipts of £50 of the £100 fee as chief steward of the duchy, £14 of a £20 annuity paid to the earl by Queen Elizabeth's receiver in Essex and Hertfordshire, and £8 for the keeping of the forest of Essex, but not for example the fees for the constableship of the tower, the keeping of the lions,

[91] ERO, D/DPr 139 m. 4 and d.; Longleat House, Wiltshire, Miscellanea xi, fol. 136r.

[92] K. Mertes, *English Noble Households from 1250–1600* (Oxford, 1988), 94–5.

[93] See below, 184–5.

[94] *The Northumberland Household Book. The Regulations and Establishment of the Household of Henry Algernon Percy, fifth earl of Northumberland, begun 1512*, ed. T. Percy (London, 1770), 46.

[95] SRO, HA6:51/4/5.3, mm. 2–4.

any profits or fees from the admiralty, nor any casual income from wardships or any other stewardships, nor from the Beaumont estates, where the earl presumably continued to employ separate receivers.[96] Such casual profits or fees 'were normally paid direct into the lord's coffers or privy purse in charge of a confidential servant, usually called a cofferer', for whom no account has survived; the earliest surviving cofferers' accounts in England date from Henry VII's reign, but only one or two are known.[97]

This means that a complete and precise figure for the earl's total income cannot be given, however, and varied over time in any case, so what follows is no more than a rough estimate. Receipts from his ancestral lands would probably have been worth around £1800 in 1485, to which purchases worth perhaps £150 p.a. could be added by 1509.[98] By 1500 in the region of a further £1000 p.a. had been added by royal patronage in the form of land, a figure comprising £300 derived from landed grants by the crown in tail male or for life, and £750 a year from Beaumont's lands until the viscount's death; from 1509 Oxford received at least £500 p.a. from the dower lands of Beaumont's widow, the earl's second wife. Therefore at the turn of the century, his total landed income was probably approximately £3000 p.a. To this should be added several hundred pounds from the French pension, the fees of his many offices and an unknown amount deriving from profits of these offices, and either the sale of wardships, or exploitation of the estates of those he retained, as well as, from 1498, a small sum each year in the exploitation of his feudal rights. At no stage can his total income have been realistically much less than £4000 p.a., and might at some periods have been higher.

While his own landed endowment was more modest than one or two of the richest and most powerful magnate families, his earnings from other sources, such as the Beaumont estates, royal office and wardship, meant that his total income is likely to have been similar to all but one of the wealthiest of the early Tudor nobility, and considerably outstripped many powerful families like the Talbots, whose estates generated around £1500 a year.[99] The second duke of Norfolk's landed revenue was estimated to be £2241 p.a. in 1524 – a sum very similar to that of Oxford's own estates a decade or two earlier.[100] The net revenue from the Percy estates in 1489, including therefore the £1096 later spent on extraordinary expenses, was estimated at £3208. They were assessed at £2920

---

[96]   ERO D/DPr 139, m. 3.

[97]   McFarlane, *Nobility of Later Medieval England*, 129. He noted the duke of Buckingham's extant account from 1503–4, and there are also several relating to Margaret Beaufort from her son's reign: WAM, 22824–6, 32390.

[98]   Fifteen years later, without the estates and offices the earl held for life or the Beaumont estates, the earldom was valued at £2260: *LP*, IV, ii, no. 4588.

[99]   Bernard, *Power of Early Tudor Nobility*, 143.

[100]   Virgoe, 'Recovery of the Howards', 18.

in the tax assessment of 1523, though this appears to underestimate the value.[101] Stanley receiver accounts of 1522–3 put the gross income of the then underage earl of Derby at £3343 p.a., but a valor a year earlier estimated his landed income at £4259; the first earl's collection of offices, which probably matched that of Oxford, would have taken his income above that of de Vere.[102] Jasper Tudor also might have been wealthier than the earl for a brief period; his landed income may have been as high as £4300 p.a. after a large number of grants in 1485–6 and his marriage to the widowed duchess of Buckingham.[103] The only man who landed resources outstripped all these magnates was Edward Stafford, duke of Buckingham, whose annual income was around £5600 by 1521.[104] Nonetheless, throughout the reign, the earl of Oxford would have been in the top three or four earners amongst the peerage – a critical fact overlooked by historians.

The earl's solvency enabled him to be generous in alienating a number of estates. Presumably in 1485 he granted his brother George the manors of Preston (Suffolk), Dullingham (Cambridgeshire) and Langdon (Essex), worth together around 100 marks in 1488–9, which the latter held until his death in 1503, and his widow until hers at an unknown date after the making of the earl's will.[105] In 1492 he also granted to his family priory at Earls Colne the manors of Hinxton (Cambridgeshire) and Crepping Hall (Suffolk), worth £50 p.a.[106] In a gesture of gratitude to his former gaoler, de Vere made a life grant to Sir James Blount of the manor of Wigston Magna in Leicestershire, worth 50 marks annually, which Blount held until his death in 1492.[107] The earl's substantial income allowed substantial expenditure, particularly on his household. Grants from the receiver-general to the controller of the household were £889 in 1488–9 and £1238 in a fragmentary account of either 1497–8 or 1498–9, and by 1507–8 the total cost was £1498, of which £213 was the wages of over one hundred servants,

[101] E179/238/95; E179/69/24a, 25, 26; J.M.W. Bean, *The Estates of the Percy Family, 1416–1537* (Oxford, 1955), 129–40; H. Miller, 'Subsidy Assessments of the Peerage in the Sixteenth Century', *BIHR*, xxviii (1955), 18.

[102] Coward, *The Stanleys*, 200–4.

[103] Thomas, 'Political Career...of Jasper Tudor', 322.

[104] Rawcliffe, *Staffords*, 133. Harris, *Edward Stafford*, 104 has £5061, and suggests certainly earlier in his life his income fell far short of this.

[105] ERO, D/DPr 139, m. 3; PROB 11/17, fol. 88r.

[106] CCR, 1485–1500, 226; C54/354, m. 20d. The calendar incorrectly dates the document to 13 May (it is actually 15 May) and the year as 9 Henry VII. While it is hard to decipher the date even under ultra-violet light, the correct date of the grant is actually 7 Henry VII, though the memorandum of acknowledgement is indeed 9 Henry VII. The calendar also omits three of the eight attorneys appointed – William Coke, William Hille and John Harry-daunce. The convent had been granted a licence at the supplication of the earl to acquire lands to the value of £40 yearly, at the cost of £200 in February 1489: CPR, 1485–94, 260. Hinxton was worth £40 p.a. in the valor of 1485–97, Crepping just under £10 in the receiver-general's account of 1488–9: NRO, Towns. 196, MS 1615, m. 2; ERO, D/DPr 139, m. 3.

[107] ERO, D/DPr 139, m. 3.

not including estate officials.[108] As noted above, his retaining at the end of his life cost £198 p.a. Despite all these burdens, however, there is little doubt that receipts were greater than expenses.

Other noble families around this time did occasionally find themselves indebted; the duke of Buckingham owed £10535 to the king in 1520, and the earl of Northumberland was borrowing on a similar scale at the same date.[109] It is easy to overplay the scale of this; Rawcliffe points out Stafford's debts were no more than the equivalent of two years' clear landed income and contemporaries did not regard borrowing on this scale excessive.[110] Yet de Vere was clearly in a different financial position. Not only did the earl appear to have the financial resources in the 1480s and 1490s to undertake extensive new building at Hedingham, and during the whole period after 1485 to purchase eleven manors and five reversions, but there is no evidence at all of substantial borrowing. Indeed at the time of his death, de Vere had £2100 in ready money and debts owing to him of £1333 6s 8d. Moreover, he had accumulated goods to the value of £4888, making a total, with debts and ready cash, of £8321.[111] This source demonstrates his great wealth; this wealth and huge territorial endowment in East Anglia, if not quite the *sine qua non*, was undoubtedly one of the foundation stones of his political pre-eminence in the early Tudor period.

[108] Longleat, Misc. xi, fols 126–136r.; ERO, D/DPr 139, m. 4; D/DPr 135A.
[109] Rawcliffe, *Staffords*, 140; Bean, *Estates of the Percy Family*, 141–2.
[110] Rawcliffe, *Staffords*, 140.
[111] 'Last Testament', 348. The scribe gives a total of £8206, of which the goods must form £4773. By my reckoning the addition (from the subtotals) is £115 short. The inventory of his goods is 'Last Testament', 320–48. The sheer accumulation of wealth in the form of plate, clothes, tapestry and other goods is staggering. One chain of gold with a mariner's whistle, presumably reflecting his office of admiral, was valued at £243 6s 8d, the annual income of a small barony. As a comparison, the inventory of the goods of Thomas Howard, duke of Norfolk at Framlingham at his death in 1524 totalled £1091: *Medieval Framlingham. Select Documents, 1270–1524*, ed. J. Ridgard (Suffolk Record Society, xxvii, Woodbridge, 1985), 129–58.

✦ 4 ✦

'His Principal Servant Both for War and Peace': Political Life under Henry VII[1]

The noble and corayiouse knyght therle of Oxinforde desired and besaught the king to have the conduyt of the fowarde, whiche the king grauntede.

His fowarde recountrede his enemyes and rebells, wher by the helpe of Almyghty God he hade the victorye. (The Herald's memoir on the battle of Stoke, 1487)[2]

Henry VII faced an immediate problem when he ascended the throne. He had only one adult male among his immediate family, his uncle Jasper Tudor, earl of Pembroke, shortly to be created duke of Bedford. Henry was unmarried in 1485, and it would therefore be a long time before he had sons to shoulder any of his burdens. He had no surviving brothers to rely on, as Edward IV had in Richard of Gloucester, or Henry V had in the dukes of Bedford, Clarence and Gloucester. While his formidable mother, Margaret Beaufort, was to become influential in parts of the midlands, she was not able to offer genuine regional leadership. This meant that he would have to work closely with the higher nobility if he were to establish order in the regions and raise troops to protect his throne in the first few years after Bosworth. The higher echelons of the peerage were numerous enough in 1485. There were three dukes, those of Bedford, Buckingham and Suffolk; one marquess, Dorset, and a second, Berkeley, was created in 1489; and fifteen earls, Arundel, Derby, Devon, Essex, Huntingdon, Kent, Lincoln, North-umberland, Oxford, Rivers, Shrewsbury, Surrey, Warwick, Westmorland and Wiltshire. However, a surfeit of numbers concealed a dearth of loyalty, ability and power. Of these twenty peers, four were minors until the late 1480s and 1490s (Buckingham, Essex, Warwick and Wiltshire), two had better claims to the throne than Henry himself (Lincoln and Warwick), one was not technically a member of the peerage, having forfeited for opposition at Bosworth, and had to wait four years for his release from the Tower (Surrey), and many were time-

---

[1]   Quote from *Francis Bacon's History of the reign of King Henry VII*, ed. R. Lockyer (London, 1971), 209.
[2]   *The Herald's Memoir 1486–90*, ed. E. Cavell (Donnington, 2009), 112, 117.

serving nonentities or political lightweights. Only two of these men had existing regional power structures – Derby in the north-west, Northumberland in the north-east. Perhaps four others had the wherewithal to build such structures – Bedford in south Wales, Oxford in East Anglia, Devon in the south-west, though he was less well endowed with land, and in the Welsh Marches and west midlands, the earl of Shrewsbury, though young in 1485, was to be ably assisted by his uncle Gilbert Talbot.[3] Buckingham, though the richest magnate, was a minor until 1498, and his great estates in south Wales were in the hands of Jasper Tudor until his death. It was perhaps a smaller group of loyal men than even Edward IV or Henry IV had had to work with in not dissimilar circumstances. It would also take a little while for two of these four potential power blocs to become viable, as neither Bedford nor Oxford had been resident in their respective regions for many years.

Henry did, however, have one substantial advantage. In 1485 he held more crown lands than virtually any other English monarch before him, including the principality of Wales, the duchies of Cornwall, York, Lancaster, Gloucester, Somerset and (temporarily) Buckingham, the earldoms of Warwick, Chester and Ulster, and a fresh round of attainders brought further substantial lands into his hands; to this could be added his own earldom of Richmond. Having great lands, but few men, Henry had various options to ensure good governance and regional security. One was to rely on those, mainly below the peerage, who had shared the hazards of exile, and to create loyal gentry groups in some areas. Certain individuals who had been with Henry on the continent did very well, being raised to the lower ranks of the peerage, men such as Giles, Lord Daubeney and William, Lord Willoughby de Broke, who were trusted by the king and had grants of land and office from him.[4] However, unlike both Edward IV and Henry IV, Henry Tudor had no large, coherent affinity backing him. Alternatively or additionally, Henry could rely on existing Yorkist regional and royal structures, portraying himself as Edward IV's political heir, partly by marrying the latter's daughter Elizabeth. However, the loyalty of those who had participated in Edward's regime could not be taken for granted, and it would take a while to win them over to Tudor rule. The absence of a loyal and powerful peerage, a stable personal retinue, and trustworthy political communities already in existence, increased the necessity of Henry following a further option, namely to rely heavily on the few great men who combined both power and loyalty, notably Oxford, Derby, his father-in-law, and Bedford, his uncle.

---

3   Bernard, 'Fourth and Fifth Earls of Shrewsbury', 7–18. Shrewsbury, aged 17, was given livery of his estates without proof of age in November 1485.
4   D.A. Luckett, 'Crown Patronage and Political Morality in Early Tudor England: The Case of Giles, Lord Daubeney', *EHR*, xc (1995), 578–95; idem, 'The Rise and Fall of a Noble Dynasty: Henry VII and the Lords Willoughby de Broke', *Historical Research*, lxix (1996), 254–65.

An early indicator of Oxford's importance in the new regime was seen within a few days of Bosworth. Arriving in London after the battle, he was importuned with 'grete suyt and labour … ffor causys towchyng solycytyng of causys unto the kyng' as well as his own matters.[5] Before he was restored to the office formally by the reversal of his attainder, he officiated as great chamberlain at the king's coronation, the first de Vere to do so since 1377.[6] The earl was also made a knight of the Garter during 1485, and during the first parliament of the reign, on 6 December 1485, his attainder was reversed, and his mother's grants to Gloucester in 1473, which he claimed were made under duress, were annulled.[7] De Vere was also the recipient of a considerable amount of patronage, including the important political offices of admiral of England, constable of the Tower of London, and chief steward of the duchy of Lancaster south of the Trent, as well as other local offices and estates in East Anglia.[8] With similar offices and estates elsewhere granted to Bedford and Derby, such patronage was part of an attempt quickly to secure Tudor power in certain regions through the medium of powerful and reliable noble supporters. In addition, such substantial patronage would have sent a strong signal to local communities about the king's intentions, and in the cases of Bedford and Oxford encouraged gentry to co-operate from the beginning with the new regional power-broker. Such clear signals from the centre, the series of grants that passed much of the control of the crown's territorial interests in East Anglia into Oxford's hands and the alliance of those interests with Oxford's own estates and a burgeoning affinity, created the possibility of regional domination. Of course, it needed adroit leadership to make such a possibility a reality.

Arraying the troops

As a usurper with a tenuous claim to the throne, Henry VII would have expected to face a number of challenges to his rule. The first stirrings of rebellion came just nine months after Bosworth when, during Easter 1486, the king received reports of the escape from sanctuary at Colchester of Richard III's friend and

---

5   *Great Chronicle of London*, 239.
6   The exorbitant sum of £101 was spent by the crown on his robe for the coronation: LC9/50, fols 135, 139v.
7   S. Anglo, 'The Foundation of the Tudor Dynasty: the Coronation and Marriage of Henry VII', *The Guildhall Miscellany*, ii (1960–8), 3–11; *The Rutland Papers. Original documents Illustrative of the Courts and Times of Henry VII and Henry VIII*, ed. W. Jerdan (Camden Society, o.s., xxi, 1842), 3–5. The grant of the chamberlainship was confirmed on the accession of Henry VIII; see *CP*, x, appendix F, 60–3; Townsend, *History of the Great Chamberlainship*, 90–4; *LP*, I, i, no. 54 (56). For the Garter, see G.F. Beltz, *Memorials of the Order of the Garter: From Its Foundation to the Present Time* (London, 1841), no. 229. For the reversal of his attainder see *Parliament Rolls*, xv, 119–22, also reported by the Colchester parliamentary burgesses: *Parliamentary Texts of the Later Middle Ages*, ed. N. Pronay and J. Taylor (Oxford, 1980), 188.
8   See above, 99.

supporter Viscount Lovell and Sir Humphrey Stafford, who promptly attempted risings in Yorkshire, Warwickshire and Worcestershire.[9] The king was able to muster a substantial body of troops, quickly dispersing the outnumbered rebels. This was, however, a prelude to the next decade of domestic disturbance and insecurity, despite the birth of the king's son and heir, Arthur, on 19 September 1486. By February 1487 Lambert Simnel had appeared in Ireland, claiming to be Edward, earl of Warwick, the son of Edward IV's brother, George, duke of Clarence. Warwick himself was alive and was displayed by Henry in London, but this made little difference as the Irish political community chose, for reasons of their own, to accept the impostor as genuine and acknowledged him as king. Worryingly for the king there were serious English backers as well. Edward IV's widow, Elizabeth Woodville, and Robert Stillington, bishop of Bath and Wells, were arrested, as was the marquess of Dorset 'to whom the kyng did sende the Erle of Oxenford to intercept him ridyng on his iourney and to conveigh him to the Towre of London, to trye his truth and prove his pacience'.[10] John de la Pole, earl of Lincoln, Richard III's nearest male heir, and perhaps the leading force behind the conspiracy, fled to the Low Countries to join Viscount Lovell. Lincoln managed to raise a force of 2000 German mercenaries, through the backing of his aunt Margaret, duchess of Burgundy, and sailed with them to Dublin. There, supported by a leading Anglo-Irish peer, the earl of Kildare, and with his force supplemented by thousands of Irish troops, an invasion of England was prepared. Henry Tudor mustered an army and waited at Coventry and Kenilworth, strategically stationed to cover an assault from the Low Countries or Ireland, while it was unclear from where the attack would emanate. Oxford appears to have been with the king throughout this period and relied on his deputies to protect the coast of East Anglia from assault. A letter to his senior retainer Edmund Bedingfield reveals the difficulties of preparing for a possible invasion from the continent and from Ireland simultaneously:

> Hys Hyghnes wull not as zytte put you to ony further labur or charge, for somoche as hys rebellys and enemyes be in to Irlande; neverthelesse hys Grace wull that the contre be redy at all tymis to do hys Hygnes service up on resonabull warnyng; for so moche as the Kynges Grace intendythe to make provysyon to sende an armi in to Irlonde in haaste.[11]

The army never departed for Ireland, but certainly Bedingfield left East Anglia with the rest of Oxford's forces after the rebels had landed in England as they fought at the decisive battle of Stoke on 16 June. Oxford was prominent throughout the campaign. At a council at Coventry to set the royal host in order the 'noble and coraygious knight the Erle of Oxenforde desired and besought the kyng to have the conduyt of the Forward, which the king grauntede and

---

[9] Williams, 'Rebellion of Humphrey Stafford', 181–9.
[10] *Hall's Chronicle*, 433.
[11] *PL*, vi, 101; *PLP*, ii, 453. Undated, but probably in May.

accompanyed him with many great coragious and lusty knights'.[12] The forward or van was the position of greatest prestige, but also where the fighting was usually fiercest. The evening before the battle the royal army was shaken by a 'great skyre' or astrological phenomenon which 'caused many cowards to flee, but therle of Oxinforde and al the nobles in the forwarde with hym wer sone in a good array and in a fayre bataile'.[13] This prompt display of courage, and the presence of their captains, settled the troops. The rebel army was around 8000 men, a mixture of experienced German mercenaries and raw Irish levies, grouped into one large battalion on the top of the hill. Raked by English longbowmen, the rebels charged down the hill at Oxford's vanguard which probably numbered 6000. Initially shaken by the assault, the vanguard rallied, and Oxford, using the lie of the land and relying on the experience and courage of his troops, counterattacked up the hill. After some tough fighting, Oxford's division broke the back of the rebels' resistance without any aid from other components of the royal army.[14] Lincoln was killed, Simnel captured and perhaps 4000 rebels were killed. After the battle the king made thirteen banneretts and fifty-two knights, among whom were many of Oxford's retainers who had fought so well.

Although national security was evidently still fragile, it might have appeared after Stoke that things were improving; certainly the next few years saw Henry going through the traditional forms and motions of medieval kingship. Following the conventional dictates of English foreign policy, he intervened in France to try to stop the French acquisition of the duchy of Brittany. Substantial forces were sent in 1489 and 1490 to prevent the complete collapse of Breton independence, and a sum of about £124,000 was spent. In April 1489, the king wrote to Oxford with 'good tidinges' of the campaign's progress,[15] but it was all to no avail – Nantes fell in March 1491 and Anne, duchess of Brittany, married Charles VIII of France in December. The collection of substantial sums in taxation for Henry's foreign policy also provoked a rebellion in the north of England, which saw Henry Percy, earl of Northumberland, murdered in 1489. Oxford wrote to Sir John Paston describing this incident:

> my lord of Northumberland having the auctorite to se the Kynges money levied in the North parties had knowleche that certeyne persones of combnes wer assembled at Topclif, and at a nother lordship of his nygh to the same, saying that they wolde pay no money; my seid Lord of Northumberland heryng therof, and that they wer but naked men, addressed hymself towardes theym withoute eny harneys in pesible maner, trusting to have appeased them. Howe be it, as hit is seid, that

---

[12] *Herald's Memoir*, 112.

[13] Ibid., 116.

[14] Among other contemporary descriptions of the battle see *The York House Books, 1461–90*, ed. L.C. Attreed (2 vols, Stroud, 1991) ii, 573. For a modern account of the battle itself, see Bennett, *Lambert Simnel and the Battle of Stoke*, 89–103, and for the political background, ibid., passim; Cunningham, *Henry VII*, 47–58; Chrimes, *Henry VII*, 72–7.

[15] *PL*, vi, 125–7.

he is distressed and that they have taken hym or slayne hym, whiche the Kyng entendeth to punysshe.[16]

To deliver the punishment, a royal army, including Oxford, marched north to quell the uprising. Although a proclamation by the rebels states somewhat vague and formulaic concerns about those persons around the king who 'for to dystroy oure suffereyn Lord the Kynge and the Comowns of Engelond, for suche unlawfull poyntes as Seynt Thomas of Cauntyrbery dyed for',[17] Oxford, in the letter above, certainly assumed that taxation was at the root of the rebellion. Michael Hicks has also argued that royal financial demands, along with other local concerns, were indeed the basis for a loyalist rebellion.[18] However, even if the rising in 1489 was prompted by resistance to royal taxation, dynastic conspiracy remained.

A new pretender, Perkin Warbeck, appeared in Ireland towards the end of 1491, presenting himself as the younger of the princes in the Tower, Richard, duke of York. His move to the French court in 1492, as well as the French appropriation of Brittany, stirred Henry into preparations for that most traditional of English royal activities – invading France. The king secured an alliance with the Archduke Maximilian of Austria, negotiated with separatist groups in Brittany, sent English fleets to harass Normandy, and then, with an army of around 15000 men, crossed to France, but in October, very late in the campaigning season, with the probable intention at that point of accepting the inevitable on the best terms he could. The French offered peace terms, including a pension, which would allow Charles VIII to retain Brittany and then concentrate on his ambitions in Italy.[19] The opinions of Oxford, Dorset, Shrewsbury and twenty-two others of the king's council regarding the terms are preserved in a document dated in the camp near Boulogne; it purports to show them urging the king to agree to the terms. The king, however, would have wanted to accept them, and the statement of the lords' opinion cannot be taken at face value, because having his leading nobles sign the document allowed the king to save face.[20] As at Stoke, Oxford was the only commander actually to undertake military action: he was entrusted with a separate command during the invasion, having overall direction

[16] Oxford to Paston, 30 April 1489: *PL*, vi, 127–8. Six days later Oxford wrote to Paston ordering his attendance with his military retinue at Cambridge on 12 May. Paston's brother, in Oxford's household, also wrote to him with a copy of the rebel's proclamation: ibid., 129–31.
[17] Ibid., 130–1.
[18] M.A. Hicks, 'The Yorkshire Rising of 1489', *Northern History*, xxii (1986), 39–62. M.J. Bennett, 'Henry VII and the Northern Rising of 1489', *EHR*, cv (1990), 34–59, has, however, suggested that the dynastic threat to Henry should not be under-estimated, especially given the substantial army which the king hurriedly raised to deal with the rebellion.
[19] S.J. Gunn, 'Henry VII (1457–1509)', *ODNB*; Chrimes, *Henry VII*, 280–2; Cunningham, *Henry VII*, 65–73. The latter, along with John Currin, '"To traffic with war"? Henry VII and the French Campaign of 1492', in *English Experience in France*, ed. Grummit, 106–31, argue that Henry's intention was to renew the dynastic war with France.
[20] E30/612.

of a contingent including the duke of Suffolk, the earls of Shrewsbury, Devon and Essex, and six other lords, which successfully carried out the king's orders concerning the 'betinge downe of Arde [Ardres]' before rejoining the main force outside Boulogne.[21] Oxford's contingent of twelve spears and 400 archers was the joint largest of the expedition.[22]

However, Henry's substantial taxation and failure to deliver any decisive victory in the Agincourt mode, following much rhetoric and propaganda, left him in a more vulnerable position at home and abroad. By the terms of the treaty of Étaples, Charles VIII promised that he would no longer harbour Yorkist rebels, and so Warbeck quickly moved to the court of Margaret of Burgundy, who enabled his access to the young Duke Philip the Fair. Henry suspended all direct trade to the Netherlands, and took steps to re-impose royal control in Ireland, sending Sir Edward Poynings with a substantial force to Dublin. None of these actions, however, prevented treason in England, and Henry became aware by the end of 1494 of a serious conspiracy within his own household circle, through Sir Robert Clifford turning king's evidence; the chamberlain of the royal household, Sir William Stanley, was tried and executed in February 1495, and the steward of the household, Lord Fitzwalter, arrested by Oxford in January, was convicted on 23 February, imprisoned at Guines and executed in 1496 after trying to escape. The treachery of such important household figures at the heart of the regime increased the general air of suspicion at court, and Henry began to draw back from the more open, traditional style of government that he had adopted previously.

Henry's breaking of the English conspiracy early in 1495 was a serious blow to Warbeck's chances of success. However, he continued to be a threat, making a landing at Deal (Kent) in July 1495 which was easily repulsed, and then disembarking in Ireland. Warbeck besieged Waterford, but was driven off by Henry's Irish deputy, Sir Edward Poynings, and fled to the Scottish court. While it is unclear whether James IV believed Warbeck's story that he was indeed Richard IV, he certainly gave Warbeck a pension, a royal cousin as a wife, and a base for another assault on Tudor England. Indeed, James himself invaded northern

---

[21] *The Chronicle of Calais in the Reigns of Henry VII and Henry VIII*, ed. J.G. Nichols (Camden Society, o.s., xxxv, 1846), 2; *Chronique de Jean Molinet*, iv, 325.

[22] The earl of Derby brought an equal contingent to that of Oxford, Shrewsbury one of ten spears and 400 archers, Arundel ten spears and 300 archers and Surrey five spears and 150 archers: Nottingham University Library, Middleton MS, Mi Dc7, m. 43; A. Cameron, 'The Giving of Livery and Retaining in Henry VII's Reign', *Renaissance and Modern Studies*, xviii (1974), 23 and n.; and see also J.R. Hooker, 'Notes on the Organisation and Supply of the Tudor Military under Henry VII', *Huntingdon Library Quarterly*, xxiii (1959–60), 19–31. For the surviving indentures for the 1492 campaign (though Oxford's is not among them) see E101/72/3/1065–1162, including de Vere's associate Sir Robert Cotton, accompanied by thirty men (no. 1077). Some wages paid for the campaign are in Henry VII's household books, including those of de Vere's retainers Sir Edmund Bedingfield and Robert Lovell, who brought eighteen and five men respectively: E36/285, fols 22v–23, 39v–40.

England in September 1496, though it turned out to be a very desultory campaign. Henry, however, could not let this pass, and after securing a promise of very substantial taxation, he began to gather a huge force for a major assault on the Scots. As Lord Daubeney finalized the assembly of a vanguard of 7000 men at Newcastle, another tax rebellion began in Cornwall. Within a few weeks the rebels had taken Exeter, and marched eastwards, reaching Blackheath by mid-June; there they were confronted by the royal army. Once more de Vere led the royal vanguard, in the last battle fought on English soil during the reign, and for the third time in twelve years, his division emerged victorious from the fray.[23] Although Warbeck landed in Cornwall in September, and brought 8000 men to Exeter, his force could not face the advancing royal army, including Oxford, and melted away. Warbeck surrendered to Henry, and a truce was made with the Scots on 30 September. Henry had survived the greatest crisis of his reign.[24]

During the troubled and insecure years between 1485 and 1497, John de Vere's role was primarily military, both as leader of a large retinue from the eastern counties, and as a battlefield commander. His military reputation, already high after Bosworth, grew during the following decade, as a result of the impressive performance of his divisions at Stoke and Blackheath. There was no great military innovation apparent in either of these battles, nor was there need for any. Oxford seems to have relied on sound military principles, such as not allowing his men to stray far from their standards, and bringing as many of his men to bear on the enemy as was possible at any one time. Certainly his men held firm against a much larger division at Bosworth and a ferocious assault by the rebels at Stoke, so as a divisional commander, Oxford was undoubtedly successful. Moreover, he did more fighting for Henry VII than any other nobleman, given that at Bosworth, Stoke and Blackheath it was primarily the vanguard that bore the brunt of the engagements, with Oxford always in command.

It was, moreover, not just as a field commander that Oxford proved his worth. He was able to bring substantial forces to the king's campaigns, though the evidence is scanty and difficult. In 1487 the earl's household books contain confusingly overlapping lists of retainers and others who were appointed to be ready to go north on 18 July to subdue rebels in the aftermath of the battle of Stoke. Numerous captains, including Lord Willoughby and twelve knights, brought their retinues, and towns such as Walden, Bury and Ipswich also sent contingents, totalling 204 men.[25] In addition, he collected almost £400 from

[23] BL, Stowe 440, fol. 82v.; *Hall's Chronicle*, 479; *Chronicle of London*, 214–5; *Great Chronicle of London*, 277; *Francis Bacon's History of the Reign of King Henry VII*, ed. Lockyer, 173–5.
[24] I. Arthurson, *The Perkin Warbeck Conspiracy, 1491–99* (Stroud, 1994), passim; Cunningham, *Henry VII*, 81–93; Chrimes, *Henry VII*, 78–92; S.J. Gunn, 'Henry VII', *ODNB*.
[25] *Household Books of John, Duke of Norfolk and Thomas, Earl of Surrey, temp. 1481–1490*, ed. J.P. Collier (Roxburghe Club, 1844), 493–6. This is a printed edition of a household book containing entries for Norfolk until 1485, and thereafter for John, earl of Oxford, not Surrey, as was pointed out by M.J. Tucker, 'Household Accounts, 1490–1, of John de Vere, Earl of

individuals, towns and hundreds in Essex and Suffolk for the wages of this force.[26] Given the absence from this source of many of his retainers, his household and his tenantry, the men involved were not just Oxford's retinue, but represented a marshalling of some of the wider military and financial resources of East Anglia under authority of a commission in July 1487, which had given Oxford alone the power to array the five counties of Essex, Suffolk, Norfolk, Cambridgeshire and Huntingdonshire.[27] The Paston letters and other sources record a number of Oxford's retainers, associates and troops from East Anglian towns being summoned for military service on various occasions.[28] This was not always popular even among his own retinue – the lack of enthusiasm in 1489 can be seen in John Paston's attempt to reduce the number of men he brought to the muster. His brother, William Paston, in the earl's service, thought he might get away with bringing only a dozen of the twenty he had promised, but Sir Edmund Bedingfield, Sir Thomas Tyrell and Sir Richard Fitzlewis were all to bring thirty, and William Paston, not wanting his brother to suffer in the earl's estimation, added that he 'wolde not ye schulde be to ferre undyr them'. Nor was John Paston the only one suffering from a certain degree of war-weariness. William related the actions of Sir William Say relating to the same muster, when Say 'sent my lorde be a servaunt of his £40 to have excusyid him and it wolde not be takyn, and that I mervell of'.[29] There is no evidence of any serious disquiet, however, among the earl's own retinue or in East Anglia more generally, not least as influence and prestige accrued from campaigns, and many of Oxford's retinue were knighted or made bannerets after Stoke and Blackheath.[30]

It is difficult to assess how large were the forces Oxford could raise. 204 men were mustered in 1487 above and beyond his own personal retinue, and the retinues of his retainers. In 1489, some of his leading retainers – Bedingfield, Tyrell, Fitzlewis and Paston – brought between twenty and thirty men each to a muster. Oxford had at least twenty-two substantial gentry followers in the 1480s and the 1490s, and had granted life annuities to fifty-five men by 1509.[31] As a conservative

---

Oxford', *EHR*, lxxv (1960), 468–74, though the household book does contain de Vere material from 1487 as well.

[26] *Household Books*, 496–501.

[27] Ibid., 501–3. For the king's aims at this time, see Bennett, *Lambert Simnel*, 106.

[28] *PL*, vi, 100–1 (Sir Edmund Bedingfield, May 1487), 122 (Sir John Paston, March 1489), 127–8 (Sir John Paston, May 1489), 145–6 (concerning Paston's sub-contracting for his retinue for France in 1492). See also Richmond, *Paston Family: Endings*, 171. For further examples of Oxford's recruitment, see *The Red Paper Book of Colchester*, ed. W.G. Benham (Colchester, 1902), 145, for a damaged copy of a summons to the town of Colchester for troops by Oxford, which, given it was written on 7 May summoning men to meet at Cambridge on a Tuesday, and thus identical to the orders given to Sir John Paston a day before, can be dated to 1489: *PL*, vi, 128–9. Oxford summoned troops from Norwich in 1491 and twice in 1497, and from the town of Ipswich on at least seven occasions: see below, 165–6.

[29] *PL*, vi, 129–30.

[30] See below, 193 and n. 87–8.

[31] See below, 184.

estimate, on the assumption that at almost any point in Henry VII's reign Oxford had twenty gentry associates who could bring twenty men each, and perhaps another thirty who could bring ten, a force of seven hundred men could be raised from his close followers. Oxford's personal retinue, comprising his tenantry and household would have further swelled any force; in March 1513, when it had been some years since a major muster had taken place, the earl's armoury could supply around 275 men, in the proportion of 120 archers, 140 halberdiers or billmen, and twenty-five men-at-arms.[32] A basic Oxfordian war retinue would probably have been in excess of one thousand men. Furthermore, this figure does not take into account any role he might have in arraying royal tenants such as those of the duchy of Lancaster in East Anglia, mobilizing urban resources, and more generally the king's loyal liegemen in the region. Those forces led by Oxford to royal musters would have been very substantial indeed, unless restricted by indenture, as was the case with the invasion of France in 1492, when he brought 412 men.

Evidence from the campaigns of 1497 confirms the size of his forces. After defeating the rebels at Blackheath, a royal army had to be raised again to deal with Perkin Warbeck's landing in the south-west. Oxford was paid twice as much as any other magnate for the wages of his force. De Vere received £998, Shrewsbury £504, Derby £433 and the earl of Suffolk just £94.[33] Although the Blackheath wage payments are more confusing, there is an indication once more of the great size of his military following. Oxford was paid exactly £400 for the wages of his retinue by a royal bill signed by Sir Richard Guildford and Sir Reginald Bray, but no numbers of his retinue are specified. Humphrey Stanley was paid £373 for bringing a force of 800 archers, while of the two men paid more than Oxford's £400, the earl of Shrewsbury had twenty-six men-at-arms or lances and 1161 archers, and was paid £559.[34] However, the payment to Oxford, unique in its format compared to the others, may have been a partial settlement, in order for Oxford to have cash in hand, and cannot be taken as an accurate guide to the size of his force. Moreover, on the occasion of both musters in 1497 some de Vere retainers indented separately, including Sir John Montgomery who had a substantial retinue of his own (himself, two half-lances and seventy-three archers), and John Paston, and it is possible that these men

---

[32] The armoury at Earls Colne in 1513 contained, among other items, 175 saletts, 101 brigandines, 124 halberds, 140 bills, 120 bows, sixty-four sheaves of arrows, eighty-three pairs of gussets, and twenty-five 'aporns' of mail, presumably an apron, or mail shirt: 'Last Testament', 323.

[33] E36/126, pp. 48 (Suffolk), 53 (Shrewsbury) 63 (Derby) 67 (Oxford). This excludes Daubeney, who took a large advance party, drawn from other sources than just his own retinue, to face the rebels, and who was paid a little over £2000 for this force.

[34] E405/79, rots. 31 (Montgomery, Shrewsbury), 33v (Stanley, Pole) & d. (Oxford). The other paid more than Oxford was Richard Pole, chamberlain to the prince of Wales. Royal expeditions in Henry VIII's reign were of a different order of magnitude – Shrewsbury's retinue in the invasion of France in 1513 was 4437 men: Bernard, *Power of the Early Tudor Nobility*, 181.

were paid for the guarding of East Anglia from invasion, not putting down the rebellion.[35] With some close associates indenting separately, yet still leading vast forces to the battles, the extent of Oxford's military power becomes apparent; Michael Bennet has noted 'the immense military power wielded by a handful of grandees, men like the earls of Derby and Oxford, whose court connections and strong regional power-bases gave them formidable followings'.[36]

An examination of the military role of Oxford also leads to interesting political conclusions. Why was it Oxford who did most of the fighting for the fledgling Tudor regime? At Stoke, large parts of the royal army did not take part in the battle at all, and Oxford's vanguard struggled for three hours on its own before the victory was won. No wonder, Sean Cunningham concluded from this evidence that despite the conclusive victory 'Henry's national security was still fragile'.[37] A decade later Oxford's troops faced the rebels at Blackheath, supported only by Lord Daubeney, trying to atone for deliberately failing to face the rebel army a few days earlier.[38] There are perhaps two major reasons for this strikingly prominent military role. Oxford proved himself a successful divisional commander; even Barnet saw him break the opposing force, just fail to control his men in the rout of Hastings' battle. But perhaps the major reason, in an age when defections on the battlefield could cause the death of kings, was that Henry trusted Oxford beyond all others to remain true to his cause.

Securing the east

The second facet of Oxford's role was to ensure the political security of East Anglia – something he achieved with some distinction throughout the reign. East Anglia was of vital strategic importance to the English realm. With a long coastline and in close proximity to France and the Low Countries, it was a promising landing ground for a hostile invasion. A further problem for Henry VII and Oxford was that all the other magnates in the region were either Yorkist by deed – such as Thomas Howard, earl of Surrey – or by blood, as in the case of the Bourgchier earls of Essex, or by both, as in the case of the de la Pole family. Such an agglomeration of potentially disloyal magnates would have been of great concern, regardless of whether the magnate might be under age or absent. While Henry posed as the continuator of the Yorkist dynasty, the threat was more limited, but it could not be ignored and it grew in scope with the rise of the impostors, Simnel and Warbeck. As will be discussed in the following chapter, Oxford's lordship in the region could not be all-encompassing, and other

---

[35] E36/126, pp. 59 (Paston), 67 (Montgomery).
[36] Bennett, 'Henry VII and the Northern Rising', 53.
[37] Cunningham, *Henry VII*, 58.
[38] For Daubeney's role at this time, see Luckett, 'Crown Patronage and Political Morality', esp. 586–9.

noble, gentry and urban interest groups co-existed alongside. Therefore, he had to manage these groups while maintaining the loyalty of the region.

The Paston letters and other evidence demonstrate Oxford's importance in ensuring the political stability of the region. In May 1486 his countess, Margaret, wrote to John Paston as sheriff of Norfolk and Suffolk to inform him that, after the failure of the rising instigated by Francis, Viscount Lovell and Humphrey Stafford, she was 'credibly enfourmed that [Lovell] is now of late resorted into the Yle of Ely to the entente by alle lykelyhod to finde the waies and meanes to gete him shipping and passage' and she encouraged Paston to keep watch on the ports and rivers for the fugitive.[39] Oxford himself was in the midlands with the king, and it appears to be to Margaret that political information was temporarily directed. So important was the security of East Anglia that Oxford could crack down hard on those in his circle whom he felt were under-performing. This can best be seen in Oxford's letter to John Paston in January 1487. The letter is written in Oxford's own hand, and its tone is set from the start: it simply states 'John Paston, I comaund me to you'. Every single other letter by Oxford to Paston has as the opening line a variant on 'Right hertly welbilovyd, I grete you wele' or 'Right worshipfull and righte intirely belovyd, I commaunde me to you'.[40] The cold greeting is likely to have sent a chill through Paston. The letter then continues:

> As for such tithynge as ye have sent hither, the Kyng had knowlech therof more than a sevyn-nyght passed. And for such names as ye have sent, supposing theym to be gone with the Lord Lovell, they be yitt in England, for he is departing with xiij personys and no moe. At the Kynges coming to London I wold advise you to see his Highnes.[41]

It was not suspicion of Paston's loyalty, but irritation and embarrassment at his man's poor performance.[42] Paston, after all, must have been Oxford's nomination as Henry's first sheriff of Norfolk and Suffolk in October 1485, and although his term as sheriff had just expired, his role as Oxford's right-hand man in Norfolk was still extremely important. One might feel a little sorry for Paston; even at this point the King had access to more sources of information than Paston did, and he was only trying to do his duty, but so serious was the matter at hand that Oxford was not in a forgiving mood. Paston's redemption came in his military service, for which he was knighted after the battle of Stoke six months later. It is worth contrasting this letter with one that was sent by Oxford to Sir Edmund

---

[39] PL, vi, 92–3. For Lovell's uprising, see Bennett, Lambert Simnel, 36–9.

[40] PL, vi, 106, 122. Contrast with the very friendly letter at some point before 1503: PLP, ii, 487.

[41] PLP, ii, 448–9; PL, vi, 93.

[42] Paston's ill-judged boat trip from Yarmouth shortly after created a 'gret rumour and mervelous noyse' and led to Lord Fitzwalter suspecting him of trying to flee the country: PLP, ii, 451. See also the following letter, 452–3; Castor, Blood and Roses, 295–6.

Bedingfield, probably in May 1487, when Bedingfield was sheriff of Norfolk and Suffolk:

> Where as I understonde by your late wrytyng un to me, that ye have right well endevyrd you to th'execusion of the Kynges comission and comawndment in preparyng your selffe with the jentylmen and other of the contre, to be redy to do the Kyng servyce, which I have shewid un to the Kynges Hyghnes, so that hys Grace ys ryght well content and right thankfully accepptyth the same, under-stondyge the ryght good myndys and dysposyschon off you and off other jent-lymen there towards hys Grace.[43]

The letters to Paston and Bedingfield demonstrate de Vere's good man-manage-ment, using criticism when necessary and reward and recognition when they were due, a skill which was crucial to Oxford's successful lordship in East Anglia.

The earl could not, of course, exercise control over the political choices made by all individuals, and some East Anglian men chose to become involved in trea-sonable activities. John, Lord Fitzwalter, was arrested for treason in connection with Perkin Warbeck, and executed after trying to escape from prison in 1496.[44] As early as 1487, Fitzwalter seems to have hesitated to act when called upon, according to a letter by Oxford's associate, Sir Edmund Bedingfield. Discussing Fitzwalter and unspecified others, Bedingfield recounted that 'they thought in asmoche as they ware the best in the shere, that every man owghte to wayte and go with them. Wherto yt was answerd that oure master [Oxford], nexte the Kynge, havynge hys commysshon, muste nedys have the jentylmen and the contre to a wayte up onhym by the vertu of the same.' Fitzwalter's response was 'yt was thought I owght not to obeye no copy of the commisshon, withoute I had the same under wexe.'[45] It is possible to construe Fitzwalter's behaviour as disloyalty, or even treason, but it is more likely that there was an element of pride and of standing on his dignity. Bedingfield's response, however, spoke volumes about his loyalty to Oxford, and he spoke for many East Anglian gentry when he replied to Fitzwalter that 'nexte to the Kynge, I answerd pleynly I was bownde to do him [Oxford] service, and to fullfylle hys commaundment to the uttermest off my powere'. By 1487, whatever Fitzwalter's pride told him, the political authority in the region lay in Oxford's hands, both through his own power and by royal delegation, and de Vere's leading role in winning the battle of Stoke would have reinforced his authority.

Oxford cannot always be seen as directly involved in the suppression of sedition in East Anglia. By the summer of 1490, French agents, keen to cause trouble for Henry VII, who was then fighting France in support of an inde-pendent duchy of Brittany, were in contact with Richard White of Thorpe by Bellingford in Norfolk, and were, Ian Arthurson has argued, seeking to contact

---

[43] *PL*, vi, 101.
[44] See Arthurson, *Perkin Warbeck Conspiracy*, 91–2.
[45] *PL*, vi, 99 (16 May 1487), and see Bennett, *Lambert Simnel*, 58–9.

Sir Robert Chamberlain of Barking.[46] Chamberlain, an experienced Yorkist and knight of the body to Edward IV and Richard III, had been under house arrest since 1487, but after contact with the French, he and several others attempted to escape, only to be captured at Hartlepool. Chamberlain was executed in March 1491; White was reprieved on the scaffold, though he was later to be executed for his participation in Warbeck's activities. In practice, despite the involvement of Chamberlain's two sons, a London esquire, two Middlesex gentlemen, and fourteen others, this episode proved no threat whatsoever to the king, whose eagerness to break Durham's judicial franchise in order to seize them was presumably in the hope that they would have information about French agents in England or other English traitors.[47] Oxford was appointed to the oyer and terminer commission investigating the affair in February 1491, but he did not attend the sitting at Stratford Langthorn in Essex on 7 March 1491, where several of the accused were condemned to death.[48] The fact that of the twenty men accused, only three, Chamberlain, Verney and Clinton, were sentenced to death also indicates a relative lack of seriousness attached to the conspiracy. Given that Oxford could raise more substantial forces than anyone else in the region at short notice, drawing not only on his own affinity but also on Tudor loyalists, there was little future in open rebellion in East Anglia, and Chamberlain found the only course open to him was to flee to foreign courts – as the earl of Suffolk was to do later in the reign.

Warbeck's supporters captured after his landing at Deal in July 1495 reflect little popular East Anglian support. Just two of fifty-one men originated from the four eastern counties which constituted Oxford's area of influence: Richard White, a long-term traitor, and William Walgrave, a merchant of Harwich.[49] Nonetheless, East Anglia remained under threat not least because it was within easy reach of the Low Countries and was suitable for a landing by foreign armies. Although some of Warbeck's troops had been killed or captured after his landing at Deal, an apprehensive letter from Great Yarmouth to Sir John Paston shows that they thought that what was left of Warbeck's forces 'woll have Yermouth or they xall dye for it', and begged Paston's 'ayde and sucowr'.[50] Paston obviously promised precisely this, as a less worried letter the next day thanked him and promised faithfully that they would 'send you word in all the hast possible up on sight of the shippis', but that the ships of the 'Kynges rebellars, they be furth out of Cambyr [Camber point, near Rye] westwards; whyder they be, thei can

---

[46] For the conspiracy, see Arthurson, *Perkin Warbeck Conspiracy*, 16–17, based on the brief account recorded in the attainder of the conspirators in *Parliament Rolls*, xvi, 123–4, but not on the indictments in KB9/390, nos 84–6, 97.

[47] The king's letter to the bishop of Durham on the subject is in *Letters and Papers of Richard III and Henry VII*, ed. Gairdner, i, 98–100.

[48] *CPR, 1485–1494*, 356; KB9/390, no. 97. Oxford was granted Chamberlain's advowson of the Norfolk church of Yelverton in tail male: *CPR, 1485–1494*, 343

[49] KB9/52, nos 1, 9, 10, printed in Arthurson, *Perkin Warbeck Conspiracy*, 220–1.

[50] *PL*, vi, 153–4

not sey.'[51] As Oxford was almost certainly either with the king at this time – at Ludlow on 12 July – or at Canterbury, where some of his retinue were, Paston was acting as Oxford's lieutenant in Norfolk, either formally as deputy admiral in the region or informally as one of the earl's trusted inner circle; the earl would certainly have wanted a reliable man to secure the vulnerable Norfolk coastline from invasion, as his brother Thomas had done in 1471.[52]

Ian Arthurson and Colin Richmond have identified an East Anglian group of Warbeck conspirators, based around men connected with the last Mowbray duke of Norfolk and his successor, Richard, duke of York, and who found their loyalty to the supposed Richard Plantagenet greater than that to Henry Tudor.[53] These men included Sir Gilbert Debenham, Sir Robert Chamberlain, and Thomas Brandon. None had been initially hostile either to Henry VII or to Oxford: William Brandon was Henry VII's standard bearer at Bosworth, and both he and Thomas Brandon had been in contact with Oxford during Risley's 'conspiracy' in 1484. Debenham had not been close to the earl, despite being a feoffee for the countess in 1472, but he had served in his retinue in 1487.[54] These men never became Oxfordians, however, and their loyalties were to Henry while he represented the continuation of the Yorkist dynasty; they became rebels when Warbeck's imposture undermined that vital ideological prop of Henry's kingship. One might argue that perhaps Oxford should have made greater efforts to draw the remnants of the Mowbray affinity into his circle, but he was never finan-cially able to retain or reward all the gentry in East Anglia, and if their oaths of fealty and military service to Henry VII were unable to bind some individuals to the Tudor dynasty, it is questionable whether annuities or stewardships in de Vere's administration would have done so instead. Dynastic or ideological loyalty was often a more powerful motivating force than personal interest, and Oxford's authority in such a wide region could not be expected to counter such decisions of conscience in every case. The earl's regional power lay in his ability to control the consequences of such decisions if they occurred rather than to eliminate them before they arose.

Oxford's role as the political guardian of East Anglia continued until the end of the reign. It was Oxford who was responsible for the arrest of Lord Fitzwalter in 1495, as a payment of £10 was granted by the king to 'My Lorde of Oxon servants for bringing up of my Lorde Fitzwater' on 20 January.[55] At a later date in 1495, Edmund Sybly of Wiggenhall 'confessed certain things to the earl of

---

[51] PL, vi, 154–5.

[52] Arthurson, Perkin Warbeck Conspiracy, 113. Paston was deputy admiral in 1491, and it is likely that he continued in the office: PL, vi, 140–3.

[53] Arthurson, Perkin Warbeck Conspiracy, 91–2; C.F. Richmond, 'After McFarlane', History, lxvi (1983), 60 n. 25.

[54] For the conspiracy and Brandon see above, 82–3; for Debenham, see Household Books, 496.

[55] Bentley, Excerpta Historica, 101.

Oxford' and was then delivered by him into the custody of a royal official.[56] When Warbeck temporarily escaped from prison on 9 June 1498, a messenger was sent the same day to Oxford and then onto Ipswich, Great Yarmouth and Bishop's Lynn, and a second messenger headed solely to the earl arrived a few days later, presumably with news of his recapture.[57] A London chronicle records that in 1498–9, 'In the borders of Norfolk and Suffolk was a newe maumet aresid which namyd hym sylf to be the forenamid erle of Warwyk, the which by sly and covert meanys essaied to hym soom adherentis, but all in vayn, in conclusion he was browgth before therle of Oxynfford, to whom at length he confessid that he was born in London … afftie which confession he was sent up to the Kyng.'[58] The impostor, named Ralph Wilford, was hanged. Accounts of the chamberlains of the town of Eye in northern Suffolk between Michaelmas 1500 and 1502 twice note the expenditure of 2s incurred in escorting a man from the town to the earl. In neither case does the account note why the men, John Clerk and John Gylis, were being sent to Oxford, but it was as likely to be suspected sedition as mere felony.[59]

Given the popular perception of Henry VII's bond and recognizance policy as being primarily aimed at the power of the nobility, it is worth noting that rather than being its victim, John de Vere was, from time to time, its agent. On at least three occasions Oxford was formally empowered to take recognizances from members of the East Anglian gentry for their allegiance. On 20 January 1488, in response to a writ of *dedimus potestatem*, Oxford wrote to the chancellor stating that he had, in person and in the presence of Viscount Beaumont, George Vere, Sir Robert Broughton and Sir William Carew, taken a recognizance for £2000 from Sir Edmund Hastings for his future loyal behaviour towards the king for the term of his life.[60] After the earl of Suffolk's final defection, forty-one bonds were taken from suspected members of his household and affinity by Oxford in person at Hedingham in the autumn and winter of 1501.[61] In 1504, another writ of *dedimus potestatem* was issued to Oxford to receive recognizances for the loyalty of Thomas Wyndham, son and heir of the Norfolk knight Sir John Wyndham, which Oxford did at Hedingham on 18 May and certified the chancery of the fact.[62] Such delegation of this particular type of business to Oxford is striking, once more reinforcing to local society that the security of the region lay in the earl's hands.

What is also clear is that Oxford applied a welcome dose of common sense to the role of securing the east, particularly in the later years of the reign when

---

[56] *CPR, 1494–1509*, 37.
[57] E101/414/16, fol. 30; Arthurson, *Perkin Warbeck Conspiracy*, 197–8.
[58] *Great Chronicle of London*, 289; Arthurson, *Perkin Warbeck Conspiracy*, 202.
[59] SRO, EE2/L2/2/24, account N.
[60] C255/8/4, nos 143–4.
[61] See below, 131.
[62] C255/8/8, nos 26–7.

the constant rumours of sedition must have been especially wearisome. Thomas Lucas, the king's solicitor, sent him a letter in late March 1508, asking him to call two men before him; one, William Wafyn, was the earl's tenant, the other, John Russell, was a tenant of the duchy of Lancaster. Wafyn and Russell were informing on several other men, who, two years previously, had been uttering treasonous words regarding Edmund de la Pole, and had criticized the king and Oxford: 'the king is but a pillor of his people and my lord of Oxford an extorcioner'.[63] De Vere, however, had a low opinion of the informers:

> so is it that I know the same Russell and Wafen to be simple personnes and of small reputation and little credens: so as I entend not to busy myself in that bihalve upon their information. But forasmoche as yee be oon of the kings councell aswell as I and oder: I send the said Russell eftsounes unto you herwith for thexamiacion and direction to be had and taken in and upon the mattier forsaid like as ye and oder of the said councell shall seme exspedient in that partie: and I fear me that bycause the said Russel and Wafen thorugh folly and mysgouernance be now dekaied and haue but small substance whereupon to lyve: they do busy their self in such causis to the trouble of the kings pouer subgetts forto haue a bribe.[64]

Lucas sent the matter onto Richard Empson, chancellor of the duchy of Lancaster, to investigate further if he so chose.[65] The earl's acerbic reply to Lucas demonstrated his pragmatic response to the security situation.

Nonetheless, the defection of the de la Pole family had important implications for political security. John, duke of Suffolk had married Elizabeth, the sister of Edward IV. While the duke made his accommodation with the new regime in 1485, his eldest son, John, earl of Lincoln, did not, and led the Yorkist forces at Stoke in 1487. De Vere's superior position vis-à-vis the de la Pole's in East Anglia was emphasized when he personally sat on a commission not recorded on the Patent Rolls concerning treasons committed by the earl of Lincoln, on 4 April 1487 at Henhowe in Suffolk.[66] The position of the younger son Edmund, who succeeded his father in 1492, was politically and financially precarious. Reduced to the status of earl, he fled abroad in July 1499; although he was persuaded to return, he fled again in 1501 and took up the Yorkist claim to the throne.[67] A letter by Oxford to Paston, and probably others, on 20 August 1499, shortly after the earl of Suffolk had fled England, demonstrated Oxford's role in securing East Anglia. Writing from the Isle of Wight, where he was with the king, the earl

---

[63] DL 3/4, N 1 c.

[64] DL 3/4, N 1 d.

[65] DL 3/4, N 1 b; referenced in M.M. Condon, 'An Anachronism with Intent? Henry VII's Council Ordinance of 1491/2', in Kings and Nobles in the Later Middle Ages, ed. Griffiths and Sherborne, 234.

[66] KB9/373, nos 3, 7.

[67] Thomson, 'John de la Pole', 528–42; Cunningham, Henry VII, 186–91; A. Hanham, 'Edmund de la Pole, Defector', Journal of Renaissance Studies, ii (1988), 240–50; Chrimes, Henry VII, 92–4.

ordered Paston to 'enquyre aswell of such persones as departid over with the seid Erle as of theim that accompanyed hym in his repayre to the see, and retornyed ageyn, or in any wyse were prevy to the same and thereupon ... to put them, and every of them, in suertie savely to be kept, and therof t'acertayn me'.[68] There is further evidence of the extent to which Oxford was involved as the king's lieutenant in such affairs. At the same time as Suffolk's return to England in the autumn of 1499, Oxford, along with his most prominent retainers, entered into two bonds in October 'for the waching of my lady Suffolk at Colchester'.[69] After de la Pole fled abroad again in August 1501, his estates were seized, and one of de Vere's most loyal retainers, Sir Robert Lovell, became the crown's receiver-general for the de la Pole lands in Norfolk and Suffolk.[70] A royal writ, dated 10 October 1501, commanded Oxford and William, Lord Willoughby to take security for the allegiance of 'the rebels ... followers of Edmund de la Pole' in East Anglia. Between 18 October and 15 January 1502 Oxford took in person forty-one bonds for 119 individuals, normally in groups of three, at set rates of £40 for a yeoman, £100 for a gentleman, and £200 for an esquire or knight, on the condition that they remain loyal to the king.[71] Despite the designation of Suffolk's followers as rebels, it is unclear to what extent there had been any sort of rising, and it seems more likely that these were men of his household and affinity, abandoned by his flight, and whose loyalty needed to be ensured. There seems to have been no thought by Suffolk of trying to raise and lead a rebellion in East Anglia: Oxford's dominance rendered such an undertaking hazardous, and flight abroad until the political circumstances were more propitious was the best option for de la Pole.

It has been suggested that it was Oxford's sudden return in 1485 and immediate political dominance thereafter that made other East Anglian nobles such as Fitzwalter and de la Pole, faced with a subordinate political role in the region, disillusioned, and inclined them to look for alternatives to Henry VII.[72] There is no doubt that Oxford's regional power, and by the early 1490s the prospect of the return of Thomas Howard to the region at some stage, had consequences for the de la Pole family. Yet the primary reason for the family's political marginalization was the earl of Lincoln's leading role on the losing side at the battle of Stoke, highlighting to the king the dynastic danger they embodied. Henry VII's insensitive handling of Edmund de la Pole after his succession to his father's title in 1492, downgrading him from a duke to an earl, followed by a level of judicial

[68] PL, vi, 160.
[69] BL, Add. MS. 21480, fol. 66v. The retainers were Sir Robert Drury, Sir Robert Lovell, Sir Richard Fitzlewis and Sir Thomas Tyrell. The bonds were 'to pay at Wysontyd next £77 4s 11d over and above £55 2s 9d paid', presumably if they failed to keep her secure.
[70] CPR, 1494–1509, 265; SRO, HA411/9/7.
[71] CPR, 1494–1509, 287; C54/376, mm. 32–6. I am indebted to Dr Sean Cunningham for this reference.
[72] Cunningham, Henry VII, 63–4.

harassment, did not help matters. For the de la Poles, as for many noble families who were heirs to fathers killed in rebellion or executed for treason, the way back to trust and influence was loyal military and administrative service, as exemplified by Thomas Howard, earl of Surrey, rather than any assumption of a rightful role in their locality. Fitzwalter, on the other hand, with substantially less wealth, could never have taken the leading role in East Anglia, given there were three more powerful and senior noble families in the region. He had forged a career for himself in Calais during Edward IV's reign, and as steward of the household from 1485 he had more than ample opportunities for advancement and influence. Fitzwalter's descent into treason must have been prompted by personal rather than local imperatives. Oxford had certainly made an effort to keep him within his circle, and to some extent trusted him; Fitzwalter acted a feoffee for two settlements of the earl's estates in 1486 and 1492.[73] Certainly such business activity suggests that it was not Oxford personally who had alienated Fitzwalter.

What would have undermined Oxford's control of East Anglia was disloyalty among his own core supporters. There are one or two hints that some were at least considering their options. The most prominent of these was Sir Thomas Tyrell. He had been promoted to master of the horse in 1483, and was a squire of the body to Edward IV and Richard III; although there is no evidence that he fought for Richard at Bosworth, he was nevertheless associated quite closely with the Ricardian regime.[74] He had moved smoothly into Oxford's circle after 1485, however, not least because of his family's good connections with the earl, was a feoffee for him in 1486, and was knighted after the battle of Stoke where he fought in Oxford's retinue. Yet he was named in a confession in March 1496, which detailed a plot to murder the king, headed by John Kendal, prior of St John in England. The confession was by Kendal's servant, a Frenchman named Bernard de Vignolles, who noted that:

> the said Prior of St. John has been two or three times, once a twelve-month, to the house of Sir Thomas Tirel to inquire after news, and discussed various matters between them, and among other things the prior began to speak how King Edward had formerly been in the said house [of Tyrell], to which the said Sir Thomas replied that it was true, and that the King had formerly made good cheer there and that he hoped by God's will that the son of the said Edward should make like cheer there.[75]

Tyrell was not implicated in the plot to murder the king, but such a positive statement of belief in Perkin's assumed identity and desire for his 'restoration' ought to have landed him in very serious trouble. This does not appear to have happened. Tyrell was neither arrested nor pardoned, and he continued in Oxford's

---

[73] RH, Boxes 38, 39.
[74] Arthurson, *Perkin Warbeck Conspiracy*, 60; and for Tyrell more generally, Wedgwood, ii, 892–3.
[75] F. Madden, 'Documents Relating to Perkin Warbeck, with Remarks on his History', *Archaeologia*, xxvii (1838), 177; Arthurson, *Perkin Warbeck Conspiracy*, 98.

service, fighting under him for the defence of Henry VII's crown at Blackheath two years later, where he was made a banneret. This would suggest that the either the confession was inaccurate, that Tyrell was able to secure forgiveness, or was protected from the consequences of his actions by Oxford. Two factors make the first the most likely explanation. If Tyrell was keeping his options open (and William Stanley had done little more), even Oxford would have been hard pressed to have defended him before the king and might not have wanted to do so; there is no evidence such as a pardon or a bond for loyalty at this date, as in other cases. Tyrell was not only doing well in the service of Oxford and Henry VII – as a key figure in Oxford's affinity he was among the most influential men in East Anglia – but as a former servant of Richard III, he was much less likely to have a sentimental attachment to Richard Plantagenet, duke of York. It was Edwardians, like Gilbert Debenham and Thomas Brandon, not Ricardians like Tyrell, whose loyalty was tested by the supposed appearance of one of Edward's sons. The balance of probabilities makes it hard to accept Tyrell's treachery, as recorded in de Vignolles' confession. However there is further evidence that Tyrell's loyalty was suspect, as eight years later, on 21 February 1504, five knights and esquires bound themselves for various sums for Tyrell's true allegiance.[76] This recognizance should not necessarily be taken as evidence of guilt. Sean Cunningham has demonstrated the widespread use of such bonds, and it may well be that Tyrell was under slight suspicion at least twice during the reign, but that on neither occasion did any further evidence come to light.[77] Certainly his association with Oxford was not disrupted – even after the bond for his allegiance was taken in 1504 Tyrell served as a feoffee in 1507, 1508 and had a life annuity confirmed in 1509, which would have been much less likely if Tyrell had been plotting against the king Oxford served so steadfastly.[78]

There is further evidence of disloyalty, this time from Oxford's own house-hold. A letter by the Scottish Lord Bothwell to Henry VII in August 1496 mentions that among defectors to Warbeck in Scotland was a new arrival: 'one Hatfeld yat was wonnt to dwell with my lord of Oxinford and tellis monys tydings'.[79] Hatfield cannot be found among the household accounts of 1490–1, or indeed in any other de Vere source, and if Lord Bothwell's information was correct, then he would have been a relatively recent addition to the household. Whether a genuine spy or a disgruntled servant dismissed from service and looking for revenge, such a defection would have been of concern to Oxford, and does demonstrate that the earl could not command total loyalty from supporters and servants.

---

[76] C255/8/5, no. 1.
[77] Cunningham, 'Loyalty and the Usurper', 459–81.
[78] See below, 237.
[79] H. Ellis, *Original Letters Illustrative of English History* (3 vols, London, 1825), i, 24; Arthurson, *Perkin Warbeck Conspiracy*, 135, 140.

The third man in Oxford's circle whose loyalty might have been tested was Sir William Waldegrave, though, unlike the other two, in connection with the earl of Suffolk in 1501 rather than with Warbeck in 1495–7. While most of his connections with the earl of Oxford were after 1500, Waldegrave had been enfeoffed with him by a third party in 1486, and de Vere may have helped to acquire the wardship of Geoffrey Gate for him and John Clopton in the same year. As noted earlier, in the autumn of 1501 Oxford took forty-one bonds for 119 individuals for the allegiance of the followers of Edmund de la Pole in East Anglia. One of those who compounded with the earl was Waldegrave. Given that within a few weeks of the bond being taken Waldegrave was a feoffee in the earl's purchase of the manor of Beaumont Berners, this is surprising.[80] Cunningham has suggested that Waldegrave may have been acting as a double agent.[81] Waldegrave was by no means the closest of Oxford's circle, having had few business dealings with him before 1500, though there is little evidence that he was closely connected with de la Pole either. The fact that he was not one of Oxford's inner circle would have been in itself a recommendation for Waldegrave playing the double agent, as anyone known to be close to the earl would be suspect. Both this and the timing of the business connection of a few weeks later might support this idea. It is worth noting that Waldegrave was knighted at the marriage of Prince Arthur on 14 November 1501, just a week before the issuing of the bond, another indicator, perhaps, that he had been acting a part rather than being genuinely disloyal, although this could hardly be described as conclusive. Waldegrave went on to become one of the closest of Oxford's retainers, being appointed an executor of Oxford's will, feed £6 13s 4d per annum by 1509, and acting as a feoffee and business associate. While Tyrell particularly, and to a lesser extent Waldegrave, may have been linked to Warbeck and de la Pole respectively, they did not appear to act on these links, and it is clear that Oxford's affinity remained generally loyal during a period when fidelity was at a premium.

Despite individual choices, especially among the nobility, and the presence of Yorkist sentiment among several groups, East Anglia remained loyal to the king, not seeing any outbreak of rebellion, as various other regions did during the reign, and its resources were mobilized by Oxford for Henry at Stoke and Blackheath. Oxford's lordship could not necessarily prevent disloyalty, although it may have discouraged some from treason. However good his governance in the east was, he could not satisfy everyone's expectations, nor could he, in the difficult circumstances of the reign of a usurping king with a weak claim to the crown faced with several genuine or pretended claims to the throne, minimize the allure of a dynastic alternative across the seas. The earl's role was primarily reactive, enforcing allegiance to the king by taking bonds, arresting dangerous

---

[80] CP40/959, rot. 415 (Hilary term, 1502); *Essex Feet of Fines*, iv, 106.
[81] Cunningham, *Henry VII*, 190, and for Henry's use of double agents, 75–8, 105, and more generally I. Arthurson, 'Espionage and Intelligence from the Wars of the Roses to the Reformation', *Nottingham Medieval Studies*, xxxv (1991), 134–54, esp. 138–40, 143–4.

individuals, and suppressing potential disorder. If one accepts that Oxford was not responsible for the decisions made by a few individuals, such as the earl of Suffolk, and given the circumstances of the reign, his success in the task of securing the east for Henry Tudor was impressive.

The court and the king

While de Vere did sterling service for Henry VII on the battlefield and in East Anglia, a third facet of his political role was at the political centre, involving his presence at court and on judicial business, and his personal relationship with the king. Clearly, as with any of the senior nobility, he could never be frequently at court: 'the needs of their estates and affinities, and the benefits to the King of the presence of trusted great men in the localities, made most peers occasional courtiers at best ... but this did not make such magnates at the thirteenth earl of Oxford or the first earl of Derby any less influential with the king when they did happen to be at court'.[82] Nonetheless Oxford was at court, wherever it happened to be, on many occasions during the reign; when he was present, he was always prominent. This was partly for political reasons, partly that his hereditary post of lord great chamberlain ensured that he played an important ceremonial role; indeed by virtue of this office, he has been described by David Starkey as Henry's 'leading courtier'.[83] The earl was present at several occasions during Henry VII's important first progress after Easter 1486, and at the St George's day feast in the same year.[84] Prince Arthur was born on 2 November 1486 and de Vere was intended to be one of the godfathers at his christening. As a consequence of the early birth, the earl was at Lavenham and while the christening was postponed for four days so he could travel to Winchester, he was further delayed as 'the season was al rayny'. On the appointed day of the christening they 'tarried iii oures largely and more after the saide erle of Oxinforde', but the king eventually started without Oxford, who in the end arrived in time to hold the prince on his right arm while the bishop of Exeter confirmed him.[85] The same source notes Oxford's participation as the queen's chamberlain at her coronation in 1487 and at the Christmas feast in the same year, when he was using the style of earl of Oxford, marquess of Dublin, Viscount Bolebec, Lord Scales, great chamberlain and admiral of England.[86] He was also prominent at the knighting

[82] S.J. Gunn, 'The Courtiers of Henry VII', *EHR*, cviii (1993), 33.

[83] D. Starkey, *Henry: Virtuous Prince* (London, 2008), 44.

[84] *Herald's Memoir*, 71, 81, 89, 107.

[85] Ibid., 100–5; 'The Christenynge of Prince Arthure' in Stowe's memoranda, *Three Fifteenth Century Chronicles*, ed. Gairdner, 104–5; Starkey, *Henry: Virtuous Prince*, 43–4.

[86] *Herald's Memoir*, 121–2, 132, 136, 152–5. Technically he was not marquess of Dublin, as the grant of that title had been revoked in 1386 when Robert de Vere was created duke of Ireland. Given de Vere's knowledge of the duke of Ireland's forfeiture, which he had had reversed in 1464, this usage seems unlikely to have been an oversight. Was claiming a ducal status too

and creation of the king's second son, Henry, as duke of York in 1494, but he did not participate in the jousting, which was a young man's game, but attended the feasts and other events, and played a prominent ceremonial role.[87] The earl was at the reception of Katherine of Aragon,[88] and her marriage to his godson, Prince Arthur, in November 1501, and on the wedding night 'the lord of Oxford and others conducted Prince Arthur to the lady Catherine's bedchamber, and left him there', the results of which night were later hotly disputed by Katherine and her second husband, Henry VIII.[89] That the earl was regularly present at court earlier in the reign is attested by the fact he witnessed seventeen out of eighteen royal charters for which there are witness lists between 1485 and 1501.[90]

Oxford played a prominent role on less convivial occasions, particularly in the judicial sphere. When the king went north after the earl of Northumberland's murder by his tenants in 1489 there was little fighting. Oxford, however, was appointed to investigate the affair, and he, along with the earls of Derby and Shrewsbury, and other lords sat on the commission on 29 May 1489 at the Guildhall in York. They oversaw a relatively lenient application of royal justice, with only five insurgents being condemned to death.[91] More important was the trial of Edward, earl of Warwick, son of the duke of Clarence, in November 1499.[92] A packed meeting of the royal council was told by Chief Justice Fineux that Warwick and two associates were guilty of treason in imagining the king's death, and conspiring with Perkin Warbeck through a hole in the floor that linked their two chambers in the Tower of London; on hearing this 'All the said Councellors and everie of theim by himself adviseth, councelleth and praieth that not onlie proces but execucon of Justice be also had, of not onlye Perkin but also of the said Edward and other offenders.'[93] An indictment was taken

presumptuous? Why also was this the only time he used the title: could Henry VII have been considering a role in Ireland for him in light of the Irish backed invasion by Lambert Simnel the preceding summer, or was the earl simply attempting to enhance his own prestige?

[87] *Letters and Papers of Richard III and Henry VII*, ed. Gairdner, i, 388–404. For other occasions when Oxford was at court see *Herald's Memoir*, 158, 159 (St George's Day, 1488), 162 (All Hallows, 1488), 171 (Whitsun 1489), 174, 176–9 (creation of Arthur as Prince of Wales, November 1489), 184 (parliamentary session, 1490).

[88] *The Receyt of the Ladie Katheryne*, ed. G. Kipling (EETS, ccxcvi, 1990), 30, 31, 42, 46, 47, 49, 50, 53, 59, 69, 70; *Great Chronicle of London*, 306.

[89] *LP*, IV, iii, no. 5774 – deposition of the earl of Shrewsbury in 1529.

[90] C53/199, nos 1, 3–7, 11, 13, 15–24; *CChR*, vi, 273–9.

[91] KB9/381, nos 38–40; and see M.A. Hicks, 'Dynastic Change and Northern Society: The Career of the Fourth Earl of Northumberland, 1470–89', *Northern History*, xiv (1978), 78–107.

[92] KB8/2, and for a summary of the trial see *Third Report of the Deputy Keeper of the Public Records* (London, 1842), Appendix 2, 216–8; *Hall's Chronicle*, 491; *Great Chronicle of London*, 291; *Plumpton Letters*, ed. Kirby, 135; Chrimes, *Henry VII*, 92; Arthurson, *Perkin Warbeck Conspiracy*, 214–5.

[93] *Select Cases in the Council of Henry VII*, ed. C.G. Bayne and W.H. Dunham (Selden Society, lxxv, 1956), 32.

before the lord mayor of London and various other commissioners of oyer and terminer, on Monday 19 November 1499.

A day after the indictment was made the king appointed de Vere as high steward of England for the trial. While this appointment added to his *dignitas*, more importantly it reinforced the impression that the king trusted the earl above all others when it came to the security of the realm. The following day, 20 November, two writs were sent out in Oxford's name, one commanding the justices to deliver the indictments to Oxford, and the other requiring the earl of Warwick to be brought before him.[94] Three days after the indictment was made, the earl sat in the Great Hall of Westminster, before the assembled nobility of England, whom Oxford had summoned as Warwick's peers 'by whom the truth shall be better known', and to associate them in the judgement that was to be made.[95] The earl's lieutenant as constable of the Tower, Sir Thomas Lovell, brought the prisoner into court, and the indictment was read. Warwick promptly pleaded guilty, and de Vere made the inevitable judgement, namely that Warwick should be executed in the grisly manner reserved for traitors.[96] The king was undoubtedly determined to get a guilty verdict in this case, as Edward, earl of Warwick, son of the duke of Clarence, had a better claim to the throne than Henry. The proceedings and judgement attracted some contemporary criticism: 'In Grete Hall of Westmynstir areygned the fforenamyd Erle of Warwyk … upon whom satt for Juge therle of Oxynford undyr a cloth of astate where without any processe of the lawe the said Erle of Warwyke for tresons by hym there confessed and doon submytted hym unto the kyngis grace and mercy whereaffytr he was adjugid to be drawyn, hangid and quartered.'[97] As Chrimes put it, 'The most innocent sprig of the white rose was thus lopped off. Tudor reason of State had claimed the first of its many victims.'[98] The earl was also present alongside most of the higher nobility on an oyer and terminer commission that found Sir James Tyrell guilty of treason in London in April 1501.[99]

Outside of the judicial sphere, Oxford seems to have attended all the parliaments of the reign, being appointed a trier of petitions in 1485, 1487, 1489, 1495 and 1497, and he was part of the Lords' deputation to the convocation asking for a clerical subsidy in 1489.[100] He also participated as feoffee or guarantor on several important occasions. The king enfeoffed him and many other lords, both spiritual and temporal, with the duchy of Lancaster in 1491, and he was again

---

94   KB8/2, nos 7–10.
95   KB8/2, no. 1d. Present among the nobility were Edward, duke of Buckingham, the earls of Northumberland, Kent, Surrey and Essex, and seventeen men of baronial rank.
96   KB8/2, no. 3d.
97   *Great Chronicle of London*, 291.
98   Chrimes, *Henry VII*, 92.
99   *CPR, 1494–1509*, 506; *Great Chronicle of London*, 318.
100 *Parliament Rolls*, xv, 91, 338; xvi, 9, 142, 284; *Register of John Morton, archbishop of Canterbury (1486–1500)*, ed. C. Harper-Bill (3 vols, Canterbury and York Society, 1987–2001), i, nos 103, 108.

a feoffee of royal manors in 1496.[101] In 1492 he stood as a feoffee for Thomas, marquess of Dorset, in an indenture between him and the king.[102] In 1507 he stood as a guarantor of the treaty concerning the marriage of Princess Mary with the Archduke Charles, later Charles V, making a bond, with Thomas, earl of Arundel, for 50000 crowns for any failure on Henry's part to fulfil his obligations under the treaty; a year later the *'illustris comes Oxonie, Magnus Camerarius et Admirallus Anglie'* was present at the betrothal.[103] He acted as surety for William Blount, Lord Mountjoy, binding himself in the sum of 200 marks for Mountjoy's safe keeping of Hammes.[104]

Given Oxford spent much of his time in East Anglia, he would have need to maintain good ties with the key men at court. His close relationship with some of Henry's courtiers is suggested by Giles, Lord Daubeney's enfeoffment of some twelve manors in Devon to Oxford, the bishops of Winchester and Exeter and others in December 1504, and indeed Oxford's grant of a £10 annuity to the influential Reginald Bray.[105] Though Bray was in receipt of annuities from several other earls, barons and a bishop, this was clearly a relationship that mattered.[106] Although the earl's social superiority was clear in the grant of an annuity, de Vere did not stand on his dignity, and, as with Thomas Lovell, another of Henry VII's inner circle who was described as 'my olde frende' in the earl's will, there is clear evidence that friendship blossomed between Oxford and Bray despite the social difference. Two letters survive among the muniments of Westminster Abbey from the earl to Bray, asking for minor favours. Both open with the phrase 'Right kind and loving frend', an unusual address, and on both Oxford scrawled in his own hand 'By yowr loving frend' before his signature.[107] A good working relationship between Oxford and men like Daubeney, Bray and Lovell should not surprise, given their mutual goal of ensuring the survival of the Tudor dynasty, but it appears friendship also evolved, no doubt to the strengthening of Henry VII's inner circle.

---

[101]   *Parliament Rolls*, xvi, 101–4, 285–6.

[102]   C54/352, m. 14d.; *Parliament Rolls*, xvi, 169–70; Lander, *Crown and Nobility*, 286–8; and for the indenture, see Pugh, 'Henry VII and the English Nobility', 102–5.

[103]   E30/1732–3, printed in summary in *Calendar of State Papers: Spanish*, i, 448–9; 'The Spouselles of the Ladye Marye', ed. J. Gardiner in *Camden Miscellany IX* (Camden Society, n.s., liii, 1895), 7.

[104]   C54/376, m. 40. See also C254/159, no. 5, which notes that both John Rochester and John Paston stood surety on the same day at Castle Hedingham, both for 100 marks.

[105]   E150/149/7 (Daubeney's inquisition *post mortem*, 1510). Lord Daubeney's son, aged around 14, visited the earl at Wivenhoe in 1507: Longleat, Misc. xi, fol. 27r. See also CP25/1/294/80/104–6, 116, 129 for Oxford along with Bray, Empson, Lovell and others as feoffees concerning the West Country estates of the Beaumonts and Bassets. For Bray's annuity see NRO, Towns. 196, MS 1615, m. 1.

[106]   S.J. Gunn, 'The Court of Henry VII', in *The Court as a Stage. England and the Low Countries in the Later Middle Ages*, ed. S.J. Gunn and A. Janse (Woodbridge, 2006), 134.

[107]   WAM, 16039, 16075.

For all Oxford's involvement in judicial and courtly events, there was one area of governmental activity where he might have been expected to be more involved than he was. It made sense for de Vere to be appointed admiral of England in 1485: he was a trusted and reliable magnate, and he had experience commanding small fleets and privateering during his 1473 campaign. Many, if not most magnates, owned a ship or two by this date, partly to hire out for trading purposes, partly for occasional use in royal fleets, although Oxford's cousin, John Howard, was exceptional in his substantial trading interests.[108] Oxford's manor and residence at Wivenhoe, at the mouth of the River Colne, acted as a port for Colchester in the sixteenth century, and was certainly a fishing harbour in the fifteenth, so the opportunity for seaborne mercantile activity was obvious.[109] The evidence, however, does not exist as to whether he owned ships and exploited these favourable circumstances.

Yet, as C.S.L. Davies has pointed out, Oxford held the office of admiral from 1485 until 1513 but 'never commanded the fleet … and had shown himself only occasionally interested in the judicial side of the office'.[110] On occasions when a fleet was needed, the king appointed a temporary admiral.[111] However, Oxford did play a role in the administrative and judicial fields, as can be seen in his correspondence with his vice-admiral, Sir John Paston; though his deputies did much of the routine administration, Oxford did not treat the office 'entirely as a sinecure'.[112] The level of local administration can be gauged by the fact that over the course of six months in 1491 alone there are five letters from Oxford among the Paston collection relating to naval administration, and it is clear that the earl took a personal interest in these maritime matters, on one occasion confessing that 'I can nat be content in my mynde to such tyme as I may here bothe you [Paston] and Barkeley to geder', and summoning them both before him.[113] On occasion he issued formal commands as admiral, ordering, for example, that all fishing smacks make surety before him for their behaviour on voyages to Iceland, after complaints received by Henry VII from the king of Denmark.[114]

---

[108] Crawford, *Yorkist Lord*, chap. 9, and see more generally G.V. Scammell, 'Shipowning in England, c. 1450–1550', *TRHS*, fifth series, xii (1962), esp. 119–20. Richmond, 'Royal Adminis-tration and the Keeping of the Seas', 250–5 notes at least forty-two noble shipowners between 1422 and 1485.

[109] *VCH Essex* (10 vols, London, 1903–2001), x, 284–5. Oxford had a barge, presumably for use on the Thames – payment of wages was made to the unnamed master of 'the barge of the lord' in 1488–9: D/DPr 139, m. 4.

[110] C.S.L Davies, 'The Administration of the Royal Navy under Henry VIII: The Origins of the Navy Board', *EHR*, lxxx (1965), 269.

[111] *CPR*, 1485–94, 239, 276, 284, 286, 344; C.S. Goldingham, 'The Navy under Henry VII', *EHR*, xxxiii (1918), 141–58.

[112] *PL*, vi, 111–2, 116–7, 128, 136–42, 146–7; *Select Cases in the Court of Requests, 1417–1569*, ed. I.S. Leadam (Selden Society, xii, 1898), cxviii, n. 113; W.E.C. Harrison, 'Maritime Activity under Henry VII' (unpublished MA thesis, University of London, 1931), 54–5 (quote).

[113] Oxford to Paston, October 1491, *PL*, vi, 141; the other four letters are 136–42.

[114] *PL*, vi, 136–7; Chrimes, *Henry VII*, 236 & n.

He also kept abreast of naval events, as is seen in an account of a naval action in 1488 related by William Paston – then in the earl's household, and written from Hedingham – to his brother, and which, given the level of detail, almost certainly used an official report made to the lord admiral.[115] The earl might also have profited from occasional casualties accruing to his office; there are several letters relating to a 'whalle fyssh' that washed up at Thornham in Norfolk, and whether Oxford was entitled to any share in it.[116] Harrison commented that the 'emoluments accruing to the earl . . . from maritime cases must have provided a substantial income in a time of increasing mercantile activity'.[117] Yet given the near complete absence of information concerning the court of the admiralty and some elements of naval administration it is rather difficult to be precise about Oxford's involvement and profits.[118]

Given Oxford's prominent role in the early Tudor polity, how close was the relationship between the king and the earl? The earl did spend time at court so there was time for a genuine relationship to be built between the two. Some of the sources hint at a friendship. While royal grants often add fulsome praise of an individual, the phrase included in the grant of the office of admiral is unusual: 'in consideration of the sincere and inward affection which the king bears him'. His loyal service was emphasized even when more conventional phrasing was used in other grants: 'in consideration of the good, gratuitous and praiseworthy services done to the King in times past and daily at the present time' or 'for the laudable and acceptable service' relating to the appointment as keeper of the lions and leopards in the Tower and as constable of the Tower respectively.[119] The earl was certainly perceived to have influence with the king; when the city of York wanted a favour from the king in 1489, letters were written to the chancellor, the keeper of the privy seal, the master secretary, the dean of York, Lovell, Bray, the earls of Oxford and Derby and the bishop of Ely – a good summary of the great men of the kingdom.[120] The king of France also appreciated Oxford's importance at the highest level. At the treaty of Étaples, Oxford was one of the twelve leading men granted substantial pensions by Charles VIII.[121]

---

[115]   *PL*, vi, 111–2.

[116]   *PL*, vi, 116–7, 128.

[117]   Harrison 'Maritime Activity', 54, 64, and see generally 49–65.

[118]   A.A. Ruddock, 'The Earliest Records of the High Court of the Admiralty, 1515–1558', *BIHR*, xxii (1949), 139–151; *Select Pleas in the Court of the Admiralty, 1390–1404 and 1527–1545*, ed. R.G. Marsden (Selden Society, vii, 1892); *Naval Accounts and Inventories of the Reign of Henry VII*, ed. M. Oppenheim (Navy Record Society Publications, viii, 1896); Goldingham, 'The Navy under Henry VII', 472–88.

[119]   C82/2, part 2, no. 252; part 3, nos 321, 322; C82/4, no. 149; and see also C82/5, no. 21; C82/6, no. 21; C82/7, no. 27; *Material for a History of the Reign of Henry VII*, ed. Campbell, i, 23, 537.

[120]   *York House Books*, ed. Attreed, ii, 665.

[121]   Giry-Deloison, 'Money and Early Tudor Diplomacy', 140. Others included Daubeney, Surrey, Shrewsbury, Bray, Thomas Lovell and Lord Willoughby de Broke.

Henry also made personal visits to the earl at Castle Hedingham. Oxford made a considerable effort on the occasion of Henry's first visit to East Anglia in 1487, as detailed in a letter by William Paston, in Oxford's household, to his brother John in Norfolk. The king's itinerary took him from Chelmsford to Castle Hedingham, Colchester, Ipswich, Bury St Edmunds, Norwich and Walsingham. As Paston relates:

> My lorde [Oxford] hathe sente on to the most parte of the gentyl men of Essex to wayte upon hym at Chelmnysford, where as he entendythe to mete with the Kynge, and that they be well apoynted, that the Lankeschere men may see that ther be gentylmen of as grete sobestaunce that thei be able to bye alle Lankeschere. Men thynke that ye amonge yow wol do the same. Your contre is gretely bostyd of, and also the inabytors of the same.[122]

On the king's second visit to East Anglia in 1498, he visited Oxford at Hedingham on 6 August, where he rewarded the earl's jester, bearward, parkers and the yeomen of his horses, and the earl appears to have accompanied him throughout his progress. On Saturday 25 August the king and queen, accompanied by Oxford, rode into the town of Bishop's Lynn in Norfolk. On the following Monday, the king, the mayor of Lynn and Oxford rode out again to hunt at Oxford's nearby manors of Middleton and East Winch.[123] A third visit occurred in May 1506, when the king stayed at Hedingham for a few days, during which time he rewarded the children of Oxford's chapel, his arras makers, and the keeper of the earl's park.[124]

The famous story of Oxford's fine for retaining originates in the work of Francis Bacon, writing in 1621. He recounts that, in an unspecified year, the king was entertained by Oxford at Hedingham:

> And at the king's going away, the earl's servants stood in a seemly manner, in their livery coats, with cognizances, ranged on both sides and made the king a lane. The king called the earl to him and said, 'My lord, I have heard much of your hospitality, but I see it is greater than the speech. These handsome gentlemen and yeomen, which I see on both sides of me, are sure your menial servants?' The earl smiled and said 'It may please Your Grace, that were not for mine ease. They are most of them my retainers, that are come to do me service at such a time as this, and chiefly to see Your Grace'. The king started a little and said 'By my faith, my lord, I thank you for my good cheer, but I may not endure to have my laws broken

[122]   PL, vi, 122, correctly redated by PLP, i, 654. There was work being done on 'the kynges chamber' at Hedingham on 9 January 1491: Household Books, 519.
[123]   E101/414/16, summarized in Excerpta Historia, 119. The king stayed at Hedingham ('my Lord of Oxon's') for a week. For the hunting and entertainment at Lynn, see NRO, KL/C7/5, fol. 17.
[124]   E36/214, pp. 59–65. On Sunday 15 May, the king left Bury St Edmunds, travelled via Sudbury, and at some point during that week arrived at Hedingham. He was back in London around 21 May.

in my sight. My attorney must speak with you'. And it is part of the report that the earl compounded for no less than 15000 marks.[125]

Superficially, Bacon's story is plausible, given Paston's report of 1487, and the fact that the king visited Oxford at Hedingham in 1498 and 1506 as well, but for a number of reasons the story is unlikely to be true. There is neither any record of such a fine being paid, nor of such a bond being made, either in Henry's chamber books, other financial records or indeed in any of the contemporary chronicles. Moreover, Bacon introduces the story with the phrase 'There remaineth to this day a report', which hardly induces confidence in the reader that the story was accurate, given it was century-old hearsay. Surely a contemporary would have picked up on the story had it occurred. Although Henry did use the 1468 legislation for retaining prosecutions, the 1487 and 1498 visits predated the king's statute of 1504 on illegal retaining, and there is evidence that the king after that date allowed peers to acquire a licence for their retinues; if some magnates had licensed retinues, then Oxford was likely to have been among them.[126] There is also the matter of probability. If Henry VII had any method behind his undoubted policy of bringing magnates to financial dependence on his goodwill, it was surely based on trust: those he did not trust were to be fined or threatened with a fine to ensure good behaviour. Henry surely trusted Oxford more than any other, and to force the earl to compound for a fine for retaining men who had fought for the king on several occasions, and on whom the security of his throne partly rested, would have been a gross insult to perhaps his most important supporter. The story is surely apocryphal, and probably originates with Bacon, whose work was designed to show Henry VII in such a light.[127]

---

[125] *Bacon's History*, 209. George Buck in his history of Richard III, written in 1619, says that the earl 'was arrested for a small offence' and was fined £30000, but gives no further detail, though he cites the source as the then earl of Arundel, Thomas Howard (d. 1646): *The History of King Richard III (1619) by Sir George Buck, Master of the Revels*, ed. A.N. Kincaid (Gloucester, 1979), 169–70. This allegation was part of a wider story of a prophecy by a hermit that Oxford would repent of his role in the execution of Perkin Warbeck. The partisan Buck's belief that Warbeck was actually the younger prince in the Tower makes his motivation in telling the story rather suspect.

[126] Cameron, 'Livery and Retaining', 25–6. One signet letter concerning licensing survives, and the retinue list of Sir Thomas Lovell was almost certainly drawn up in response to such a licence: *Report on the Manuscripts of his Grace the Duke of Rutland* (Historical Manuscripts Commission, xxiv, 1908), iv, 559–66. Margaret Beaufort obtained a pardon for previous retaining in 1505 and at the same time was given permission under the privy seal to continue doing so: KB27/976, rex rot 3. For a discussion of licensed retinues, see D.A. Luckett, 'Crown Office and Licensed Retinues in the Reign of Henry VII', in *Rulers and Ruled in Late Medieval England*, ed. R.E. Archer and S. Walker (London, 1995), 223–38.

[127] Geoffrey Elton also describes the fine as 'probably apocryphal': *England under the Tudors* (third edition, London, 1991), 51; Cunningham states that 'it is a plausible story of Henry's reaction, but unlikely to be true': *Henry VII*, 213. A.F. Pollard, 'Council, Star Chamber and Privy Council under the Tudors', ii, *EHR*, xxxvii (1922), 526 and n. argues the story is true. For Bacon's career, see *Bacon's History*, ed. Lockyer, 7–13. Lockyer argues that in Bacon's view

Nor is there other evidence to show Oxford embroiled in a web of bonds and obligations designed to hamper his freedom of action or ensure his loyalty to the king. Oxford is known to have entered into just four bonds with Henry VII's government. Two emanated from the purchase of royal wards, and simply guaranteed the payment of the sums in question (respectively 800 marks for the wardship of Clement Harleston in 1498 and 1000 marks for the Trussell wardship in 1507) over a few years. Doubtless the earl could have paid either debt in one lump sum if he had wished to do so, but it was in his financial interest to spread the repayment out over a few years, and no political motive should be read into it, so typical was the practice in English society.[128] A third bond, for 200 marks, was on behalf of Lord Mountjoy and the safekeeping of Hammes castle. The last, while certainly more political, was for such a small sum (the earl and several retainers were bound for a total of £125 for the watching of the countess of Suffolk) that it could not possibly affect the earl's actions.[129]

While Bacon's story is unlikely to have taken place, and there is no evidence of other punitive bonds, royal administration and comital power did occasionally collide, but neither the king nor the earl would have wished to become embroiled in a genuine dispute. In January 1505, as a result of a statute in the previous year against illegal retaining, and as part of a rash of similar returns across England, a Cambridgeshire jury indicted five men, Roger Love of Newmarket, Henry Bocher, of Great Abington, labourer, Thomas Sewall of Little Wilbraham, yeoman, John Fernham of Hinxton, yeoman and Stephen Swan of Hinxton, junior, yeoman, all of whom had been the earl's servants in his household, but who had left his service, for continuing to wear his livery. They also indicted a sixth man, John Whitall of Newmarket, for wearing a gown of the earl's livery, because though he was a 'continual provisor of the household . . . to supply victuals' he did not 'daily live in the household' though the jury admitted that they did not know if Whitall 'is in other ways of the earl's household, or whether the earl gave him the gown'.[130] None of these men was paid either in the household account of 1507–8 or in the will of 1509, but three were de Vere's tenants at Abington and Hinxton. The earl himself was carefully excluded from any blame in the indictments, nor was he the only one – in Suffolk Margaret, countess of Richmond had her livery worn by those not part of her household, and indictments elsewhere also included the 'servants' of the duke of Buckingham, and

'once again a new dynasty had come to the throne and King James, like his illustrious predecessor, was asserting the royal prerogative and trying to hold in check unruly subjects': ibid., 12. Fining a leading supporter for infringing the law was an example of the 'ruthless use of the royal prerogative', Bacon clearly thought James (and Prince Charles) could usefully follow.

[128]   Horowitz, 'Policy and Prosecution in the Reign of Henry VII', 414.

[129]   See above, 131.

[130]   KB9/436, no. 14. There are two further indictments for illegal wearing of the de Vere device of a 'molett' against John Steven of Gestingthorpe, smith, and John Williamson of St. Ives, Cambridgeshire, shoemaker: ibid., nos 8, 9.

the earls of Derby, Essex, Northumberland and Shrewsbury.[131] For these reasons – the small number of men involved, the exclusion of the earl from blame, the other magnates in the same position – the evidence from the indictment cannot support Bacon's story of the earl's fine for illegal retaining.

The only known example of a genuine legal case brought by the royal administration against de Vere dates from the last years of the reign, but it owed more to an administrative oversight rather than an attack by the king on the earl's interests. In the Trinity term of 1508, the king's solicitor general, John Ernley, brought a case in the court of Common Pleas for a trespass by the earl in seizing a royal ward.[132] Ernley claimed that Nicholas Barrington, whose father, Nicholas, had died on 20 November 1505, and whose wardship and marriage pertained to the king, had, with force and arms, been seized and abducted by the earl on 1 December 1505, against the king's peace.[133] In response the earl asked for licence to imparl, but in the following term further pleadings were entered in the court. Ernley rehearsed the trespass, and detailed the fact that Barrington's father, Nicholas Barrington, senior, had held the manor of Thriplow in Cambridgeshire of the king in chief. The earl, by his attorney John Jenour, responded that Nicholas senior had held the manor of Chigwell in Essex of the earl, and that Barrington did not hold Triplow of the king, and the wardship and marriage of Nicholas junior consequently pertained to him.[134] The sheriff was therefore ordered to procure a jury to decide the matter, but did not return the writ, whereby the case was postponed until the following Hilary term, where no trace of it occurs on the plea roll.

The accusation of a seizure with force and arms can be discounted as the words *vi et armis* were obligatory in any case of trespass, and it is unclear when, or indeed if, de Vere actually took possession of Barrington, as the crown case was weakened by an error in the date of Barrington's death, which Ernley stated as 20 November. This date probably came from the later Cambridgeshire inquisition *post mortem*, but returns from other, even more belated, inquisitions gave the date as 19 September, and probate to Barrington's will was granted on 25 October.[135] Other evidence confirms that Barrington's manor in Thriplow had long been held of the honour of Mandeville, parcel of the duchy of Lancaster, while on 2 January 1499 Barrington had paid the earl 50s relief for half a knight's fee he held of him in Chigwell.[136] However, one contemporary source that ought to have confirmed these details does not appear to have done so. No writ of *diem*

---

[131]   Pugh, 'Henry VII and the English Nobility', 71; Luckett, 'Crown Office and Licensed Retinues', 231–3.

[132]   Condon notes two other cases of crown prosecution of magnates for this offence: 'Ruling Elites', 122, 138. For the legal position see J.M.W. Bean, *The Decline of English Feudalism* (Manchester, 1968), 8–9.

[133]   CP40/985, rot. 345d.

[134]   CP40/986, rot. 557.

[135]   *CIPM Henry VII*, iii, 328, 330, 431, 487; PROB11/14, fol. 301v.

[136]   *VCH Cambridgeshire*, viii, 242; Bodleian, Rawl. B 319, fol. 21; *VCH Essex*, iv, 26–7.

clausit extremum, the standard writ ordering the escheator to take inquisitions *post mortem*, was issued from the chancery. The escheator in Cambridgeshire took an inquisition by virtue of his office nine months after Barrington's death, and returned that Barrington held Thriplow of the crown. However, the escheator of Essex and Hertfordshire did not do likewise at this time; there is an escheator's inquisition, *virtute officii*, for Hertfordshire on 4 December 1507, but none for Essex. The later returns of a commission of concealments (13 November 1508) touched on Barrington's holdings in Essex, but did not mention Chigwell.[137] In the absence of a full inquisition *post mortem*, there are two possibilities as to why the crown initiated the court proceedings. The first is that the case was genuine, and Oxford had taken possession of Barrington, and, perhaps as a result of the delay in the holding of the inquisition in Cambridgeshire, de Vere may have been in ignorance of the paramount royal right to the wardship. The second possibility is that the case was collusive, and having sorted out their differences beforehand, the pleadings were designed to enter de Vere's feudal rights concerning Chigwell, omitted entirely from the inquisitions, as well as the crown's right to the wardship, in a court of record. Given the delay between Barrington's death in autumn 1505 and the initiation of the court case in summer 1508, the collusive action is more likely, and this impression is reinforced by the ridiculous legal argument put forward by the earl that Nicholas did not hold Thriplow, and therefore was not the king's ward, which neither he nor his lawyers could have thought a serious argument by that date. A product of ignorance and/or administrative oversight, the case cannot be read as the crown attacking Oxford's interests. Technically, the earl was in the wrong if he had actual custody of Barrington at any stage, not being legally entitled to the wardship and marriage, but the case seems likely to have been collusive, especially as it was not pushed through to a conclusion.[138]

There is no doubt that, in his last years on the throne, Henry oversaw 'a pre-emptive political and financial clampdown on the abilities of England's most powerful subjects to destabilise his throne. His own ill-health and spectre of dynastic failure made Henry's final years an unpleasant exercise in the reten-tion of power.'[139] Indeed, Edmund Dudley noted how 'the pleasure and mynde of the kinges grace … was much sett to haue many persons in his danger at his pleasure … wherefore divers and many persons were bound to his grace … in great somes of money.'[140] If one discounts Francis Bacon's story of the fine, the earl was relatively unaffected by this – of all 'England's most powerful subjects'

---

[137] *CIPM Henry VII*, iii, 328, 330 (concealments), 431 (Cambs.) 487 (Herts.).
[138] The absence of the case from the Hilary term plea roll (CP40/987) can be read as evidence of the case being allowed to lapse, though the king's death during the following term would have ended any ongoing process.
[139] Cunningham, *Henry VII*, 109.
[140] C.J. Harrison, 'The Petition of Edmund Dudley', *EHR*, lxxxvii (1972), 86–7; and for contemporary comments on Henry's avarice, see *Anglica Historia of Polydore Vergil*, 126–31.

left in the last decade of the reign, Henry must have had least suspicion of his most faithful supporter.

Even if personally unaffected, Oxford is unlikely to have approved of Henry's increasing rapacity, avarice and growing isolation in the last decade of the reign, or, as the most powerful representative of the old nobility and one who grew up in rather different political circumstances, Henry's policy of binding many magnates to him by financial constraints.[141] If Oxford disapproved of such a policy, it could explain a growing distance between Oxford and Henry that might be inferred both from Oxford's increasingly infrequent attendance at council, and from the fact that he was not appointed to be an executor of Henry's will in 1509, alongside men such as the earl of Arundel and the earl of Surrey, the lord treasurer.[142] He does not appear to have been excluded on grounds of age, as two of the executors, Surrey and the king's mother, Lady Margaret Beaufort, were both born only a year later than Oxford. It may be that he declined the honour, citing infirmity or age, but it is perhaps more likely that he was not asked.

To a certain extent Oxford may have ceased to be of so much use to Henry. In the years after 1497, Henry may have felt that there was less need for a seasoned battlefield commander, and the security of East Anglia was less of a priority. Moreover, during the latter part of the reign a powerful royal affinity was created, in which loyal knights like Sir Thomas Lovell were encouraged to build up their military resources through grants of royal office. With knights like Lovell reportedly able to raise a military retinue of 1300 men, Henry's new arrangements could provide substantial forces for the defence of his kingdom. This development should not be overstated: noblemen like Oxford were not excluded, especially when they already held crown offices, such as the steward-ship of the duchy of Lancaster south of the Trent or keeper of Colchester castle, and this aspect of noble power has been underplayed in recent historiographical discussion of Henry's licensed retinues.[143] Furthermore, this was a development right at the end of the reign; in 1497 Oxford's forces were still four times the size of those of Lovell.[144] However, it must have been clear by 1500 that the king was seeking to foster alternative recruiting and leadership structures and that by 1509

[141]   For discussions of this policy, see Carpenter, *Wars of the Roses*, 226–8; Pugh, 'Henry VII and the English Nobility', 67–81; Chrimes, *Henry VII*, 212–6; Cunningham, 'Establishment of the Tudor Regime', passim; J.P. Cooper, 'Henry VII's Last Years Reconsidered', *Historical Journal*, ii (1959), 103–29.

[142]   M.M. Condon, 'The Last Will of Henry VII: Document and Text', in *Westminster Abbey: The Lady Chapel of Henry VII*, ed. T. Tatton-Brown and R. Mortimer (Woodbridge, 2003), 99–140, and for the executors, 137–8. He was a feoffee of the duchy of Lancaster estates and therefore had a role to play, but the enfeoffment had occurred in 1491: ibid., 125, and see above, 137.

[143]   For example, Luckett, 'Crown Office and Licensed Retinues', 223–38 does not discuss the nobility at all, ignoring the obvious point that many crown offices were held by peers.

[144]   E36/126, pp. 64 (payment to Lovell of £245 for his retinue), 67 (£998 to Oxford).

the nobility may not have been the primary contributors to royal military forces that they had been for much of the preceeding two centuries.

Oxford, apparently, did not wish to compensate for any diminution in his military role by becoming more involved in central administration, as, for example, Surrey did, or as a regular councillor to the king or being frequently at court. One wonders how much input into royal policy Oxford had in the last decade of the reign. As Margaret Condon has pointed out, while Henry did not exclude the nobility from his council, and actively cultivated their presence at court, few peers could claim any significant influence with him, though by 1500, Oxford was perhaps the only senior peer to be able to do so.[145] Yet, like many peers, Oxford was an occasional councillor during the whole of the reign, rather than a regular one, and it also seems likely that his council attendance became less frequent after 1497. Of the sixteen occasions when it is known that he was present at council, all but three were between 1486 and 1494, with his attendance noted after the latter date on 6 November 1498, 12 November 1499 and 9 July 1504.[146] This may have signalled disapproval of Henry's policies, but it could be that Oxford, aged fifty-eight in 1500, was less inclined to travel to court, and wished to enjoy the hard-earned comforts of Hedingham and Wivenhoe. Nonetheless, backed by the authority of two decades of regional ascendancy, his undiminished power in East Anglia meant that he retained a national status. It is worth noting that it was Oxford, not the court-based Surrey, Empson, or Dudley, who the Flemish ambassadors described as 'one of the great, and as we are told, the principal personage of this kingdom' as late as 1508.[147]

The Flemish ambassadors were correct in underlining Oxford's continuing importance in the realm as the events of Henry's death demonstrated. The earl was not present at court when Henry VII died late in the evening of 21 April 1509. The king's leading councillors were not told until the afternoon of the next day. Early the following morning, the late king's most hated servants, Empson and Dudley, were arrested. This appears to have been done before Oxford reached court, though it was not likely to have been unwelcome news to him. Assuming Oxford was in Essex,[148] a message must have been sent to the earl as soon as the council was aware of the king's demise, as it is sixty miles from Westminster to Castle Hedingham, and Oxford had reached London by 24 April. At the Tower, where Henry VIII had gone for greater security, 'was ordeyned a right honourable wache ... therll of Oxinford beyng always and other gret lordes and noble

---

[145] Condon, 'Ruling Elites', 121.

[146] *Select Cases in the Council of Henry VII*, 7–37. The court was also occasionally entertained by his players: see S. Anglo, 'The Court Festivals of Henry VII', *Bulletin of the John Rylands Library*, xliii (1960–1), 27, 32, 33, 41.

[147] *Letters and Papers of the Reigns of Richard III and Henry VII*, i, 371.

[148] He might have been expected to be present at Windsor on the 23rd, St George's Day, as a knight of the Garter, but Wriothesley's account (see following footnote) does not mention him in the list of those present.

men attending apon the sayd yong king'.[149] As constable of the Tower, Oxford had a role to play in the immediate security of the king in the safest royal residence in London, but the importance of Oxford's presence is not surprising in the fraught days after Henry VII's death, partly as, along with Fox, Surrey and Margaret Beaufort, Oxford represented the noble political establishment, but also as Oxford still provided much of the military capacity on which the security of Henry VIII's new throne depended. It was not just political but dynastic uncertainty that made the succession in 1509 potentially dangerous, and the Spanish ambassador commented that Henry's mortal illness 'left this kingdom not without danger'.[150]

Once Henry VIII's accession was assured, Oxford resumed his more withdrawn role, though perhaps for different reasons. While there was no diminution in his prestige, he appears to have been an infrequent visitor to court, except on state occasions. All his grants from Henry VII were confirmed by the new king within a few days of the funeral, and he was at a chapter of the Garter on 18 May at Greenwich. He officiated as great chamberlain at the coronation, receiving two silver basins with the king's arms worth £28 6s with which he had presumably served the king, and he was also at a committee meeting shortly before where the 'rate of the lyverees of Scarlet [cloth]' granted to each duke, earl and other ranks was decided by Margaret, countess of Richmond, Oxford, the earl of Shrewsbury and others in Margaret's chamber. The earl was also present at the opening of the first parliament of the new reign on 21 January 1510, and bore the king's train.[151] He very occasionally dealt with governmental business in the first three years of the reign, but given the fact that he was in his late sixties in 1509, it is not surprising that he was not regularly at court, where younger men close to the king became responsible for the direction of royal policy.[152]

Conclusion

Unlike previous usurpers in the later Middle Ages, Henry VII brought very little to his occupation of the throne. He had neither a good claim to the throne (unlike Edward IV), nor any powerful affinity backing him (Henry IV, Richard III), nor male heirs to succeed in the event of an early death (Henry IV, Edward IV), nor significant military experience (Henry IV, Edward IV, Richard III). If he was, in Antonovics' phrase, Henry VII, King of England, 'By the Grace of Charles

---

[149] Wriothesley's account is BL, Add. MS. 45131, fols 52–3, printed in S.J. Gunn, 'The Accession of Henry VIII', *Historical Research*, lxiv (1991), 287–8.

[150] Quoted in Gunn, 'Accession of Henry VIII', 280–1.

[151] *LP*, I, i, nos 11 (12), 20, 37, 54 (11–14, 56), 81, 82 (1–2); 'Last Testament', 333.

[152] *LP*, I, i, nos 406 (23 March 1510); 442 (27 April 1510); 784 (16) (10 May 1511); H. Miller, *Henry VIII and the English Nobility* (Oxford, 1986), 105–6. He appears twice (10 May and 1 July 1511) as a witness out of the nine royal charters in the early years of Henry VIII's reign for which there are witness lists: C53/200, nos 14, 15; *CChR*, vi, 278–80.

VIII of France',[153] he only remained king by the grace of a few key supporters among the nobility, one of whom was Oxford. For the first half of Henry's reign, from Bosworth to the battle of Blackheath in 1497, Oxford's crucial role on the battlefield and in East Anglia was partly responsible for securing his throne. The second half of the reign, from 1497 until 1509, though seeing little diminution in Oxford's prestige, saw less need for his skills as a battlefield commander and guarantor of East Anglia political loyalty. Moreover, both contemporaries and historians have seen a growing avarice in Henry's policies, as he instigated a clampdown on his more powerful subjects. This was a policy of which Oxford, though not a victim, was unlikely to have approved.

Like all members of the nobility, de Vere's public role was multi-faceted, and played out on a local and a national stage. Few, however, shouldered such responsibility as did Henry VII's earl of Oxford during the first half of the reign. The earl was not alone in having oversight of an entire region – Stanley in the north-west, Jasper Tudor in south Wales and Percy, then Surrey, in the north also had such regional roles. However, the earl was as successful as any of these men in such a demanding task. Yet he played a key role on the battlefield as well. As a divisional commander in 1485 and thereafter, he put himself and his troops in the forefront of each battle, unlike Thomas Stanley or Jasper Tudor; furthermore his troop-raising capacity was unsurpassed by any other magnate. He certainly embodied the idea that 'war was the supreme expression of the social purposes for which the military aristocracy existed'.[154] This combination of military service, along with his sure hand in keeping East Anglia quiescent, made the earl perhaps the most valuable servant of the early Tudor dynasty.

---

[153] A.V. Antonovics, 'Henry VII, King of England, "By the Grace of Charles VIII of France"' in *Kings and Nobles in the Later Middle Ages*, ed. Griffiths and Sherborne, 169–84.
[154] A.R. Bridbury, 'The Hundred Years War: Costs and Profits', in *Trade, Government and Economy in Pre-Industrial England*, ed. D.C. Coleman and A.H. John (London, 1976), 82, and see also, Bernard, *Power of the Early Tudor Nobility*, chapter 4.

✦ 5 ✦

Oxford's 'Satrapy' – East Anglia, 1485–1513[1]

the counties wherof his heighnesse be for tyme hath yeven me the rule and governanus.
(Oxford to the authorities of Norwich and Ipswich, 30 March 1497)[2]

There is consensus among historians that Oxford held sway over East Anglia during Henry VII's reign.[3] Dairmaid MacCulloch argues that 'there was no one to challenge him in his control of the region'. Christine Carpenter comments that 'Oxford may have been given regional authority in East Anglia, and especially in Essex'. Roger Virgoe states that 'From 1485, John, 13th earl of Oxford, was the dominant figure in Norfolk and Suffolk, as well as in the neighbouring counties'. Such historiographical agreement demands acceptance. Yet, given that no previous earl of Oxford had ever been the foremost magnate in the region, how did John de Vere gain such ascendancy, by what means did he maintain it, and what did his role in the region entail?

East Anglia was one of the wealthiest areas of England in the later Middle Ages. The wool trade had brought substantial prosperity to the region, and with few upland areas, it had little marginal land. Its prosperity can be seen by a comparative assessment of the wealth of English counties in 1515. Essex was, in terms of lay wealth, the third richest county, Suffolk the seventh, Hertfordshire the eighth, Norfolk the twelfth, and the small county of Cambridgeshire the twenty-first.[4] For all its productivity and commercial prosperity East Anglia was not a place for the politically timorous in the later Middle Ages. In the second half of the fifteenth century it was home to an impressive array of temporal and spiritual magnates, two substantial population centres in Norwich and Colchester, and wealthy, numerous, quarrelsome and litigious gentry commu-

---

[1]   Quote from Gunn, 'Henry Bourgchier', 154.
[2]   NRO, NCR, case 16d. 1491–1553, fol. 44; SRO, C/2/10/3/4, p. 9.
[3]   D. MacCulloch, *Suffolk and the Tudors: Politics and Religion in an English County, 1500–1600* (Oxford, 1986), 55; Carpenter, *Wars of the Roses*, 225; Virgoe, 'Recovery of the Howards', 8.
[4]   Figures from R.S. Schofield, 'The Geographical Distribution of Wealth in England, 1334–1649', *Econ HR*, xviii (1965), 504.

nities. The interplay between these often conflicting groups was complex, and additionally the region was close enough to Westminster that the crown could, and did, interfere in East Anglian politics. Ecclesiastically, there were three separate jurisdictions – the bishopric of London covered Essex and Hertfordshire, the bishop of Norwich held sway over Norfolk and Suffolk, and the much smaller bishopric of Ely was roughly contiguous with Cambridgeshire. In the monasteries of Bury St Edmunds and St Albans, the region had two of the wealthiest religious houses in the country.[5] The bishopric of Norwich was not the wealthiest see, but earlier in the fifteenth century receiver-general's accounts for the bishop recorded receipts of £600–£700 annually, enough for the bishop to be a significant temporal power in the region if he so chose.[6] The region had four major noble families: the Mowbray/Howard dukes of Norfolk, the de la Pole earls of Suffolk, the Bourgchier earls of Essex and the de Veres. The lesser magnate families in 1485 included the Lords Fitzwalter and Lord Willoughby de Eresby.[7]

Roots

Aside from Oxford, however, in the autumn of 1485 there were only two adult members of the upper ranks of peerage in East Anglia at liberty. They were both de la Poles. Though the head of the family, the duke of Suffolk, was a political lightweight, their Yorkist blood made the family a clear danger to Henry VII. When the duke's son and heir, the earl of Lincoln, was killed at Stoke in 1487, it would have been clear that the family would not be able to challenge the earl of Oxford's regional leadership for the foreseeable future. Of the other peerage families, the earl of Essex was a minor until 1493, the earl of Surrey was imprisoned in the Tower for loyalty to Richard III at Bosworth, one lesser family, the Lords Scales, had died out and their lands had been partly subsumed into the earldom of Oxford, and Lord Fitzwalter was initially Oxford's ally. This power vacuum, combined with the prospect of no competition from other lay magnates in the near future, was one reason why de Vere was able to fill the role of the region's leading lord in the first few years after Bosworth. There were two others; his own estates in East Anglia naturally brought him power and influence and, as it was clearly in Henry VII's interests to back him, royal support was forthcoming.

---

[5] *Valor Ecclesiasticus temp Henry VIII*, ed. J. Caley (6 vols, Record Commission, 1810–34), i, 451 (St Albans, net £2102 p.a.); iii, 459–465 (Bury, net £1656); *VCH Suffolk*, ii, 69.

[6] £597 in an account of 1428–9, £674 in one of 1450–1: NRO, DN EST 15/1; BL, Add. Ch. 16544.

[7] Lord Willoughby held a fair amount of property in Norfolk and Suffolk, and appears to have been resident in Suffolk for at least part of the time: *CIPM Henry VII*, ii, 19–22; C142/80/143, 144. Lord Dinham acquired some of the Fitzwalter estates through marriage, and was subsequently resident at Woodham Walter for part of the year.

Traditionally magnate dominance of a region arose from possession of considerable landed estates, especially those which were inherited. As has already been discussed, by 1490, with the partition of the Scales estates and the granting of some land by the king, Oxford had a landed income of around £2300, not including his control of the Beaumont estates; 84 per cent of his income was generated by his lands in the four counties of Essex, Suffolk, Norfolk and Cambridgeshire. Such a level of regional landed endowment matched that of the Percies and the Nevilles of Middleham in the north-east of England.[8] Nearly half of de Vere's landed income (42 per cent) came from Essex, with Suffolk producing 14 per cent, Norfolk 19 per cent and Cambridgeshire 9 per cent.[9] These lands were, of course, not evenly distributed – some areas such as southern Essex or northern Suffolk had little de Vere land, but the total was impressive, and his lands were so concentrated in East Anglia that no other magnate came close rivalling his holdings there, especially when Oxford's control of the Beaumont estates is also taken into account. In comparison, Thomas Howard, earl of Surrey, held East Anglian lands worth £560 net in 1495, and after the death of Elizabeth, duchess of Norfolk, in November 1506, he inherited perhaps another £600 worth. Thus Howard had a total income from East Anglian lands of a little over half de Vere's, though his lands in Suffolk and Norfolk were more extensive than those of Oxford, a factor that only became important in the last decade of the reign when he was resident at Framlingham.[10] Henry Bourgchier, earl of Essex was assessed at £568 per annum in a tax assessment of 1523.[11] Nor could the de la Poles, a neglible political force, match Oxford's total. In 1436 William de la Pole, earl of Suffolk, was assessed at £1667 a year, of which £359 was in annuities.[12] By 1504–5, by which time the de la Pole estates were in royal hands, the family lands in Norfolk and Suffolk produced £858 gross annually.[13] Additionally, while a de Vere had never previously been the leading figure in East Anglia, the thirteenth earl was the heir to a comital line that stretched back before the limit of legal memory, and his lordship in the region was 'natural' in a way that no outsider or newcomer could match, a category that, for example, included the Howards.

Besides his own territorial power-base, royal patronage cemented Oxford's position. Henry VII's grants were partly in land, and partly in offices, and were largely focused in East Anglia. The landed grants included three manors in Essex, two in Hertfordshire and five Howard manors in Suffolk, although de Vere generously surrendered these back to Howard in return for an annuity of

---

[8]   Pollard, *North-Eastern England*, 91, estimated the Percies to have land in the north-east worth a little over £2000 p.a. and the Nevilles £1900 annually.
[9]   Figures from his inquisition *post mortem*: C142/28/2, 83, 88, 123; E150/299/8.
[10]   Virgoe, 'Recovery of the Howards', 13, 16.
[11]   Gunn, 'Henry Bourgchier', 134.
[12]   Gray, 'Incomes from Land', 617.
[13]   SRO, HA 411/9/7.

100 marks.[14] His control of the Beaumont estates, through a royal grant, added thirteen manors in Norfolk, five in Suffolk and one in Hertfordshire.[15] In addition, the grant of the office of chief steward of the duchy of Lancaster gave him the potential of considerable influence in northern Norfolk, where the extensive estates of the duchy, worth around £960 annually, were concentrated.[16] Castor has argued at the end of the fourteenth century that no magnate had sufficient estates to dominate the shire, except perhaps the duke of Lancaster;[17] by the end of the fifteenth, the alliance of the duchy interest with de Vere's own estates, and the thirteen manors of Lord Beaumont in Norfolk, gave Oxford the opportunity to exert real leadership over the county. Lesser positions, such as steward of Castle Rising in Norfolk or constable of Colchester castle, gave him more local influence in parts of East Anglia, as well as opportunity for his retainers to enjoy authority and financial rewards as his deputies. The earl was also appointed to virtually every royal commission in the reign that dealt with East Anglia,[18] including every commission of the peace in Essex, Cambridgeshire, Suffolk, Norfolk and Hertfordshire, to all those in Buckinghamshire, Kent and Oxfordshire where he was a minor landowner, and in Huntingdonshire, where he held no lands at all.[19] He did make his presence felt on the judicial bench on occasion, especially early in the reign. He sat on the Kentish bench at Canterbury on 17 and 18 December 1485, in Suffolk on 4 April 1487, at Hadleigh on 23 May 1493 and Sudbury on 28 September 1493 and he certainly intended to be at sessions at Ipswich on 15 April 1491, where matters concerning a dispute between his retainer Sir Edmund Bedingfield and William Yelverton were to be discussed. He attended sittings of the Essex commission of the peace at Colchester on 11 January 1486, at Chelmsford on 17 December 1488, on 14 December at Halstead and 16 December at Colchester in 1489, and on 26 April 1490 at Braintree.[20] He does not appear, however, to have sat as a JP after about 1493, perhaps feeling after the first few years of the reign that his authority could be exercised at such sittings through his retainers rather than in person.

Such royal grants of land and office, added to the numerous appointments to commissions, amounted to a policy towards Oxford's lordship. It was more

[14] See above, 98.

[15] C142/24/62, 85, 86; E150/615/18.

[16] Such influence appears to have been used indirectly, as he rarely appears in duchy sources; see Cunningham, 'The Establishment of the Tudor Regime', 193–4. For the duchy estates, see Castor, *Duchy of Lancaster*, 54–5.

[17] Castor, *Duchy of Lancaster*, 55.

[18] *CPR, 1485–94*, 40, 103, 106 bis, 162, 179 bis, 278–9, 281, 283, 319, 324, 348–9, 356–7, 397, 417, 434, 438; *1494–1509*, 29–30, 32, 53, 87, 180, 194, 287 bis, 289, 290, 357, 359 bis.

[19] *CPR, 1485–94*, 481–2, 486, 488–90, 494, 497, 501; *1494–1509*, 631–2, 638, 642–4, 651, 654–5, 659.

[20] KB9/369, nos 35, 40; 374, no. 13; 375, nos 49, 61; 380, no. 53; 398, no. 37; KB27/917, rex rot. 6; E137/11/3, mm. 6, 7d.; E137/42/3 (unnumbered); *PL*, vi, 135–6. Given the poor survival rate of returns from commissions and quarter sessions, he may have attended many more.

than just Henry reflecting the existing political situation in East Anglia; Oxford was fulfilling an important role for Henry VII, both in the 'stabilisation of traditionally volatile county societies',[21] and in ensuring that they remained loyal, enabling their military resources to be used for the defence of the kingdom. As far as it was possible for Henry to aid Oxford in this task while his throne remained insecure, it was in his interests to do so – indeed Roger Virgoe has commented that in East Anglia in the years after 1485 'there was no conflict of interest between the interests of the king and the local magnate [Oxford], who was acting virtually as his lieutenant in the region.'[22]

In addition to royal patronage bolstering Oxford's lordship, it is striking how little royal government appeared to touch East Anglia during Henry VII reign at the highest level. It should be emphasized that the region was not among the political peripheries of late medieval England. It had neither a long tradition of judicial independence (as did Lancashire and Durham), nor the political latitude of a frontier region (the North and the Marches of Wales). It is only one hundred miles from Norwich to London, and rather less from Ipswich or Colchester, compared to 200 miles from York or 175 from Exeter or Chester to the capital. However, some of what might be considered routine royal activities passed into Oxford's hands during the first half of the reign at least, during what was a period of weakness for the crown. It was Oxford who negotiated with the city of Norwich for troops at several periods during the reign. There were avenues for the king to use if he so wished; he could have negotiated directly via letter, or asked the sheriffs in the city to pass on his wishes, but instead he appears to have entrusted the task to the earl. This seems to have been common enough for smaller towns, but for the second largest city in the kingdom, it is perhaps surprising.[23] It was Oxford who raised money and troops in East Anglia for a royal campaign in 1487, and while this was in response to a commission of array, the commission was addressed solely to him. This was not a minor task, as Oxford was to all intents and purposes raising the armed forces of a large part of England. The limitations of royal interference in East Anglia can be seen at most stages of the reign. For example, it has been suggested by J.R. Lander that the period 1494–5 saw a remodelling of the commissions of the peace in almost every English county. Among the few that did not see substantial intrusions

---

[21] Bennett, *Lambert Simnel*, 58–9. These societies were not, according to Philippa Maddern's survey of East Anglia between 1422 and 1442, particularly violent, though obviously the magnate feuding of the later 1440s and 1450s temporarily changed this picture: P. Maddern, *Violence and Social Order. East Anglia, 1422–42* (Oxford, 1992). Norfolk, Suffolk and Essex were, however, wealthy counties and rather litigious, as any examination of the records of the courts of Common Pleas or King's Bench during the period will make abundantly clear.

[22] R. Virgoe, 'The Crown, Magnates and Local Government in Fifteenth-Century East Anglia', in *The Crown and Local Communities in England and France in the Fifteenth Century*, ed. J.R.L. Highfield and R. Jeffs (Gloucester, 1981), 76.

[23] S.J. Gunn, D. Grummit and H. Cools, *War, State and Society in England and the Netherlands 1477–1559* (Oxford, 2007), 111–2.

of non-resident peers and royal councillors, designed to 'galvanise the habitués of complacent, self-interested ... local establishments into somewhat greater honesty and efficiency, possibly even loyalty' were the counties of Essex, Suffolk and Norfolk.[24]

Oxford considered that he had been granted the rule of East Anglia by Henry VII. In 1497 when summoning troops from the city of Norwich for a royal campaign against the Scots, he explicitly said so:

> For asmoche as the kyng oure souereigne lorde ... entendyng to make an army and vyage ryall both by see and by londe towardys the parties of Scottlond and for the accomplysshment of the same hath yeven me in commaundement in myn owen person with a certeyn nombre by his grace appoynted at his wagies to geve hym attendanus and to accomplish my seid nombre of thenabitaunts of *the counties wherof his heighnesse be for tyme hath yeven me the rule and gouernauns* as wele of knyghtys, esquires, gentylmen, citezeins and burgesys as of other able yomen with in the same.[25]

This bears comparison with the proclamation of the duke of Norfolk in the early 1450s in which he stated that servants of Lord Scales had said that:

> We wolde abyde but a short tyme her [Norfolk], and aftir our departynge he wolde have the rewle and governaunce as he hath had affore tyme. We lete yow wete that nexst the kynge our soverayn Lord be his good grace and licence we woll have the princypall rewle and governance throwh all this schir, of whishe we ber our name whyls that we be lyvynge, as ferre as reson and lawe requyrith.[26]

The implication of both statements is the same – that the natural rule of those regions was in the hands of a nobleman, through the grace or licence of the sovereign, and reflect Bishop Russell's statement that 'the polityk rule of every region wele ordeigned stondithe in the nobles.'[27] Yet it is striking how different the two superficially similar statements by Norfolk and Oxford are. Norfolk's proclamation was asserting a rule over a single shire that was not yet extant and never really became so. Oxford's less bombastic, more assured, assertion of his governance over several shires was based on political reality. He may have found it politic to remind the city of Norwich of his position, at a time when national royal authority, though not his comital regional authority, was at a low ebb. This did not indicate any weakness in Oxford's position.

Henry VII was not in the business of creating new franchises, or setting regional precedents, so there was no likelihood of Oxford heading something

---

[24] J.R. Lander, *English Justices of the Peace, 1461–1509* (Gloucester, 1989), 127, and more generally see 112–9, 124–40.

[25] NRO, NCR, case 16d. 1491–1553, fol. 44 (my italics).

[26] *PL*, ii, 259. See Watts, *Henry VI*, 64–6 for a discussion of this claim, and the weakness of Norfolk's position.

[27] *Grants etc from the Crown during the Reign of Edward the Fifth*, ed. J.G. Nicols (Camden Society, o.s., lx, 1854), xliii.

like a 'Council of the East', or being made 'Warden of the March towards Flanders'. Henry preferred to use existing structures, such as the council in the north, where they already existed, and this meant that Oxford was not to have an overarching judicial commission or a palatinate *in lege*. However, he had the *de facto* rule of 'the counties wherof his heighnesse be for tyme hath yeven me the rule and gouernauns'. He may have had to exercise his power via more informal methods than, for example, Surrey did as lieutenant in the north, such as through his own retainers, as an arbiter, as a landlord, as the king's councillor and general, through limited formal appointments, such as a commissioner of oyer and terminer, of array, of the peace, and through royal offices in his control, but exercise authority and power he did.

Similarities in approach in Henry's response to the need for strong regional leadership can be seen in his attitude towards Jasper Tudor, though the details differed. The king's uncle received a considerable amount of landed patronage in Wales and the nearby English counties, most notably the lordships of Glamorgan and Abergavenny, and he held important offices such as that of chief justice in South Wales.[28] However, in March 1486 he received the extraordinary grant of 'Power, during pleasure, to appoint justices to enquire of all treasons and offences in Herefordshire, Worcestershire, Gloucestershire, and in the Marches of Wales, as also in south Wales and West Wales, to hear and determine the same, with power to assemble men at arms, archers and other fencible men in the counties of Wales and the Marches thereof for the safeguard of his person and the repression of malefactors and to come to the king with them arrayed in thousands or hundreds if necessary'. No precedent was created here, but this was a substantial delegation of royal power, done 'as a symptom of Henry VII's desire to improve the administration of law and order in Wales' and reflecting the 'great trust and confidence he had in his uncle'.[29] The lack of something similar in writing to de Vere (there may have been a more informal, oral equivalent) may be explained by Jasper Tudor's consanguining with Henry VII and the regular royal grants of authority over Wales to others, such as the Prince of Wales. Such a grant (during pleasure) to the king's childless uncle was one thing, to an unrelated nobleman, however trusted, was perhaps something more. Occasional earlier precedents of written grants to non-royal noblemen, such as Richard III's grant to Buckingham of the virtual rule of Wales in 1483, were not ones Henry would have wanted to copy.[30] Unofficial power structures, to aid the good governance of particular

---

[28] *CPR, 1485–94*, 47, 64, 220 and various commissions e.g. 85–6, 106–7, 284, 319, 353–7, 441. For Tudor after 1485, see Thomas, 'Political Career … of Jasper Tudor', esp. 322–48.

[29] *CPR, 1485–94*, 84; Thomas, 'Political Career … of Jasper Tudor', 333; R.A. Griffiths, 'Wales and the Marches', in *Fifteenth Century England, 1399–1509*, ed. S.B. Chrimes, C.D. Ross and R.A. Griffiths (Manchester, 1972), 163–4.

[30] Griffiths, 'Wales and the Marches', 162. The indenture for the Stafford marcher lordships in 1504 was aimed at increasing royal control rather than delegating it: T.B. Pugh, '"The Indenture for the Marches" between Henry VII and Edward Stafford (1477–1521), Duke of Buckingham', *EHR*, lxxi (1956), 436–41.

regions and to trusted men, were, however, part of Henry's method of govern-ment, and in addition to Oxford in East Anglia, others can be seen in the Stanley domination of the north-west, based firmly on the Stanley estates as well as royal favour, in Sir Rhys ap Thomas's position in south Wales especially after Jasper Tudor's death,[31] and to a lesser extent in Margaret Beaufort's influence in some Midland counties. The latter's landed estate, though worth £1960 p.a. in 1487–8 was too scattered for regional leadership; estates in Devon and the lordship of Kendal formed substantial portions of her income. She had influence in certain counties however, such as Lincolnshire, and her obviously close relationship with the king would have bolstered her power.[32] Surrey's domination in the north was solely built on royal favour and office, since he had no estates of his own in the region.[33]

Henry VII's position in the early years of his reign meant that he would obvi-ously have to rely heavily on the earl in East Anglia; conversely, factors such as the absence of competition, as well as his own power, meant regional leadership devolved on the earl almost by default. Whether he would remain the region's leading lord in the longer term would depend on his success in suppressing sedition and leading the military forces of the region (discussed in the previous chapter), in building a powerful and reliable affinity (discussed in the following chapter), as well as on external factors such as Henry VII making a success of his kingship. Additionally, he needed to succeed in tasks such as keeping disorder to a minimum and in maintaining good relations with other interest groups – the good governance of East Anglia.

Relations

The easiest of Oxford's relations in East Anglia was with the ecclesiastical magnates, of whom the most important for the region was usually the bishop of Norwich. In contrast to the politically active Walter Lyhert, bishop from 1446 to 1472, James Goldwell (bishop from 1472 to 1499) was politically inactive: 'After Henry VII's accession he retired from all but the most formal of public duties; but age, as much as the change in dynasty, may have led to his concentrating his

---

[31] R.A. Griffiths, *Sir Rhys ap Thomas and his Family: A Study in the Wars of the Roses and Early Tudor Politics* (Cardiff, 1993), 44–9, where it is argued that 'there can be little doubt that it was Sir Rhys who had effective overall charge of the southern part of the principality of Wales', though under Jasper's overall authority, and in 1496 'he was appointed justiciar of south Wales in Jasper's place, thereby giving him formally the authority which he had most likely enjoyed in practice for a decade past'.

[32] M.K. Jones and M.G. Underwood, *The King's Mother. Lady Margaret Beaufort, Countess of Richmond and Derby* (Cambridge, 1992), 67–74 (for her relationship with the king), 87–90 (for a discussion of her influence, though the case for her council being an 'unofficial council of the midlands' does not quite convince), and 125–36 for a case study in Lincolnshire.

[33] Tucker, *Thomas Howard*, 52–70.

energies in his diocese.'[34] Richard Nix or Nykke, bishop from 1501 to 1535, had benefited from the patronage of Bishop Richard Fox, keeper of the privy seal, and one of Henry's leading ecclesiastical supporters. Nix was already a councillor of the king by 1498, and as political allies there is no record of Nix impinging on Oxford's interests in any way.[35]

It was primarily the lay nobility who would determine the extent of Oxford's lordship in the region. Closest to Oxford's Hedingham seat, the Bourgchier family had escaped the dangers of Richard III's usurpation and downfall through a minority, but when Henry Bourgchier, second earl of Essex, came of age in 1493, he found himself completely overshadowed by Oxford. While Bourgchier's lands might have allowed him to compete with de Vere in Essex, as Steven Gunn has stated, 'Henry VII's debt to Oxford was too great for a prudent rival to do anything other than accept the king's will. When Henry VII wanted something done in Essex he wrote to John de Vere; when he visited the county … he visited John de Vere.'[36] Indeed, Bourgchier accepted the situation and was content to play a subsidiary role, serving under Oxford's command in France in 1492, and this ensured harmonious relations with Oxford until the latter's death, as evidenced by the fact that several men named both earls as feoffees.[37] A second great noble family in the region, the de la Poles, as a consequence of their Yorkist blood and some disastrous political choices, suffered greatly during Henry VII's reign, to the point of extinction as members of the English nobility, and they were not able to offer any substantive lordship in the region at any point after 1485.[38] Among the lesser peerage, William Lord Willoughby of Eresby had a major residence at Parham in Suffolk, and also held land in Norfolk. Willoughby and Oxford cooperated in taking bonds of former de la Pole men in 1501, and the good relations between them are most evident in Oxford heading the list of feoffees in a major settlement of Willoughby's lands on 26 November 1504.[39]

Thomas Howard, earl of Surrey, however, was, or could have been, Oxford's greatest rival for lordship in East Anglia, given his landed wealth and his substantial estates in the region. However, fighting at Bosworth on Richard III's side cost him four years in the Tower, and when he was released he was busy on the king's council in the north until 1500.[40] From the very start Oxford's policy towards his family was conciliatory rather than confrontational, and his magnanimous

[34] R.J. Schoeck, 'Lyhert, Walter (d. 1472)'; R.C.E. Hayes, 'Goldwell, James (d. 1499)', *ODNB*.

[35] N.P. Tanner, 'Nix, Richard (c. 1447–1535)', *ODNB*.

[36] Gunn, 'Henry Bourgchier', 154.

[37] For France, see above, 119–20. Essex visited Oxford at Whitsun 1508: C49/29 (Suffolk v. Haworth and Powis). For the feoffees – Hugh Naylynghurst, esq.: *CIPM Henry VII*, i, 321; John Middleton; C1/335/33; C1/340/33; William Thornton, clerk and John Peke: ERO, D/DU 23/47; see Gunn, 'Henry Bourgchier', 154.

[38] See above, 130–2.

[39] Lincolnshire Archives, 2ANC3/A/30. Feoffees also included James Hobart, Richard Empson and Robert Drury, knights. For 1501, see above, 131.

[40] Virgoe, 'Recovery of the Howards', 12–15.

actions in the aftermath of Bosworth earned him the respect and goodwill of the Howard family. On 3 October 1485, Elizabeth, countess of Surrey wrote to John Paston from the nunnery of Minster in the Isle of Sheppey, where she had taken refuge after Bosworth: 'I have fownde myn lord of Oxenforth singuler very good and kynde lord to myn lord and me, and stedefaste in hys promys, wher by he hath wonne myn lordys service a longe as he leevyth, and me to be hys trewe beedwoman terme of myn lyve; for hym I drede mooste, and yit as hyther to I fynde hym beste.'[41] It is hard not to agree with Colin Richmond concerning Oxford's attitude in this letter that 'If we knew nothing else about the thirteenth earl of Oxford . . . [this] would be enough to esteem him.'[42] After Surrey's political restoration in 1489, Oxford also settled for an annuity in exchange for the six Howard manors that he had been granted in 1486 which was cheap at the price. Nor was Thomas Howard's return from his time as lieutenant in the north in 1500 a threat or designed as a counter-balance to Oxford's dominance in the region. Surrey returned to London, to fulfil the demanding role of lord treasurer,[43] not directly to East Anglia, and while he must have spent some time at Framlingham, it was not envisaged that he would play a major role there immediately; for example, Surrey was not reappointed to the commissions of the peace in Norfolk and Suffolk until 1504.[44] He was almost constantly at court, and missed only two recorded meetings of Henry VII's council after 1501.[45] If anything the restoration of the Howards was with an eye on the next generation, as it was not necessarily in the interests of the Tudor dynasty for such a large region to be dominated by one family, and while Oxford's loyalty was not in question, the loyalty of his successors could not be guaranteed. Howard did not challenge Oxford's lordship while he lived, and the amicable relations between the two families were cemented in 1511 by the engagement of Oxford's nephew and heir to Surrey's daughter, Anne.

While the marriage alliance was a symbolic and practical demonstration of the friendly relations that existed between the Howard and de Vere families despite the reversals of fortune in the civil war and the opposition of the two families at times during this period, it was also an important business transaction. The marriage contract does not survive but there is evidence in the earl's will as to some of the arrangements. 'Endenturis of covenants' were made on 16 November 1511, and the marriage was 'nowe solempnysed' by the time of the making of the

---

[41] *PL*, vi, 87–8. Some evidence of the local problems of Elizabeth, duchess of Norfolk, can be seen in KB27/897, rot. 5; 898, rot. 6d.; 901, rot. 30d.

[42] Richmond, *Paston Family: Endings*, 167. See also Crawford, 'Victims of Attainder', 71–2.

[43] 'The treasurership was no sinecure. In the mid fifteenth-century there can have been few more thankless tasks': L. Clark, 'The Benefits and Burdens of Office: Henry Bourgchier (1408–83), Viscount Bourgchier and Earl of Essex, and the Treasurership of the Exchequer', in *Profit, Piety and the Professions in Later Medieval England*, ed. M.A. Hicks (Gloucester, 1990), 119–36, quote 133.

[44] *CPR, 1494–1509*, 651–2, 659–60.

[45] Tucker, *Thomas Howard*, 76.

will on 1 September 1512.[46] It is not known how much the earl of Surrey paid the thirteenth earl for the marriage of his nephew and heir. There were provisions made in the will for 'suche persons ... as stonde and are bounde by theyr writting obligatory att my desire and for me unto the forsaid Erle of Surrey for the repayment of suche summes of money as must be repaid to the same Erle or to his executors if suche chaunce doo fall or happen as be remembred and exppressid in the fore rehersid endenture made between me and hym towching the saide marriage'.[47] Such repayment was likely if the marriage ended childless. It may be that the sum of 2000 marks that was owing to Oxford at his death eighteen months after the marriage agreement was drawn up was part of Surrey's payment for the marriage.[48] In a reversal of the arrangement in 1532 when a de Vere daughter, Frances, married Norfolk's son and heir, Henry, earl of Surrey, the fifteenth earl agreed to pay 4000 marks, and the sum that changed hands in 1511 was unlikely to have been much less.[49] In return for what is likely to have been a very substantial payment, Oxford agreed a jointure for Anne and her new husband. A balanced group of feoffees, eight named by Oxford, seven by Surrey, recovered in the court of Common Pleas against Oxford eleven manors in six counties which were to go to Anne and John in jointure immediately on the earl's death, and three more on the death of Margaret, John's mother.[50] The marriage was not finalized, however, by the time of the earl's death. In May 1514 a royal letter patent stated that 'Whereas the espousals' between the fourteenth earl and Anne Howard 'were, during the life of the said late [thirteenth] earl, celebrated according to the laws of the church, the said earl then and after the late earl's death being within marriageable age viz within fourteen years, it pertains to the king's prerogative to offer him another woman for wife, and the king lately offered him Margaret Courtenay, who he utterly refused'.[51] Henry VIII thereupon granted the wardship and marriage to Surrey, now duke of Norfolk, who continued with the planned marriage of John to Anne. After Oxford's death, Surrey acquired the wardship of the fourteenth earl, and his family inherited Oxford's dominant position in Norfolk and Suffolk, maintaining it for most of the sixteenth century.

There is often a sense of inevitability in the historiography that Oxford's domination of East Anglia was a short hiatus in the normal hegemony of the dukes of Norfolk, and that the last decade at least of Oxford's childless life was the prelude to the return of the Howards to regional pre-eminence. Roger

---

[46] CP, x, 245; PROB11/17, fol. 87v.
[47] PROB11/17, fol. 89v.
[48] 'Last Testament', 348.
[49] E211/83.
[50] PROB11/17, fol. 87v, 88r. Surrey's seven were Edward Howard, Thomas Knyvet, Thomas Boleyn, Philip Calthorpe, Philip Tilney and Thomas Wyndham, knights and Thomas Bleverhasset, esquire.
[51] LP, I, ii, no. 2964 (80).

Virgoe has stated that 'the duke of Suffolk in the 1430s and 1440s used his court position to dominate East Anglia and temporarily eclipse the influence of the Mowbray duke of Norfolk. In the early years of the reign of Henry VII the earl of Oxford likewise replaced the Howard duke. But in neither case was the power permanent. The inherent landed strength and traditional authority of the dukes of Norfolk survived both periods of eclipse.'[52] Arguably, this view does not reflect the realities of politics in either the 1440s or in Henry VII's reign. In the earlier period Rowena Archer has demonstrated that the Mowbrays were by no means restricted to East Anglia, and had little regional presence by the death of the second duke in 1432.[53] The dukes, their estates burdened by long-lived dowagers, thereafter promised more than they delivered in terms of regional leadership, until the last Mowbray duke died in 1476. There followed a seven-year minority (although Earl Rivers may have exercised some authority on Prince Richard's behalf in East Anglia),[54] just two years when John Howard was duke[55] and his son and heir was either imprisoned or absent for the following fifteen years. When Thomas Howard returned south in 1500, a generation had passed since a duke of Norfolk had exercised any regional leadership for more than a year or two, and prior to which the Mowbray family had had a relatively poor track record for responsible and effective local government.

The explanation for Howard's recovery in East Anglia 'at Oxford's expense' is usually described not only as the return of this natural order of things, but because 'the earl of Oxford … was now ageing and childless, and men were bound to look to the future which accidents apart, had to lie with the Howards.'[56] Surrey was virtually the same age as Oxford, and although, unlike Oxford, he had a son, de Vere was not without a male successor: his nephew and heir, John, who was thirteen at his uncle's death. Surrey's longevity meant that during the seven and a half years of the de Vere minority he was the undisputed regional lord, but there was nothing inevitable about his position once the fourteenth earl came of age. That Surrey did maintain his regional power can be ascribed to three factors: the thirteenth earl's successor was extravagant and incompetent, not just youthful; after the fourteenth earl's early death in 1526, his successor and cousin, the fifteenth earl, was not the heir to Elizabeth Howard's estates, and the de Veres' East Anglian patrimony was substantially reduced; lastly, both the earl of Surrey and his son and heir, the third Howard duke of Norfolk, were able and vigorous men who were able to take advantages of their opportunities in East Anglian and national politics. The fourteenth earl is best described as

---

[52] Virgoe, 'Crown, Magnates and Local Government in East Anglia', 84. MacCulloch, *Suffolk under the Tudors*, 54–5, paints a different picture.

[53] Archer, 'Mowbrays', esp. 149, 283, 284.

[54] E.W. Ives, 'Andrew Dymmock and the Papers of Anthony, Earl Rivers, 1482–3', *BIHR*, xli (1968), 216–29.

[55] For Howard in East Anglia between 1483 and 1485 see Crawford, *Yorkist Lord*, 113–25.

[56] Virgoe, 'Recovery of the Howards', 15 (quote); Cunningham, *Henry VII*, 190–1.

an incompetent wastrel. So far had both the situation in East Anglia and the balance of power between nobility and crown changed under Henry VIII that in 1523, just ten years after the thirteenth earl's death, the twenty-four-year-old earl of Oxford, as a result of his financial incompetence, was ordered by Wolsey to 'incontinentlie discharge and breake his household, sojourning hee and the lady his wife, their family and servants hereafter to be mentioned, with his father-in-law the duke of Norfolk'. In addition, his household was limited to twenty men and women, he was forbidden to make any grants of annuities or offices, he was commanded to moderate his excessive hunting, and to drink less wine, not stay up late, eat less meat, forbear excessive and superfluous apparel, and ordered to treat his countess kindly. Not only did the adult earl, possessor of one of the larger noble patrimonies in the kingdom, accept these patronizing and humili-ating strictures, but he thanked Wolsey for them.[57] Such a fate for the de Vere family was not inevitable, however, but the result of the feckless character of the fourteenth earl.

The other noble families in East Anglia were not the only powers in the region and the thirteenth earl of Oxford tried to maintain a good relation-ship with his urban neighbours, not least as towns were a source for cash and troops. Equally, the towns and cities were anxious to remain on good terms with him, not least to access the influence he wielded at court.[58] The parliamentary borough of Maldon seems to have enjoyed a close relationship; Oxford had a manor next to the town, and at least four men connected with Oxford sat for the borough in parliament – Sir Richard Fitzlewis, Sir William Say, Thomas Hintlesham and Richard Churchyard. The townsfolk also sent him a presumed spy in 1502–3 and passed important letters to him in 1507–8.[59] There was a regular exchange of presents between the earl and Colchester. In 1510–11 the chamberlain's accounts of Colchester record a 'present sent to my lord of Oxford; Swanys, Teelys, Oxbirds etc', and in return Oxford's minstrel John Brown played before the bailiffs, and the town received some bucks from him.[60] The bailiffs of Yarmouth in Norfolk wrote to John Paston in 1491 of their 'old special good lord of Oxford, in whom we founde as gret favour be the mediacion of your maystir-ship, as ever we had of any creature, as we have wryting to shewe, in recumpens of whiche at all tymes sethyn hise lordshyp hathe had our preyeris', and while

[57] 'Copy of an Order Made by Cardinal Wolsey, as Lord Chancellor, Respecting the Manage-ment of the Affairs of the Young Earl of Oxford', ed. H. Ellis, *Archaeologia*, xix (1821), 62–5. Correspondence between the earl, his countess and Wolsey can be seen in *LP*, III, ii, no. 2932.
[58] For urban-magnate relationships more generally, see R. Horrox, 'Urban Patronage and Patrons in the Fifteenth Century', in *Patronage, the Crown and the Provinces in Later Medieval England*, ed. R.A. Griffiths (Gloucester, 1981), 145–66.
[59] ERO, D/DB 3/112, fol. 61; Gunn, 'Henry Bourgchier', 158.
[60] ERO, D/Y 2/3, fols 6, 8, 13. See Hicks, *Bastard Feudalism*, 80–1, for the common gifts from towns to lords.

they could not wait upon him in person at the time, they sent him a porpoise.[61] Bury St Edmunds and Mettingham in Suffolk had visits from Oxford's players.[62] Letters and presents were exchanged with the University of Cambridge, and early in 1496 three officials, including the vice-chancellor and senior proctor, travelled to Hedingham to discuss the new act passed by parliament on weights and measures.[63]

Norwich, on the other hand, appears to have had a less easy relationship with the earl. Oxford appears to have relied heavily on those members of his affinity with Norfolk and Norwich connections, such as Sir Ralph Shelton, Sir Robert Lovell and James Hobart, who was also recorder of Norwich, to impose the king's will in the city. In 1491 letters were delivered to the city by Shelton and Lovell and in 1497 by Shelton and Hobart. It was Hobart, rather than the earl directly, who was often a recipient of gifts from the city.[64] One reason for this is that the earl was rarely near Norwich. He does not appear to have used much one of his father's favourite residences, at East Winch in Norfolk, and spent most of his time in northern Essex or southern Suffolk when not at court.[65] Perhaps the most interesting episode illustrating the city's relations with Oxford concerns the raising of troops for service against the Scots in 1496–7. Norwich had consistently been reluctant to raise and pay for troops throughout the fifteenth century, and in 1487 had objected to Lord Fitzwalter's request for troops, which may have been why it was Oxford who was making the requests by 1491.[66] Oxford wrote to the mayor and aldermen in September 1496 informing them that 'I am acerteyned that the Scotts and other straungers accompanyed with the Kyng's rebellys approch the marches and bordes of England ther to make their interesse to the finall distruction of the same', and asked the city to prepare troops to serve against them.[67] The city agreed that twenty men should be raised, but in the end no royal force set out that autumn. On 30 March 1497 Oxford wrote

[61] *PL*, vi, 138–9, and see *PLP*, ii, 465 for references to Yarmouth's business.

[62] *Records of Plays and Players in Norfolk and Suffolk, 1330–1642*, ed. D. Galloway and J.M. Wesson (Malone Society, Collections xi, 1980–1), 148, 188. Towns in Kent, such as Sandwich, Dover, Hythe and New Romney, were also entertained by Oxford's minstrels and players: *Records of Plays and Players in Kent, 1450–1642*, ed. G.E. Dawson (Malone Society, Collections vii, 1965), 29, 85, 127, 147, 148; *Historial Manuscript Commission Fifth Report* (London, 1876), 549, 550. Oxford's troupe was good enough to have performed at the royal court twice between 1496 and 1498: Anglo, 'Court Festivals', 30–4.

[63] They also dined with Robert Tyrell, controller of the household and other gentlemen of the earl's household on their return journey: *Grace Book B*, ed. M. Bateson (2 vols, Cambridge, 1903–5), i, 95–6, and for other correspondence and presents sent to and from the earl, 10, 97, 137, 173, 194, 195. For the act of 1495: *Parliament Rolls*, xvi, 241–3.

[64] L.C. Attreed, *The King's Towns: Identity and Survival in Late Medieval English Boroughs* (New York, 2001), 119.

[65] For residence patterns, see below, 214–16.

[66] Attreed, *King's Towns*, 186–90, 200.

[67] NRO, NCR, case 16d. 1491–1553 (Assembly folio book of proceedings), fol. 43. I am indebted to Dr David Grummit for this reference.

again, explaining the king's proposed invasion of Scotland 'for the repressing of the presumption and males of the Kyng of Scotts', and commanding that the city raise a force of soldiers 'aswell archers as bylles with sufficient and able harneys and other necessary hablements of were'. The earl did not specify how many men should go, though he did argue for greater numbers: 'the moo in your nombre be cause the wages shalbe at the kyngs charge'. He gave 'full power and auctorite to my ryght welbeloued frende', James Hobart, 'with you to common and conclude for the furnishing of your seid nombre'.[68] The use of Hobart, the city recorder, in dealing with Norwich denotes his sensitivity in dealing with the city, since the next letter from Oxford might be taken to show the reluctance of the city to respond to the earl's demands.[69] Oxford, having been informed that some of the city's soldiers chosen to serve in Scotland 'a loyne them selffes and feyne such unresonable excuses so as thei in no wyse wyll serve the king in the seid viage', required that such troops as had been agreed should be sent straightaway.[70] However, there is something strange about these two letters. The first request for troops was written on 30 March at Castle Hedingham in Essex. The second, having theoretically heard of the unreasonable excuses, was dated the following day from the same place. It would seem surprising if someone had travelled the 120-mile round trip between Norwich and Castle Hedingham in a day. Both letters were delivered on 7 April by Ralph Shelton and James Hobart, and were then discussed by the council. Had the earl drafted several letters to be used at the discretion of Shelton and Hobart, and was there a third, not used, praising the loyalty and efficiency of the city? Whatever the practicalities of the situation, Oxford's letters seemed to have had the desired effect as the city agreed to send the twenty soldiers to the earl.

The incompetence, rather than the reluctance, of the city council is evident in that it took them an inordinately long time to equip even the small number of soldiers they had agreed to send. On 5 June 1497 the city received an urgent letter from Ralph Shelton, reporting that the king had written to Oxford saying that 'in all hast possible that he shulde geue hym attendanus at Banbury' on 8 June, with his retinue. Shelton continued that 'wherfore my lorde have wreten and comaunded me to send on to you for such retinue as ye have granted on to hym'. When the city responded, it was found that two months after the initial request there were not sufficient harnesses for the soldiers.[71] Eventually, on 9 June they dispatched their twenty soldiers to Oxford, and probably to the surprise of all concerned, they arrived in time to be of use, reaching the earl on Tuesday 13 June, when they were put under the command of William Yelverton, gentleman, and, as a note in the city council's proceedings states, four days later the king emerged

---

[68] Ibid., fol. 44.
[69] Gunn, Grummitt and Cools, *War, State and Society*, 112.
[70] NRO, NCR, case 16d. 1491–1553, fols 44–6.
[71] Ibid., fol. 45.

victorious from the battle at Blackheath.[72] There was considerably less tarrying or hesitation among the city council in Norwich in 1502 when Hobart, Lovell and Robert Drury were among those appointed to a commission to raise men in the city to resist Edmund de la Pole in 1502; fifty men were quickly sent to the earl of Oxford or his chief deputy.[73] Oxford's letters in 1497 might indicate a reluctance on the city's behalf to respond, but nationally it was this campaign that saw a rebellion in the south-west based on a refusal to serve or pay taxation for the Scottish campaign, so such passive resistance to the king's will, as expressed through Oxford, does not reflect so badly on Oxford's lordship.

While twenty soldiers may seem a paltry number of armed men for the city to equip for the 1497 campaign, it has been noted that the 'towns in general supplied astonishingly few men to the armies of the civil war' and that York, after an appeal in 1485 from Richard III, 'produced no more than eighty men at this supreme crisis in its patron's fortunes'.[74] The city of Exeter produced between sixteen and thirty men for various campaigns in the later fifteenth century.[75] Indeed the only times that Norwich ever strained its resources were when its own interest was directly affected: when a French invasion of the East Anglian coast was threatened in 1457 it undertook to supply 600 men. Oxford probably expected few more from Norwich, and indeed as 'English urban troops consisted of small bands of badly trained amateurs' may not have been too concerned at the limited numbers he received.[76]

The financial records of Ipswich no longer survive, so it is not clear if there was a regular exchange of presents with the earl, but the surviving administrative records indicate that the town, in contrast with Norwich, showed little reluctance to supply the earl with troops whenever requested. The terse great court records generally only note that a certain number of troops had been granted to serve the king in Oxford's retinue, though on a couple of occasions they note that the royal request for troops was delivered via letters from Oxford, and it is likely, as with other East Anglian towns, that this was the usual practice. Ipswich agreed to supply ten men in February 1487, six in 1489, ten in May 1489, an unspecified number of horses and men in April 1491, ten more mounted men in March 1495 and eight soldiers at Michaelmas 1496.[77] Interestingly, almost the only document copied in full in the town's court books is a further request from

[72] Ibid., fol. 46.

[73] Ibid., fols 57v–58.

[74] Ross, *Wars of the Roses*, 149; Attreed, *King's Towns*, 181; W.I. Haward, 'The Economic Aspects of the Wars of the Roses in East Anglia', *EHR*, xli (1926), 184–9.

[75] H.W. Kleineke, '"þe Kynges Cite": Exeter in the Wars of the Roses', in *The Fifteenth Century VII: Conflicts, Consequences and the Crown in the Late Middle Ages*, ed. L. Clark (Woodbridge, 2007), 148–9.

[76] Attreed, *King's Towns*, 181.

[77] SRO, C/2/10/3/1 (Borough of Ipswich Composite Court Book, 1486–91), pp. 1, 30, 174, 276; C2/10/3/1 (1493–6), pp. 76, 166; *Ipswich Borough Archives, 1255–1835. A Catalogue*, ed. D. Allen (Suffolk Record Society, xliii, 2000), 188–9. See also Nathaniel Bacon, *The Annalls*

Oxford for soldiers, this time in March 1497 for the Scottish campaign. Parts of it – the opening justification of the Scottish campaign, the description of Oxford's rule and governance of East Anglia by royal grant, are identical to the letter dispatched to Norwich at the same time, although in the case of Ipswich, rather than letting the town authorities set the number of troops themselves, the earl stated that 'I therfor have appoynted you to sende to me for your township xx able men aswele archiers as billes defensibly in fourme of warre addressed to do the Kyng servyce in my company and retynew.'[78] The town authorities agreed to supply the twenty men the earl demanded without demure. One wonders, nonetheless, if the circumstances of 1497 – the unpopular Scottish campaign, the subsequent Cornish rising – explain why this letter was the only one to be copied into the Ipswich records, and whether Oxford himself made a special effort in his correspondence to justify royal demands for troops in his region, although it may also be explained by the large contingent demanded of the town. Certainly, the earl had good relations with Ipswich, being made a freeman and one of the brethren of a guild in the town in 1491.[79] He was also capable of gracefully conceding defeat on the odd occasion. In 1493, the earl, as lord admiral of England, ordered the arrest of a ship in the roads of Ipswich, which the bailiffs refused to do, and sent a copy of the town charter, on which they based their refusal, to the earl at Hedingham castle. The earl discussed the matter with Sir Robert Drury, Sir James Hobart, John Yaxley and Thomas Appleton, who, with the exception of the latter, were connections of the earl, but who also were prominent in Ipswich society.[80] It was agreed that the town was in the right and Oxford backed down; yet in conceding defeat, the earl would have generated goodwill amongst the Ipswich elite for doing so.

Law and disorder

One of the earl's most important roles, alongside the forestalling and/or containment of sedition, was the suppression of disorder in East Anglia and the enforcement of the law. This was partly as regional governor by the king's command, but also partly as one of the leading landowners, as disorder was detrimental to all the propertied classes. As Bishop Russell put it 'to you then my lordys perteynthe principally the office of herynge of the state of every case fallynge a mong ... the people under yowe', and these people were to receive true justice.[81] The earl and his council offered a source of appeal and arbitration, but he had no major judicial franchise, and thus needed to work through the common law, and for

of Ipswche: The Lawes, Customes and Governmt of the Same, ed. W.H. Richardson (Ipswich, 1884), 161, 168, 171, 174, 178.

[78] SRO, C/2/10/3/4 (1496–7), p. 9.

[79] *Annalls of Ipswche*, 162.

[80] Ibid., 166; Horrox, 'Urban Patronage and Patrons', 152.

[81] *Grants etc from the Crown*, ed. Nicols, xliii.

most of county society, the effectiveness of the common law, and the curbing of serious disturbance, were the benchmarks by which the effectiveness of a regime was measured.

De Vere had an immediate advantage compared to William, duke of Suffolk, in the 1440s in that Oxford's affinity was not involved in anything like the violence and intimidation that certain of Suffolk's henchmen were, and so he did not need to exercise his influence in protecting his guilty associates. Additionally, his own lack of pressing local issues or rivalries meant that he was not himself a source of local disorder as well as the cure. There was no equivalent of John Mowbray's siege of the Paston castle of Caister in 1469. Oxford accepted with equanimity Thomas Howard's slow return to East Anglia in the last decade in the reign, and through his magnanimous and conciliatory behaviour towards the family earlier in the reign, was partly responsible for it. In contrast to, for example, Lord Abergavenny in Kent or various of the Stanley family in Lancashire, Oxford at no stage needed to resort to violence to either assert his own lordship, or to attempt to quash pretenders to it.[82] This is in part a reflection of the fact that East Anglia was more stable in Henry VII's reign than the last two decades of Henry VI's, but that was very much down to the earl's sound lordship. The Paston letter collection after 1485 makes a striking contrast to the family's letters during the period 1445–75 which are full of complaints about manipulation and abuse of the law.

Petitions to the earl asking that he ensure that justice be done probably occurred on a regular basis; their informal nature means that most have not survived. Those that have are mainly in the Paston letters. One example is an undated letter by the earl to Paston, in which he states that 'one Thomas Charlys of Norwiche late hathe presentid unto me a bille of complaynte agaynste Symonde White gentylman . . . shewing by the same such wrongis as the saide Symonde hathe done and daily dothe to the said Thomas, as by the saide bille, which I sende you with this, more playnely apperith'. The earl instructed Paston to deal with the matter: 'I therfor desire and pray you that ye woll do calle the saide parties byfore you, and ... ye shall take suche direction as may acorde with righte and gode consciens, so the saide Thomas Charlis heraftur have no cause to resorte to me complaynyng'.[83] As the last phrase makes clear, it was of little importance to a busy magnate like Oxford, but he nevertheless conscientiously passed the bill for the attention of his retainer and JP for Norfolk. Further examples are seen in the Paston collection, such as the letters of Thomas Andrew to William Paston, Oxford's squire, in 1488, in which he beseeched Paston to 'speke with my lord to know of his good lordchepe how we shall demene ourselff in that be half' over various criminalities in Norfolk which touched not only a oyer

[82] See below, 172–3.
[83] *PL*, vi, 143.

and terminer commission but the rights of the duchy of Lancaster.[84] Paston was a regular intermediary, but doubtless other men deemed to be influential around the earl received such requests. Equivalent appeals to the Plumpton family, and by them, 'in the same cringing way', towards Henry, earl of Northumberland, demonstrate that this was a staple of noble lordship, and if other gentry letter collections survived, the full scale of such business might illuminate this key aspect of noble power.[85]

The earl acted through the agency of justices of the peace at quarter sessions, gaol deliveries and commission hearings, and in doing so offered a source of redress through the medium of the common law in the region he ruled. Equally, there was something that might be termed an equitable side to his lordship. As Carole Rawcliffe has argued, formal arbitration by a lord's council was 'quicker, cheaper, more effective and generally more acceptable than the traditional methods hitherto offered by the king's court'.[86] More formal arbitrations are likely to have occurred on a fairly regular basis, but only two heard by Oxford, between Sir James Tyrell and Thomas Lucas in 1501 and between Robert Straunge and Henry Sharborn at some point between 1485 and 1503, are known.[87]

A third method involved exerting his personal authority over his own retainers, ensuring disputes concerning them did not get out of hand. At the sessions of the peace at Ipswich on 15 April 1491, the earl 'purpose then certaynly to be, and to have aswell the matere by twene Sir Edmounde Bedingfield and Yelverton there to be harde and commenyd, as diverse othre great maters in the contrey necessary to be had in commynycacion'.[88] Oxford's purpose in writing to Paston was to make sure that Paston brought Yelverton, his brother-in-law, to Ipswich so that the problems between him and Bedingfield, whom Oxford was to ensure was present, could be discussed. Such a matter was important for Oxford's personal good lordship, because Bedingfield was a important retainer of his, but also in ensuring order in the region.

The earl did occasionally initiate legal cases, but they were no of serious consequence for the earl's lordship, and were the kind that most landowners faced on a reasonably regular basis. The total number of his causes in the Westminster courts was also rather low. Carole Rawcliffe, assessing the cases brought by the

---

[84] PL, vi, 113–5. Further examples of Oxford's involvement in such matters include PLP, ii, 479 and PL, vi, 166–7.

[85] For other examples of Paston being approached to intercede with the earl on minor matters, see PLP, ii, 479, 496; PL, vi, 166–7; C. Rawcliffe, 'Baronial Councils in the Later Middle Ages', in Patronage, Pedigree and Power, ed. Ross, 87–8. For Plumpton and Percy, see Pollard, North-Eastern England, 121–2.

[86] C. Rawcliffe, 'The Great Lord as Peacekeeper: Arbitration by English Noblemen and their Councils in the Later Middle Ages', in Law and Social Change in British History. Papers Presented to the Bristol Legal History Conference 14–17 July, 1981, ed. J.A. Guy and H.G. Beale (London, 1984), 34.

[87] See below, 192.

[88] PL, vi, 135–6; Lander, English Justices of the Peace, 70.

nobility in the court of Common Pleas between Hilary 1513 and Michaelmas 1515, found that Henry, earl of Northumberland brought thirty-four cases, with Edward, duke of Buckingham only just behind with twenty-six. Most magnates, however, had less than ten. For an equivalent period in 1494 and 1495, at the height of his power, Oxford had only two cases in Common Pleas, and none at all over those two years in King's Bench.[89] In the former court, in response to an attack on 16 April 1491 on his servant Thomas Elyndore, he sued William Crouche, of Wetherden in Suffolk, gentleman, and claimed damages of £100. Crouche appears to have settled out of court. This is likely to have been less serious than it at first appears, as it took four years for the case to appear in court, and the legal case may just have been another avenue for the earl to pursue the issue to a successful conclusion. The second case involved the earl suing his former bailiff at Frettenham, John Hawes, for unpaid rents totalling £23, and a jury found in the earl's favour.[90] In 1505, the story remained the same, with just two cases (excluding enfeoffment by collusive action) in Common Pleas, and none in King's Bench. The earl was suing nine men from the neighbouring manor of Dedham for damaging a mill at his manor of East Bergholt, and claiming damages of £40, and also had an action apparently ongoing against a certain John Elyce, over a trespass. His attorney in the latter case was noted, but no process or pleading of the case has been found.[91]

What is striking is when the earl, or more likely his council, decided to crack down. In Michaelmas term 1499 there was a flurry of legal activity. Cases of debt were brought against William Taylor of Dovercourt, husbandman, for 10 marks, Robert Keel of Barton, Lincolnshire, Richard Morley of Barton, merchant of the staple of Calais, Thomas Bradley of Barton, yeoman, and John Fereby of Barton, chapman, collectively for £100, and in the following term, against Walter, abbot of Langley and George Makworth of Empingham, Rutland, gentleman, for 100 shillings, and against Richard Restwold, esquire, for £20.[92] In addition, he brought a suit against Robert Neubery of St Albans, and two other Hertfordshire men, and breaking into his park at the More and taking an unspecified number of onions, and another plea against John Forde of Great Oakley, gentleman, for breaking into his park at Great Oakley, and taking hay to the value of 100 shillings.[93] None of these cases would have been considered too serious by the earl and his advisors. There may have been simply a mild outbreak of misdemeanours, but given other evidence suggesting that he was attempting

[89] For the records covering 1494–5, see CP40/930–3; KB27/933–6; Rawcliffe, *Staffords*, 175.
[90] CP40/930, rots. 96, 100d., 278 (Crouche), 180d. (Hawes); CP40/932, rot. 193d (Hawes – verdict). The earl's office of steward of the liberty of Bury St Edmunds made it necessary for him to appear twice (by attorney): CP40/930, rots. 97, 274d.
[91] CP40/970, rot. 511 (enfeoffment), 550 (damage to the mill), attorney rots (Elyce); CP40/970–3; KB27/973–6.
[92] CP40/950, rots. 171d., 507; CP40/951, rots. 63, 64d. The following term (Easter) de Vere changed his suit and sued the abbot and Makworth separately, each for 100 shillings.
[93] CP40/950, rots. 9d. ('sepas', from 'cepa', an onion), 208.

to maximize his income around this date, the debt cases may have resulted from a new financial policy.

No systematic survey of violence and disorder has been done at this period for East Anglia, nor does this work attempt to do so. Comparisons between East Anglia and other regions are also difficult as the only basis on which to do so would be the records of the central courts of King's Bench and Common Pleas, but there are a number of reasons why some regions would be over-represented in these records, and others under-represented.[94] Although these caveats make regional comparison on a systematic basis difficult, two years of King's Bench indictment files have been used to give at least an impressionistic comparison for the whole of England. Within those two years (Michaelmas 1489–90 and Michaelmas 1500–1), East Anglia showed little evidence of disturbance or serious violence.[95] It saw fewer murders than any other region, indeed just one of the forty-four total indictments for that crime in 1500–1, and none of thirty-seven in 1489–90. Riotous assemblies or serious disturbances of the peace occurred infrequently (just six in 1489–90 and 1500–1 combined), and none of these could be categorized as a serious threat to the stability of county society, by involving senior gentry, or provided a *cause célèbre*, unlike other regions at the same date. In 1489–90 Staffordshire saw a treble murder committed by three vicars of the cathedral church of Lichfield and five others, aided and abetted by hundreds of other ecclesiastics and laymen in July 1489; in Yorkshire a major riot by one hundred persons and assaults on gentry servants occurred in March 1490; in Middlesex, one of the Stanley family, described as John Stanley, of the king's household, esquire, and servant of the earl of Derby, murdered a local man, Leonard Petreson.[96]

This is not to say there were not incidents in East Anglia that would have concerned those in authority. The most serious incident occurred in Norfolk, at Thetford on 30 June 1500, where Peter Larke of Thetford and up to ninety others assaulted William Tylles, understeward of Thomas Lovell and James Hobart, stewards of the duchy of Lancaster in Norfolk, though no serious harm appears

---

[94] Distance from Westminster obviously made a difference as to the numbers of indictments, and areas under special jurisdiction, such as Durham, Cheshire and Lancashire, saw very few cases in the Westminster courts, and Cornwall, the Welsh Marches and the north, where the Prince's council and the council in the north offered an alternative source of justice, are under represented. The severity of the crime also tended to dictate whether the case came to Westminster. The increasing use of the bill of Middlesex to speed up the legal process also distorts the figures: M. Blatcher, *The Court of King's Bench, 1450–1550. A Study in Self Help* (London, 1978), chapter 7, though a note of caution was sounded by Susan Jenks, 'Bills of Custody in the Reign of Henry VI', *Journal of Legal History*, xxiii (2002), 197–222.

[95] KB9/383–6; KB8/3, parts 1–4.

[96] KB9/383, nos 47, 92 (damaged); KB9/385, no. 52; KB9/386, nos 38, 47. There was a riotous assembly by twenty or so men in Cambridgeshire, culminating in an assault on three men, but the indictment is damaged, the date is missing, and therefore details and context are elusive: KB9/386, no. 3.

to have come to Tylles. This might well have concerned de Vere, not only as chief steward of the duchy south of the Trent, but also as Lovell and Hobart were his appointees in the office, though both were now influential in their own right.[97] Nonetheless, it was a local matter – the attack took place at a view of frankpledge in the town of Thetford, mainly by Thetford men and seems to have been personal against Tylles, rather than any direct threat to the authority of the duchy. In 1500, Suffolk provided one of those comic moments that occurred in the medieval justice system, where the men responsible for imposing justice could also be the most prominent offenders. At an inquisition at Bungay, before John Wingfield and Sir John Audeley, justices of the peace for the county, a jury presented that the same Sir John Audeley, along with four yeomen, with force and arms had assaulted and wounded Philip Booth, esquire, on 27 October 1500; what Audeley's expression was as he sat in judgement on himself was not recorded. It was a local dispute no doubt, and one that is unlikely to have concerned de Vere overly.[98] Certainly, there was no East Anglian violence that would have worried the earl in the way that any one of several incidents in the north might have concerned the king and council. For example, a session of the peace held before Sir Marmaduke Constable and others at Howden, Yorkshire, on 8 January 1500 saw a jury allege that Sir Walter Griffith, Roger Kelke, gentlemen, twenty other named men, and 150 others, not named, riotously assembled at Beverley and murdered Sir Ralph Ellerker of Risby. Not content with this indictment, those who had suffered apparently took matters into their own hands, according to a suspiciously partisan looking indictment three weeks later. In sessions of the peace at Drypool on 4 February 1500, in the presence of Sir Walter Griffith, indicted at the earlier session and Thomas Gower, JPs, a jury alleged that on 9 January, just a day after the hearing at Howden, Sir Marmaduke Constable, Sir Ralph Ellerker (presumably the deceased's son) and forty-six named others murdered Roger Kelke in revenge. Among the jurors who presented the indictment was one Roger Kelke, junior. This was the sort of gentry violence that would have worried the king's council. Such incidents needed firm central control, or powerful local magnate authority, to contain, and to the historian of the mid-fifteenth century, accustomed to evidence concerned with the breakdown of Lancastrian authority, this might have a suspiciously familiar ring.

Other judicial sources give a similar impression concerning the lack of serious disturbance in the east. Indeed the region was hardly discussed in the surviving sources for the king's council.[99] Perhaps only a serious quarrel in 1489 between

---

[97] KB8/3, part 2, no. 33.

[98] KB8/3, part 2, no. 22. For Booth, see *Estate and Household Accounts of William Worsley*, ed. Kleineke and Hovland, 134–5. He acted as a mainpernor for Worsley's future good behaviour in 1495.

[99] *Select Cases in the Council of Henry VII*, 1–59. There are references to minor East Anglian problems on 14, 19.

Sir Christopher Willoughby and Sir John Wingfield would have caused concern for the king and council, and it was to the earl of Oxford they turned, commissioning him to take sureties that they would keep the peace towards each other.[100] However, the case was already being dealt with in one of the equity courts, and did not cause a major disturbance. Again this can be contrasted to other regions: northern lords were rioting in late autumn 1488, and there were serious problems between the earl of Northumberland and the archbishop of York in 1504.[101] There is some overlap between the council registers and the extant sources for the judicial arm of the king's council, Star Chamber; certainly the sources for the latter support the impression of an eastern region largely free of serious disorder. During Henry VII's reign, there were forty-three cases for the five counties of Essex, Hertfordshire, Suffolk, Norfolk and Cambridgeshire, approximately 10 per cent of the 412 surviving, though the east comprised more than 10 per cent of English counties and total population, yet almost all were routine litigation, which ended up in that court as opportunistic or well connected landowners sought quick and favourable solutions to legal problems.[102]

It is clear that other regions saw grave problems in Henry VII's reign. Christine Carpenter has emphasized 'the truly terrible crisis of order in the north midlands in the first ten years of the reign', where the king 'deputed too much and too little, allowing local forces too much freedom and yet failing to give anyone enough power to act as a sub-ruler for the king'.[103] Sean Cunnningham has traced the increasing loss of royal control in Kent, an area usually dominated by the royal household, in the middle of his reign. He notes how Lord Abergavenny, a Kentish landowner, 'was able to become more assertive precisely because the grip of royal control in Kent weakened. The political resources of the king's household officers such as [Sir Richard] Guildford and [Sir Edward] Poynings became more thinly spread.' He traced the growth of violence between Abergavenny and Guildford, and the king's eventual acceptance of Abergavenny's power in the county, though his famous fine of £70650 for illegal retaining enabled the king to maintain some control over the troublesome peer.[104] In Lancashire, after the fall of Sir William Stanley, the region became considerably more disturbed, as Stanley power was eroded by royal suspicion and consequent favouring of

[100] The problem was clearly a flare-up of an old dispute. The council proceedings refer to 'bills and answers' suggesting the case came before Chancery, or more likely Star Chamber, but no trace can be found: ibid., 22.

[101] *Select Cases in the Council of Henry VII*, 20, 39, 41, 44.

[102] STAC1 (Star Chamber Proceedings, Henry VII), STAC2 (Star Chamber Proceedings, Henry VIII). There is a list of 277 cases in STAC 2 redated to Henry VII's reign in the paper introductory note to the series at the National Archives. There is some duplication of cases among STAC 2, so the total figure may be a little lower. There were thirty-nine rural English counties, and twelve incorporated boroughs, though most of the latter generated very few cases to Star Chamber.

[103] Carpenter, *Locality and Polity*, 592, 595, and generally chapter 15.

[104] Cunningham, *Henry VII*, 174-80, quote from 177.

the assertion of rights to local influence by other north-western families, such as the Savages and Butlers.[105] Dominic Luckett has suggested that the participation of Lord Audley and at least twenty-five members of the Somerset and Dorset gentry communities in the 1497 rebellion is evidence that not only 'that they considered something to be very wrong', but also of the loss of crown control in the region.[106]

From the work that has so far been done on East Anglia at this period – by Roger Virgoe on the Howards, by Colin Richmond on the Pastons, and here on the de Veres – based on common law sources, council and Star Chamber records, and on more informal evidence such as the Paston letters, there is no real evidence of major, prolonged gentry or magnate disorder, such as has been posited for other regions. Where problems occurred, such as de la Pole's 'rebellion', they were dealt with swiftly, often by de Vere in person. While many other violent incidents occurred, they tended not to escalate into prolonged feuding, but were dealt with either within the framework of the common law, or by more informal methods which are harder to trace. While it is clear from the Paston letters that Oxford dealt with many problems informally, the survival of one family's letters has not been matched by the dozens of others whom Oxford is certain to have had similar correspondence with. Nevertheless, the earl was probably not involved in the settlement of the majority of disputes directly, but he did provide a framework of authority and power in the region which inhibited serious disorder.

Conclusion

So much of lordship relied on personal relationships and the informal use of influence, that it is now very difficult to assess just how influential a lord was in the later Middle Ages. Nevertheless, from the surviving evidence, and on such indicators as the numbers of retainers or associates who were sheriffs or MPs,[107] it does seem that Oxford enjoyed dominance in Essex in particular, and to a slightly lesser extent in Norfolk, Suffolk and Cambridgeshire, partly through his own territorial stake, partly through office-holding, royal and private, and partly through influential retainers. Additionally, the power and prestige that emanated from the national, as opposed to the regional, role that de Vere played, as the leading battlefield commander, clearly influential with the king in the early years of the reign, prominent at court and council, would have reinforced the earl's regional authority. Very little challenge was offered to Oxford's position as the leading magnate in these counties, and what challenge there was came when Oxford was attempting to impose the king's commands on reluctant shires,

---

[105] Ibid., 180–6.
[106] Luckett, 'Crown Patronage and Political Morality', 586.
[107] See below, 195–7.

towns or individuals. The challenges that occurred, such as the difficulties with Norwich over supplying troops in 1497, or the passive resistance of the inhabitants of two Essex hundreds to financial impositions,[108] or even Fitzwalter's questioning of Oxford's authority in 1487, all related to royal demands to raise troops and cash for distant campaigns. Even then, local resistance to royal demands in East Anglia was far more limited than seen elsewhere. The tax rebellions of 1489 in the north and in 1497 in the west were not echoed in the east, and this reflects wells on Oxford's good lordship. Moreover, nothing Oxford did during the reign of Henry VII in East Anglia generated the level of local resentment and discontent that Suffolk's rule did in the 1440s. As Colin Richmond has put it: 'What more telling way is there of demonstrating the corrupt rule of William de la Pole, duke of Suffolk, in East Anglia in the 1440s than to indicate its good governance by John de Vere, earl of Oxford, between 1485 and 1513?'[109]

De Vere's domination in East Anglia was not imposed or created by the king, as to a large extent that of Lord Hastings was in the midlands under Edward IV, or certainly Charles Brandon's was in Henry VIII's reign. His own estates and military reputation allied to the absence of serious competition and royal favour combined to make him the leading lord, but his seems to have been a personal lordship, relying as much on informal and personal connections, than on structural features such as heavy retaining, or the absorption of leaderless affinities, such as Mowbray/Howard in 1485, Fitzwalter in the 1490s, or de la Pole in the first few years of the sixteenth century, into his own. It was also a rather light lordship, not touching all corners of the region and not interfering in every gentry cause. In this it echoes Westervelt's views of Lord Hastings's regional influence in Edward IV's reign, which was 'not intrusive' and did not exercise power in every dispute, but which imposed order on the region, though, unlike Hastings, his East Anglian followers were one of the sources of his power and

---

[108] An undated letter to the council by Oxford, Roger Wentworth, Giles Capell, Henry Makwilliam, John Barnes, and Thomas Audeley recorded their summoning at various times of all the inhabitants of the two Essex hundreds of Hinckford and Freshwell with incomes of £20 or more, 'accordyng to the kyngs comysson and instructions [and] advysed them to accomplise the kyngs desyr', but they 'moche lament and bewayle that it lyth not in there possible powers nowe to serve the kynge accordyng to his dysire': SC1/52/61. Oxford then forwarded their names so they could be called before the council. The letter may well date to the collection of the 1491 benevolence. There are no surviving lists of commissioners for 1491 enrolled on the patent roll for Essex, unlike for most counties, but a commission of six men headed by a peer would be similar to that in most other shires: Chrimes, *Henry VII*, 203–4; *CPR, 1485–94*, 353–5. The letter is unlikely to date from the forced loan of 1496 for which the Essex commissioners are known: Hannes Kleineke, '"Morton's Fork'? – Henry VII's "Forced Loan" of 1496', *The Ricardian*, xiii (2003), 325 for the commissioners, and 315–27 more generally.

[109] Richmond, 'East Anglian Politics and Society', 200.

not just a means of exercising his authority.[110] However, when needed, Oxford was prepared to act, and the absence of major rebellion and disorder in the region over the space of twenty-five years and the successful marshalling of its military resources when required, meant that Oxford had done a successful job, and little more could be asked of him in this task.

[110]   T. Westervelt, 'The Changing Nature of Politics in the Localities in the Later Fifteenth Century: William Lord Hastings and his Indentured Retainers', *Midland History*, xxvi (2001), 96–106, quote 102.

6

'My Retainers … Come to Do Me Service' – The Earl's Affinity[1]

I desire and pray you that ye woll in all godely haste, upon the sighte hereof, prepare youre selfe to be in a redinesse with as many persones as ye herbyfore grauntid to do the Kyng service in my company diffensibeley arrayed and there-upon so to resorte unto me in all godely haste possible upon a day warnyng …
(Oxford to Sir John Paston, 12 March 1489)[2]

When assessing the following of a late medieval magnate, it is inevitable that the historian will concentrate on those who can be proved to be connected to the nobleman directly; in practice this usually means where a cash fee, either as a retainer or in return for administrative or legal service can be traced, or where other non-financial bonds, such as an enfeoffment, are identified. With the affinity often described in terms of a series of concentric circles, these followers are part of the inner rings of a magnate's following.[3] This study is no different – perforce it must concentrate on those closest to the earl, those retainers, admin-istrators and key household officials, whose positions, fees and close associations are provable through estate and household accounts, business transactions and Paston letter evidence. Obviously, those on the outer fringes of a magnate's circle, well-wishers and acquaintances, are far harder to trace. Yet, as Michael Hicks has stated, the thirteenth earl relied for 'regional hegemony' on 'the vaguer goodwill and co-operation' of the 'most ancient families of the gentry whom [he] had not retained, as well as those [he] had'.[4] In providing a large percentage of the earl's wider military following and in their co-operation in keeping the peace and local administration, such families were crucial. This qualification underpins

---

[1] *Bacon's History*, 209. Further information and sources for most individuals within the earl's affinity are included in the Appendix, see 228–39.
[2] *PL*, vi, 122.
[3] C. Carpenter, 'The Beauchamp Affinity: A Study of Bastard Feudalism at Work', *EHR*, xcv (1980), 515.
[4] Hicks, *Bastard Feudalism*, 161.

what follows, even though this chapter concentrates on the earl's inner circle of retainers and servants.

The early years

When John de Vere was finally given livery of his lands in January 1464 he did not also inherit a large, coherent affinity. Traditionally, the de Veres had not had a large following among the gentry, and certainly one reason why the de Vere affinity between 1400 and 1462 does not appear to be either extensive or comprehensive among the upper Essex gentry is the very limited resources that the earls could devote to being 'good lords' to their affinity. This was a consequence of the fact that they were not among the richest of the peerage, which placed restrictions on the number and size of fees that could be paid, and also because of the lack of other patronage at their disposal. Perhaps the major reason why the Courtenay earls of Devon in the late fourteenth and early fifteenth centuries were able to maintain a large and cohesive affinity was the large well of patronage pertaining to the duchy of Cornwall that was made available to them, as well as a lack of any rival magnate in the region, and one major reason why they lost control of the affinity was the fact that this patronage had been diverted to William, Lord Bonville and others by the 1430s.[5] The de Vere earls in the first half of the fifteenth century had nothing similar to offer the East Anglian gentry. Neither the eleventh nor twelfth earls of Oxford spent much time at court nor were closely connected in blood to the king, both of which aided the placement of crown resources at the disposal of magnates. Earl Richard's early death in 1417, before the conquest of Normandy, meant the twelfth earl, unlike others among the nobility, had no lands in the duchy, nor captaincies of castles in France, which could provide more opportunities for ambitious or military-minded men. Without the ability to appoint men to lucrative posts or sinecures, they could only attract a few men with cash fees, or with offices in their own estate administration, a limited pool, and most such posts required hard work to make the comital administration effective.

The earls could still be 'good lords' to their followers, but largely through their personal connections and on an ad hoc basis, rather than through institutional patronage. A letter to John Paston by the twelfth earl, written before 1461, saw the earl inform Paston that 'William Mathew of Norwich, Bocher hath brought an accion of dette agayn Nicholas Hert, a tenaunt of myn', an action claimed to be unjust, and Oxford asked Paston to 'calle the jurry before you that arn impanellid betwen thaym, and opne thaym the mater at large at myn instaunce, and desire thaym to do as concyens wole and to eschue perjury'.[6] It is precisely at

---

[5] M. Cherry, 'The Courtenay Earls of Devon: The Formation and Disintegration of a Late Medieval Aristocratic Affinity', *Southern History*, i (1979), 91.

[6] *PL*, iii, 259.

this level that the twelfth earl could be a good lord to his household servants and tenants, lending his influence and authority to matters which did not directly concern him, and in fact letting the more influential members of the affinity do the work for which he paid them.

A more revealing example of the workings of good lordship, as well as the possible dangers of advancing one's servants, is illustrated by the career of Thomas Denys. The twelfth earl wrote to John Paston, probably on 17 May 1450, asking Paston to use his influence to persuade a Norfolk gentlewoman, Agnes, widow of Thomas Ingham the younger, to marry his servant Denys because, he added somewhat ironically, Denys's 'love and effeccion which he hath to a gentil-woman not ferre from yow, and which ye be privy to, as we suppose, causith hym alwey to desire toward your cuntre, rather than toward suych ocupacion as is behovefull to us'. He adds that 'if the comyng thider of our persone self shuld be to plesir of hir, we wole not leve our labour in that'.[7] The involvement of Oxford and Paston was needed as it was not an equal match. As Paston reminded the earl a few years later:

> remembre sche was maried be you and be my meanes, be your comaundement and writyng, and draw therto full sore ageyn her etent in the begynnyge; and was worth 500 marc and better, and shuld have had a gentilman of this contre of a 100 marc of lond and wele born, ne had be your gode Lordshep and writyng to her and me.[8]

The value of the marriage was very great to Denys, and if Oxford, through Paston, achieved this for his relatively humble servant, then this was indeed an exercise of good lordship, although such a marriage could hardly fail to benefit Oxford as well.

It is, of course, dangerous to assume that because men were connected with the earl that they did not have their own interests, as the example of Thomas Denys after his marriage demonstrates. Denys, as a result of his matrimonial endeavours, found himself in dispute with the Ingham family. The dispute was over £260 that Thomas Ingham, junior, owed to his father, Thomas senior. Agnes, as the younger Thomas's widow and executrix, became responsible for the debt. Shortly afterwards, she married Denys, and according to Ingham, they refused to repay the sum. There had been threats and a scuffle between the two parties in Chancery Lane in London, and, to add to the bitterness, Denys found himself subpoenaed to appear in chancery, partly because of the actions of Thomas's brother, Walter Ingham, upon whom Denys chose to avenge himself.[9] In 1454,

---

7   Ibid., ii, 151–2.
8   Ibid., ii, 306. Paston to Oxford, 31 March 1454.
9   C1/22/130 (Thomas Ingham the elder v. Denys and his wife, over the debt); C4/26/3 (Ingham v. Denys, further debt proceedings, and depositions concerning the fight); C.F. Richmond, 'The Murder of Thomas Dennis', *Common Knowledge*, ii (1993), 85–98; unpublished article on 'Thomas Ingham' by C.E. Moreton, History of Parliament Trust, 1422–1504 section.

according to Walter, Denys 'contryved a lettre in the name of my Lord of Oxenforde, he not knowyng of ony suche lettre, commaundyng your seyde besecher
to be with the seide Lorde at Wevenhoe'. As Ingham travelled to Wivenhoe in
response to the false summons, Denys ambushed him and 'grevosly bette and
woundet' him.[10] Oxford was unsurprisingly furious, and he and the Chancellor,
Cardinal Kemp, sent both Denys and his wife to the Fleet prison in London.
John Paston acknowledged to the earl the gravity of the crime when he wrote
'I know wele that Walter Ingham was bete, the mater hangyng in myn award,
right fowle and shamefully; and also how the seid Thomas Denys hath, this
last terme, ageyn your nobill estat, right unwyseley demend hym to his shame
and grettest rebuke … where fore it is right wele do his person be ponysshed as
it pleaseth you.'[11] Nonetheless, Denys was a useful man, especially with greater
financial resources as a result of his marriage, and two years later Denys had not
only been released from prison, but was back in the earl's good graces, serving as
a feoffee in the major settlement of estates in 1456.

In all probability the de Veres in this period were rather more widely connected
and certainly paying more fees than the extant evidence records. Despite the
presence of other baronial families in close proximity, up to 1461 the earls of
Oxford were the acknowledged leaders of Essex society. It was to them that
the crown looked for leadership on important royal commissions, such as that
following Cade's rebellion in 1450, and the de Vere earls personally served on
these occasions. The earls had greater wealth and rank than any other person
primarily resident in Essex during this period, including Henry Bourgchier, and
their ancient title would only have added to their prestige. However, the upper
gentry of Essex were very wealthy, and while a few were drawn into the de Vere
circles, the most obvious being Thomas Rolf, Richard Baynard and Edward
Tyrell, most had connections with other magnates as well as the de Veres.[12] The
earls used many Essex gentry for legal business, as feoffees, attorneys, and secu-
rities, but Linda Clark's conclusion on Henry Bourgchier and Sir John Tyrell
holds good for the de Veres' relationship with most of them: 'Naturally men of
such character could not be regarded as anyone's servants, except perhaps the
king's … the Bourgchiers could not expect a real hold over Tyrell.'[13] They thus
used men of lesser wealth and social standing to run their estates, and even to
transact much business. Similarly, few of the upper gentry fought in de Vere
military retinues, but the de Veres had no problems finding men to fulfil their
indentures – it was just that many of them were of undistinguished birth.[14]
There is no evidence that the de Veres at any stage did not have a retinue or

[10] *PL*, ii, 302–3.
[11] Ibid., ii, 307.
[12] Ross, 'De Vere Earls', 218–25.
[13] Woodger, 'Henry Bourgchier', 261.
[14] See the author's 'Essex County Society and the French War in the Fifteenth Century', in
Fifteenth Century VII, ed. Clark, esp. 57–62.

household that was not commensurate with their wealth and status, though it may be that there was a lower level of gentility among their following than in some other noble households.

Much can change over half a century, and any comparison made between the affinity of the twelfth earl in 1450 and that of the thirteenth earl in 1500, would reach the conclusion that change, both in terms of type and number of retainers, rather than continuity, was the dominating characteristic. Most importantly, the quality of the evidence is such that firmer conclusions can be reached about numbers, payments and the roles of those connected to the earl after 1485. Yet, the shape and extent of the affinity in the early years of John de Vere's career remains obscure. The earl certainly needed administrators and feoffees during this period, and he continued to use the services of his parent's servants and associates; such association across generations seems to have been common.[15] On 1 July 1466, the earl enfeoffed James Arblaster and John Power of eight manors in five counties.[16] Arblaster was a devoted servant of the twelfth earl and his countess, while John Power was paid an annuity of 66s 8d a year by Countess Elizabeth at the same period.[17] Witnesses to the 1466 enfeoffment included Sir Thomas Montgomery, who had been feed by the twelfth earl in 1461 but was now a knight of the royal household, Thomas Tyrell, the son of Sir John Tyrell of Heron, one of the twelfth earl's most prominent connections and a staunch Lancastrian, and the earl of Essex, his father's longstanding colleague.[18] Henry Robson, esquire, appeared as the earl's attorney in a legal case in 1465, and was a feoffee for the Dowager Countess Elizabeth, but most of the evidence of his association with the earl comes from after 1485.[19] Both the earl and his mother stood as feoffees for William Paston in 1464.[20] Perhaps the best evidence for association with the earl at this stage comes from the returns of a commission in 1472 headed by Henry Bourgchier, earl of Essex, identifying those who committed treason in fighting for King Henry at Barnet. In addition to mentioning the leading figures, Exeter, Montagu, Warwick and Oxford himself, a number of men from East Anglia are identified. Given the territorial interests of the Readeption magnates, virtually all those men from East Anglia would have fought under Oxford's banner at Barnet. Those named in the returns were the Essex men Sir John Marney of Layer Marney, Robert and Thomas Bendish of Steeple Bumpstead, John Darcy, esquire, of Tolshunt Darcy, William Godmanston, esquire, of Little Bromley, who was killed and afterwards attainted,[21] William Eden,

[15] Hicks, *Bastard Feudalism*, 95–100.
[16] BL, Harl. Ch. 57 C14.
[17] DL29/295/4848.
[18] For Essex see above, 33–4; for Montgomery, see below, 234. For Tyrell (d. 1476), see Wedgwood, ii, 891–2.
[19] BL, Add. Ch. 28620; CCR, 1468–76, 334–5. For the period after 1485, see below 235.
[20] Bodleian, Norfolk charters a.8734; Richmond, *Paston Family. First Phase*, 190.
[21] *PL*, v, 100; *Calendarium Inquisitionum Post Mortem Sive Escheatorum* (4 vols, Record Commission, 1828), iv, 373–4.

esquire, John Smith of Colchester, gentleman, William Benbury of Takeley and John Buliman of Braintree, and from other counties Henry Elveden, esquire, of Bragbury, Hertfordshire, Roger Dolyngham of Cambridgeshire, Thomas Tey of Tattingstone, Suffolk, yeoman, and Thomas Miller of Holbroke, Suffolk.[22] The list contains a number of feudal tenants whose presence is unsurprising – the two Bendishes, Tey and Miller all held land in a de Vere manor, and Marney was Earl John's cousin. Benbury of Takeley was one of those who received a pardon for service with the earl at St Michael's Mount.[23] It is known from other evidence that John Paston fought with the earl at Barnet, being wounded by an arrow in his right arm,[24] and Sir William Fyndern, later a close associate of the earl, also fought, suffering forfeiture of his lands.[25] Sir William Tyrell was killed fighting at Barnet, probably in Oxford's retinue, as was Lewis John II, Oxford's cousin.[26] A few other men were attainted with Oxford and his brothers in 1475: Robert Harlyston of Shimpling, Suffolk, John Durrant of Collyweston in Northamptonshire and Robert Gybbon of Wingfield, Suffolk.[27] There were, of course, many others who served in the campaign of 1471 with Oxford, and who helped him secure East Anglia for the Readeption regime, but their names are not recorded in the indictments nor have sources from de Vere's own administration survived for this period.

The affinity after 1485 – personnel

Membership of the affinity of the thirteenth earl of Oxford after 1485 brought together many disparate types of men. Poorer tenants, who would have filled his military retinues as archers or billmen, and who might have aspired to service in the lower household, formed a part of the affinity, as did East Anglian knights, whose wealth, power and status was equal to many in the baronage. Between these two extremes were men of every social gradation – esquire, gentleman, yeoman, clerk – and wealth, sometimes united solely by service to the lord, sometimes by bonds of kinship and friendship, often forged in the earl's service. Some men were paid cash annuities for life while some were paid wages for

[22] KB9/41, nos 34, 49, 51; KB27/847, rot. 38.
[23] C81/1507, no. 49.
[24] *PL*, v, 99.
[25] *CPR*, *1467–77*, 336; Wedgwood, ii, 327. His father had been attainted in 1461, but he managed to have the attainder reversed in 1478: *Parliament Rolls*, xiii, 43–50; xiv, 369–70.
[26] *Warkworth's Chronicle*, 16. Probably Sir William Tyrell of Beeches, third son of Sir John Tyrell (d. 1437) of Heron, though possibly Sir William Tyrell of Heron, grandson of Sir John and son of Sir Thomas (d. 1476): unpublished article on 'William Tyrell II' by C.E. Moreton, History of Parliament Trust, 1422–1504 section; W.E. Hampton, 'Sir James Tyrell', *The Ricardian*, 4:63 (1978), 9–11; for John see *CPR*, *1467–77*, 267; unpublished article on 'Lewis John, alias Fitzlewis' by C.E. Moreton, History of Parliament Trust, 1422–1504 section.
[27] *Parliament Rolls*, xiv, 299–301.

service in a particular office, held during the pleasure of the lord, while members of the household were rewarded through the sustenance they received from the earl's table, as well as a small cash fee. The earl's affinity, while naturally reflecting the particular areas where he held land, also brought together men from all over East Anglia.

The household of the thirteenth earl was built on a grander scale than his father's, and was more of a drain on his resources.[28] The contrast between the two households is seen most sharply in the scale of the expenditure. In 1431–2 payments for the wages, food and other expenses incurred by the steward of the household totalled just over £340 over twelve months. From 1 January to 31 December 1507, the same expenses incurred by the controller of the household totalled £1498, some 60 per cent of the earl's annual landed income from his own estates, a figure that seems to be typical of the higher nobility.[29] In 1431–2 there were fifty-one waged servants, who cost the twelfth earl £76 10s; in 1507–8 there were 124, whose wages ran to just over £213.[30] Indeed, the personnel and the expenses would have been higher earlier in the thirteenth earl's career, and would be later, for the simple reason that the earl had recently become a widower by January 1507, but remarried within a few months of the end of this household account. Of the 124 paid throughout the year, only just over one hundred were paid in any one quarter, and not all were therefore in residence at one time: in March 1507 there were 107 men paid; in June 102; in September 101; in December 102.[31] Rotation such as this can be seen in the earl of Northumberland's household at the same date.[32] Bearing in mind the earl's status as a widower, this was a large household staff – compare the fifty that the earl of Essex had in 1533. It was perhaps a little smaller than that of Edward, third duke of Buckingham and his family early in Henry VIII's reign, when they required a staff numbering 225, of whom eighty-six were assigned to the duchess, although no more than 150 appear to have been in residence at any one time; however, Buckingham had perhaps the largest household in England, excluding that of the king.[33]

---

[28] For a discussion of the organization of the various departments of the household of the two earls, see Mertes, *English Noble Households*, 35.

[29] The 1431–2 account is ERO, D/DPr 137, printed in *Household Accounts*, ed. Woolgar, the total expenses are in vol. ii, 548. The account of 1431–2 was very early in the twelfth earl's career, and likely to have been the lower household only – for a more detailed discussion, see Ross, 'De Vere Earls', 209–10. The 1507–8 account is Longleat, Misc. xi, fols 126–35. For the 60 per cent figure, see C. Given-Wilson, *The English Nobility in the Late Middle Ages* (London, 1987), 94.

[30] For 1431–2, see *Household Accounts*, ed. Woolgar, ii, 537; Longleat, Misc. xi, fols 126–35.

[31] Longleat, Misc. xi, fols 126–35, and see fol. 143r for six men who joined the household during the year.

[32] C.M. Woolgar, *The Great Household in Late Medieval England* (New Haven, CT and London, 1999), 38.

[33] Gunn, 'Henry Bourgchier', 148; Rawcliffe, *The Staffords*, 88–9. For other comparisons, which suggest 100 as a slightly above average figure, see McFarlane, *Nobility of Later Medieval England*, 109–13; Given-Wilson, *English Nobility*, 87–90.

The wage payments in the household account overlap considerably with the life annuitants listed in the earl's will of 1509, and also with the hundred or so men granted one-off rewards in the same document. Of the fifty-nine life annuitants, sixteen were paid in the 1507–8 account, generally those on the higher wages and several were of gentle birth.[34] Of the hundred men paid single rewards, ninety-three are named, and of these forty-five are paid in the household account.[35] Why only approximately half the household were paid rewards in the will is unclear; a few men named in the will may have entered the earl's service through his wife's household at the time of the earl's second marriage at some point between November 1508 and April 1509. The three women granted rewards in the will, Margaret Ryder, Elizabeth Wingfield and Margaret Harleston, almost certainly joined the household in this manner, as only one woman was paid in the household account of 1507–8.[36]

While the senior officials of the twelfth earl's administration were shadowy figures, of little status, the same is not true of most of the administrators of the thirteenth earl, many of whom saw long service with de Vere, and rose accordingly in local society. Henry Smith, controller of the household between at least 1488 and 1489, was later appointed to the office of controller and clerk of the king's works at Windsor.[37] Robert Tyrell (d. 1508), who held the same office of controller between at least 1493 and 1495, and who was in receipt of a life annuity of 53s 4d, was knighted in the earl's service at the battle of Blackheath. His son held the office of controller in 1513.[38] Robert Rochester, esquire, was controller of the household from c. 1495 until his death in 1508 at the fee of £10 a year, and was a business associate of the earl. Clement Heigham, receiver-general from 1485 to about 1500, was the second son of Thomas Heigham of Heigham (d. 1481), an important Suffolk landowner, though Clement, as a younger son, probably inherited little land, so that service to the earl was a way, like a career

---

[34] William Oakley (on an annuity of £10) was paid £4 in expenses; Thomas Tyrell, junior (annuity of £3 6s 8d) was paid 53s 4d in expenses; John Danyell (£10), was paid £5 6s 8d in wages and expenses; William Sandes (£3 6s 8d) was paid 53s 4d wages; John Barners (£3 6s 8d), was paid £5 6s 8d in wages and expenses; Anthony Danvers, Henry Radcliff, William Pirton, jun., and Thomas Lathbury (all on 53s 4d) were paid 53s 4d in wages; Roger Neve and Henry Watson (40s) were paid 40s wages; George Reynew and William Dixson (40s) were paid 26s wages; Robert Dedyk (40s) was paid 80s in wages and a subsistence allowance ('prebend'); and John Hewet (40s) was paid 53s 4d in wages: Longleat, Misc. xi, fols 126–35, and see below, 238–9 for annuities.

[35] See Appendix, 239.

[36] Overwhelmingly male households were the norm: Hicks, *Bastard Feudalism*, 45; Mertes, *English Noble Households*, 57–9.

[37] ERO, D/DPr 139, m. 4; *Household Books*, 510; *CPR, 1485–1494*, 330; *1494–1509*, 200. He was a feoffee of the earl in 1486: RH, Box 39.

[38] For the son's office, see CP40/1002, rots. 510, 510d. (Hilary term 4 Hen VIII) where, as controller of the household, he sued six men for debts to the household totalling just over £60.

in the church, for such men to make their way in the world. With wages of £10 a year as receiver-general, it was not a bad living either.[39]

There were perhaps between fifty and seventy gentry families in any county, so for East Anglia at the end of the fifteenth century there might some 250 families. However, the county gentry elites were a small fraction of these numbers – by the mid-fifteenth century there were only thirteen 'greater gentry' families in Nottinghamshire , and allowing for the greater wealth of East Anglia, there might have been sixty to seventy heads of major families.[40] Oxford chose, for sound financial reasons, not to retain more than about a third of this gentry elite, but secured the active co-operation or passive acquiescence of many of the others in his role as the king's lieutenant in the region.

Oxford's codicil to his will of 1509 contains a list of annuities to be paid for life, though it is by no means a complete record of his retaining over the course of Henry VII's reign, a number of his most important retainers having died at some point before that date.[41] Furthermore, as the will was looking towards the period after his death, partly on behalf of his successors and partly as reward for service already done, it is possible both that the numbers of annuities and the size of the fees paid were deliberately less than was the case during Oxford's lifetime, even as late as 1509. Despite these caveats, the will is the key document in understanding de Vere's affinity. The codicil lists thirteen knights and thirty-three esquires and gentlemen who received fees ranging between £10 and 53s 4d, plus two members of his family and eleven household men, the latter mainly on 40s p.a. This was a total spending of £220, somewhere a little under 10 per cent of his landed income in 1509. This figure was probably rather less than it had been around 1500, and some members of the affinity were clearly not paid annuities from de Vere's central administration, but either from the proceeds of his royal offices, or at manorial level for local offices. However, it should be noted that a total cash expenditure of £220 in 1509 on retaining was not a particularly high level of expenditure. For example, John Holand, earl of Huntingdon, was spending £170 12s on twenty-six annuitants in 1436, from a landed income of little

---

[39] ERO, D/DPr 131; 139, m. 4.

[40] C. Given-Wilson, 'The King and the Gentry in Fourteenth Century England', *TRHS*, fifth series, xxxvii (1987), 100; S. Payling, *Political Society in Lancastrian England. The Greater Gentry of Nottinghamshire* (Oxford, 1991), 14–16, 221–6, 244–5; C.F. Richmond, 'An English Mafia?', *Nottingham Medieval Studies*, xxxvi (1992), 238–9; Pollard, *North-Eastern England*, 89–91.

[41] Close associates and likely annuitants who died before 1509 included Sir Thomas Montgomery (d. 1495), Sir Edmund Bedingfield (d. 1496), John Clopton, esq. (d. 1497, though his son Sir William was an annuitant), Sir Ralph Shelton (d. 1499), Thomas Cotton, esq. (d. 1499, though his son Sir Robert was a annuitant), Sir William Carew (d. 1501), Sir John Paston (d. 1503) and Sir Robert Broughton (d. 1506, but both his sons are given bequests in the will, 316). Reginald Bray (d. 1503) was paid an annuity of £10 p.a.: NRO, Towns. 196, MS 1615, m. 1. Thomas Fynas or Fiennes was also an annuitant, paid £10 in the 1480s and 1490s at least: see above, 107, n. 84.

over £1000. The far wealthier duke of Buckingham was spending £465, approximately one-tenth of his income, on eighty-three annuitants in 1442.[42] Nonetheless, such a level of retaining ensured de Vere influential supporters in each of the East Anglian shires. Evidence from their inquisitions *post mortem* reveal that most of the men paid annuities in the will were very substantial landowners, with lands in several shires, though most can be identified as being primarily resident in one.[43] Men such as Sir William Waldegrave (landed income of at least £242 p.a.), Sir William Carew, Sir Robert Drury (£115 p.a.) John Clopton (£49 p.a.) and his son Sir William, and Sir Robert Broughton (£600 p.a. in an inquisition *post mortem*, £1000 estimated in a chamber book), were all Suffolk landowners and residents. Norfolk men included Sir John Paston, Sir Edmund Bedingfield (£209 p.a.), Sir Ralph Shelton (£84 p.a.) Sir Robert Lovell and Robert Brewes, esquire, and his son Thomas (£93 p.a.) and those in Cambridgeshire were Sir William Fyndern (£162 p.a.), Thomas Cotton (£86 p.a.) and his son and heir Sir Robert (£145 p.a.), Sir Robert Payton (£196 p.a.), and Sir Giles Alington (£124 p.a.). As might be expected most of the rest were Essex men, including probably the earl's two most important retainers Sir Richard Fitzlewis and Sir Thomas Tyrell (£129 p.a.) as well as other men, such as Tyrell's son Thomas, Sir Thomas Montgomery (£47 p.a.), Sir John Grene (at least £110 p.a.), Sir Roger Wentworth and Sir Henry Tey (£60 p.a.). Many of those who became Oxford's annuitants were the more important and richer gentry in each county, and Oxford's lordship enhanced the status granted by their own land and power.

The reason that Oxford could retain so many powerful men for the small total of £220 a year was that the fees he paid were modest, both compared to other peers and to the income of most of these men. The duke of Buckingham spent £465 a year in the 1440s retaining among others eight knights and twenty-six esquires; Oxford spent £220 retaining among others twelve knights and thirty-three esquires and gentlemen.[44] Sir William Fyndern's annuity of £5 p.a. was only about 3 per cent of his annual landed income of £162, as was Sir William Waldegrave's annuity of 10 marks, compared to an income of £242 p.a. They appear not to be designed to be a significant addition to the retainer's income as far as most of the senior members of the affinity were concerned, but were more of a symbolic link between the earl and his feed men. This was similarly true of the Beauchamp affinity in the first half of the fifteenth century, where for example Sir William Mountford, with an annual income of £258 was feed just £26 13s 4d, though his fee was more than double any that de Vere paid to men outside his family, as well as the affinity of the third duke of Buckingham,

---

[42] Stansfield, 'Holland Family', 271; Rawcliffe, *The Staffords*, 73. The earl of Devon was able to give livery to 130 persons, though many were estate officials and household servants, from an income of about £1350: McFarlane, *Nobility of Later Medieval England*, 111.
[43] Sources for income for the following men are included under their entries in the Appendix.
[44] Rawcliffe, *The Staffords*, 73.

whose fees ranged from £2 to £20.[45] As attractive as cash, in many cases, was the patronage and good lordship Oxford could offer. It also helped that de Vere did not face much competition in recruiting members of the gentry during much of Henry VII's reign, since he would have had to pay rather more to ensure the retainer's primary service if this had been the case.

As the most prominent lord in East Anglia for much of Henry VII's reign, de Vere's service was always likely to attract many of the gentry, but the earl was in a much better position to reward followers than his father had been. This was not simply a result of his greater landed wealth, but also to the considerably greater reservoirs of patronage available to him. It was his numerous royal offices that gave him an opportunity to place many of his followers in positions of influence and reward – John Paston was his deputy in the admiralty, John Radcliffe, Lord Fitzwalter, his deputy as constable of the Tower, succeeded by Sir Thomas Lovell.[46] De Vere's stewardship of the duchy of Lancaster south of the Trent, especially, provided opportunities to promote associates to office. John Tey, described as of Castle Hedingham in 1498–9, and probably, therefore, a member of the earl's household, held the office of feodary of the duchy in five counties from 1510 to 1523, having succeeded Richard Churchyard in the same office. Churchyard, MP for Maldon in 1497, for which he was almost certainly indebted to the earl, had been a feoffee in 1486 and was a senior member of the earl's estate administration, holding the office of supervisor of all the earl's lands in four counties in 1488–9 at the annual fee of 53s 4d. Sir Robert Drury, Sir Thomas Lovell, and Sir James Hobart all held posts in the administration of the Duchy.[47] One or two royal offices were held by the earl in perpetuity: Sir Richard Fitzlewis, and the earl's cousin, John de Vere, were Oxford's deputies in his hereditary office of steward in the royal manor of Havering atte Bower.[48] Sir John Raynesforth, who may have been retained by the earl, held the position of deputy in de Vere's hereditary office of master forester of Essex.[49]

The earl's own administration also provided a number of similar posts, and, as Michael Hicks has argued, such offices were 'an important means of recruiting retainers from the gentry', though they were not sinecures.[50] Fitzlewis, Paston, Thomas Heigham, Churchyard, John Josselyn and Clement Heigham all held important posts within the central administration, and there were many other manorial posts available which provided reasonable remuneration. The office of parker at Earls Colne carried with it fees of just over £6 a year, and was held by, among others, John Tey between 1496 and 1501 and Thomas Tyrell, junior,

[45] Carpenter, 'Beauchamp Affinity', 519; Harris, *Edward Stafford*, 138.
[46] Radcliffe: *Select Cases in the Exchequer Chamber before all the Justices of England*, ed. M. Hemmant (2 vols, Selden Society, 1945–8), ii, 120; KB145/9/1. Lovell: KB8/2, mm. 1d., 3d.
[47] Somerville, *Duchy of Lancaster*, i, 263, 431, 595.
[48] E150/299/8.
[49] E150/299/8; *Household Books*, 493.
[50] Hicks, *Bastard Feudalism*, 53.

between 1508 and 1510.[51] There would have been a number of other comparable posts, carrying substantial fees, but the survival of manorial accounts for Earls Colne is not matched by those of Wivenhoe, Lavenham, East Winch or Castle Hedingham which all had parks. Financial advantage could also be given by the grant of the position of bailiff of a manor or through farming a manor for a fixed rent: James Hobart, for example, was bailiff of the manors of Waltons in Mucking and Gobins in Tilbury in 1488–9, and James Arblaster was bailiff of Chelsworth in Suffolk at the same date.[52] Robert Tyrell, later controller of the household, was the farmer of Downham in 1488–9 and 1499–1500, and Roger Wentworth, Thomas Arblaster, John Josselyn and Sir Roger Townshend all farmed de Vere manors for the earl.[53]

In contrast to his father, the thirteenth earl was able to call upon the exclusive service of the bulk of his affinity, with few having significant connections with other members of the nobility. Sir Robert Broughton, who, with an income of over £600 from lands in ten counties, was one of the richest non-baronial land-owners in England, can be connected with no magnate except Oxford, under whose banner he fought at Stoke, where he was knighted. In February 1502 and June 1504, Broughton made two enfeoffments of his estates to the earl, Sir Reginald Bray, Robert Drury and others, and he also made the earl the supervisor of his will.[54] This pattern is repeated elsewhere. Men like Sir William Fyndern, Sir Richard Fitzlewis, Sir John Paston, Sir Robert Payton, Sir Henry Tey, Sir John Grene, Sir William Clopton and Sir Robert Cotton cannot obviously be connected in their public dealings to magnates other than Oxford, in contrast to the Beauchamp affinity earlier in the century.[55] Even where some of his men acted for other magnates their primary loyalties appear to have remained with the earl. For example, while Sir Robert Lovell was a feoffee of Richard, Lord Latimer in 1499,[56] Latimer himself was obviously close to the earl, having grown up as his ward at Castle Hedingham between 1486 and 1491, serving at Stoke in 1487 and in the north after the earl of Northumberland's murder in 1489, in both

---

[51] ERO, D/DPr 124, mm. 4–6; 131, mm. 4, 5; 133; 134. The accounts for Earls Colne are patchy at this period, and these individuals may have held the office for longer periods. It is worth noting in some cases that the wages appear to have been in addition to the retaining fees paid in the will, as Tyrell at least was paid £6 20d (*sic*) in wages as parker, but 53s 4d as an annuity.

[52] ERO, D/DPr 139, mm. 2, 3.

[53] Ibid., mm. 1–3; for Tyrell in 1499–1500, see ERO, D/DBm M501, m. 3d.; for Josselyn: PROB11/22 Porche, fol. 19v. In general, however, the farming of manors was not done by the wealthier or more important members of the de Vere affinity.

[54] *CIPM Henry VII*, iii, 142–3, 259; *Testamenta Vetusta*, ed. Nicolas, ii, 489; Wedgwood, ii, 118; see also *CCR, 1485–1500*, 108; *1500–9*, 76; *CPR, 1485–94*, 168, 283, 438; *1494–1509*, 185, 287, 659. Broughton may have married a bastard daughter of the earl called Katherine: BL, Add. MS 19121, fols 12, 14 (pedigree of the Broughton family by David Davy in the nineteenth century).

[55] Carpenter, 'Beauchamp Affinity', 517.

[56] *CCR, 1485–1500*, 357–60.

cases probably as part of Oxford's retinue.[57] Both John Clopton and Sir Thomas Montgomery were feoffees of the estates of Henry Bourgchier, earl of Essex, but this dated back to the period before 1483.[58] Sir Thomas Tyrell[59] and Sir William Waldegrave[60] can be connected with very few other nobles, despite their wealth and status. Perhaps only Sir William Say could be described as having equally close links with other magnates, as his daughters and co-heiresses, Mary and Elizabeth, married Henry Bourgchier, earl of Essex and William Blount, Lord Mountjoy, respectively.[61]

The earl's only significant competitor was the king himself, and several of Oxford's associates graduated to royal service. Sir Robert Drury was a close associate of the earl throughout Henry VII's reign, but was also from about 1504 a councillor of the king, receiving a number of grants of land and wardships from Henry VII.[62] Nonetheless, in Carole Rawcliffe's words, 'Drury's association with the de Veres no doubt helped him to secure a place on Henry VII's council, but he was not tempted to seek out any other major patrons, remaining staunchly loyal to his original benefactor.'[63] Sir Robert Lovell was described as the king's servant in 1501,[64] as was Thomas Cotton in 1486.[65] There were also two men, Sir James Hobart and Sir Thomas Lovell, who, though they were closely connected with de Vere from 1485, rose primarily through service to the crown rather than to the earl. Hobart was bailiff of two de Vere manors in 1488–9, a regular feoffee, and an executor of the earl's will, and both Hobart and Lovell served as deputies to de Vere as chief steward of the duchy south of the Trent. However, Hobart was from 1486 a privy councillor, and later attorney-general.[66] Lovell was another executor, and received a bequest of a 'salt of silver and gilt, with a pearl weighing 25 ounces' in the earl's will, where he was described as 'my olde frende'. However,

---

[57] CPR, 1485–94, 339. See also Michael Hicks 'Richard Lord Latimer, Richard III, and the Warwick Inheritance', The Ricardian, xii (2001), 314–20; L.L. Ford, 'Neville, Richard, second Baron Latimer (c. 1467–1530), ODNB; Household Books, 519–20 (work was being done on Latimer's chamber in 1491).

[58] CCR, 1485–1500, 85.

[59] Tyrell enfeoffed two Essex manors to Oxford and also to Thomas, earl of Arundel; E150/299/6, and earlier, in 1479, during de Vere's imprisonment, his Hampshire estates were enfeoffed to, among others, John, Lord Dinham: E150/963/6.

[60] In 1486 Thomas, earl of Ormond, was a feoffee of a Suffolk manor and in 1499 John, Lord Berners, was among Waldegrave's feoffees of his Suffolk estates: CCR, 1485–1500, 49; E150/630/12.

[61] CCR, 1500–1509, 238-9; CP, v, 159.

[62] 'Last Testament', 318; CPR, 1494–1509, 368, 388, 466, 506, 522; Bindoff, ii, 57–8.

[63] C. Rawcliffe and S. Flower, 'English Noblemen and their Advisors: Consultation and Collaboration in the Later Middle Ages', Journal of British Studies, xxv (1986), 165.

[64] CPR, 1485–94, 271; 1494–1509, 265.

[65] CPR, 1485–94, 14, 99.

[66] ERO, D/DPr 139, m. 2; D/DMh/T34; RH, Boxes 38–9; Somerville, Duchy of Lancaster, i, 595; Wedgwood, ii, 458–9; Lander, English Justices of the Peace, 36–7. For the appointment of executors see 'Last Testament', 318.

he was speaker of the House of Commons in 1485, knight of the body, Chancellor of the Exchequer and treasurer of the household, and although associated with Empson and Dudley in the latter part of Henry VII's reign, he escaped their fate in 1509.[67]

Given the unusual circumstances of 1485, when Oxford, having been absent from local politics since 1471, suddenly became the leading figure in East Anglia, it is worth asking to what extent the affinity that served him so well was a construct, built to ensure the loyalty of the area and to provide him with troops, or was it a natural response from groups of local gentry to the growth of de Vere power? Certainly some members of the affinity were men who were likely to be drawn into his orbit. This category included family, such as his brother George, and his cousins Sir John Marney and Sir Richard Fitzlewis, and there were families with whom his father had had connections, most notably the Pastons and the Cloptons. In addition, amongst his life annuitants there were feudal tenants, including Sir William Fyndern, Sir Edmund Bedingfield, Sir William Waldegrave, Sir Roger Wentworth, Thomas Heigham, Humphrey Wingfield and William Pirton.[68] Sir Robert Broughton was a close associate, although it is not known what fee (if any) he received, and also a feudal tenant.[69] While the feudal bond may not in itself be responsible for any association between the earl and the landowner in question, such a connection usually indicates neighbouring estates or at least manors in close proximity to one another, an important factor as it was unusual for lords to retain men from areas where they did not hold land. It may have assumed greater significance when the feudal lord was a leading magnate – the tenant had a greater interest in remembering that the tie existed. Oxford's enforcement of his feudal dues may also have brought this connection into prominence. However, by no means all Oxford's circle were relatives, tenants or neighbours, and some were drawn in from further afield.

Men of differing political persuasions were also drawn into his circle, former Edwardians, Ricardians and Lancastrians, but Oxford's lordship was inclusive enough to be able to absorb these men into his affinity. In particular, the earl was magnanimous enough in the years after Bosworth to retain or be associated with a number of men who had been involved in Richard III's regime, the most prominent of whom was Sir Thomas Tyrell, made master of the horse in 1483, and squire of the body to Edward IV and Richard III.[70] However, from early in Henry VII's reign he appears to have become one of Oxford's closest retainers.

---

[67] 'Last Testament', 313, 318; Wedgwood, ii, 555–6; S.J. Gunn, 'Sir Thomas Lovell (c. 1449–1524): A New Man in a New Monarchy?', in *End of the Middle Ages?*, ed. Watts, 117–53.

[68] E150/302/1 (Fyndern); *CIPM Henry VII*, ii, 8–11 (Bedingfield); E150/311/3 (Waldegrave); C142/72/74 (Wingfield); *CIPM Henry VII*, i, 262–3; C142/81/297 (Pirton). For the others, Bodleian, Rawlinson B 319, fols 5v, 84r, 86r, and for the full range of feudal tenants, see B 319 passim.

[69] *CIPM Henry VII*, iii, 259–60, 284.

[70] Wedgwood, ii, 892–3.

Tyrell appeared as a feoffee in 1486, and was one of a number of the earl's retinue who were knighted after the battle of Stoke the next year; he was involved in a number of property transactions with Oxford, was appointed a feoffee in a major settlement of de Vere estates in 1492, by which time he had a permanent chamber at Hedingham, and was feed £6 13s 4d for life by 1509. Oxford got the service of a wealthy, powerful member of the gentry, in his council chamber and on the battlefield; Tyrell was knighted for his service in de Vere's retinue at Stoke, while at Blackheath he was made a banneret. While Tyrell was the most important of those former Ricardians who were to become retainers or associates of the earl he was by no means the only one. Sir William Say, knighted by Richard III and given a grant of the manor of Sawbridgeworth, Hertfordshire, in 1484, brought twelve men at his own cost to Oxford's muster at Cambridge on 20 July 1487.[71] Sir Henry Wentworth, despite having Lancastrian sympathies during the 1460s and at the time of the Readeption, received a £5 pension as the 'king's servant' and was a squire of the household in 1484. However, he was twice a witness of Oxford's enfeoffments in 1486 and 1492, and may have raised men for Oxford's muster in 1487.[72] Such a policy of reconciliation can only have bolstered Oxford's reputation as a good lord.

There were almost no kinship or marriage ties between members of his affinity in 1485, but this was to change.[73] As early as 1489, Sir Ralph Shelton was arranging the marriage of his daughter with Sir Richard Fitzlewis, and after Shelton's death Fitzlewis acquired the wardship of his heir.[74] By 1497 Sir John Grene's daughters, Margaret and Agnes, had been married to Sir Henry Tey and Sir William Fyndern respectively.[75] Sir Robert Broughton was married between 1487 and 1490 to Dorothy, daughter of Henry Wentworth,[76] and Sir Roger Wentworth married into the Tyrell family.[77] Both Thomas and Clement Heigham married into the Cotton family.[78] Sir Giles Alington's son and heir, another Giles, married Ursula, Sir Robert Drury's daughter, in 1515.[79] One reason that the affinity that was in place within a few years of 1485 had almost

[71] Wedgwood, ii, 747–8; *Household Books*, 493, 495.

[72] Wedgwood, ii, 933–4; *Household Books*, 495.

[73] Sir William Say married Thomas Waldegrave's widow, mother of Sir William Waldegrave, at some point after 1472, and probably before 1485: Wedgwood, ii, 748.

[74] ERO, D/DP T1/1505, business arrangements for a jointure, 1489, with considerable numbers of Oxford's circle acting as feoffees; Rawcliffe and Flower, 'Noblemen and their Advisors', 172. Fitzlewis, Sir Robert Clere and Nicholas Shelton paid £266 for the wardship in 1499, shortly after Sir Ralph's death: E101/414/16, fol. 102r.

[75] *CIPM Henry VII*, ii, 27–30.

[76] *CIPM Henry VII*, ii, 594, where the first name of her father is missing, but only Henry is of the correct generation; Wedgwood, ii, 118.

[77] He married Anne, daughter of Humphrey Tyrell, brother of Sir Thomas, the earl's retainer: *Visitations of Essex*, ed. W.C. Metcalfe (2 vols, London, 1878), i, 110–15; Wedgwood, ii, 935, and for Humphrey (d. 1517), see C142/32/59.

[78] *Visitation of Suffolk, 1561*, ed. J. Corder (2 vols, Harleian Society, 1981–4), ii, 394–5.

[79] Bindoff, i, 307.

no kinship ties in its early years was the wide geographical spread of his retinue. There were always stewards and receivers for outlying estates, and de Vere had these too – Robert Power, the steward of the earl's Buckinghamshire manors, was one example – but usually the core was geographically more concentrated and few affinities had at their centre men from more than one or two counties.[80] However, Oxford had annuitants and close associates in Cambridgeshire, Suffolk, Norfolk, Essex, and to a lesser extent Hertfordshire.

In addition to increasing kinship and marriage links, most members of de Vere's affinity served as feoffees and executors for one another and were associated together in financial transactions such as bonds and recognizances; a similar phenomenon among the Beauchamp retinue earlier in the fifteenth century 'helped cement political alliances made through the affinity'.[81] Groups of retainers acquired the wardships of sons of others, or helped pay livery fines – Sir Robert Drury, Sir William Waldegrave, Sir Robert Cotton and Giles Alington paid 3500 marks for the special livery of John Broughton, son and heir of the very wealthy Sir Robert Broughton, who was aged fifteen at his father's death in 1506.[82] Occasionally, more personal ties can be seen; Thomas Tyrell left money in his will for prayers to be made for the souls of Thomas Montgomery and his wife, despite Montgomery having died seventeen years earlier.[83]

While some of the gentry in Essex and Suffolk were drawn into the affinity of most de Vere earls, that of the thirteenth earl was at least partially a construct, so that in each of the East Anglian counties, the earl had several powerful, wealthy men, who could be relied on in the event of a crisis and who could exercise the earl's authority in his absence. It is clear that in 1485 the earl did not inherit a coherent affinity, either from his father's old associates or from another magnate,

---

[80] In contrast with the Bourgchier affinity in Essex, the Talbots in Shropshire and the Beauchamps in Warwickshire, the Mowbray affinity between the 1390s and the 1430s was 'representative of the breadth of Mowbray possessions'. The dukes could 'count on staunch supporters in Lincolnshire, East Anglia, Sussex and the Midlands': Archer, 'Mowbrays', 279–80, and more generally 266–311.

[81] See virtually all inquisitions *post mortem* cited in individual entries in Appendix 1, and their respective biographies in Wedgwood and also, for example, CP25/1/30/101, nos 4 (Fyndern, Thomas Cotton, Clement and Richard Heigham), 11 (Fyndern, Thomas Cotton), 12 (Drury and Cotton); CP25/1/170/195, nos 2 (Paston, Bedingfield, Hobart), 26 (Drury and Hobart); CP25/1/224/125, nos 51 (Pirton, Hobart, Ralph Josselyn), 69 (Drury and William Clopton), 94 (Drury and Waldegrave), 99 (Drury, Thomas Lovell); C67/53, mm. 26 (Sir William Say's feoffees), 41 (Sir Robert Payton's feoffees); KB27/909, rot. 110 (Daubeney, John Clopton, Drury and others); BL, Add. MS 21480, fols 47v (Drury, Waldegrave and Alington), 53v (Drury, Robert Tyrell), 60v (Drury and Waldegrave), 75v (Drury, Payton and Thomas Bedingfield), 78v (Robert Tyrell, Marney, Roger Wentworth), 94r (Thomas Tyrell and Richard Wentworth); E36/214, pp. 461 (Henry Tey and Pirton), 462 (Thomas Tyrell and Henry Marney); E36/215, fol. 330r (John Vere, John Josselyn and Humphrey Wingfield). For the Beauchamps, see Carpenter, 'Beauchamp Affinity', 522–4.

[82] E36/215, fol. 327r and see above, 190 n. 74.

[83] PROB 11/17, fol.1.

a point illustrated by the near-complete lack of kinship ties between his future retainers in 1485. But if the earl did not inherit a homogenous following those drawn into his orbit quickly became one, despite their diffusion across the whole of East Anglia and differing connections to the lord, and they soon became a group tied by more than just loyalty to the earl. Personal and familial bonds were formed, accelerated by their shared military and administrative service to their lord.

The affinity after 1485 – types of service

Like every other nobleman, de Vere needed members of his affinity to serve in his military retinues, administer his estates, to advise on his legal cases, and to transact a wide range of business. The more senior retainers served in most of these capacities, often simultaneously: some men held a senior post in the household or estate administration, acted as the earl's deputy in a royal office, gave counsel or legal advice, and followed the earl's banner onto the battlefield when required. It is clear types of service could be fluid, but such distinctions of household, administration, and politico-military service are nonetheless useful as the basis for discussion of how the earl employed his affinity.

Legal business was one area that occupied some of the time of the earl's retainers, both the trained lawyers and some of the senior gentry. A type of business that may well have been common can be glimpsed in occasional surviving documents. The earl was asked to arbitrate in a dispute between Sir James Tyrell and Thomas Lucas concerning the ownership of a Suffolk manor. By 8 January 1501 the earl and his council came to a decision that Sir George Vere, Sir Robert Broughton, Sir Richard Fitzlewis, Sir Robert Lovell, John Mordaunt and Thomas Frowyk were to be enfeoffed of the manor in question to the use of Tyrell, who was to have the manor as long as he paid Lucas 650 marks.[84] While the lawyers debated the legal points, the senior gentry added their weight to the decision, and, standing as feoffees, guaranteed its implementation. Less successful was the arbitration undertaken by the earl and his 'councell learned' between Robert Straunge and Henry Sharborn; although he took 'suche direction as bothe parties were therwith agreed as I then supposed', but 'of late I am enformed a breche to be bitwenee theym in the said mattier by reason wherof privie sealis have ben sued'. As the dispute lay before the royal council, the earl wrote to Reginald Bray on the matter desiring that 'suche good end therein be taken as may stond with justice and the rather at this myn instans'.[85] The earl did not have a large number of cases in the Westminster courts, but he certainly had a few, and, as referenced in the arbitration between Straunge and Sharborn, the earl echoed the royal practice of having a 'consilium in lege eruditum', a

[84] BL, Add. Ch. 16570.
[85] WAM, 16075. No year given.

council learned in the law. William Ayloff and Richard Heigham, serjeant-at-law, were members of this body in 1499, when they are mentioned in a legal suit in Common Pleas concerning a debt owed by Sir John Grene to the earl.[86] Such men would not just give counsel on civil or criminal cases in the courts, but were also crucial in advising on how to avoid such suits, how to acquire a secure title to property when purchasing land, as the earl did on a number of occasions, and in the settlement of estates. It is clear from the length (over 6000 words) and complexity of the arrangements in the earl's will for the descent of his lands that many lawyers were employed in drafting it.

Most noble affinities had at their core a few trusted men who might be used in a military capacity, but few retinues were designed primarily as a military force, to be used for campaigning and for local 'peace-keeping' duties. Here de Vere's affinity appears to depart from the norm. From the aftermath of Bosworth to Blackheath the earl's retinue was mustered on at least five occasions (twice in 1487, 1489, 1492, twice in 1497), and must have been on high alert throughout each summer in Henry VII's insecure early years. One needs only to look at the lists of knights made after Stoke, where up to seven of de Vere's affinity were knighted, and Edmund Bedingfield made a banneret,[87] and after Blackheath, where four were made bannerets, and a further seven knighted,[88] to understand the military service his followers performed. It did not appear to matter whether an annuitant was a lawyer by training, like Robert Drury, or an administrator, such as Richard Churchyard, the man in question was expected to, and did, see service on the battlefield. It is interesting to note the multi-faceted roles that men like Drury, Churchyard and Fitzlewis played. Carole Rawcliffe has discussed the fact that 'gentry' councillors played important roles in the earl's council and legal business, and that the professional abilities of lawyers were 'usefully complemented on the council board by the special influence and knowledge of their colleagues from the upper ranks of the gentry'.[89] Such distinctions tend to blur in the affinity of the thirteenth earl, where men like Fitzlewis and Paston played important legal and administrative roles, yet still raised thirty and twenty men respectively for the campaign of 1489, and were knighted for their military service.

De Vere was also able to draw on the wider resources of East Anglia for royal campaigns. To take one example from many discussed earlier, the household books for 1487 detail forces raised in July of that year. One list contains men and

[86] CP40/949, rot. 103d.

[87] Carew, Fitzlewis, Paston, Broughton, Thomas Tyrell, and possibly also William Sandes, who may have fought under Oxford's banner, and whose son was later in the earl's service, and Thomas Lovell, though he may have fought in the king's retinue: *Herald's Memoir*, 119–20; W.C. Metcalfe, *A Book of Knights, Knights of the Bath and Knights Bachelor* (London, 1885), 13–15.

[88] The bannerets were Thomas Lovell, Fitzlewis, Broughton and Thomas Tyrell, the knights were Robert Lovell, Robert Tyrell, Drury, Henry Tey, Payton, Grene and Roger Wentworth: Metcalfe, *Book of Knights*, 27–9.

[89] Rawcliffe and Flower, 'Noblemen and Their Advisors', 172.

the forces they raised under the heading 'These personys folwyng shall brynge the personys folwyng, at the charges of the Kyng and my Lord.'[90] Another much shorter list contains four men who were to bring men at their 'propre costys and charges.'[91] The first list contains a number of men who were amongst the earl's closest associates – Fitzlewis, Tyrell, Broughton and four others – as well as some men who cannot otherwise be connected to the earl. It contains men from Essex, Suffolk and Cambridgeshire, though not Norfolk, and cannot be taken to represent the earl's entire military following, given the absence of some of his retainers, his own household and tenantry. It does however list twenty-two captains, including eleven knights, nine esquires, one yeoman, and two without title, who, bar two, were to serve in person, and it contains details of a force to number 204 men. The rebellion of 1489 in Yorkshire that saw the murder of the earl of Northumberland required a stern response from the king, and some of Oxford's followers are listed as they joined the king at Northampton on 15 May. Those named in the Herald's account were Sir John Wingfield, Fitzlewis, Broughton, Tyrell, Carew, Philip Lewis, Simon Wiseman, Roger Hastings, John Raynesforth, Robert Tyrell, John Colt, and John Peke. Again some of these names are familiar, though Wingfield, Wiseman, Hastings, Colt and Peke were not in the earl's close circle, but for a royal campaign the earl would naturally have drawn upon the wider military resources of East Anglia for his retinue, including those outside of his orbit.[92]

Service on a political level was also important. This might take the part of serving as MPs and sheriffs for East Anglian counties or other more miscellaneous and ad hoc service. For example, Sir Robert Drury, Sir Robert Lovell, Sir Richard Fitzlewis and Sir Thomas Tyrell entered into bonds with the earl in 1499 for watching the countess of Suffolk after her husband had fled abroad. Several of the bonds for allegiance taken from suspect East Anglian knights had de Vere retainers standing as sureties, such as the one Sir Gilbert Debenham made in 1499, for which Sir John Paston and Robert Brewes undertook that role. While some of these may have been natural and longstanding associations, it also allowed Oxfordian retainers some oversight over untrustworthy locals, and by obligating the latter to the former for large sums, may have given the de Vere retainers some input into the future behaviour of these individuals.[93] It is also clear from such examples as Paston's reassurance to Great Yarmouth in 1495, Bedingfield facing down a peer in 1487 to carry out the commands of Oxford and the king, and the subtle exercise of influence by Shelton and Lovell

---

[90] *Household Books*, 494.

[91] Ibid., 495.

[92] *Herald's Memoir*, 167; Bennett, 'Henry VII and the Northern Rising', 56.

[93] C255/8/7, nos 39–40. From the extant files of bonds in C255, there are two further examples: Robert Drury stood as surety for Fitzwalter in 1489 (C255/8/5, no. 160) and William Waldegrave, esquire and Thomas Appleton, gentleman, for Thomas Cressener (C255/8/7, no. 68).

in discussions with Norwich, that de Vere expected and received good political service from these men in his absence, and that his own lordship across the whole region was reinforced by his affinity.

Part of the duty of the earl's retinue was to demonstrate his worship and power. When Oxford ordered that 'the gentyl men of Essex to wayte upon hym ... as he entendythe to mete with the Kynge, and that they be well apoynted, that the Lankeschere men may see that ther be gentylmen of as grete sobe-staunce that thei be able to bye alle Lankeschere', such display would not only reflect well on the gentlemen, but on him as their lord.[94] The daily expense for the household at Wivenhoe dropped by approximately 40 per cent during the earl's sojourn with the king at Cambridge in late July 1507, suggesting the earl was accompanied by forty to fifty members of his household to demonstrate his worship, and one would assume that many of his retainers not normally resident in the household and others of the region's gentry would have accompanied him to see the king, as occurred in 1487.[95]

De Vere's retaining, patronage and good lordship ensured that a number of the most important offices in each shire were filled by his retainers or associates. In terms of one of the more prestigious steps on the *cursus honorum* for the local gentry, that of representing a shire or a borough in parliament, most of the county seats in East Anglia were filled by Oxford's men. In Essex only four men are known to have sat in parliament during Henry VII's reign, though Sir Henry Marney did so three times (1491–2, 1497, 1504). Three, Fitzlewis (MP in 1495), Thomas Tyrell (1495) and Henry Tey (1491–2) were feed by Oxford, and Marney was a feoffee.[96] In Suffolk the situation was similar – of the five known MPs three, Sir Robert Broughton (MP 1489), Sir William Waldegrave (MP 1495) and Sir Robert Drury (MP in 1491–2, 1495, when he was Speaker, 1497, and 1504), were annuitants, Sir William Carew (1489) almost certainly was, and only Simon Wiseman (1487, 1491–2) was apparently not a close associate.[97] In Norfolk only four MPs are known to have sat in parliament during the reign of the first Tudor king – Sir Thomas Lovell in 1485, Sir Robert Brandon and Sir Philip Calthorpe in 1491 and Sir Robert Clere in 1495. Of these only Lovell was connected to the earl.[98] Only two Cambridgeshire MPs are known for Henry VII's reign:

94 *PL*, vi, 122.

95 Longleat, Misc. xi, fols 49r–52v. Average expenses on meat and fish were in the region of 100–120 shillings a week. In the earl's absence from Wivenhoe, the controller of the house-hold paid only 60s in the week covering 25–31 July, and 83s in the following week, towards the end of which the earl returned. Clearly the expenses of the travelling household were not the controller's responsibility and another official would have accounted for them.

96 Wedgwood, i, 642. For Marney, a feoffee in 1486, later raised to the baronage, see Wedg-wood, ii, 575–6. He fought at Stoke and Blackheath, probably under Oxford's banner, and received a mention in Oxford's will: 'Last Testament', 317.

97 Wedgwood, i, 684; and see also Virgoe, 'Recovery of the Howards', 11. Wiseman did serve with the earl in 1489: see above, 194.

98 Wedgwood, i, 660–1; ii, 102, 148–9, 190, 555–6.

John Burgoyne (MP 1491–2) does not appear to have had any connections with Oxford but Sir William Fyndern (MP 1491–2 and 1495) was Oxford's retainer.[99] Overall, of the known returns to parliament of knights of the shire in Henry VII's reign in Essex, Suffolk, Norfolk and Cambridgeshire, de Vere's annuitants or feoffees filled seventeen of the twenty-three seats for which evidence survives between 1485 and 1504.[100] The parliamentary borough of Maldon also saw de Vere men being returned – of the six known parliamentary returns between 1485 and 1510, Sir Richard Fitzlewis (1487) and Richard Churchyard (1497) were certainly the earl's men, Sir William Say (1504) and Thomas Hintlesham (1504, 1510), were connected to the earl, and Robert Plummer (1491–2), had done homage for the lands he held of the earl, though he was more closely connected with the earl of Essex.[101] There is no evidence to suggest that de Vere actively sought the election of his men, nor would one expect it, despite the benefits magnates derived from their presence in parliament.[102] Both the wealth and prominence of the earl's retainers and Oxford's virtually unchallenged position in East Anglia meant that the election of his men to parliament would have been a natural process at this period.[103] In contrast with the period before 1485, there is no evidence of disputed elections in the region, such as those of 1461 or 1483, nor indeed of much manipulation of the elections as occurred in 1450 or 1483.[104]

With respect to the shrievalties, Oxford's clientele did not dominate the office as they dominated the parliamentary representation of the region. Of the nineteen men who filled the office of Sheriff of Essex and Hertfordshire in the reign of Henry VII, four were retainers, four others were certainly connected with the earl, and of the remaining ten, several were men primarily resident in Hert-

---

99   Ibid., i, 619–20; ii, 137, 327–8.

100   There are no known MPs for the parliaments of 1510 and 1512 for Essex, Cambridgeshire or Norfolk, and only one MP (Robert Drury) is suggested for Suffolk in 1510: Bindoff, i, 40–1, 88–90, 148–9, 189–91.

101   P.R. Cavill, 'Henry VII and Parliament' (unpublished DPhil thesis, Oxford University, 2005), 230–2; Wedgwood, i, 643–4, and ii, 185 for Churchyard, 688 for Plummer, 747–8 for Say; Bindoff, ii, 365 for Hintlesham. Plummer had sat for the borough three times before 1485. For the homage, see above, 105 n. 78.

102   See the discussion in P.R. Cavill, *The English Parliaments of Henry VII* (Oxford, 2009), 125–8.

103   For the position earlier in the century, when perhaps 14 per cent of MPs in general, and 39 per cent of shire knights in particular, had known links with magnates, see L. Clark, 'Magnates and Their Affinities in the Parliaments of 1386–1421', in *The McFarlane Legacy*, ed. R.H. Britnell and A.J. Pollard (Stroud, 1995), 127–53.

104   R. Virgoe, 'Three Suffolk Parliamentary Elections of the Mid Fifteenth Century', *BIHR*, xxxix (1966), 185–96; idem, 'An Election Dispute of 1483', *Historical Research*, lx (1987), 24–44; idem, 'The Cambridgeshire Election of 1439', *BIHR*, xliv (1973), 95–101; C.H. Williams, 'A Norfolk Parliamentary Election, 1461', *EHR*, xl (1925), 79–86; K.B. McFarlane, 'Parliament and Bastard Feudalism', in idem, *England in the Fifteenth Century*, 3–11. The general disappearance of election indentures after c. 1475 makes the possibility of disputed elections harder to discern, however.

fordshire, where de Vere held less land, or appear to have been outsiders to the
counties, presumably appointed by the king.[105] Among the sheriffs of Norfolk
and Suffolk, the first four sheriffs of Henry VII's reign, Sir John Paston, Sir
Edmund Bedingfield, Sir Ralph Shelton and Robert Lovell, were close associates of Oxford's, perhaps indicating that he had used his influence with the
king to secure the appointment of men he could trust in this difficult period, or
that Henry had asked Oxford's advice, unfamiliar as the king was with his new
realm. Later, only a few men connected with Oxford were appointed, a reflection of his smaller territorial stake, though he may also have taken a decision
not to exert himself in such matters as he felt that he could work effectively
with anyone, given the alignments of royal and comital interests in East Anglia
at this period.[106]

Further evidence of the earl's general disinterest in the selection of sheriffs
is contained in a mutilated document among the warrants for the great seal,
dating from 1497, and which contains a list of three men for each county shrievalty, one of whom in most cases went on to become sheriff. However, in a few
cases the king added a fourth name, usually of a household knight, who was
selected as sheriff, and then signed the document.[107] It has been argued that the
list reflected local opinion, and in certain cases Henry overrode county sensibili-
ties by inserting outsiders, though it is not clear where the list of names originated from and whose opinion it represented.[108] Norfolk and Suffolk was one
shrievalty where the three original knights – William Boleyn, Robert Clere and
Philip Calthorpe – were ignored in favour of a fourth name, Edmund Arundel,
a household knight. Although Essex and Hertfordshire did not have a fourth
name added by the king, all three nominees, Edmund Danyell, John Pirion and
William Tendring, were ignored, and a household knight, Sir John Verney, was
made sheriff. The selection of Verney, who, though primarily a Buckingham-

---

[105] De Vere's retainers were Sir Henry Tey (twice sheriff), Sir Richard Fitzlewis, Sir Roger
Wentworth (twice sheriff), and William Pirton, esquire. Those he had connections with were
Sir Henry Marney (see above, 195), John Leventhorp (who supplied troops in 1487), Sir
John Verney (steward of Chesham in Buckinghamshire in 1485–97 at the fee of 66s 4d:
NRO, Towns. 196, MS 1615, m.2) and Humphrey Tyrell, brother of de Vere's retainer Sir
Thomas. Those who appear to be Hertfordshire landowners, from the evidence of appoint-
ments as JPs, were John Boteler, Robert Turbeville (sheriff in 1490, he was not appointed to
the Essex bench until 1498, but was on the Hertfordshire Bench in 1489), William Pulter,
Robert Newport and William Skipworth. Those who were not appointed to either Bench
were John Berdefield (1491), Thomas Peryent (1497), Verney (1498), Robert Darcy (1505), and
John Broket (1506): *List of Sheriffs for England and Wales, From the Earliest Times to A.D. 1831*
(London, 1898), 45; *CPR, 1485–94*, 486, 488; *1494–1509*, 638–9, 642–3.

[106] After 1488 the men appointed with connections with Oxford were Philip Lewis, esquire
(1490), Sir William Carew (1493), John Shelton, son of Sir Ralph (1504) and Sir Richard
Wentworth (1509). For Paston as sheriff, see Richmond, *Paston Family: Endings*, 165–6.

[107] C82/180; Condon, 'Ruling Elites', 125–6, 140 n. 84; Arthurson, *Perkin Warbeck*, 167.

[108] Condon, 'Ruling Elites', 125–6. The document (C 82/180) is in a standard chancery hand.
Might it have been the product of a council meeting?

shire man, owned four manors in Hertfordshire, was not likely to have been opposed by de Vere because he was the steward of Oxford's manor of Chesham in Buckinghamshire and may indeed have been the earl's suggestion.[109] While it is obvious that the choice of sheriff was of interest to the king, what this also suggests is that Oxford had not paid much attention to the selection: none of the original six names put forward for the two shrievalties had any connection with Oxford, and neither had either sheriff been Oxford's man in the preceding few years.[110] By the autumn of 1497, the king may have been thinking rather less of East Anglia's security, and rather more of efficient administration and increased revenue.

The mutual benefits that multi-faceted military, administrative and legal service to the earl could provide are illustrated by the career of Robert Tyrell (d. 1508). Third son of Sir Thomas Tyrell of Heron (d. 1476), he was no more than adequately endowed by his father, as even by the end of his life his inquisition *post mortem* records only his tenure of the manor of Coggars in Corringham, Essex, worth £10 p.a., and some smaller holdings holding in Thaxted and elsewhere totalling another £7 13s 4d a year. His marriage to Christina, widow of Edward Makwilliam, brought him further estates in Essex worth nearly £20 annually. He was therefore no more than moderately affluent in terms of landed revenue, and compared to many other East Anglian knights he was relatively poor. As a result Tyrell was in a position where service to the earl of Oxford was a desirable goal, and he undertook virtually every role in the earl's administration. He was the parker of the earl's manor of Castle Camps, Cambridgeshire, for a period in the 1480s, and farmed the Vere manor of Downham in 1488–9 and 1499–1500, and probably for the intervening period as well. He took his turn in one of the major and more demanding offices of the administration, serving as controller of the household from at least 1493 to 1495, and he was associated with the earl's property settlements, being appointed as an attorney in the grant of estates to Earls Colne priory in 1492 and as a feoffee in 1507.[111] However, he was not just an administrator. He served in person with two men in the campaign of 1487, and was knighted for his military service at Blackheath. He was almost certainly the earl's annuitant throughout the period, and he introduced his son to the earl's service, as the younger Robert was paid an annuity of 53s 4d a year in the earl's will, and indeed was serving in his father's old office of controller of the household in 1513. Thus for a total of perhaps £15–£20 a year in annuities and wages (an annual fee of £10 was the going rate for controller of the household), and the odd other favour, such as a grant of a wardship, the earl got the exclusive service for more than two decades of an able, hardworking member of the

---

[109] Wedgwood, ii, 905–6; *CIPM Henry VII*, iii, 30, 463.

[110] Sir Richard Fitzlewis, sheriff for Essex and Hertfordshire in 1493–4, and William Carew, sheriff of Norfolk and Suffolk in the same year, were the last close connections.

[111] NRO, Towns 196, MS 1615, m.2; ERO, D/DPr 139, m. 2; D/DBm M501, m. 3d.; D/DPr 124, m. 3; D/DPr 131, m.2; *CCR, 1485–1500*, 226; RH, Box 39.

gentry, who was also ready to risk life and limb for the earl and the king on the battlefield.[112] On Tyrell's part, he not only probably added a third to his annual income but also won personal prestige and a knightly title in the earl's service, both on the battlefield and in the council chamber at Hedingham, and secured a bright future for his son. Both benefited from such an association, and they may even have become friends over their twenty-three-year working relationship.

Such politico-military service became less important after the turn of the century, as de Vere became less evident at court, and the need for military service less pressing: for this reason that the affinity became less militarized. A group of younger, less distinguished and less affluent professional lawyers and administrators began to fill the gaps left in the earl's affinity by the deaths of a number of the older county gentry. Men such as Humphrey Wingfield, William Ayloff, John Aspelon, John Josselyn, John Danyell and William Oakley emerge into prominence at this time. Some were younger sons, while several were not scions of the existing county gentry, but were new men, who founded landed families in Essex. The influence of this new generation was noticeable: Josselyn, Danyell and Oakley were the highest paid members of the affinity outside the earl's family, all being in receipt of £10 p.a., and all of these men were prominent in the earl's last major set of enfeoffments.[113] It is also noticeable that of the ten men, excluding the earl's wife and his cousin John Vere, appointed executors of the earl's will, three, Wingfield, Danyell, and Oakley, were relatively new to the earl's affinity, one, Josselyn, had risen through the ranks to the important position of executor, two more, Thomas Lovell and James Hobart, were professional lawyers and administrators in royal service, though of long acquaintance with de Vere, and only three, Robert Drury, William Waldegrave and Robert Lovell, were of the older generation of county gentry.[114] By 1512, with the Tudor dynasty well established, the smooth administration of the earl's estates and the competent performance of his will would have been as much a priority as large military retinues; younger lawyers and administrators were a sound choice for this purpose.

Both the older generation of county gentry and the newer administrators viewed the earl himself with respect and affection judging by the evidence of wills and letters. At least five of those who died before the earl appointed him supervisor of their will (James Arblaster, Thomas Montgomery, Robert Broughton, William Carew and John Clopton). In 1492 Arblaster appointed the

---

[112] Tyrell and another unnamed man were granted the wardship of Richard, son of Thomas Bendish, in January 1502: Bodleian, Rawlinson B 257, p. 2.

[113] Oakley and Danyell were members of the earl's household in 1507–8: see below, 231, 234, 239; Rawcliffe and Flower, 'Noblemen and their Advisors', 165–6. It might be that several of these men were holding important positions in the earl's administration, but there are no estate accounts around this time.

[114] 'Last Testament', 318. The tenth was Dr William Cooke, who had been associated with de Vere since 1471: PL, v, 94; RH, Box 38.

earl as supervisor in return for the 'love and service' he had shown the earl since childhood, and asked to be buried at the foot of the tomb built for the twelfth earl and his countess.[115] Five years after the earl's death, Oxford was clearly still remembered with respect by John Danyell, who, in making his will in May 1518, specified that the chantry priest at Felsted shall 'specilly pray for the soule of the full noble and valyant knyght my late singuler good lorde and maister John de Veer, late erle of Oxenford'.[116] Friendly relations existed between the earl and several of his affinity, both those in the wider circle whom he directly called 'friend', such as Thomas Lovell, and in the inner circle, evidence of which can be seen in the letter to John Paston which fulsomely thanks him for a gift and that the earl 'would be right glad to se you in these parties' and if not, he would shortly be going to 'to se you in those parties, and than to thank you for your right gode and louyng remembraunce … which shall nat be in my behalue forgotyn'.[117] It is easier to exercise leadership if the leader is respected and liked.

Conclusion

For all de Vere's unusual political dominance in East Anglia the extant evidence for his retaining and household would suggest a more typical magnate, rather one who dominated four counties, with the exception of the unusually wide geographical spread of the affinity. His retaining, with the proviso that he may have spent more a decade or two earlier than he did in 1509, suggests an affinity of moderate size, and his expenditure was a typical 10 per cent. Certainly de Vere cannot be compared to the fourth Percy earl of Northumberland, who was spending over £1000 on extraordinary fees in 1489, approximately 25 per cent of his income, though de Vere had the political dominance of an equally large region. Nor does Oxford's retinue compare to the ninety men, including two peers, nine knights, fifty-nine esquires and twenty gentlemen retained by William, Lord Hastings, in Edward IV's reign.[118] Despite de Vere spending over £200 a year on annuities for twelve knights and thirty-three esquires and gentlemen, the fees he paid were in general rather low, and this was in any case a small percentage of the county gentry in the four counties of Essex, Cambridgeshire, Norfolk and Suffolk. However, posts in his administration and as deputies in his royal offices may have been equally remunerative and probably were used in many cases as alternatives to cash fees.

Yet this average cash expenditure masks the sheer power of his affinity which

[115]   PROB 11/9, fol. 124v.
[116]   PROB 11/19, fol. 102r.
[117]   *PLP*, ii, 487.
[118]   Bean, *Estates of the Percy Family*, 129; W.H. Dunham, *Lord Hastings' Indentured Retainers, 1461–83. The Lawfulness of Livery and Retaining under the Yorkists and Tudors* (New Haven, CT, 1955), 27.

secured East Anglia and played a major role on English battlefields at the end
of the fifteenth century. In part, a lesser level of expenditure was compensated
for by the fact that he was retaining many of the most prominent men in the
region, for while many were knighted as a result of their military service with
the earl, the upper ranks of his followers comprised very wealthy men. For those
whose incomes can be established, three had incomes of over £200, six more
between £100 and £200 and three more between £50 and £100.[119] These were
the 'gentylmen of as grete sobestaunce that thei be able to bye alle Lankeschere',
and the wealth and power of his affinity should not be underestimated, especially
since almost all were exclusively in his service.[120] If there were between sixty
and seventy heads of greater gentry families in East Anglia at the end of the
fifteenth century, at least a third were retained, employed or closely associated
with the earl.[121] Association with the earl did not guarantee compliance with his
commands, but direct refusal would have been more difficult as it would have
put a knight in opposition to not only Oxford, but his own peer group, and
potentially against the king as well.

The earl's competence in assembling, managing and maintaining a coherent
affinity for two decades should not be understated. It was clearly loyal; during a
reign when many men found their allegiances severely tested, none of Oxford's
associates deserted to Yorkist pretenders or claimants. The affinity's multi-
faceted service allowed it to be one of the major foundations of his political
power in East Anglia, comprise the bulk of his military following, keep disorder
to a minimum and not form one of the causes of such disorder, manage the earl's
estates and household, deputize for him in numerous offices, and counsel him in
legal issues. Lastly, he managed all this without expending more than an average
sum on formal retaining fees. Taken together, this was an impressive achievement; the earl was clearly a good judge of men, and adept at managing them.

As discussed at the outset, this chapter on the earl's affinity, has, for obvious
reasons, focused on those who can obviously be identified as being members of
his household, administration, or whom he retained. Of course, such paid officials and feed retainers are only half the picture. If Lord Hastings paid cash to
only two of his sixty-nine indentured retainers, instead substituting 'good lordship' in place of a fee, then Oxford, while still paying considerable numbers of
annuitants, may also have promised to be a good lord to a number of men to

---

[119]   See directory in the Appendix, 229–39. Those whose incomes cannot be established, such
as William Carew, John Paston, Robert Lovell, Richard Fitzlewis, and Roger Wentworth,
were almost certainly of equivalent wealth to these men.
[120]   *PL*, vi, 122.
[121]   Heads of greater gentry families included Alington, Bedingfield, Brewes, Broughton,
Carew, Clopton, Cotton, Drury, Fitzlewis, Fyndern, Grene, Lovell, Montgomery, Paston,
Payton, Shelton, Say, Tey, Tyrell, Waldegrave and Wentworth (21), younger sons included
Humphrey Wingfield, and the Heigham family might or might not be included in the elite
group.

whom he was not paying life fees.[122] He was able to draw on the resources of those to whom he cannot otherwise be connected to assemble a large fighting force, following the evidence of the household books of 1487 and the Herald's account in 1489 – presumably he was able to continue to do so throughout his later life. A full military retinue list has not survived, and this might well show just how widely Oxford was able to recruit. More generally, it may be that more informal connections which can no longer be reconstructed, which had favour and 'good lordship' as their basis rather than cash, as well as strong personal links with those outside his immediate circle were equally important in the earl's political dominance.

---

[122] Dunham, *Hastings' Indentured Retainers*, 9. However, Hastings may well have been the exception rather than the rule in the composition of his indentures: M. Jones and S. Walker, 'Private Indentures for Life Service in Peace and War, 1278–1476', *Camden Miscellany XXXII* (Camden Society, 5th series, iii, 1994); M.A. Hicks, 'Lord Hastings' Indentured Retainers', in his *Richard III and his Rivals*, 229–46.

7

Private and Public

Despite the earl's relatively well-documented public career, he remains something of a shadowy figure in terms of his personality. Oxford perhaps has more sources than most late medieval noblemen, though in quality or quantity they do not match those of his cousin, John Howard, but no full personal study could be written – the best that can be done in terms of appraising his character is to survey what we know of his activities outside of the political sphere, which allows a glimpse of a more rounded individual. Some of the evidence for such activities does, however, come from the earl's last testament, which must be treated with caution, as preparations for the afterlife are not necessarily the best guide to an individual's outlook on life being lived. Other sources, such as household expense accounts, provide detail on his day to day life, but were written by his officials, rather than the earl himself. In light of the lacunae in the evidence, much of what follows must be suggestive rather than conclusive.

Family relationships

It is clear that Oxford had a strong sense of his lineage, and that his relationships with members of his family mattered a great deal. One immediate reason why his family was so important to him may have been that he had lost so many members of it during his lifetime. In 1485, when forty-three, he had neither surviving grandparents nor parents, and three of his four brothers were dead. Although he had no children of his own, his sole surviving brother did produce children after 1485, but the earl was already looking further afield for family. As early as 1490, his cousin John, grandson of the brother of the twelfth earl, and aged around eight, had been placed in the earl's care by his parents, and was being educated for future service; he was second in line to the comital dignity by 1503.[1] The earl kept his sole surviving brother close to him after his return

---

[1]   The vicar of 'Kocsall', probably Coggeshall, was paid for the board of John Vere, and two other boys, Nicholas Wentworth and John Pilkington: *Household Books*, 508, 509. They may have been at a local school.

to England; it is likely that George was primarily resident at his family home at Hedingham, rather than on one of the three scattered manors in Essex, Suffolk or Cambridgeshire that formed his endowment from his brother. Clearly present on some formal occasions, George's absence from the enfeoffments that otherwise provide the best evidence of who was around the earl may be explained that as the then heir male and a likely beneficiary of whatever settlement was being made, he was not appropriate as a feoffee.[2] George's second marriage to Margaret, daughter of William Stafford of Frome, produced three daughters and one surviving son and heir, John, born in 1499. George was clearly sought after as an influential man; for example, he was appointed chief steward of the abbey of St Osyth by 1491 at the fee of £5 p.a.[3] George died in 1503.[4]

One crucial area of his personal life, his relationships with his two wives, remains difficult to gauge. He might have resented his first wife Margaret, if the marriage took place in the early 1460s, as the sister of the then Yorkist Warwick, but he followed Warwick enthusiastically soon after, and marriages of political convenience were the norm. The only extant letter between the two, written in the aftermath of Barnet, was composed at such a desperate time that nothing should be read into the juxtaposed businesslike practicalities and unconvincing reassurance.[5] Almost no other evidence survives as to their relationship, though Countess Margaret acted as his deputy in East Anglia when the earl was absent, writing a practical and authoritative letter to John Paston in 1486 on the receipt of news of the fugitive Lord Lovell, and she was also frequently at court with the earl in the first few years of the reign.[6] Margaret died between 20 November 1506 and 14 January 1507; on the latter date the earl's household account notes the delivery on that date of 'suche things as was about the herse at Colne of my lady'.[7] This brought to an end approximately forty years of marriage, although fourteen

---

[2] For occasions when George was present: C255/8/4, nos 143–4; BL, Add. Ch. 16570.

[3] R.C. Fowler, 'A Balance Sheet of St. Osyth Abbey', *TEAS*, n.s., xix (1927), 190.

[4] *CP*, x, 244. His will, naming the earl as the supervisor and containing bequests to his children and a number of religious institutions, is printed in *TEAS*, n.s., xxi (1933–4), 261–3; *Hall's Chronicle*, 452, reports a brother (no first name given) of the earl dying at the naval assault on Sluys in 1492. George is the only known brother alive at this date, but the wage and expense accounts record a John Veer, joint captain of a Spanish ship called 'La John de St. Sebastiane', who disappears towards the end of the campaign: E 36/208, pp. 16, 67, 71. If this man was an Englishman, he could, perhaps, be an illegitimate brother of the earl. I am grateful to Dr Steven Gunn for the suggestion and reference.

[5] *PL*, v, 101–2. See above, 67–8.

[6] *PL*, vi, 92, for the Lovell letter, and she also wrote a friendly missive to Paston, in his capacity as a Norfolk JP, on behalf of her servant, John Malpas, at some point after 1485: ibid., 165. For her presence at court see *Herald's Memoir*, 131, 141, 147, 151, 153, 154.

[7] Longleat, Misc. xi, fol. 143r. Former date from an account of funerals by Wriothesley: BL, Add MS 45131, fol. 161; A. Payne, 'Sir Thomas Wriothesley and his Heraldic Artists', in *Illuminating the Book Makers and Interpreters*, ed. M.P. Brown and S. McKendrick (London, 1998), 156. I am grateful to Christian Steer for bringing this to my attention.

of the first twenty had been spent apart. Evidence from the household account
hints at a lengthy mourning period that could indicate a degree of happiness to
the marriage. The earl and the entire comital household remained stationary at
Wivenhoe for at least seven months, from the start of the account on 1 January
1507 until 20 July when a marginal notation stated that 'the lord rode to the
lord king at Cambridge', in whose company he remained until 6 August when
he returned to Wivenhoe.[8] While noble households were increasingly stationary
by the late fifteenth century (though the use of two or three residences annually
was more usual), such a lengthy stay by the earl is surprising for a normally busy
noblemen, who might have been expected to have journeyed with his travelling
household, for business or leisure, much more frequently.[9] It is suggestive that
he spent the period in mourning, and the fact that the sojourn was at a hitherto
less frequented residence could indicate that their regular home at Hedingham
reminded him too much of his deceased wife, though this can only be specula-
tion.

Grief at the loss of his wife might be one explanation that de Vere put off
remarriage, though he was childless and sixty-four at his wife's death, until two
years later, when approximately a year after William, Lord Beaumont's death, he
married his widow, Elizabeth, daughter of Sir Richard Scrope.[10] The marriage
took place around November 1508, when the earl settled property on her.[11] One
is tempted to suggest that this was a match made for reasons other than policy
or profit, despite her substantial dower, not least as, born around 1468, she would
have been close to the end of her child-bearing years. She and her husband
had been living in Oxford's care, mainly at his manor of Wivenhoe, since 1487,
and there would have been opportunity for affection to grow between them.
However, the earl's second marriage may simply have been a way of retaining as
many of the Beaumont estates as he could, and Elizabeth's dower may have been
more of an attraction than her person. Although there is no surviving marriage
settlement, it is clear from the evidence of the earl's will that Oxford agreed that

[8]   Longleat, Misc. xi, fols 49r, 52v. The earl took short trips to his lodge at Lavenham for
ten days in September, spent five days later the same month at St Osyth's, presumably with
the abbot, to whom there are other references in the account, and was absent from 6 to 22
October, though where is not specified: ibid., fols 58r–64r.
[9]   For increasingly stationary great households and mobile travelling households, such as that
of the duke of Buckingham, see Woolgar, *Great Household*, chap. 4. There is little evidence for
the other obvious explanation for the prolonged sojourn at Wivenhoe, a lengthy illness: there
are no payments to physicians in the 'foreign' expenses section of the household account and
he made at least four trips to the parish church, rather than use his private household chapel
which one might expect if he was very unwell.
[10]   J. Ward, 'Elizabeth Beaumont, Countess of Oxford (d. 1537): Her Life and Connections',
Transactions of the Monumental Brass Society, xvii (2003), 2–13; H.W. Lewer, 'The Testament
and Last Will of Elizabeth, Widow of John de Veer, Thirteenth Earl of Oxford', *TEAS*, n.s.,
xx (1933), 7–16.
[11]   The earl's settlement was on 28 November. They were certainly married by the making of
his will on 10 April 1509: C142/28/83; 'Last Testament', 310.

Elizabeth should receive a substantial jointure of twenty-seven manors in East Anglia according to 'suche covenants as are therof expressed and comprised in certeyn endentures made betwene me on the oon party and Rauff Scrope, doctor of divinitie, Sir Roger Wentworth knight and Sir Richard Wentworth knight, on thoder party concernyng the marriage had bitwene me and my said wif'.[12] This was generous of the earl, as she was already in possession of dower estates from her first husband worth over £500 p.a., and she was to be entitled to dower from those of Oxford's estates which were not enfeoffed to use.

Oxford's familial relationships were not just with the living; his actions towards his deceased parents demonstrate something of the earl as a man. Echoing Warwick's reburial of the earl of Salisbury and Edward IV's of York and Rutland, all three killed at or just after the battle of Wakefield in 1460, and despite the reinterment of his father in 1464, Oxford chose to move the twelfth earl, his countess Elizabeth and, presumably, his brother Aubrey from their graves at the Austin Friars in London to the family mausoleum at Earls Colne. The will of the devoted de Vere servant James Arblaster, made 5 July 1492, requests that he be buried 'at Colne Priory even at the foot of the tombe that is nowe made for my Lorde of Oxenford fader and my especiall good lady his modre.'[13] A bequest later in the will of 10 marks to the thirteenth earl 'to his charge warde to bring my Lady his modre is bonnys to Colne' shows that Countess Elizabeth, interred in 1473 alongside her husband in the Austin Friars, had not yet been reburied.[14] That the thirteenth earl carried out the planned reburial of his father is confirmed by a set of antiquarian notes on the family, now in the British Library. Written about 1571, before the dispersal and destruction of the tombs at Earls Colne, the author saw the effigies there, and his recording on the inscription of the tomb of the twelfth earl at Colne may be taken as accurate.[15]

[12] PROB11/17, fol. 87r. Twenty-five manors in Essex and Hertfordshire were acquired by a group of feoffees in several separate collusive actions in Common Pleas in the Trinity term of 1507. At this stage they were enfeoffed for use for the performance of the earl's will, as Viscount Beaumont did not die until December 1507, but their use was altered by the earl: CP40/981, rots. 519, 581. Countess Elizabeth received two other manors, East Bergholt and Weeting, in jointure but it is not clear from the will as to whether this was part of a marriage settlement or a later arrangement: PROB11/17, fol. 87v.

[13] PROB11/9, fol. 124r.

[14] PROB11/9, fol. 124v. According to the deposition of John Power in 1495, she died at the nunnery of Stratford at Bow in Essex, but two days later, in the presence of the duke of Gloucester, John Howard and others, she was entombed before the high altar in the Austin Friars: Hicks, 'Last Days', 95.

[15] BL, Cott.Vesp. B XV, fol. 85v notes that at the time of writing Edward, seventeenth earl of Oxford, was in the ninth year of his earldom. Edward succeeded his father in August 1562. Various seventeenth-century antiquarians, including John Weever and Daniel King, saw the remnants of the tombs at Colne, and none mentions that of the twelfth earl, but the dispersal and destruction of some of the tombs occurred between the sale of the estate by Edward earl of Oxford in 1592, and a survey taken in 1598, by which date the priory church had been destroyed: see the detailed and comprehensive description by F.H. Fairweather, 'Colne

The inscription stated that 'Here lieth the noble Lord John Veer Erle of Oxford and viscount Bulbeck which for his true minde and suer allegians due unto King Henry 6th under King Ed 4th suffred death at the towre the 26 February in the year of Christes incarnation 1461'.[16]

The earl granted two manors in May 1492 to Earls Colne priory for 'the honour of God, the Virgin Mary and St John the Evangelist [the latter two being the patron saints of the priory], for the health of my soul and those of my ancestors'.[17] Given the close correspondence in the dates between the grant and the 'tombe nowe made' in July, it is likely that this was connected with the planned reburial; as the thirteenth earl was on campaign in France in the autumn of that year, winter 1492 or spring 1493 was the most likely date for the reinterment. What no source states is what ceremony took place at the reburial, how much the earl spent, and whether he made it a public spectacle for East Anglian society, though this seems likely. The reburial of Richard, duke of York, at Fotheringhay in 1476, though certainly on a more magnificent scale than Oxford could have managed, gives some indication of the type of ceremonial possible. The hearse stopped each night at a parish church on route, where alms were given to all who came; 400 poor men on foot accompanied the body, as well as mounted men of higher social status. A life-size effigy of the duke, on a hearse covered in innumerable candles, heraldic badges and images of kings and saints, was the focus of the interment ceremony at the final destination, while at the final feast 5000 people were given alms.[18]

It is should not be seen as surprising that the earl waited so long to translate the bodies. It would have been impolitic to have done so between 1464 and 1469, when the reburial of traitors to Edward IV would have been a charged political action; the first reburial in 1464 made sure the conspirators in 1462 were 'sumptuously interred' at the Austin Friars, a high status church with a number of other earls and important men buried there.[19] Equally, the early years of Henry VII's reign were fraught, and Oxford was busy hanging onto his newly recovered earldom by supporting the usurping Tudor, and perhaps did not have the leisure to contemplate moving the previous incumbent.

What are we to make with Oxford's concern with, and knowledge of, his family lineage and history throughout his life? Certain actions make obvious political sense – the reversal of an attainder would have been a priority of most

---

Priory, Essex, and the Burials of the Earls of Oxford', *Archaeologia*, lxxxvii (1937), 275–95. A number of other epitaphs given in Cotton Vesp. B XV correspond to later accounts of them by Weever and King.

[16] BL, Cott. Vesp. B XV, fol. 75v.

[17] C54/354, m. 20d; *CCR, 1485–1500*, 226; *CPR, 1485–1494*, 260. For the dating of the close roll entry, see above 112 n. 106.

[18] *The Reburial of Richard Duke of York, 21–30 July 1476*, ed. A.F. Sutton, L. Visser-Fuchs and P.W. Hammond (Richard III Society, 1996), 8–19, 37–40.

[19] Weever, *Ancient Funeral Monuments*, 418; *A Survey of London: by John Stow*, ed. C.L. Kingsford (2 vols, Oxford, 1908), i, 178–9.

noble families, especially as it might have led to the recovery of estates, and the earl's actions in 1464 in repealing the duke of Ireland's attainder are understandable in the light of the change of dynasty, though it is interesting that the twelfth earl did not ask the malleable Henry VI to do the same. The antiquity of his family, and their more recent sufferings for the house of Lancaster, would have been a point worth emphasizing in the reign of Henry VII; the reburial of his parents in 1492 may have been a reminder of both to East Anglian society. His distinguished descent, however, was a theme picked up by contemporaries. A poem by one Thomas Rotheley, using a boar to stand for the earl (playing on the Latin verres/Vere, and indeed an image the earl himself used),[20] emphasizes ancient lineage, as well as his devotion to a cause:

> In hys persone ys founde so pure verité
> And standyth so clene wyhtowte transgresse
> That all England may ioy hys natiuité.
> Of contynewyng trwth he standyth pereles,
> Hys Progenie neuer distayned with falsenes.
> Syth hys fyrst day he hathe contynwyd so demure
> Unto now that he is here colowred with azure
>
> Now unto thys blew bore honour and grace,
> Ioy, laude, and praysyng, fortune and magnyfycens.
> Criste graunt hym of such grace suche ioy to purchace
> As may be worthy unto hys reuerence.
> Foreuyre in feyfull trouth hathe ben hys permanence;
> Wherefore now of all England he hathe avauntage,
> Owte excepte the blode ryall the most trwyste lynage.[21]

The earl's own interest in his lineage was clear. In the preface to a later work the printer and scholar Caxton noted that at the request of Oxford himself,

[20] In the inventory of his goods there were a number of expensive items incorporating the blue boar badge: 'Last Testament', 328; see *Heraldic Badges in England and Wales*, ed. M.P. Siddons (3 vols in 4, Woodbridge, 2009), ii.2, 300–1 for the use of the boar badge and 301 for the use of a mullet (see following footnote).

[21] Hanna and Redworth, 'Rotheley, the de Vere Circle and the Ellesmere Chaucer', 33. Hanna and Redworth suggest a date earlier than 1485 (p. 26), while Ethel Seaton dates it to 1468–9: *Sir Richard Roos, c. 1410–1482: Lancastrian Poet* (London, 1961), 424. Yet the references to the de Vere star that 'nowe hathe dominacion' and 'Cryste graunt the contynewyng tyme and space that the mollet may resplende ouer euery region' would suggest a period when de Vere was in the ascendancy, such as the Readeption or after 1485, though why at either period the poet would be in prison, as he explicitly states he is, is not clear. Hanna and Redworth identified several Rotheleys at this period, but as a result of their earlier dating went for a John Rotheley, perhaps of West Caister, Norfolk. However, with a later dating, the most likely candidate to have written the poem is probably Thomas Rotheley of Witham, Essex. The Essex location is one reason, and he had a connection once removed to the earl, having served as an attorney in a feoffment made in 1489 by Sir Thomas Montgomery, a de Vere annuitant: *A Descriptive Catalogue of Ancient Deeds in the Public Record Office* (6 vols in 7, London, 1890–1915), iv, 205, 208. Seaton dismisses any Rotheley as a candidate for authorship and opines that the poem must have been written by Sir Richard Roos (pp. 422–4).

he had translated a French life 'of one of his predecessors named Robert Earl of Oxford toforesaid with diverse and many great miracles'.[22] No copies of the original French manuscript or the printed translation have survived, but, as there is a reference to miracles in the work, the subject is most likely to have been Robert, sixth earl, 'whose government both in peace and warre was so prudent, his hospitalitie and other workes of charitie so wisely abundant; and his Temperance with a religious zeale so admirablie conioyned, that he was surnamed the good Earle of Oxford; and the vulgar esteemed him as a saint'.[23] There was clearly a public aspect to Oxford's request if it was printed, and it could only further publicize his ancestry. Yet there may have been a very personal motive behind this and many of his activities connected to his family history were more private, such as the bequests in his will to nineteen religious institutions founded by his ancestors.

Other family business necessitated parliamentary or public acts. Although the reversal of the earl's attainder in 1485 included a revocation of all releases made by the countess of Oxford to Richard of Gloucester, this did not end the matter. In the parliament of 1495 Countess Elizabeth's enforced grants of her lands to Duke Richard in 1473 were formally annulled again.[24] Although the 1485 act made void any release or grant by the countess to Gloucester, and it 'was, still is, fully and publicly known by a great part of this realm' that the grants were made by compulsion, coercion and imprisonment, 'yet there was no mention made on record of any witness or proof of it'. Therefore 'various worshipful and trustworthy persons have come to this present parliament at the instance and desire of the said earl' to testify to it. Regardless of other considerations, one motivation was surely that placing further detail on the formal rolls of parliament documented his family's suffering at the hands of Gloucester, and emphasized the Lancastrian credentials of the de Vere line. The particular timing of this move, however, probably had more prosaic considerations. Michael Hicks has suggested that it may have been Thomas Howard's parliamentary business in 1495, which restored many estates granted by Richard III to his father, John Howard, that prompted Oxford's efforts to ensure that his title to his mother's estates, including Wivenhoe (purchased by John Howard), was unassailable.[25] Ownership to three other estates, which St George's, Windsor allegedly discussed with him not long before his decease and laid claim to after his death, might also have prompted a search for a stronger legal position.[26] It is interesting, however, that de Vere chose not to allow St George's to have the manors, certainly by the tenor of his acts in parliament, if not an outright refusal at the end of his life.

---

[22] Quoted in G.D. Painter, *William Caxton. A Quincentenary Biography of England's First Printer* (London, 1976), 164–5.

[23] Weever, *Funeral Monuments*, 616.

[24] *Parliament Rolls*, xvi, 171–3; Hicks, 'Last Days', 297–316.

[25] Hicks, 'Last Days', 300–1.

[26] For the case, and the deliberate inaccuracies uttered by St George's in pursuing their spurious claim, see the author's 'Richard, Duke of Gloucester, and the de Vere Estates', 29–30.

When contrasted with his generosity to other ecclesiastical institutions, discussed below, it was clear that the earl required religious patronage to be on his terms.

This sense of family can be seen in the earl's long will of 1512 which sought to settle his estates after his death.[27] The will made a number of short-term arrangements. In summary, Oxford's wife Elizabeth, if she survived him, was to have twenty-seven manors and smaller holdings in jointure during her life, with the manors to descend after her death to the earl's heirs. The remaining manors were evenly split between feoffees for the performance of his will, and the heir male. The earl left the possibility of a male child with his new wife open, but the strong likelihood at nearly seventy years of age was that the estates would descend to his nephew, son of his brother George, with a second reversion in the event of his nephew not having male children to his cousin John. Forty-two manors were to be held for between twenty and twenty-four years for the performance of his earlier testament of 1509, and only then descend to his heir male.[28] Eleven manors were to go in jointure to his nephew and male heir John and his wife, Anne Howard, and the remaining thirty-two 'of the olde inheritance of myn Erldom' were to descend immediately to his male heir. Three manors continued to be held for life by Margaret, widow of his brother George, and were then to descend to John and Anne jointly. However, Countess Elizabeth was entitled to dower from those estates not enfeoffed to use; these comprised the thirty-two manors designated for the heir male. Ten manors and other property in five counties were assigned from this group to Elizabeth for her dower between July and October 1513, extended at £237 p.a.[29]

The descent of the estates of the earldom in the longer term was carefully considered. Most estates were to descend eventually to his nephew, John. Should his nephew die without male offspring, the earl followed the male line of descent, with lands he inherited from the de Vere line or had purchased to descend to his cousin John and his male offspring, and, in default of such issue, to the right heirs of his grandfather, Earl Richard. However, the estates of his mother were, if his nephew failed to have any children, to descend to the right heirs of his mother's body, then to his nieces; the next male heir, his cousin John, was not an heir to Elizabeth Howard's estates. Following the blood lines, rather than trying to divert estates away, was designed to avoid future law suits. To ensure that all this was legal and to break any previous enfeoffments, Oxford, in a series of collusive actions in the court of Common Pleas in Trinity term 1507, had legally lost many of his manors to a select group of feoffees, and had recovered them in the same court in Michaelmas term 1512, a process known as a common recovery.[30] These actions had close scrutiny by the earl's council, his lawyers, and Sir Robert Reed, chief justice of Common Pleas, who 'at his last being with me'

---

[27] PROB11/17, fols 86v–90r.
[28] PROB11/17, fols 86v–90v.
[29] C142/28/153–7.
[30] CP40/981, rots. 515 (Cambs.) 516d. (Bucks.), 518 (Suffolk), 519 (Herts.), 581 (Essex).

had discussed the tactics to be employed.[31] Other members of his family were not forgotten; his younger nieces, Dorothy and Ursula, were to have '600 markes that is to sey to either of theym 300 markes the same to be delivered unto either of theym at their agis of 24 yeres or bifore if they be married'.[32]

The fourteenth earl proved to be an unmitigated disaster as a successor, but at least his period as earl was short. He died aged just twenty-six and childless, and was succeeded by his cousin, John, an eventuality foreseen in the thirteenth earl's will. The complexity of the settlement of the estates in 1512 did not forestall a further re-arrangement of the estates between the fifteenth earl and the three sisters of the fourteenth earl and their husbands, who were heirs to Elizabeth Howard's inheritance, but not to the older estates of the earldom. A huge jointure granted to the fourteenth earl's widow complicated the picture further, and there was some violence committed by the fifteenth earl against her estates before a high powered committee, including the dukes of Norfolk and Suffolk, induced a settlement. After much bargaining, some of Elizabeth Howard's estates stayed with the earldom and some of the older estates of the earldom went to the female co-heirs.[33]

Religion and interests

It is notoriously difficult to assess an individual's personal beliefs, and in an age where outward conformity to religious norms was obligatory, it is sometimes only when exceptional or excessive behaviour is found that one can comment. The only conclusion that one can reach on the piety of the thirteenth earl of Oxford is that he appears to have been conventional in his religious beliefs and followed standard forms in their expression. Such is the case with the arrangements made in his will for the celebration of 2000 masses to be said for his soul by any priest or friar within 'any house of Religion of the foundacion of any of myn auncesters', in return for 3s 4d for each mass, at a total cost of £333.[34] Other evidence supports the notion of conventional belief. He undertook a pilgrimage to Walsingham at some point before 1503 and he owned a number of religious works.[35]

---

[31] PROB11/17, fol. 87v.

[32] 'Last Testament', 316. The eldest niece, Elizabeth, had presumably already married Anthony Wingfield and received a marriage portion at that date.

[33] For the political background, see S.J. Gunn, *Charles Brandon, Duke of Suffolk, c.1484–1545* (Oxford, 1988), 84–5. Copies of the division of the estates can be found in WARD2/36/144/2 and E41/220, and enrolled on the statute roll: *Statutes of the Realm* (11 vols, London, 1810–28), iii, 412–5.

[34] 'Last Testament', 310–11.

[35] *PLP*, ii, 487. Oxford to John Paston, datable only to before John Paston's death in 1503. For the books, see below 218–19.

The earl's patronage of a large number of monastic institutions might also be evidence of a conventional piety, or of his dynastic and familial interests, or both. He was generous throughout his life to religious institutions. His grant of two manors to the family priory of Earls Colne in 1492 shortly before his parents' reburial increased that institution's landed endowment by a third.[36] His will records a large number of bequests to religious houses, generally founded by his ancestors, either in the male line or other families who married into the comital dynasty. They were the Benedictine priory of Earls Colne, which received an enormous bequest of goods and chapel gear, the Black Friars of Cambridge, the Black Friars of Oxford, the White Friars of Lynn, 'which houses of freers be of the foundacion of myn Auncesters', the abbey of St Osyth (Essex), Woburn (Bedfordshire), Medmenham (Buckinghamshire), the nunneries of Swaffham Bulbeck (Cambridgeshire), Castle Hedingham (Essex), Blackborough (Norfolk) and Ickleton (Cambridgeshire), the priories of Hatfield Broadoak, Thremhall, Blackmore (Essex), Bromehill, Hempton (Norfolk) and Royston (Hertfordshire), all 'beyng of the Foundac[i]on of myn Auncestres aswell men as women', the abbeys of St John's Colchester and Syon (Middlesex), the nunnery of Bruisyard (Suffolk), and the Charterhouses at Sheen and London. There was also a bequest to the Cathedral of St John the Baptist at Amiens in Picardy, either somewhere he visited in exile, or evidence of a particular attachment to St John, whose head was believed to be buried there. The bequests to these houses, with one or two exceptions, and also to 'suche p[ar]isshe churches where I have Mano[r]s, lands and tene[ment]s' was of 'the stuff of my chapell', and if that should not suffice, his executors should provide from his estates.[37] The nineteenth-century editor of the earl's will expressed startlement at the sheer amount of chapel material owned by the earl, but if one considers there were at least three chapels within Castle Hedingham itself, and residual material at other residences, the quantity is less surprising.[38] All bequests were made in return for prayers for the earl's soul, and those of his wife, his children (if he had any), his father, mother, brothers, sisters and all of his ancestors. Such a varied list of institutions to be patronized – two orders of friars, two Cistercian abbeys, six houses of Augustinian canons, two houses of Benedictine monks, and four of nuns, and one Franciscan nunnery – showed no particular attachment to any monastic order. The patronage was focused on the houses founded by his ancestors, to which he clearly felt he had a responsibility, and not about religious attachments to any particular house or order (with the possible excep-

---

[36] The net value of the priory of Earls Colne by the dissolution was £156 p.a.: *Valor Ecclesiasticus*, i, 444. The two manors were worth £50 net in the 1480s.

[37] 'Last Testament', 311–13. Exceptions included 20 marks to Bruisyard for repairs, and specific bequests of particular chapel items to Woburn, Colchester, Amiens and the Black Friars at Cambridge.

[38] 'Last Testament', 301. In ascending order of size, the closet, the keep, and a free standing chapel in the bailey: Mertes, *English Noble Households*, 47.

tion of the Carthusian houses at Sheen and London), though obviously prayers for his soul wherever undertaken were to be welcomed. Of the houses, only Earls Colne, Hatfield Broadoak, and Hedingham nunnery had been founded by ancestors in the male line; two had been established by widowed countesses of Oxford (the Blackfriars at Oxford and Cambridge), while a further nine were founded by ancestors in the female line (Bolebec, Sandford, Mountfichet, Plaiz, Scales). However in at least five cases it is not entirely clear what relationship he claimed to the reputed founder.[39] One can only presume he had an extremely good knowledge of a family tree extending back centuries, or that the institutions in question sought out the contemporary representatives of their founders. The earl also made a bequest of an antiphoner to the parish church at Stoke-by-Nayland, Suffolk (a Howard residence), and £20 each to the (re)building of the churches of Lavenham and Harwich (both de Vere manors).[40]

The earl was also associated with two guilds in Essex, being a member of that of St John the Baptist at Thaxted, along with his associates Robert Tyrell and John Grene, and others in 1507.[41] He was involved with a second guild, that of St Helen in Colchester, where in 1510 property was leased by the guild to the prior of the Crutched or Crossed Friars in Colchester in return for masses to be said by two friars daily for the souls of Henry IV and V, and prayers for the welfare of Henry VIII and for the 'prosperity and heath of the illustrious Lord John, earl of Oxford, lord high admiral'. The deed was assented to, and signed by, the earl and Thomas Bonham, esquire, 'fundatores'. Oxford was not a founder of the guild, though he was probably a member, but was a benefactor of the Friars, as, according to the Essex antiquary Morant, they had been reinstated in the hospital of St Helen's early in Henry VII's reign by Oxford and James Hobart.[42]

Day-to-day evidence of his religious life, while reinforcing the theme of a conventional religiosity, had less connection with his family's foundations, and could indicate a certain degree of piety. The earl's household accounts in 1507 record several payments during Lent to various religious for sermons preached in the presence of the earl in the parish church at Wivenhoe. The provincial of the Black Friars of Cambridge received 10s for preaching, as did a friar of Oxford.[43] Other payments, at the lower rate of 6s 8d a sermon, included those to a bachelor of Theology at Cambridge, a Master Buckenham of Cambridge, to Dr Brynkley of Bakewell on the feast of the Annunciation of the Virgin Mary, and

[39] The White Friars at Lynn (Bardolf), St Osyth (Richard, bishop of London), Ickelton (Valoignes), Hempton (Roger de St. Martin) and Royston (Eustace de Merk/Ralph de Rochester): 'Last Testament', 313. The editor of the will, Hope, gives the founder of Ickelton as perhaps Aubrey de Vere in 1190, but see *VCH Cambridgeshire*, ii, 223.

[40] 'Last Testament', 317. The earl notes he had given £20 previously to Lavenham church, where the de Vere arms are very prominent on the magnificent building.

[41] ERO, D/Dsh/Q1.

[42] ERO, D/DRg 6/8; Morant, 'Colchester', in his *History of Essex*, i, 150, and, in less detail, *VCH Essex*, ii, 181–2.

[43] Longleat, Misc. xi, fol. 116.

to a friar of Colchester on an unspecified date in March.[44] At Easter itself, one Talbot, a doctor of Theology, preached in the presence of the earl in his chapel at Wivenhoe, on both Good Friday and Easter Sunday. He was paid in total 13s 4d, with the price of the word of God being put at 6s 8d a time. Other evidence from the same account includes the purchase of bread to celebrate mass in the 'chapel and in the closet of the lord'.[45] The gift of 6s 8d to the parish priest of Wivenhoe by 'mandate of the lord in honour of St. Nicholas the bishop', probably on the saint's feast day (6 December), might be taken as piety or perhaps, if the gift was related to the widespread practice of appointing a boy 'bishop' or a St Nicholas bishop, whose irreverent role was to preside over services or performances and perhaps even give sermons, was evidence of the earl's engagement in local parish affairs, and possibly of his sense of fun.[46]

The earl's choice of residence indicates an attachment to his family roots. The earl had plenty of potential abodes among his estates, and both the recently acquired Middleton in Norfolk and the More in Hertfordshire had new, impressive and comfortable houses that many would have used as preferable to Wivenhoe or his mansion at Earls Colne, which, while sizeable, were somewhat outdated, as was Castle Hedingham in 1485. Rather than use these existing houses built by others, de Vere chose instead to extensively rebuild and modernize his rather cramped seat at Hedingham; though he did not construct quite on the scale of the duke of Buckingham at Thornbury, his upgraded castle at Hedingham was large and comfortable enough that he entertained Henry VII thrice there.[47] Only the twelfth-century keep and a beautiful Tudor bridge spanning the inner and outer bailey now survive at Hedingham, but evidence from a survey made in 1592, just after the estate was sold, and from archaeological excavations, record that the earl built from scratch the bridge and 'a great brick tower', probably rebuilt another tower and the gatehouse, as well as the great hall (the new hall was about 83 feet by 37) and associated service buildings, and probably much or all of the curtain wall, as almost all the extant foundations are of late fifteenth or

[44] Longleat, Misc. xi, fols 116r–17r. These men were presumably William Buckenham (Buckingham is given in the account but this was a common variant), fellow of Gonville Hall, Cambridge in 1488, incepted for Doctor of Theology, 1506–7, and master of Gonville, 1514, and perhaps Richard Brynkley, a friar minor of Cambridge, who may or may not have completed his doctorate in Theology at Cambridge in 1505–6: Emden, *Biographical Register of Cambridge*, 103–4.

[45] Longleat, Misc. xi, fols 117v, 118v. Probably John Talbot, who eventually had the distinction of three doctorates, though not that of Theology at the date of the account; he was Doctor of Medicine 1498, Doctor of Canon Law by 1507 and Doctor of Theology by 1518: Emden, *Biographical Register of Oxford*, 1845–6.

[46] Longleat, Misc. xi, fol. 123r. I am grateful to Dr Steven Gunn for this suggestion. For the practice see R. Hutton, *The Rise and Fall of Merry England* (Oxford, 1994), 10–12, 53–4.

[47] Harris, *Edward Stafford*, 85–9.

early sixteenth century date.[48] He even added a brick dome to one of the turrets on the old keep. This was a huge programme of construction, but it was clearly a priority for the earl; building appears to have started soon after 1485 as repairs were being done to the 'ledde on the new towre, and the ledd of the dongen' on 20 December 1490.[49] The additional accommodation in the new tower(s) and the new great hall reflected the greater size of his household and his increased status after 1485, and might have been necessary anyway, but what is unclear is what state the castle was in after fourteen years of disuse after 1471; it might have been in a semi-ruinous condition, and this would explain the thorough overhaul. Hedingham, the traditional family seat, now comfortable and modernized, was his favourite residence for most of Henry's reign. Of the fifteen letters in the Paston collection which Oxford or his countess wrote between 1485 and 1502, six were written from the court or on the king's business, while of those written from one of the earl's homes, seven were written from Hedingham, and two from Lavenham in Suffolk, where the earl had a 'lodge'.[50] Two further letters addressed to Bray before 1503 were written at Hedingham, while it was at his ancestral home that he died.

It is only later in the earl's life that there is much evidence for the use of his other Essex residences at Earls Colne and Wivenhoe. The inventory of his goods suggests that he did use the former, as a large proportion of his household goods was there, and particular chambers had been assigned to William Waldegrave, his cousin John Vere, and others.[51] No other evidence for its use exists however, and it is unknown whether any work to improve the century old house had been done.[52] Wivenhoe, some twenty miles as the crow flies from Hedingham, did have the advantage of being on the coast and close to the largest urban centre in Essex, Colchester. The Essex antiquarian Morant described Wivenhoe as a 'large and elegant seat, having a noble gate-house, with towers of a great height that served for a sea mark'.[53] It was initially used by the Walton family in the late

---

[48] *TEAS*, i (1858), 79 for the survey; *An Inventory of the Historical Monuments in Essex* (4 vols, London, 1916–23), i, 51–7.

[49] *Household Books*, 515.

[50] At London and in company with king: *PL*, vi, 95, 124, 128, 140, 160, 167. Homes: *PL*, vi, 92–3, 106, 122, 128–9, 135–6, 138, 142–3, 165. The lodge (ibid., 106) was probably a hunting lodge as the earl had a park on the manor.

[51] 'Last Testament', 320–8.

[52] The amateur archaeological excavations undertaken episodically between 1929 and 1935 focussed on the church and monastic buildings and not on the site of the lay house(s): Fairweather, 'Colne Priory', esp. 278–9. Leland wrote that 'a little besides Colne Priorie yn Estsax, wher the Erles of Oxford usid to be buried, was a manorplace of theirs, the dikes and the plotte wheof yet remayne, and berith the name of the Haulle Place. Syns the ruin of this manor place the Erles hath buildid hard by the priory': *John Leland's Itinerary. Travels in Tudor England*, ed. J. Chandler (Stroud, 1993), 162. Leland is unclear as to when Hall Place fell out of use and another house was constructed. For other sources see Fairweather, 'Colne Priory', 293–4.

[53] Morant, *Essex*, ii, 188; *VCH Essex*, x, 281.

fourteenth century, but was a favourite home of the twelfth earl and his countess, the Walton heiress. No archaeological work has been done on the site, but it is likely that the expansion work that made it a 'large and elegant seat' was done in the fifteenth century by either the twelfth or the thirteenth earl, as there appears to have been no problem in accommodating the earl's hundred-plus household; in 1507 the earl was resident almost exclusively there for most of the year. The earl did also own and use one or two London inns. His grandfather owned a 'mansion in the parish of St Augustine on the Wall', which ought to have descended to him; in 1486 he was also granted the 'great inn called "Le Herber" in the parish of St Mary Bothowe' formerly owned by the duke of Clarence.[54] The earl did not specify, however, where 'my place in London' was when he wrote to John Paston, nor does his inquisition *post mortem* return for London survive.[55]

The best sources for reconstructing elements of his home life are the surviving household accounts. A full account, running to 143 folios, and covering January to December 1507, details the day by day purchase of meat and fish, and also contains monthly accounts of the acquisition of corn, ale, beer, wine, spices, candles, oxen, sheep, salted fish and firewood, the expenses of the stable, 'foreign' expenses, and quarterly payments of the wages of the earl's household.[56] While a formal account, it cannot necessarily be taken as a typical year, for the earl's wife had died just before the commencement of the account, and perhaps as a result the great household was stationary at Wivenhoe for the entire year, and the earl himself for all but six weeks of it. A more problematic document survives for the period 1490–1. Written in the name of Philip Lewis (or Fitzlewis), though his servant Edmund Gilbert clearly wrote some entries, it is not a formal account. Added into the back of the household account book of John Howard, duke of Norfolk, and therefore presumably acquired when the earl was granted Howard's residence of Framlingham in 1486, it takes the form of jotted notes of expenditure, mainly in and around Castle Hedingham in 1490 and 1491. However, there are chronological lacunae; no entries are made for February, March, almost all of April, July, August or October 1490. Further, it is not clear precisely what post Philip held within the household administration, as the account, lacking any heading or *summa*, does not make it clear. Henry Smith was the controller, one of the senior financial officials of the household, as he is referenced as such in Lewis's account on 8 November.[57] Lewis could have been the treasurer of the household (the controller was the deputy to this post) or the steward of the household, who was the *major domus*, responsible for household policy and discipline. These were the three senior financial officials of the household, and all three existed in the de Vere administration, as the account of the earl's funeral

54   *CIPM*, xx, 201; *CPR*, 1485–94, 121.
55   PL, vi, 167 (probably 1503–4).
56   Longleat, Misc. xi. The opening heading states that the account runs from 1 January 1507 to 31 January 1508, but the daily and monthly accounts of purchases end on 31 December 1507.
57   *Household Accounts*, 510.

mentions their offices.[58] Equally Lewis might have been the earl's cofferer, with responsibility well beyond the household itself. Son of Sir Lewis John and Alice, daughter of Aubrey, tenth earl of Oxford, and uncle of Sir Richard Fitzlewis, Lewis was well-born enough to have held any of these roles.[59] Interesting as it is, its problematic nature means Lewis's book of payments can be only be used for its details, not in a thoroughly analytical way.

How did the earl spend his time when he was at one of his homes? The earl was keen on music. There are frequent disbursements for minstrels' services in the accounts. In 1507 these included payments to two minstrels of Prince Henry in January, four minstrels of the king in May, two minstrels of Lord Scrope and one of Lord Darcy in June, three of the earl of Arundell on 20 September, two of the Prince's in October and six in December, and in 1490 there were also frequent payments.[60] The earl maintained a top-class chapel establishment, partly as a choir, perhaps partly for theatrical entertainment; the quality can be established from the fact that Oxford's chapel appeared at the royal court in May 1506, the only noble chapel to do so.[61] There were ten or twelve boys in his chapel in 1490, under the guidance of one Richard Wood; there were similar numbers in 1507.[62]

Outdoors entertainment was not neglected. There is some evidence for participation in that most aristocratic of pastimes, hunting. As a young man the earl certainly hunted with John Howard, the two spending a week at the chase together between 21 and 28 August 1465 at Lavenham, Suffolk, and again

---

[58] See below, 223; Mertes, *English Noble Households*, 22, 23; Woolgar, *Great Household*, 18.

[59] Unpublished article on 'Lewis John' by C.E. Moreton, History of Parliament Trust, 1422–1504 section; *CCR, 1468–76*, 399–400. He was also lieutenant of Dover castle by 1481: *CPR, 1476–85*, 283. Although again his post within the de Vere administration was not specified, the context of his inclusion in the receiver general's account in the following year increases the likelihood of Philip being cofferer; in an obscure section of the account, literally 'payments to the lord's receipt' he received £110 from the official for unspecified purposes, although he was also granted 68s 4d for the repayment of several small domestic disbursements, very similar to the type of expenditure seen in Lewis's account in the following year: ERO, D/DPr 139, m. 4d.

[60] Longleat, Misc. xi, fols 114r, 118v, 119r, 121r, 122r, 123v. In 1490–1, 10s was paid to the earl of Arundel's minstrels on 20 September, 26s 8d was paid to minstrels on All Hallows, 6s 8d to the players of Chelmsford on 26 December, and 20d to unnamed minstrels, possibly his own troupe, around New Year's day and 40s to the players of Lavenham on 7 January, *Household Books*, 509, 510, 516, 517.

[61] Anglo, 'Court Festivals of Henry VII', 41. For the role of the chapel in entertainment as well as a choir, see S.R. Westfall, 'The Chapel: Theatrical Performance in Early Tudor Great Households', *English Literary Renaissance*, xviii (1988), 171–93.

[62] R. Bowers, 'Early Tudor Courtly Song: an Evaluation of the Fayrfax Book' and F. Kisby, 'Courtiers in the Community: The Musicians of the Royal Household Chapel in Early Tudor Westminster', both in *Reign of Henry VII*, ed. Thompson, 188–212, 229–60. For Wood and the boys see *Household Accounts*, 511–12; Longleat, Misc. xi, fols 117r–19v. Other indoors entertainment included chess as the earl paid 8d for two chessboards in 1490: *Household Books*, 514.

between 29 March and 10 April 1466.[63] The earl had parks at Hedingham, Earls Colne, Lavenham, Castle Camps, Stansted Mountfichet, Gibbecrake, Great Canfield, Great Oakley and probably elsewhere available for hunting, but how much personal use he made of them is difficult to ascertain; they certainly fulfilled other functions such as supplying venison for the earl's table.[64] He owned a boar spear, and had hawks in 1490, when three falconers took a pair of hawks for training at a river for a fortnight.[65] Earl John was a man in tune with courtly fashions, in this case tennis, a leisure activity made fashionable by Henry VII, as he had a court built at Hedingham. An entry in the earl's receiver-general's account notes the payment of 9 shillings to two men for the carrying of a certain quantity of 'sopeasshes pro le Tennesplay'.[66] It cannot be certain that the earl himself personally participated in any of these leisure activities – tennis, listening to minstrels, watching plays, or hunting or hawking – but it is likely. These were typical aristocratic pursuits – John Howard's household accounts detail his expenditure on hawking, listening to music, chess and also reading, for which there is evidence of Oxford's interest.[67] Again, while there is no record of the earl partaking in a joust, the fact that his jousting helm survives, improbably as far afield as Florence, suggests that he did at some point participate.[68]

The earl could read in at least three languages. There is at least one English letter in his own hand dating from 1487;[69] he owned French books, and two sojourns at the French court in 1471–3 and 1484–5 would make it likely that he was at least a competent French speaker; in signing his household accounts, it can be presumed not only that he had mastered some arithmetic but that he could comprehend the Latin in which the accounts were written, and the ubiquity of the language in religious and administrative circles make a certain familiarity probable. The earl owned vernacular books of a non-religious variety. The inventory of his goods after his death records 'A Chest full of frenshe and englisshe bokes', valued at £3 6s 8d. They were not expensive high status volumes at that price, and it would be intriguing to know what they were. Religious works owned by the earl included five mass books, two of which were printed, nineteen 'Prick' song books, and various other religious tomes.[70] The song books suggest a man once more in tune with the latest fashions of the court. The only vernacular

---

[63] *Household Books of John Howard*, ed. Crawford, 301, 385.

[64] Parkers on all of these estates brought deer during January 1507 for feasting: Longleat, Misc. xi, fols 2r, v, 4r, 7v.

[65] 'Last Testament', 323; *Household Books*, 508.

[66] ERO, D/DPr 139, m. 4; Gunn, 'Courtiers of Henry VII', 25.

[67] Crawford, *Yorkist Lord*, 154–6.

[68] B. Thomas and L.G. Boccia, *Armi Storiche del Museo Nazionale di Firenze, Palazzo del Bargello, restaurate dall'Aiuto Austriaco per Firenze* (Florence, 1971), 52.

[69] *PLP*, ii, 448.

[70] 'Last Testament', 342. For equivalent examples from testamentary evidence, see K.B. McFarlane, 'The Education of the Higher Nobility in Later Medieval England', in *Nobility of Later Medieval England*, 236–7.

work that can be proven to have been owned by the earl was a poetic life of the Virgin Mary by Lydgate.[71] He was both interested in at least one piece of chiv-alric literature, and a literary patron; Caxton translated the Charlemagne cycle *The Four Sons of Aymon,* 'out of Frenche . . . at ye request and commandment of ye right noble and vertus Erle, John Erle of Oxford, my goode, synguler and especial Lorde'. De Vere was also responsible for introducing Caxton to Henry VII, and his name appears in the dedication to Caxton's *Faytes of Arms* in 1489, where Caxton, noting that Henry VII had desired him to translate the work into English, casually added that the earl of Oxford was then waiting on the king, clearly indicating his status as a secondary patron at that time.[72] The earl's second wife also owned two collections of moralizing and contemplative works, now in the British Library and the Bodleian.[73] It cannot be assumed, however, that Oxford read his wife's devotional tracts.

It is clear that most years the earl spent Christmas and New Year at one of his homes, rather than at court, but that his circle were expected to be with him, not at their homes.[74] In December 1507 the earl's council, en masse, were entertained by players at Wivenhoe, and John Clopton's receiver paid £22 in cash to his master at Hedingham on 31 December 1495, while his son, Sir William, received sums on 1 January 1502 at the earl's castle.[75] As the standard of the entertainment and food was likely to be rather better in the earl's household, this may not have been a hardship for his affinity. Large-scale entertainment, a feature typical of aristocratic households during this period, is conspicuous in the earl's accounts during the festive season.[76] On 20 December 1490 purchases included eighteen yards of linen cloth that 'M[aster] Leynthorpe hade for dysg-ysyng', while a payment of 16d was made to an unnamed servant 'when he went to Bury [St Edmunds] to fach stuff for dysgysers on Saynt Stevens day [26 December]'; payments to minstrels, the players of Chelmsford and for a pageant were all made in late December or early January 1490–1. This is to say nothing of the purchase of 16s worth of ale, or the 6 tuns of wine brought from Colchester on 22 December, all of which would have added up to a merry Christmas.[77] In 1507, December also saw much entertainment and jollity. Four players of

---

[71] BL, Harley MS 3862. The evidence for ownership is that it bears the earl's arms: Hanna and Redworth, 'Rotheley, de Vere Circle and Ellesmere Chaucer', 21.

[72] H.S. Bennet, *English Books and their Readers, 1475–1557* (Cambridge, 1970), 45; N.F. Blake, *Caxton: England's First Publisher* (London, 1976), 50, 199.

[73] BL, Harleian 1706; Bodleian, Rawlinson lit. fol. 37. See A.I. Doyle, 'Books Connected with the Vere Family and Barking Abbey', *TEAS*, xxv (1958), 222–43.

[74] For example he was not at court at Christmas 1486, 1488 or 1489, though he was in 1487: *Herald's Memoir*, 107, 152–5, 164–5, 182.

[75] WAM, 3305, mm. 2, 6 (account of the receiver of John and William Clopton for the estates of their ward Geoffrey Gate, 10–17 Henry VII). For 1507, see footnote 72 below.

[76] For entertainment in aristocratic households at this period, see S.R. Westfall, *Patrons and Performance. Early Tudor Household Revels* (Oxford, 1990).

[77] *Household Accounts*, 516–17.

Sudbury put on a pageant in the hall at Wivenhoe, while five Colchester men were paid for 'disgising' in the same venue, on both occasions before the whole household. Presumably more refined entertainment was put on later in the same month for the earl's council in the hall, when they were amused twice by four players of Lavenham and once by four players of Bocking.[78] Over £7 was paid in December to the earl's servant William Oakley in London to purchase frivolous decoration, including items such as gold and silver paper, 'tynn foile' and counterfeit pearls. External players were responsible for much of the entertainment, in contrast to the earl of Northumberland's revels in 1515 which were organized by the household itself.[79] Without knowing the content of the entertainment, or the plays performed, it is difficult to ascertain whether there was any overtly political or propagandist message either in the entertainment for the whole household or that for the council – at Christmas it may have been religious in nature or just good natured fun. There may have been a more subtle message conveyed in such events, however, which would have spoken of the earl's largesse, prestige and his artistic patronage. Particularly when his council, retainers and household were all present, such revels may have fostered a communal spirit among his men.[80]

It would have been expected, in an age of conspicuous display, that de Vere himself cut an impressive figure, and he does not appear to have been parsimonious in this regard. Clothes were very important in aristocratic self-definition, and his apparel, described in the inventory of goods made after his death, included such items of lordly dress as 'A gowne of blake tynsell satteyn furrid with sables', valued at £20, and 'the Robe of estate furrid with myniver of crymsyn velvett with mantell tabbard and circuit and a hode', valued at £15. The earl paid Cipriano de Furnariis, a Lombard of London, £13 for sarcenet and other silks in 1488–9.[81] Oxford's inventory contains details of ten gowns, an exceptionally high number compared to other aristocratic inventories and wills at this date.[82] He owned various items of jewellery including 'A greate cheyne of gold, with a maryners whistell', probably reflecting his office of admiral of England, worth £243 6s 8d and an elaborate 'colar of fyne gold of xxvij S and ii Porteculeisse with a greate diamount in a red Rose and a Lion hanging uppon the same Rose with ii Rubies and a diamount uppon the said Lion and ii greate Rubies/ and iiii diamounts & ix greate perles uppon the S' which was valued at £98, and whose Lancastrian and Tudor symbolism might even be said to be overdone.[83] Such high-quality work was likely to be made in London, and in 1488–9, one Herman

---

[78] Longleat, Misc. xi, fol. 124v.

[79] Woolgar, *Great Household*, 94–5.

[80] Westfall, *Patrons and Performance*, 205–8 emphasizes the propaganda possibilities, as well as the prestige accruing to the lord.

[81] ERO, D/DPr 139, m. 4.

[82] M. Hayward, *Rich Apparel. Clothing and the Law in Henry VIII's England* (Farnham, 2009), 177. The mean number of gowns mentioned in the wills and inventories of a sample of twenty-four members of the nobility was 1.33.

[83] 'Last Testament', 331, 332, 342, 343.

Seales of London, goldsmith, was paid £4 3s 6d for diverse works.[84] Expensive tapestries hung on the walls of his homes, often incorporating heraldic images and de Vere badges. Two examples of such badges, the blue boar and the de Vere mullet, were prominent in a number of expensive items, including: 'v tapettes of tapestry damaske werke paly Redde and yelowe with cheyres of estate blue bores and molettes in clowdes w^t a skochion of my lordes armes and my olde Ladies in gartures and thelmet above' worth £53 6s 8d.[85]

Leisure and entertainment were part of the earl's life, but he also kept an eye on his finances and administration, and, like Henry VII, personally oversaw his expense accounts. The account of the controller of the household in 1507–8 was signed by the earl at the end of every weekly section, by the monthly totals under various sub-headings and the overall *summa*; there are in total 179 places in the account when the earl added his characteristic and idiosyncratic 'Oxynford'. This would have taken some time – if only a cursory check was needed, there was little need for so many signatures – so it can be surmised that this was a thorough assessment. Other annual accounts, including those of the receiver-general, survive in fair copy, and it can be assumed that the earl would have carefully checked these as well, even if he did not sign all of them.[86]

Conclusion

If much of the evidence for Oxford's interests, leisure, piety and day-to-day life appears to be conventional, then this should not surprise us – he was, after all, a man of his age. This picture is dependent on the available evidence, largely comprising accounts of expenses or instructions for the use of cash and goods after the earl's death, and is therefore slanted in certain directions and not always insightful, even if it can show a more rounded individual. Hard though it is to read too much into the thin evidence for the earl's personality, certain themes emerge. He clearly cared about his familial inheritance and honour, probably as a result of the execution of two members of his family while he was at the impressionable age of nineteen. This can be seen as a major reason for his political actions during Edward IV's reign, and while a less immediate motivating factor after 1485, his reburial of his father and brother, and a knowledge of his family's religious foundations, indicate a continuing interest both in his immediate heritage and ancient lineage, something that contemporaries picked up on. There is also enough evidence to suggest that the earl was a generous man. A large jointure for his second wife, a comfortable one for his brother's widow, a manor for life to thank his former gaoler, Sir James Blount, for releasing him from Hammes

[84] ERO, D/DPr 139, m.4.
[85] 'Last Testament', 328.
[86] McFarlane, 'Education of the Higher Nobility', in *Nobility of Later Medieval England*, 230–1.

castle, two manors to Earls Colne priory, and goods worth hundreds, if not thousands, of pounds granted to religious houses in his will, all indicate largesse was a facet of his character. Generosity, mingled with gratitude, was presumably behind the letter he wrote to Reginald Bray in January 1486 when he asked Bray to seek the preferment of one William Page to the office of one of the tellers of the king's receipt, as before Bosworth Page had 'demeanyd hym aswell to his grace as unto his frends and was right loving to me and myne which causeth me the rather to write and entreat for hym'.[87] Bray acceded to the request. Little touches such as the payment in a household account to one of his servants, John Watson, of 6s 8d, 'toward hys maryage, be my lordys comaundement', reinforce this impression.[88] The earl was magnanimous towards the Howard family in the aftermath of Bosworth; this is obvious in the countess of Surrey's letter when she told John Paston 'hym I drede mooste and yit as hyther to I fynde hym beste'.[89] A further character trait that might well be attributed to the earl was personal bravery, given his leading role at four battles between 1471 and 1497, the latter two of which he asked for his division to be in the van where the fighting would be fiercest. While one does not sense the humour of which his father was capable, at least in the Paston letter evidence,[90] generosity, magnanimity, bravery and familial loyalty are all appealing characteristics. When such personal virtues were allied with more political ones, it goes some way to explaining his success in East Anglia and on the national stage after 1485.

---

[87] WAM, 16039. William Page had acquired the office by Michaelmas 1486: E405/75, mm. 15, 22.
[88] *Household Accounts*, 505, 506.
[89] *PL*, vi, 88.
[90] For example, *PL*, ii, 111–12 (the rather whimsical 'for he [the twelfth earl] seid if he were sent to for to come ... if it kepe faire weder he wold not tarye, and if it reygned he wold not spare') and 151 (see above, 178).

Conclusion

This great honour, this high and noble dignity, hath continued ever since in the remarkable surname of de Vere, by so many ages, descents and generations, as no other kingdom can produce such a peer in one and the self same name and title.

For where is BOHUN? Where's MOWBRAY? Where's MORTIMER? Nay, which is more, and most of all, where is PLANTAGENET? They are entombed in the urns and sepulchres of mortality.
    And yet let the name and dignity of de Vere stand so long as it pleaseth God.[1]

John de Vere, thirteenth earl of Oxford, died at nine in the evening on 10 March 1513 at his ancestral home of Castle Hedingham at the age of seventy-one.[2] A detailed account of his funeral survives. On 22 April the corpse 'was born out of his chappelle by vi gentlimene and so layd in a cheaire well covered with black velvet and garneshed with scocheones of his arms and of his mariages and viii baner roles of his descent', and taken to the parish church at Hedingham accompanied by the:

> parson and mynesteres of the chorche and the deane of my Lord's chappelle with all the mynesteres of the same and then nexte a gentliman beringe the standarde afore him with the stuarde, tresorer and comptrolere, all the esquirers, gentlimene and all other offyceres of the house aftere them, a gentlimane bearing the healme and creste, then the coate of armes borne by Richeamont herold, then a gentilman bering my Lord's banor, then the executors, then Clarenshouxe Kyng of Armes, then the chaire and iiii baneres of Saints borne by iiii gentlimene at the iiii corneres of the chayre and the vi gentleman that weare assistaunts to the corse rode all the waye by the chaire, and then next after the chaire my yong Lorde of Oxeford as cheefe mornere by him selfe then the other vi morneres ii and ii, then alle the

---

[1] *Chief Justice Crew on the Earldom of Oxford* (Cambridge, 1928), 4–5.
[2] BL, Harl. MS 295, fols 155r–56r; a nineteenth century transcript of this is ERO, D/DMh/ F36. The Harleian MS is a collection of loose tracts, mainly relating to Spain, containing some originals and some transcripts. The hand which transcribed the account of the funeral is later sixteenth century, but the account itself is likely to be contemporary, as it refers to 'our sovereigne lord' Henry VIII.

knights and esquires of the contre nexte to them, all the yeomen of the contre and all the lords and gentlemens servants.[3]

As many as 900 black gowns were given to mourners, demonstrating the scale of the event, though this could not match the funeral of the duke of Norfolk in 1524, when as many as 1900 liveries of hoods and gowns of black cloth were distributed.[4] The funeral cortege made its way from Hedingham to the earl's family priory at Earls Colne, where he was buried before the high altar in the Lady Chapel in great state, in the presence of the bishop of Norwich, Lords Fitzwalter and Willoughby and many knights and esquires, with the ceremonials appropriate for his rank, including the offering of his shield, sword and helmet to the bishop, who then gave them to the heir, who in turn passed them to the heralds. A mounted knight, armed with an axe, was led into the choir by two knights and delivered the axe to the bishop, who gave it to the heir. A final sermon 'declared the great vertues and nobleness that was in the same nobleman'.[5] The delay in his funeral was partly because of the proximity of Easter on 27 March, but also to the fact that 'his counselle and executores weare so occupied in the tyme by the Kyng's commaundements in many and greate matteres', a reflection on his importance in the period after 1485.[6] Oxford left no children, and was succeeded by his nephew John, son of his brother George.

It is worth at this stage putting the thirteenth earl's eventful career into the context of his family background. In contrast to the generally low-key, unspectacular existence of the heads of the de Vere family from the early thirteenth century to the 1370s, the long fifteenth century was something of a spectacular sequence of catastrophes and triumphs for the earls. Of the five earls from Robert, ninth earl and duke of Ireland to the thirteenth earl, one died in exile, one by the axe, while three died respected in their beds, two of them in their seventies. Yet while Robert, duke of Ireland and the twelfth earl suffered political disaster during this period, none of the careers of the other de Vere earls compare to the extraordinary highs and lows of the thirteenth earl's long life, as he became drawn into civil war, suffered the disaster of Barnet, exile and imprisonment, followed by the most unexpected release from prison, the victory against long odds at Bosworth, and the rapid development of his rule in East Anglia. Nor were the changing fortunes of the family confined to the arena of

---

[3] BL, Harl. MS 295, fol. 155r. The ceremonial in the church bears close similarities with other accounts of burials of earls, such as those of the earl of Salisbury in 1464 and William Courtenay, earl of Devon, in 1511: 'The Burying of an Earl', in *The Antiquarian Repertory*, ed. F. Grose and T. Astle (4 vols, London, 1807–9), i, 314–17; BL, Egerton 2642, fols 192v–193r.
[4] T. Martin, *The History of the Town of Thetford* (London, 1779), appendix 8.
[5] BL, Harleian MS 295, fols 155r–156r. For discussion of these ceremonials, see A.F. Sutton, L. Visser-Fuchs and R.A. Griffiths, *The Royal Funerals of the House of York at Windsor* (London, 2005), 27–9.
[6] BL, Harleian MS 295, fol. 155r. For a financial account of his executors during 1513–7 see RH, Box 125.

warfare and national politics. Between 1413 and 1513 the landed estates of the earls nearly trebled in numbers from forty-three to 116, and overall revenue from their estates approximately doubled from c. £1200 to c. £2300. In terms of total income, that of the thirteenth earl was, from the profits of royal office-holding and patronage as well as landed estates, between three and four times that of his grandfather. The local power and influence of the earls also underwent a drastic change – from Richard whose lordship, as far as the evidence shows, barely extended beyond northern Essex, to his grandson, who was virtually unchallenged in his hegemony across the whole of East Anglia. This was reflected in the lack of influential gentry in the military retinues of 1415 and 1441, and again contrasts with the powerful, wealthy men who exclusively served the thirteenth earl. Essex was not a county easily dominated by one noble family, in contrast to Warwickshire, and between the 1370s and 1485 the de Veres amicably shared power with the Bohuns, the Bourgchiers and the Fitzwalters. Yet once more, the thirteenth earl became the exception, the unusual circumstances of 1485 allowing the domination of the county, and the whole region, by just one man. However the thirteenth earl is compared to his predecessors, he was the greatest of the de Veres – wealthier than any other, with greater estates, and more servants and retainers, and with a national importance for twenty-eight years after Bosworth that stands in direct contrast, for example, with Robert, duke of Ireland's brief ascendancy.

This study has not looked at the theoretical position of the nobility as a whole vis-à-vis the crown, not least as it had not really changed a great deal in contemporary perception. While the power of the nobility in practical terms waxed from the minority of Henry VI to the late fifteenth century, it waned somewhat under the first two Tudors, but the place of the nobility in English political society was similar in 1530 to what it had been in 1450. Where Bishop Russell in 1483 could describe 'the noble persons' as the islands of 'ferme grounde' without which there could be no good rule, Thomas Starkey in the 1530s could declare that the office and duty of the 'nobylytie and gentylmen … ys chefely to see justyce among theyr servantys and subiectys and to kepe them in unytie and concorde'.[7] George Bernard's description of an England 'divided into spheres of [noble] influence' in the mid-Tudor period mirrors England in the reign of Edward IV or Henry VII, though politics and religion had changed by then.[8] However, the practical power of the nobility did fluctuate depending on the outlook of an individual monarch, and there is no doubt that Henry VII's reign saw a limited resurgence of royal power, and in parts of the country a diminution in noble influence, yet the key

---

[7] *Grants etc from the Crown*, ed. Nicols, xl; T. Starkey, 'A Dialogue Between Cardinal Pole and Thomas Lupset', ed. J. M. Cowper in *England in the Reign of King Henry the Eighth*, ed. S.J. Herrtage (EETS, extra series, XXXII, 1878), 190, though the dialogue is critical of the contemporary generation of the nobility for their extravagance and frivolity.

[8] Bernard, *Power of the Early Tudor Nobility*, 179 (quote), and 185–97 for the theoretical position of the nobility.

point is that, as East Anglia during the reign exemplifies, royal and noble power were not antithetical to each other. The nobility usually functioned as a 'governing class' beneath the monarch, who could not 'control society directly through [his] own agents'.[9]

Historians 'should be slow to pronounce on their subjects, especially when their subjects have been dead for ... centuries', but none the less must offer 'if not a final verdict; at least a summing up'.[10] If this work has laid much emphasis on de Vere's prominence during the reign of Henry VII, that is, hopefully, not a result the biographer of becoming too close to the subject, but as an investigation, for the first time, of the reasons for the earl's importance, and also as the thirteenth earl's career after 1485 challenges a number of commonly held assumptions about the first Tudor king. Despite his reputation, Henry VII was prepared to give regional power and autonomy to a nobleman, and while that in the end came down to trust, and acceptance of an existing situation, Henry was not a king necessarily hostile to independent noble interests, as he has sometimes been portrayed – he did not necessarily harbour 'deep suspicions of the nobility, particularly members of old magnate families that dominated unruly peripheral areas of the kingdom'.[11] Such royal patronage and trust were not unique to Oxford – the Stanleys had the same until disloyalty prompted a reappraisal of royal policy towards them,[12] as did Bedford before his death and to a lesser extent the earl of Shrewsbury – but Oxford repaid the king, putting his life and those of his retinue at risk on three campaigns after 1485, and by his efforts to ensure that East Anglia was not to be a centre for sedition and treason against the new dynasty. The regional dominance that Oxford achieved was within the compass of the political culture of the fifteenth and sixteenth centuries. Not all noblemen would have aspired to have ruled their regions, but some would have done, and a few achieved such an aspiration. While regional rule by handful of noblemen is more closely associated with the reign of Edward IV, it was also a feature of parts of England under Henry VII.

What stands out about John de Vere, thirteenth earl of Oxford was that he was one of the last of the great medieval noblemen, a late representative in a tradition that went back to the Norman Conquest of hugely powerful, wealthy magnates, capable of raising vast forces, and influential in the direction of royal policy, his power based on his own estates and affinity, not just royal favour and royal office. Even his close contemporary, Thomas Howard, earl of Surrey, was one of a new breed, that of the noble Tudor servant, exercising power as a lieutenant in a region that was not familiar to him, exerting influence as lord

---

[9] G.L. Harriss, 'Political Society and the Growth of Government in Late Medieval England', *Past and Present*, cxxxviii (1993), 32–3.

[10] M. Morris, *The Bigod Earls of Norfolk in the Thirteenth Century* (Woodbridge, 2005), 184.

[11] Harris, *Edward Stafford*, 212.

[12] Cunningham, 'Henry VII, Sir Thomas Butler and the Stanley Family', 220–41; idem, *Henry VII*, esp. 180–6.

treasurer, and only towards the end of his life, among other things, a force in the region where he held the bulk of his estates. Under Henry VIII the centralization of the distribution of royal patronage at court and the increase of direct contact between crown and gentry made 'aspiring magnates of necessity court patrons'.[13] The Reformation, which brought the crown vast territorial gains, but increased diplomatic insecurity, and changed political and religious circumstances, consolidated these existing trends, involving the nobility in a much more court-based world than Oxford and his predecessors ever were.

In the context of much of the historiography of Henry VII's reign, being a great medieval nobleman would make de Vere an anachronism – one of the last overmighty subjects in a reign which saw the end of them; a noble landowner, in a reign that saw the bypassing of such feudal dinosaurs, with the king's professional administrators, dependent solely on royal favour, taking over the running of the shires; a battlefield commander who served in the reign of an accountant. There is an element of truth in much of this, but obviously such a caricature of the reign does not begin to cover the complexity of the overall picture. Part of the value of studying John de Vere is that it shows that Henry VII, in attempting to secure his dynasty, used methods other than the much discussed bonds and recognizances, including the generous dispersal of patronage, did not set out to destroy the power of his nobility, and had a much more conventional view of how power should be exercised than is often said to be the case – Henry was the last medieval king, as well as the first early modern one. De Vere repaid Henry's trust in him, not only ruling East Anglia on his behalf, but risking his life in the thick of the mêlées at Stoke and Bosworth.

[13] Gunn, *Charles Brandon*, 226.

Appendix – The de Vere Affinity

What follows is a guide to the most prominent of the wider de Vere affinity, and the most important administrators and lawyers in the comital household and administration. A full list of those paid annuities in the will of 1509 can be found below, 00–00; a list of those in the household paid a one off bequest in the will, below, 000.

Each entry in the directory below is concerned primarily with the subject's interaction with the earl, and his landholding, not necessarily with the wider career of the individual.

References to enfeoffments, annuities and executors
In the following appendix, reference will be made to de Vere's feoffees, executors and annuitants. The **enfeoffments** will be referred to by date:

1486 (RH, Box 39 – eight manors in Essex, Suffolk and Cambs.)

1492 (1) (RH, Boxes 38–9; Harvard Law School Library, English Deeds, BHG0634 – some fifty manors in various counties, for performance of his will)

1492 (2) (CCR, 1485–1500, 226 – de Vere's grant to Earls Colne priory, with witnesses and attorneys)

1492 (3) (ERO, D/DMh/T34 – exchange of lands in Belchamp Otten and Gestingthorpe with William Fyndern)

1501 (RH, Box 51 – demise to joint tenure of Aston Sandford, Bucks., to the earl and Countess Margaret)

1502–4 (CP40/959, rot. 415; Essex Feet of Fines, iv, 105–6; CCR, 1500–9, 126 – purchases of manors of Beaumont Berners and Gibbecrake in Purleigh)

1507 (CP40/981, rots. 514d. (Bucks.), 515 (Cambs.), 518 (Suffolk), 519 (Herts.), 581 (Essex); BL, Add.Ch, 41711; RH, Box 39 – enfeoffment of eighteen manors in Essex, four in Herts., one in Cambs., two in Bucks., and one in Suffolk, for performance of will)

1508 (Essex Feet of Fines, iv, 116 – purchase of Sheriffs)

Annuities – unless stated otherwise, all references are to the codicil of the will of 1509: PROB 11/17, fol. 86r, v, printed below, 00–00 (and 'Last Testament', 318–19).
Executors – all references are to the will of 1509, 'Last Testament', 318.
Valor – all references to the valor of 1485–97 are to NRO, Towns.196, MS 1615.

Directory of senior annuitants and administrators

Alington, Sir Giles

In April 1486 de Vere acquired Giles' wardship after the death of his father, who held three manors in Cambridgeshire of the earl, when Giles was just three. Although the wardship was sold to Richard Gardiner, the association continued as Giles was feed £3 6s 8d by 1509, and was a feoffee and business associate in 1507: see above, 100 n. 54. He had an annual income of around £124 p.a.: C142/36/16 (Cambs.); *CIPM Henry VII*, i, 13–14 (Herts., Norfolk, Suffolk, Cambs.).

Arblaster, James

Arblaster's impeccable record of service saw him acting in a variety of capacities in the de Vere administration before 1462, as a feoffee of Countess Elizabeth in the 1470s, and by 1473 he was paid an annuity of 100s a year: ERO, D/DPr 138; KB9/313, no. 11; RH Attic, box marked 'Manorial Records, Cambs., Essex and Suffolk'; DL29/295/4848; and see also *PL*, ii, 294–5; Hicks, 'Last Days', 306; *CIPM Henry VII*, i, 392–3. Arblaster survived to see the countess's son regain his estates in 1485, and become a feoffee in 1486 and bailiff of Chelsworth, Suffolk in 1488–9: ERO, D/DPr 139, m.3. In his will Arblaster appointed the earl as supervisor in return for the 'love and service' he had shown the earl, and was buried at the foot of the tomb built for the twelfth earl and his countess: PROB 11/9, fols 124r, v. He died 28 November 1492; *CIPM Henry VII*, i, 392–3. For his career, personality and relations with the Pastons, see Richmond, *Paston Family: Endings*, 179–85.

Aspelon, John

Aspelon (d. 1513) was paid an annuity of 53s 4d in 1509, and had been a feoffee in 1507. His landed holdings in Essex were valued at just over £3 at his death: C142/27/119.

Ayloff, William

Ayloff, feed 53s 4d a year, was a feoffee in 1507 and 1508. Admitted to Lincoln's Inn in July 1484, he was a member of the earl's 'council learned in the law' in 1499: *The Records of the Honourable Society of Lincoln's Inn: Admissions from A.D. 1420 to [A.D. 1893, and Chapel Registers]*, ed. W.P. Bailey (2 vols, London, 1896), i, 23; CP40/949, rot. 103d.

Bedingfield, Sir Edmund

Bedingfield (d. 1496) married Sir Thomas Tuddenham's sister and heir. He was the earl's feoffee in 1486 and 1492 (1) and his feudal tenant. His estates were valued at £209 p.a.: *CIPM Henry VII*, ii, 8–12, 63, 65, 66 (Norfolk, Suffolk, Yorks., Cambs., Beds.). For his role during the Stoke campaign in 1487, his knighting at Stoke, and his military contribution in 1489 see above, 117, 122, 126, 193.

Brewes, Robert, esquire, and his son Thomas
Robert (d. 1513) and Thomas (d. 1514) were both feed 53s 4d p.a., and Thomas was a member of the household in 1507–8. Thomas's estates were valued at £93 p.a., and for both their inquisitions *post mortem* see E150/617/6, 7; 618/17, 18 (Norfolk and Suffolk), and also Coppinger, *Suffolk*, vi, 114–15. See Wedgwood, ii, 108 for Robert.

Broughton, Sir Robert, and his sons John and Robert
Broughton (d. 1506) was the earl's feoffee in 1491 (1), 1492 (2), 1501 and 1502–4. He enfeoffed many of his lands to the earl, and several of the earl's retainers, and was a feudal tenant in Ashdon, Essex, and Stony Stratford, Bucks. He was the earl's deputy as constable of Clare castle, Suffolk in January 1496: Trinity College, Dublin, MS 1208/438.65. His inquisition *post mortem* valued his estates at £600 p.a., a chamber book of the king's at £1000 p.a.: *CIPM Henry VII*, ii, 594–5; iii, 104–6, 142–3, 180–1, 257, 259, 284–5, 470–1, 537 (Cambs., Suff., Norf., Devon, Leic., Herts., Essex, Bucks., Beds., Hunts., Berks.); E36/214, fol. 635. He made the earl supervisor of his will: Nicolas, *Testamenta Vetusta*, ii, 489; Wedgwood, ii, 118. In the earl's will Broughton's son and heir John received a bequest of two silver flagons weighing 173 ounces. His younger son, Robert, was feed 53s 4d, and given a bequest of £40: PROB 11/17, fol. 84v. In 1507 John was a feoffee.

Carew, Sir William
Carew (d. 1501) was knighted after serving with the earl at Stoke, and came in person with a retinue of twelve men to the muster a month later: Wedgwood, ii, 516–17; *Household Books*, 493. He also made the earl supervisor of his will. No inquisition *post mortem* survives for him, but his will records that he held estates in Devon, Suffolk, Essex and Worcestershire: PROB 11/12, fol. 86v. Being de Vere's associate, and probably annuitant, did not prevent the earl bringing an action against him in Michaelmas 1495 in the Exchequer of Pleas, in Carew's capacity as sheriff of Norfolk and Suffolk, regarding repayment of a tally for £39 6s 6d: E14/3 (Mich. 11 Hen VII); E5/5/23.

Churchyard, Richard
Churchyard, MP for Maldon in 1497 for which he was almost certainly indebted to the earl, had been a feoffee in 1486, and had a key role in the management of the earl's estates, holding the office of supervisor of all the earl's lands in four counties in 1488–9 at the fee of 53s 4d p.a. and was otherwise busy with the earl's administration during the same period: Wedgwood, ii, 185; ERO, D/DPr 139, mm. 1, 4; RH, Box 39. He raised a retinue of six men for the 1487 campaign: *Household Books*, 494, 498.

Clopton, John, esquire, and his son Sir William
John Clopton (d. 1497) had been a feoffee for the twelfth earl as early as 1456, became involved with the conspiracy of 1462, and was advising the earl in 1470:

C140/10/23; *PL*, v, 89, and see above, 42. He was a regular feoffee until his death, serving the earl in that capacity in 1486 and 1492 (1), 1492 (2) and 1492 (3), and see also *CCR, 1485–1500*, 44; *Visitation of Suffolk, 1561*, i, 20–8. He made the earl supervisor of his will, in addition to giving him 'in pore remembraunce a paire of karvyng knyves, the haftis gilt and enalmed, and a ryng of gold wherin is set a grete counterfet diament': PROB 11/11, fols 142–4v. John's inquisition *post mortem* recorded an income of £49 p.a. from lands in Suffolk: *CIPM Henry VII*, ii, 70–1. His son, Sir William, was also a feoffee in 1486 and 1507, was part of the household in 1490, and was feed £3 6s 8d in 1509: *Household Books*, 510.

Cotton, Thomas, esquire, and his son Sir Robert

Thomas Cotton (d. 1499) was a feoffee of the earl in 1486, 1492 (1) and 1492 (2). He served as the chief steward of the earl in Cambridgeshire in the valor of 1485–97, m.2, for which he received a fee of 53s 4d. His estates were valued at £86 p.a.: *CIPM Henry VII*, ii, 181–2, 197–8, 291–2. His son, Robert, a feoffee in 1507, was feed £3 6s 8d in 1509. His estates were valued at £145 p.a.: E150/71/9; 303/1; 625/3 (Cambs., Essex, Suffolk).

Danyell, John

Danyell of Felsted, Essex (d. 1519), paid an annuity of £10 p.a., was also made, on 28 October 1506, constable of the castle of Hedingham, and the annuity may be the payment for this office: E150/299/8. He had been granted the steward-ship of the More in 1504 (*CPR, 1494–1509*, 521), and was a feoffee in 1507. His landholding as mentioned in his will comprised two manors (including Felsted) leased from the monastery of Syon for a set term and rent and the tenement of Woodes and 'all other landes and tenements I have purchased lying and being within the parisshe of Felsted'. Danyell remembered the earl in his will (PROB 11/19, fols 102r, v and see above, 200). For his family connections, see Morant, *Essex*, ii, 176–7; *Visitation of Suffolk, 1561*, i, 9–12. His son John was a receiver of the earl's widow at the time of her death in 1537, receiving a bequest worth £40: Lewer, 'Testament and Last Will', 13.

Drury, Sir Robert

Drury (d. 1535) was feed £6 13s 4d, and was an executor and regular feoffee – 1492 (1), 1492 (2), 1501, 1502–4, 1507 and 1508. He was admitted to Lincoln's Inn in Trinity 1473: *Lincoln's Inn: Admissions*, ed. Bailey, i, 18. He was steward of the courts of the earl in Suffolk in the valor of 1485–97, m.1., and received a fee of 53s 4d for this office. He was also the earl's deputy chief steward in the duchy of Lancaster south of the Trent from 1499: Somerville, *Duchy of Lancaster*, i, 263, 431; and see Bindoff, ii, 57–8. For his estates, worth £115 p.a. see E150/635/3, 4; C142/57/40 (Norfolk, Suffolk), and also *CIPM Henry VII*, iii, 328 (he held the manor of Graces, Essex, of the earl); Rawcliffe and Flower, 'English Noblemen and their Advisors', 165; MacCulloch, *Suffolk under the Tudors*, 225; P. Hyde, 'Drury, Sir Robert', *ODNB*.

Fitzlewis, Sir Richard
Fitzlewis (d. 1528) was feed 10 marks as steward of all Oxford's lordships in Essex in 1488–9: ERO, D/DPr 139, m.4. He was involved in nearly all Oxford's business dealings (1486, 1492 (1), 1492 (3), 1501, 1502–4, 1507, 1508 and see *CCR, 1485–1500*, 44; Rawcliffe and Flower, 'English Noblemen and their Advisors', 172). His military retinue in 1487, at thirty men, was the joint largest individual retinue of Oxford's muster; *Household Books*, 493, 494; *PL*, vi, 130 (1489 muster – also thirty men). See also the biography in Bindoff, ii, 140. He is not mentioned in the earl's will, which is extremely surprising given his close links. His son, John, who predeceased him, was a business associate of the earl's in 1507. Only the inquisition *post mortem* returns for Richard's lands in Norfolk (£14) and Suffolk (£8) have survived: E150/631/1, 2. He held at least nine manors in southern Essex, which he enfeoffed Oxford and Sir Thomas Tyrell with in 1489: CP40/910, rot. 353. His uncle, Philip Lewis, wrote the earl's household books in 1490–1: *Household Books*, 506.

Fyndern, Sir William
His father had been attainted in 1461, but he was able, despite serving with the earl on the Lancastrian side at Barnet, to have the attainder reversed in 1478: see above, 181 and Wedgwood, ii, 327–8. Fyndern was feed £5 p.a., and was a regular feoffee and business associate in 1486 (witness only), 1492 (2), 1492 (3), 1502–4, 1507 and 1508. He also brought four men to the muster in 1487: *Household Books*, 494. He died in 1517, when his estates were worth £162 p.a.: E150/70/2; 302/1; 620/9 (Cambs., Essex, Suffolk).

Gate, Geoffrey, esquire
Gate (b. 1484), whose wardship de Vere may have helped acquire for the benefit of his associates William Waldegrave and John Clopton in 1486 (*CPR, 1485–94*, 88; E404/80/591), was paid an annuity of 53s 4d in 1509 and was a feoffee in 1507. Landholding estimate of £35 p.a. from his father's IPM: *CIPM Henry VII*, i, 11–12.

Grene, Sir John
Grene, feed £3 6s 8d a year, held four Essex manors of the earl, and was a feoffee in 1507. His inquisition *post mortem* does not survive but his mother held lands worth £36 in Suffolk and Essex: *CIPM Henry VII*, i, 446–7.

Heigham, Clement
Clement (d. 1520) was the earl's receiver-general from 1485 to about 1500, paid £10 as the wage for that office, feoffee 1486, 1492 (1), 1501 and attorney for the 1492 grant to Earls Colne: ERO, D/DPr 131, 139; RH, Box 38; *CCR, 1485–1500*, 226. He was the second son of Thomas Heigham of Heigham (d. 1481), an important Suffolk landowner: *Visitation of Suffolk, 1561*, ii, 391–8. His inquisition *post mortem* records that he held the manor of Gifford in Suffolk, worth £20

p.a.: C142/35/123. Surprisingly, Heigham is absent from the de Vere documents after 1501, and no annuity is recorded in the earl's will.

Heigham, Richard

Heigham (d. October 1500) was the brother of Clement, the earl's receiver-general, Thomas (see below) and William, bishop of Ely (d. 1490): *Visitation of Suffolk, 1561*, ii, 391–8. He was a member of the earl's council learned in the law in 1499: CP40/949, rot. 103d.

Heigham, Thomas, and his son Thomas

Thomas Heigham (d. perhaps 1492), brother of the receiver-general, Clement, had a son, also named Thomas (d. 1504): *Visitation of Suffolk, 1561*, ii, 391–8. One of the two Thomases was steward of all de Vere's lordships in Suffolk in 1488–9 (ERO, D/DPr 139, m. 4), and parker of Lavenham in the valor of 1485–97 (m. 1).

Hobart, Sir James

Hobart was bailiff of two de Vere manors in 1488–9 (ERO, D/DPr 139, m.2), a feoffee in 1486, 1492 (1), 1492 (3), and 1501, and an executor of the earl's will. Hobart served as steward of the duchy of Lancaster in Norfolk, Suffolk and Cambridgeshire from 1489, and deputy to de Vere as chief steward of the duchy south of the Trent. From 1486 he was a privy councillor of the king and attorney-general: ERO, D/DPr 139, m. 2; Somerville, *Duchy of Lancaster*, i, 595; Wedgwood, ii, 458–9; Lander, *English Justices of the Peace*, 36–7; E.W. Ives, 'Hobart, Sir James', *ODNB*.

Josselyn, John

Josselyn had been the earl's auditor in 1488–9 (ERO, D/DPr 139, m. 4), but only came to be a feoffee in 1502–4 and 1507. He farmed the manor of Great Canfield for the earl on a lease of at least nineteen years: PROB 11/22, fol. 19v. He made a good marriage with Cecilia Molyneux, widow of Eustace Fitzherbert, and acquired her lands in Gloucestershire, Staffordshire and Warwickshire. After her death he married Philippa, daughter of William Bradbury, esquire. His landed income by the end of his life was £83 according to his inquisition *post mortem*: C142/43/21; C142/45/9, 48, 124; C142/48/105 (Herts., Essex, Gloucs., Staffs. and Warws.). He was an executor of the earl's will.

Josselyn, Ralph

Elder brother of John, both sons of George Josselyn, esquire (*Visitation of Essex*, i, 224). Feoffee 1502–4, when described as 'gentleman', and secretary to the earl, c. 1505–7 (DL3/4, N1 b, c).

Lovell, Sir Robert

Lovell (d. 1521), an executor and annuitant (£6 13s 4d) was another feoffee and business associate in 1492 (1–3), 1501, 1502–4; and see also *Household Books*, 493, where he signed the retinue list. He was the brother of Sir Thomas Lovell: *Visitations of Norfolk, 1563, 1589 and 1613*, ed. W. Rye (London, 1891), 190–1.

Lovell, Sir Thomas

Lovell served as steward of the duchy of Lancaster in Norfolk, Suffolk and Cambridgeshire from 1489 and as joint deputy to de Vere as chief steward of the duchy south of the Trent. Lovell was an executor, and received a bequest of a 'salt of silver and gilt, with a pearl weighing 25 ounces' in the earl's will, where he was described as 'my olde frende'. He was also a knight of the body, Chancellor of the Exchequer, treasurer of the chamber, and speaker of the House of Commons in 1485: Wedgwood, ii, 555–6; Gunn, 'Sir Thomas Lovell', 117–53.

Montgomery, Sir Thomas

Sir Thomas Montgomery (d. 1495), K.G., was a feoffee in 1486 and 1492 (1) and (3). He brought twelve men to the muster of 1487, and made the earl supervisor of his will: *Household Books*, 493; Nicolas, *Testamenta Vetusta*, ii, 396. He was, however, an inveterate time-server, serving every government and king between 1450 and 1495, in itself an impressive achievement: Wedgwood, ii, 605–6. He had been given a life annuity by the twelfth earl in 1461, and in 1484 was granted Castle Hedingham and six other de Vere manors by Richard III; see above, 45, 91. Montgomery's estates in Essex were worth £47 p.a.: *CIPM Henry VII*, i, 447.

Oakley, William

Oakley was a feoffee in 1507, and was paid as a member of the household in the same year, Longleat, Misc. xi, fol. 126v. He was an executor of the earl's will and was given a £10 annuity in the same document. He was described as being late a yeoman of the earl's household in a pardon of October 1510: *LP*, I, i, no. 1803 (1); C67/60, m. 6.

Paston, Sir John III

For all his posthumous fame, Paston was by no means the most important of the earl's retainers. He was steward of all the earl's lordships in Norfolk in 1489, at the fee of 53s 4d a year, a feoffee in 1486, and the earl's deputy in the admiralty: ERO, D/DPr 139, m. 4; for the admiralty see above, 129, 139–40; Wedgwood, ii, 665. However, Paston did not participate in much business that others did, such as the major enfeoffment in 1492, or the grant to Earls Colne in 1492. He was, nonetheless, busy on the earl's diverse affairs: Rawcliffe, 'Baronial Councils in the Later Middle Ages', 96; Richmond, *Paston Family: Endings*, 164–72.

Payton, Sir Robert

Payton (d. 1518) was a feoffee in 1507, and feed £3 6s 8d in 1509. His estates were valued at £196 p.a.: E150/303/5; 475/6; 621/10; C142/33/109 (Essex, Kent, Suffolk, Cambs.).

Peke, John, esquire

Peke (d. by 1506) was a feoffee in 1486, and brought a retinue of himself and twelve men to the muster in 1487: *Household Books*, 494. In 1504 the earl and Countess Margaret granted him, in survivorship with John Danyell, the stewardship of the More (Moor Park), Hertfordshire, with wages of £10 a year: *CPR, 1494–1509*, 52.

Pirton, William senior, and William junior

Two William Pirtons were paid 53s 4d in the will. William Pirton senior was the son and heir of William Pirton, esquire, and grandson of Sir William Pirton; see *Visitations of Essex*, i, 92–3. He was a witness to the enfeoffment in 1486, and a feoffee in 1507. William Pirton, junior, his son, was part of the earl's household in 1507 (see below, 239), when he was in his late teens, as his father's inquisition *post mortem* in 1533 records William junior, then knighted, as being forty years or more. Pirton inherited land in Essex worth £53 p.a.: C142/81/97; *CPR, 1494–1509*, 418, 478, 638.

Power, John and Robert

John Power was paid an annuity of 66s 8d a year by the Dowager Countess Elizabeth: DL29/295/4848. He was bailiff of Lavenham in the valor of 1485–97, at the yearly wage of £4 11s 3d. He may be related to Robert Power, feoffee in 1492 (1) and 1501, and who was 'steward of the lord' in Buckinghamshire in the valor of 1485–97 (m. 2), at the wage of 40s. Power held land in the de Vere manor of Whitchurch: *VCH Buckinghamshire*, iii, 446.

Robson, Henry, esquire

Robson appeared as the earl's attorney in a legal case in 1465, and was a feoffee for the Dowager Countess Elizabeth: BL, Add. Ch. 28620; *CCR, 1468–76*, 334–5. He mainprised the manor of Bushey to the earl in 1486 (*CFR, 1485–1509*, 34), was a feoffee in 1486 and 1492 (3), and a witness to the grant to Earls Colne in 1492.

Rochester, Robert, esquire

Rochester was controller of the earl's household from c. 1495 until his death in 1508, at the fee of £10 a year: ERO, D/DPr 124, 131, 135A; Longleat, Misc. xi, fol. 2. He was a business associate of the earl in 1502 and 1507. Rochester had estates in Essex worth £60 p.a. at his death: *CIPM Henry VII*, iii, 316–17.

Rotheman, Thomas

Described as of Hadleigh (Suffolk), gentleman, in a Chancery case dating from between 1518 and 1529 (C1/542/16), he served as the earl's receiver-general from c. 1500 to 1513: ERO, D/DPr 131. Paid an annuity of 53s 4d in the will of 1509.

Say, Sir William

Say brought twelve men at his own cost to Oxford's muster at Cambridge on 20 July 1487: *Household Books*, 493, 495. He was also involved with the earl and others of his affinity in 1486 concerning the manor of Benington, Hertfordshire: *CCR, 1485–1500*, 44. For his career see Wedgwood, ii, 747–8.

Shelton, Sir Ralph

Shelton (d. 1499), described as a 'councillor' in a letter written between 1487 and 1499 (*PL*, vi, 143), was a feoffee in 1486 and 1492 (1) and (2). His estates were valued at £84 p.a.: *CIPM Henry VII*, ii, 144–7 (Norfolk, Suffolk).

Smyth (Smith), Henry

Controller of the earl's household in 1488 and 1490: ERO, D/DPr 139, m. 4; *Household Books*, 510. He was a feoffee of the earl in 1486.

Smyth (Smith), Robert

Smyth (d. 1493) paid 40s for the wages of one man in 1487 retinue, was the farmer of the de Vere manor of Wiggenhall, Norfolk, in 1488–9, and an attorney for the 1492 enfeoffment. He was a feudal tenant of the earl's in Wiggenhall: *Household Books*, 495; ERO, D/DPr 139, m. 2; RH, Box 38; *CIPM Henry VII*, i, 391.

Tey, Sir Henry

Henry (c. 1455–1510), was paid an annuity of £5 a year, and was also a feoffee in 1507. For his career see Wedgwood, ii, 845; Bindoff, iii, 436–7.

Tey, John

Described as of Castle Hedingham in 1498–9, and probably, therefore, a member of the earl's household, Tey held the office of feodary of the duchy of Lancaster in five counties from 1510 to 1523: Somerville, *Duchy of Lancaster*, i, 609. Tey died in Countess Elizabeth's residence at Wivenhoe in 1534; PROB 11/25, fols 121r–22r; Bindoff, iii, 437.

Tey, Thomas senior, and Thomas junior

Of the two Thomas Teys paid 53s 4d a year in the will, the senior was the son and heir of Sir Henry, and is described as being twenty-seven or more at his father's death. Thomas senior was a feoffee in 1507. Thomas junior (aged thirteen or more in 1502), was the son of William Tey (d. 1502) of the cadet branch of the Tey family based at Layer de la Haye in Essex, and was a feudal tenant of the earl at Aldham in Essex: E150/296/4 (Essex); *CIPM Henry VII*, ii, 386–7; Wedgwood, ii, 845; Bindoff, iii, 436–7.

Tyrell, Sir Robert and his son Robert

See above, 198–9.

Tyrell, Sir Thomas, and his son Thomas
Sir Thomas (d. 1512) was paid an annuity of £6 13s 4d in 1509, and was a feoffee
in 1486, 1492 (1), 1492 (2), 1502–4, 1507 and 1508. For Tyrell's military retinue
in 1487 and 1489 see *Household Books*, 493 (he arranged to serve in person, and
with twenty men) and *PL*, vi, 130 (30 men). In 1491 work was being done on Sir
Thomas Tyrell's chamber at Hedingham; *Household Books*, 520. His will made
reference to legal advice being given to him by the 'councell of my Lorde of Oxinforde': PROB 11/17, fol. 1. For his estates, valued at £129 p.a.: E150/64/2; 299/6;
963/6 (Cambs., Essex, Hants.). His son and heir, another Thomas, feed £3 6s 8d
in 1509, was part of the earl's household and was a feoffee in 1507.

Vere, Thomas
Paid an annuity of 53s 4d in the will. Possibly a younger brother or son of the
earl's cousin John de Vere. He was a member of Lincoln's inn between 1506 and
1509, where on 8 May 1509 he assaulted the butler with his dagger, and used
contumelious words in the presence of the governors: *The Black Books of Lincoln's
Inn, 1422–1586* (Lincoln's Inn, 1897), 152; *Lincoln's Inn: Admissions*, i, 32.

Waldegrave, Sir William and his sons George and William
Waldegrave (d. 1527), appointed an executor of Oxford's will, was feed £6 13s
4d p.a., and was a feoffee and business associate in 1502–4, 1507 and 1508. He
had been enfeoffed with the earl by a third party in 1486, and the earl may have
helped acquire the wardship of Geoffrey Gate for him and John Clopton in 1486:
CCR, 1485–1500, 44, 53, 96; *CPR, 1485–94*, 88; E404/80/591. Income of £242
p.a. from E150/311/3, 630/12, 692/7; C142/46/44, C142/47/18 (lands in Essex,
Suffolk and Northants.), and see Wedgwood, ii, 914–15. His eldest son, George,
was a feoffee and annuitant in 1507 and another William Waldegrave, probably
George's younger brother, was feed 53s 4d for life in the will.

Wentworth, Sir Henry, and his son Richard
Wentworth (d. 1499) was twice a witness of Oxford's enfeoffments in 1486 and
1492, and may have raised men for Oxford's muster in 1487: Wedgwood, ii,
933–4; *Household Books*, 495. His son, Richard, was enfeoffed by the earl in 1507.

Wentworth, Sir Roger
Roger (d. c. 1540), paid an annuity of £5, was the farmer of the de Vere manor
of Brokehall, Suffolk in 1488–9 (ERO, D/DPr 139, m. 3), and was a feoffee
in 1507. His inquisition *post mortem* has not survived, but by the terms of his
marriage settlement in 1497 he and his wife, Anne, daughter of Humphrey Tyrell
and granddaughter of John Helion, were to have lands in Helions Bumpstead,
Wix and Finchingfield, Essex; *CCR, 1485–1500*, 301. In addition on the death
of Anne's grandmother, Edith, Anne was to inherit lands in Essex worth £60:
CIPM Henry VII, ii, 27–30.

Wingfield, Humphrey

Wingfield (c. 1481–1545) is recorded as being the twelfth son of Sir John Wingfield. Unsurprisingly, he appears to have inherited little from his family, but was at his death holding lands worth about £20 yearly in Suffolk: C142/72/74. A lawyer by training, he was an executor of the earl's will, an annuitant (53s 4d p.a.), and a feoffee in 1507 and 1508. See also Bindoff, iii, 640–1, though this biography surprisingly omits any mention of the thirteenth earl.

Annuitants in the will of 1509 and household staff, 1507–9

Annuitants, 1509: PROB 11/17, fols 86r, v

This is the codicell of me John de Veer, Erle of Oxinford videlicet I woll that all thies persones whose namys be especified here under this clause shall receyve and have every oon of theym an yerely annuytie for terme of their lyvys according to the some annexid unto eche of their namys, thesame to goo owt and be paid of suche my landes and tenements as myn executors or the more part of theym shall therunto appoynt: Sir Thomas Tyrell, knyght, £6 13s 4d, Sir Robery Drury, knyght, £6 13s 4d, Sir Robert Lovell, knyght, £6 13s 4d, Sir William Waldegrave, knight, £6 13s 4d, Sir Roger Wentworth, knight, 100s, Sir William Fyndern, knight, 100s, Sir Henry Tey, knight, 100s, Sir Robert Payton, knight, £3 6s 8d, Sir John Grene, knight, £3 6s 8d, Sir William Clopton, knight, £3 6s 8d, Sir Robert Cotton, knight, £3 6s 8d, Sir Giles Alington, knight, £3 6s 8d, my cousyn John Veer over and besides myn other bequestis in my testament and last will £20, John Josselyn £10, John Danyell £10, William Okeley £10, Robert Brews 53s 4d, John Goldingham 53s 4d, William Ayloff 53s 4d, John Aspelon 53s 4d, Humfrey Wingfeld 53s 4d, William Pyrton thelder 53s 4d, John Fowhell 53s 4d, Geffrey Gate 53s 4d, George Waldegrave 53s 4d, Thomas Tyrell the sonne of Sir Thomas £3 6s 8d, Richard Appulton 53s 4d, William Sondes £3 6s 8d, John Barners £3 6s 8d, Antony Danvers 53s 4d, Thomas Veer 53s 4d, Henry Radclif 53s 4d, Thomas Brews 53s 4d, Robert Tyrell 53s 4d, William Waldegrave 53s 4d, Thomas Tey, senior, 53s 4d, Thomas Tey, junior, 53s 4d, William Pirton, junior, 53s 4d, Richard Wryght £4, Thomas Lathbury 53s 4d, Thomas Rotheman 53s 4d, Thomas Radclif 53s 4d, Robert Skern 53s 4d, Robert Dedyk 40s, Lewes Blodwell for keping of Campis mewse over and besides his fee for keping of the parc there 60s 10d, Laurence Younge 40s, Roger Neve 40s, Griffith Gough 40s, George Reynew 40s, George Traas 40s, John Swayn 60s 10d, Henry Watson 40s, John Hewet 40s, William Dikson 40s, Robert Broughton 53s 4d, Laurence Forster 53s 4d, Frances Burton 100s, Robert Goldingham 53s 4d.

The Household in 1507: Longleat, Misc xi, fols 126v–135r

Of the 123 men who were part of the household in 1507, fifteen were annuitants, and at least forty-three were paid a singular reward in a second codicil to the earl's will.

Annuitants
Thomas Brewes, Anthony Danvers, John Danyell, Robert Dedyk, William Dixson, John Hewet, Thomas Lathbury, Roger Neve, William Pyrton, junior, William Okeley, Henry Radclif, George Reynew, William Sandes, Thomas Tyrell, junior, Henry Watson.

Paid rewards in the will[1]
Richard Baker, James Baldwin, Peter Bernham, John Brand, John Brown, lutor, Robert Bryan, Robert Bukton, John Cole, miller, Richard Cook, John Doye, Simon Dyestar, William Elyston, Thomas Estay, Thomas Eyer, Anthony Freman, Simon Gatward, John Greenleaf, John Harrison, George Hesketh, Laurence Houghton, Oliver Hunt, Thomas Jackson, Nicholas Jeve, Richard Jeweller, John Kempe, John Lavers, John Legge, Thomas May, John Nash, Hugh Pigg, John Pigge, Thomas Porter, Thomas Revelay, David Rodderford, Peter South, Walter Symond, Cornelius Thomson, John Tolton, George Turner, John William, Lewis Williams, Richard Wilton, John Wood.[2]

Others in the household account
William Addeson, John Barneys, John Bowman, John Braxsted, Thomas Brett, John Brian, Alexander Broun, Gilbert Brynkley, Thomas Bukley, John Butler, Henry Carpenter, Robert Cotes, John Curby, William Davyson, John Dixson, Roger Dyrik, Thomas Elyott, John Ewres, William Ferror, Richard Fitch, Thomas Fletcher, Thomas Freman, John Garrold, John Glamvild, Geoffrey Gryffith, Hamond Hunt, Henry Hunt, George Jagger, William Jakson, Robert Jegon, Robert Keen, Robert Keler, Thomas Kyng, John Lewes, John Lytyll, John Man, John Mason, John Maw, Thomas Meryman, Robert Moore, Thomas Munden, Thomas Myller, Thomas Neve, William Nicoll, William Piggott, James Popelay, George Powntays, Andrew Reveley, Martin Richold, William Ryngar, John Saunder, Thomas Smeton, Thomas Sporne, William Stanley, Cely Sunham, Robert Sunham, William Swift, messenger, John Tailor, William Turner, John Tye, John Vowell, Walter Wingfield, Henry Witeman, and a laundress ('Lotric hospicii')

---

[1]   Houghton, a 'Hakys', George Turner, a child of the chapel and Robert Bukton, a craftsman, all appear in the household accounts of 1490–1: *Household Books*, 504, 505, 511.
[2]   Ninety-nine men in total were paid rewards in the will. In addition to the forty-three that can be clearly identified by name as being part of the household, John Cole, the miller, paid in the 1507–8 account may well be 'the Miller' paid 40s reward in the will and John Kempe in the account is probably 'Kemp the gardener' in the will. In addition the seven men not named but given job descriptions in the will (two grooms of the stable, a 'groom chariotman, a groom brewer, a groom cator, a groom slaughterman and a groom of the scullery') may be men named, but not given job descriptions in the account: 'Last Testament', 319; Longleat, Misc. xi, fols 126v–35r.

Select Bibliography

Unprinted Primary Sources

The National Archives: Public Record Office
CHANCERY
C 1 (Early Chancery Proceedings), C 4 (Court of Chancery, answers etc before 1660), C 47 (Chancery Miscellanea), C 53 (Charter Rolls), C 54 (Close Rolls), C 66 (Patent Rolls), C 81–2 (Warrants for the Great Seal, Series I and II), C 138–42 (Inquisitions *Post Mortem*), C 145 (Inquisitions Miscelleaneous), C 254 (Writs of Dedimus Potestatem), C 255 (Chancery Files, Tower and Rolls Chapel Series, Miscellaneous Files and Writs)

COURT OF COMMON PLEAS
CP 25 (Feet of Fine), CP 40 (Plea Rolls)

DUCHY OF LANCASTER
DL 1 (Court of Duchy Chamber: Pleadings), DL 3 (Court of Duchy Chamber: Pleadings, Depositions, and Examinations), DL 29 (Ministers' Accounts)

EXCHEQUER
E 13 (Exchequer of Pleas: Plea Rolls), E 28 (Council and Privy Seal Records), E 36 (Miscellaneous Books), E 101 (Accounts Various), E 137 (Estreats), E 150 (Exchequer Inquisitions *Post Mortem*), E 159 (Memoranda Rolls), E 372 (Pipe Rolls), E 401 (Receipt Rolls), E 403 (Issue Rolls), E 404 (Writs and Warrants for Issue), E 405 (Tellers' Rolls).

KING'S BENCH
KB 8 (Baga de Secretis), KB 9 (Ancient Indictments), KB 27 (Plea Rolls), KB 29 (Controlment Rolls), KB 145 (Recorda)

PREROGATIVE COURT OF CANTERBURY (PCC)
PROB 11 (Will Registers)

PRIVY SEAL OFFICE
PSO 1 (Signet and other Warrants for the Privy Seal, Series I), PSO 2 (Series II)

SPECIAL COLLECTIONS
SC 1 (Ancient Correspondence), SC 6 (Ministers' Accounts), SC 8 (Ancient Petitions), SC 11 (Rentals and Surveys)

COURT OF STAR CHAMBER
STAC 1 (Star Chamber Proceedings, Henry VII), STAC 2 (Star Chamber Proceedings, Henry VIII)

STATE PAPER OFFICE
SP 1 (State Papers, Henry VIII)

Bodleian Library (Oxford)
MS Rawlinson B 248 (De Vere Cartulary); Rawlinson B 257, Rawlinson B 319 (Accounts relating to the honour of Castle Hedingham)

British Library (London)
Additional Charters, Additional MSS, Harleian MSS, Cotton MSS, Egerton MSS, Lansdowne MSS, Stowe MSS.

Cambridgeshire Archives (Cambridge)
Various Collections

Essex Record Office (Chelmsford)
D/DPr (De Vere/Bayning Papers)
Various manorial, urban and family collections

Longleat House (Wiltshire)
Miscellanea xi (De Vere household account, 1507)

Norfolk Record Office (Norwich)
Norwich City records
King's Lynn Borough Records
Townshend MSS

Raynham Hall (Norfolk)
Boxes 1–125, and Attic Miscellany (Estate and Family Papers)

Suffolk Record Office (Ipswich and Bury St Edmunds)
C/2/10/3/1–8 (Ipswich borough composite court books, 1486–1513)
Various manorial, urban and family collections

Westminster Abbey Muniments
Bray/Beaufort papers, and miscellaneous items

St George's Chapel, Windsor
XI, XV (Records relating to Gloucester's grant of de Vere manors to the college in 1480)

Printed Primary Sources

The Anglica Historia of Polydore Vergil, A.D. 1485–1537, ed. D. Hay (Camden Society, third series, lxxiv, 1950)

Annales or a Generall Chronicle of England, ed. J. Stow (London, 1615)

The Armburgh Papers, ed. C. Carpenter (Cambridge, 1999)

'The Ballard of Bosworth Field', in *Bishop Percy's Folio Manuscript*, ed. J.W. Hales and F.J. Furnivall (London, 1868), 233–59.

The Black Book of the Admiralty, ed. T. Twiss (4 vols, Rolls Series, 1871–6)

A Book of Knights, Knights of the Bath and Knights Bachelor, ed. W.C. Metcalfe (London, 1885)

The Brut or the Chronicles of England, ed. F.W.D. Brie (2 vols, EETS, 1908), ii.

Calendar of Documents Relating to Scotland (Edinburgh, 1881–1986)

Calendar of Inquisitions Miscellaneous (8 vols, London/Woodbridge, 1916–2003)

Calendarium Inquisitionum Post Mortem Sive Escheatorum, vol. iv, ed. J. Cayley and J. Bayley (Record Commission, 1828)

Calendar of Inquisitions Post Mortem (23 vols, London/Woodbridge, 1904–2004)

Calendar of State Papers: Milan, vol. i, ed. A.B. Hinds (London, 1913)

Calendar of State Papers: Spanish, vol. i, ed. G.A. Bergenroth (London, 1862)

Calendar of the Charter Rolls (6 vols, London, 1916–27)

Calendar of the Close Rolls (45 vols, London, 1892–1954)

Calendar of the Fine Rolls (22 vols, London, 1911–62)

Calendar of the Patent Rolls (52 vols, London, 1891–1916)

Cartularium Prioratus de Colne, ed. J.L. Fisher (Colchester, 1946)

The Chronicle of Calais in the Reigns of Henry VII and Henry VIII, ed. J. G. Nichols (Camden Society, o.s., xxxv, 1846)

Chronicle of Iohn Hardyng, together with the Continuation by Robert Grafton, ed. H. Ellis (London, 1812)

'The Chronicle of John Stone', ed. W.G. Searle, in *Christ Church Canterbury* (Cambridge Antiquarian Society Publications, xxxiv, 1902), 1–119

A Chronicle of London from 1089–1483, ed. N.H. Nicolas (London, 1827)

Chronicle of the White Rose of York, ed. J.A. Giles (London, 1845)

The Chronicles of London, ed. C.L. Kingsford (Oxford, 1905)

A Chronicle of the First Thirteen Years of the Reign of King Edward IV, by John Warkworth, ed. J.O. Halliwell (Camden Society, o.s., x, 1834)

Chronicon Angliae Temporis Henrici VI, ed. J.A. Giles (London, 1848)

Chronique de Jean Molinet, ed. J.A. Buchon (5 vols, Paris, 1827–8)

La Chronique d'Enguerran de Monstrelet, ed. L. Douet-d'Arcq (6 vols, Paris, 1859)

The Cornish Lands of the Arundells of Lanherne, ed. H.S.A. Fox and O.J. Padel (Devon and Cornwall Record Society, n.s, xli, Exeter, 2000)

The Crowland Chronicle Continuations; 1459–1486, ed. N. Pronay and J. Cox (Gloucester, 1986)

A Descriptive Catalogue of Ancient Deeds in the Public Record Office (6 vols in 7, London, 1890–1915)

Domesday Book: Cambridgeshire; Essex; Suffolk, ed. A. Rumble (Chichester, 1981–6)

Domesday Book: Huntingdonshire; Middlesex, ed. J. Morris (Chichester, 1975)

An English Chronicle, ed. J.S. Davies (Camden Society, o.s., lxiv, 1856)

The Estate and Household Accounts of William Worsley, Dean of St. Paul's Cathedral, 1479–1497, ed. H. Kleineke and S.R. Hovland (Donnington, 2004)

Excerpta Historica, ed. S. Bentley (London, 1831)

The New Chronicles of England and France, by Robert Fabyan, ed. H. Ellis (London, 1811)

The Fane Fragment of the 1461 Lords' Journal, ed. W.H. Dunham (New Haven, CT, 1935)

Feet of Fines for Essex, ed. P.H. Reaney and M. Fitch (4 vols, Colchester, 1899–1964)

Foedera, Conventiones, Literae ..., ed. T. Rymer (The Hague, 1745)

Francis Bacon's History of the Reign of King Henry VII, ed. R. Lockyer (London, 1971)

The Great Chronicle of London, ed. A.H. Thomas and I.D. Thornley (London, 1938)

The Grey of Ruthin Valor, ed. R.I. Jack (Sydney, 1965)

Hanserecesse, 1431–1476, ed. G. van der Ropp (Lubeck, 1890)

The Herald's Memoir 1486–90, ed. E. Cavell (Donnington, 2009)

The Historical Collections of a London Citizen, ed. J. Gairdner (Camden Society, n.s., xvii, 1876)

Historical Poems of the Fourteenth and Fifteenth Centuries, ed. R.H. Robbins (New York, 1959)

'Historie of the Arrivall of King Edward IV A.D. 1471', ed. J. Bruce, in *Three Chronicles of the Reign of Edward IV*, ed. K. Dockray (Gloucester, 1988)

Household Accounts from Medieval England, ed. C.M. Woolgar (2 vols, Oxford, 1992–3)

Household Books of John, Duke of Norfolk and Thomas, Earl of Surrey, temp. 1481–1490, ed. J.P. Collier (Roxburghe Club, London, 1844)

The Household Books of John Howard, Duke of Norfolk, 1462–71, 1481–3, ed. A. Crawford (Stroud, 1992)

The Household of Edward IV. The Black Book and the Ordinance of 1478, ed. A.R. Myers (Manchester, 1959)

Ipswich Borough Archives, 1255–1835. A Catalogue, ed. D. Allen (Suffolk Record Society, xliii, 2000)

'John Benet's Chronicle', ed. G.L. Harriss and M.A. Harriss, in *Camden Miscellany XXIV* (Camden Society, fourth series, ix, 1972), 151–233

Johannis Lelandi Antiquarii de Rebus Britannicis Collectanea, ed. T. Hearne (6 vols, London, 1774)

'The Last Testament and Inventory of John de Veer, Thirteenth Earl of Oxford', ed. W.H. St John Hope, *Archaeologia*, lxvi (1914–15), 310–48

Letters and Papers, Foreign and Domestic, of the Reign of Henry VIII, ed. J.S. Brewer, R.H. Brodie and J. Gairdner (23 vols in 38, London, 1862–1932)

Letters and Papers Illustrative of the Reigns of Richard III and Henry VII, ed. J. Gairdner (2 vols, Roll Series, 1861)

Letters and Papers Illustrative of the Wars of the English in France during the Reign of Henry VI, King of England, ed. J. Stevenson (2 vols, Roll Series, 1864)

Material for a History of the Reign of Henry VII, ed. W. Campbell (2 vols, Rolls Series, 1873–7)

The Northumberland Household Book. The Regulations and Establishment of the Household of Henry Algernon Percy, Fifth Earl of Northumberland, Begun 1512, ed. T. Percy (Reprinted London, 1905)

Oeuvres de Froissart, ed. K. de Lettenhove (26 vols, Brussels, 1867–77)

Parliament Rolls of Medieval England, 1275–1504, general editor C. Given-Wilson (16 vols, Woodbridge, 2005)

The Paston Letters, ed. J. Gairdner (6 vols, London, 1904)

Paston Letters and Papers of the Fifteenth Century, vols I and II, ed. N. Davis (Oxford, 1971–6); vol. III, ed. R. Beadle and C.F. Richmond (EETS, Special Series, xxii, Oxford, 2005)

The Plumpton Letters and Papers, ed. J. Kirby (Cambridge, 1996)

Proceedings and Ordinances of the Privy Council of England, ed. N.H. Nicolas (7 vols, London, 1834–7), iii–vi.

The Reburial of Richard Duke of York, 21–30 July 1476, ed. A.F. Sutton, L. Visser-Fuchs and P.W. Hammond (Richard III Society, 1996)

The Receyt of the Ladie Kateryne, ed. G. Kipling (EETS, ccxcvi, 1990)

Records of the City of Norwich, ed. W. Hudson and J.C. Tingey (2 vols, Norwich/London, 1906–10)

Recueil des Chroniques et Anchiennes Histories de la Grand Bretagne a Present Nomme Engleterre par Jehan de Waurin, ed. W. Hardy (5 vols, Rolls series, 1864–91)

The Red Paper Book of Colchester, ed. W.G. Benham (Colchester, 1902)

Register of John Morton, Archbishop of Canterbury (1486–1500), ed. C. Harper-Bill (3 vols, Canterbury and York Society, 1987–2001)

Register of the Great Seal of Scotland, ed. J.M. Thomson and J.B. Paul (11 vols, Edinburgh, 1814–1914), vol. ii

Registrum Abbatiae Johannis Whethamstede, ed. H.T. Riley (2 vols, Rolls series, 1872–3)

Rotuli Parliamentorum (6 vols, London, 1767–77)

The Rutland Papers. Original Documents Illustrative of the Courts and Times of Henry VII and Henry VIII, ed. W. Jerdan (Camden Society, o.s., xxi, 1842)

Select Cases in the Council of Henry VII, ed. C.G. Bayne and W.H. Dunham (Selden Society, lxxv, 1956)

Select Cases before the King's Council in the Star Chamber, ed. I.S. Leadam (Selden Society, xvi, 1963)

'The Spouselles of the Ladye Marye', ed. J. Gairdner, *Camden Miscellany IX* (Camden Society, o.s., liii, 1895)

Statutes of the Realm (11 vols, London, 1810–28)

The Stonor Letters and Papers, ed. C.L. Kingsford (2 vols, Camden Society, third series, xxix–xxx, 1919)

'The Testament and Last Will of Elizabeth, Widow of John de Veer, Thirteenth Earl of Oxford', ed. H.W. Lewer, *TEAS*, xx (1933), 7–16.

Three Books of Polydore Vergil's English History Comprising the Reigns of Henry VI, Edward IV and Richard III, ed. H. Ellis (Camden Society, o.s., xxix, 1844)

Three Fifteenth Century Chronicles, ed. J. Gairdner (Camden Society, n. s., xxviii, 1880)

The Union of the Two Noble and Illustrious Families of Lancaster and York, by Edward Hall (Menston, 1970)

Valor Ecclesiasticus temp Henry VIII, ed. J. Caley (6 vols, Record Commission, 1810–34)

The Visitations of Essex, ed. W.C. Metcalfe (2 vols, London, 1878)

The Visitation of Norfolk in 1563, ed. G.H. Dashwood *et al.* (2 vols, Norwich, 1878–95)

The Visitation of Suffolk, 1561, ed. J. Corder (2 vols, Harleian Society, 1981–4)
William Worcestre: Itineraries, ed. J.H. Harvey (Oxford, 1969)
The York House Books, 1461–90, ed. L.C. Attreed (2 vols, Stroud, 1991)

Secondary Sources

Anderson, Verily, *The de Veres of Castle Hedingham* (Lavenham, 1993)

Anglo, S., 'The Foundation of the Tudor Dynasty: the Coronation and Marriage of Henry VII', *Guildhall Miscellanea*, ii (1960), 3–11

——, 'The Court Festivals of Henry VII', *Bulletin of the John Rylands Library*, xliii (1960–1), 12–45

Antonovics, A.V., 'Henry VII, King of England, "By the Grace of Charles VIII of France"', in *Kings and Nobles in the Later Middle Ages. A Tribute to Charles Ross*, ed. R.A. Griffiths and J. Sherborne (Gloucester, 1986), 169–84

Archer, R.E., 'Rich Old Ladies: the Problems of Late Medieval Dowagers', in *Property and Politics. Essays in Late Medieval English History*, ed. A.F. Pollard (Gloucester, 1984), 15–35

Armstrong, C.A.J., 'Politics and the Battle of St. Albans, 1455', *BIHR*, xxxiii (1960), 1–72

Arthurson, I., *The Perkin Warbeck Conspiracy, 1491–99* (Stroud, 1994)

Attreed, L.C., *The King's Towns: Identity and Survival in Late Medieval English Boroughs* (New York, 2001)

Bailey, M., *Medieval Suffolk: an Economic and Social History, 1200–1500* (Woodbridge, 2007)

Baldwin, D., *The Kingmaker's Sisters. Six Powerful Women in the Wars of the Roses* (Stroud, 2009)

Bean, J.M.W., *The Estates of the Percy Family, 1416–1537* (Oxford, 1955)

Bennett, M., 'Henry VII and the Northern Rising of 1489', *EHR*, cv (1990), 34–59

——, *The Battle of Bosworth* (Gloucester, 1985)

——, *Lambert Simnel and the Battle of Stoke* (Stroud, 1997)

Bernard, G.W., 'The Tudor Nobility in Perspective', in idem, ed., *The Tudor Nobility* (Manchester, 1992), 1–48

——, *The Power of the Early Tudor Nobility: A Study of the Fourth and Fifth Earls of Shrewsbury* (Brighton, 1985)

Bindoff, S.T., ed., *History of Parliament: the Commons, 1509–1558* (3 vols, London, 1982)

Blomefield, F., *An Essay Towards a Topographical History of Norfolk* (11 vols, London, 1805–1810)

Britnell, R.H., *Growth and Decline in Colchester, 1300–1525* (Cambridge, 1986)

Cameron, A., 'The Giving of Livery and Retaining in Henry VII's Reign', *Renaissance and Modern Studies*, xviii (1974), 17–35

Carpenter, C., 'The Beauchamp Affinity: A Study of Bastard Feudalism at Work', *EHR*, xcv (1980), 515–32

——, 'Who Ruled the Midlands in the Late Middle Ages?', *Midland History*, xix (1994), 1–20

——, 'Henry VII and the English Polity', in *The Reign of Henry VII*, ed. B. Thompson (Stamford, 1995), 11–30

——, *Locality and Polity: A Study of Warwickshire Landed Society, 1401–99* (Cambridge, 1992)

——, *The Wars of the Roses. Politics and the Constitution in England, c. 1437–1509* (Cambridge, 1997)

Castor, H.R., 'The Duchy of Lancaster and the Rule of East Anglia, 1399–1440: A Prologue to the Paston Letters', in *Crown, Government and People in the Fifteenth Century*, ed. R.E. Archer (Stroud, 1995), 53–78

——, 'Vere, John de, twelfth earl of Oxford (1408–1462)', *ODNB*

——, *The King, the Crown and the Duchy of Lancaster. Public Authority and Private Power, 1399–1461* (Oxford, 2000)

——, *Blood and Roses* (London, 2004)

Cavill, P.R., *The English Parliaments of Henry VII* (Oxford, 2009)

Cherry, M., 'The Courtenay Earls of Devon: the Formation and Disintegration of a Late Medieval Aristocratic Affinity', *Southern History*, i (1979), 71–93

——, 'The Struggle for Power in Mid-fifteenth-century Devonshire', in *Patronage, Crown and the Provinces in Later Medieval England*, ed. R.A. Griffiths (Gloucester, 1981), 123–44

Chrimes, S.B., *Henry VII* (London, 1972)

Clark, L., 'Magnates and their Affinities in the Parliaments of 1386–1421', in *The McFarlane Legacy*, ed. R.H. Britnell and A.J. Pollard (Stroud, 1995), 127–54

Cokayne, G.E., *The Complete Peerage or a History of the House of Lords and all its Members from the Earliest Times*, ed. V. Gibbs *et al.* (14 vols in 15, London, 1910–98)

Condon, M.M., 'Ruling Elites in the Reign of Henry VII', in *Patronage, Pedigree and Power*, ed. C.D. Ross (Gloucester, 1979), 109–42

——, 'An Anachronism with Intent? Henry VII's Council Ordinance of 1491/2', in *Kings and Nobles in the Later Middle Ages. A Tribute to Charles Ross*, ed. R.A. Griffiths and J. Sherborne (Gloucester, 1986), 228–53

——, 'The Last Will of Henry VII: Document and Text', in *Westminster Abbey: The Lady Chapel of Henry VII*, ed. T. Tatton-Brown and R. Mortimer (Woodbridge, 2003), 99–140

Cooper, J.P., 'Henry VII's Last Years Reconsidered', *The Historical Journal*, ii (1959), 103–29

Coppinger, W.A., *The Manors of Suffolk* (7 vols, London/Manchester, 1905–1911)

Coward, B., *The Stanleys, Lords Stanley and Earls of Derby, 1385–1672* (Manchester, 1983)

Crawford, A., 'Victims of Attainder; the Howard and de Vere Women in the Late Fifteenth Century', in *Medieval Women in Southern England*, ed. K. Bate and M. Barber (Reading Medieval Studies, xv, 1989), 59–74

——, *Yorkist Lord. John Howard, Duke of Norfolk, c. 1425–1485* (London, 2010)

Cunningham, S., 'Henry VII, Sir Thomas Butler and the Stanley Family: Regional Politics and the Assertion of Royal Influence in North-West England, 1471–1521', in *Social Attitudes and Political Structures in the Fifteenth Century*, ed. T. Thornton (Stroud, 2000), 220–41

——, *Henry VII* (Abingdon, 2007)

Currin, J., '"To Traffic with War"? Henry VII and the French Campaign of 1492', in *The English Experience in France, c.1450–1558: War, Diplomacy and Cultural Exchange*, ed. D.A. Grummit (Aldershot, 2002), 106–31

Davies, C.S.L., 'The Administration of the Royal Navy under Henry VIII: The Origins of the Navy Board', *EHR*, lxxx (1965), 268–88

——, 'Bishop John Morton, the Holy See, and the Accession of Henry VII', *EHR*, cii (1987), 2–30

Davies, R.R., 'Baronial Accounts, Incomes and Arrears in the Later Middle Ages', *Econ HR*, xxi (1968), 211–29

Doyle, A.I., 'Books Connected with the Vere family and Barking Abbey', *TEAS*, xxv (1958), 222–43

Dugdale, W., *The Baronage of England or an Historical Account of the Lives and Most Memorable Actions of our English Nobility* (2 vols, London, 1675–6)

Dunham, W.H., *Lord Hastings' Indentured Retainers, 1461–83* (New Haven, CT, 1955)

Elton, G.R., 'Henry VII: Rapacity and Remorse', *The Historical Journal*, i (1958), 21–39

——, 'Henry VII: A Restatement', *The Historical Journal*, iv (1961), 1–29

Emden, A.B., *Biographical Register of the University of Cambridge to 1500* (Cambridge, 1963)

Fairweather, F.H., 'Colne Priory, Essex, and the Burials of the Earls of Oxford', *Archaeologia*, lxxxvii (1937), 275–95

Fisher, W.R., *The Forest of Essex* (London, 1887)

Giry-Deloison, C., 'Money and Early Tudor Diplomacy. The English Pensioners of the French Kings (1475–1547)', *Medieval History*, iii (1993), 128–46

Given-Wilson, C., *The English Nobility in the Late Middle Ages* (London, 1987)

Gransden, A., *Historical Writing in England: c. 1307 to the Early Sixteenth Century* (London, 1982)

Gray, H.L., 'Incomes from Land in England in 1436', *EHR*, xlix (1934), 607–39

Griffiths, R.A., 'Wales and the Marches', in *Fifteenth Century England, 1399–1509*, ed. S. Chrimes, C.D. Ross and R.A. Griffiths (Manchester, 1972), 145–72

——, 'The King's Council and the First Protectorate of the Duke of York, 1453–4', *EHR*, xcix (1984), 67–83

——, *The Reign of King Henry VI: The Exercise of Royal Authority, 1422–1461* (London, 1981)

——, *Sir Rhys ap Thomas and his Family: A Study in the Wars of the Roses and Early Tudor Politics* (Cardiff, 1993)

Griffiths, R.A. and Thomas, R.S., *The Making of the Tudor Dynasty* (Stroud, 1985)

Grummitt, D., 'Henry VII, Chamber Finance and the "New Monarchy": Some New Evidence', *Historical Research*, lxxii (1999), 229–43

——, 'The Court, War and Noble Power in England, c. 1475–1558', in *The Court as a Stage. England and the Low Countries in the Later Middle Ages*, ed. S.J. Gunn and A. Janse (Woodbridge, 2006), 145–55

Gunn, S.J., 'Chivalry and the Politics of the Early Tudor Court', in *Chivalry and the Renaissance*, ed. S. Anglo (Woodbridge, 1990), 107–28

——, 'The Accession of Henry VIII', *Historical Research*, lxiv (1991), 278–88

——, 'Henry Bourgchier, Earl of Essex, 1477–1540', in *The Tudor Nobility*, ed. G.W. Bernard (Manchester, 1992), 134–79

——, 'The Courtiers of Henry VII', *EHR*, cviii (1993), 23–49

——, 'Sir Thomas Lovell (c.1449–1524): A New Man in a New Monarchy?', in *The End of the Middle Ages? England in the Fifteenth and Sixteenth Centuries*, ed. J.L. Watts (Stroud, 1998), 117–53

——, 'Vere, John de, Thirteenth Earl of Oxford (1442–1513)', *ODNB*

——, 'The Court of Henry VII' in *The Court as a Stage. England and the Low Countries in the Later Middle Ages*, ed. S.J. Gunn and A. Janse (Woodbridge, 2006), 132–44

——, 'Henry VII in Context: Problems and Possibilities', *History*, xcii (2007), 301–17

——, *Charles Brandon, Duke of Suffolk, c.1484–1545* (Oxford, 1988)

——, *Early Tudor Government* (Basingstoke, 1995)

Gunn, S.J., Grummitt, D. and Cools, H., *War, State and Society in England and the Netherlands 1477–1559* (Oxford, 2007)

Halliday, R., 'Robert de Vere, Ninth Earl of Oxford', *Medieval History*, iii (1993), 71–85

Hammond, P.W., *The Battles of Barnet and Tewkesbury* (Stroud, 1990)

Hampton, W.E., 'Sir James Tyrell', *The Ricardian*, 4:63 (1978), 9–22

Hanham, A., 'Edmund de la Pole, Defector', *Journal of Renaissance Studies*, ii (1988), 240–50

Hanna, R. and Redworth, A.S.G., 'Rotheley, the de Vere Circle and the Ellesmere Chaucer', *Huntington Library Quarterly*, lviii (1995), 11–35

Harris, B.J., *Edward Stafford, Third Duke of Buckingham, 1478–1521* (Stanford, CA, 1986)

Harrison, C.J., 'The Petition of Edmund Dudley', *EHR*, lxxxvii (1972), 82–99

Harriss, G.L., 'The King and his Magnates', in idem, ed., *Henry V: The Practice of Kingship* (Oxford, 1985), 31–52

——, 'Political Society and the Growth of Government in Late Medieval England', *Past and Present*, cxxxviii (1993), 28–57

Hatcher, J., *Plague, Population and the English Economy, 1348–1530* (London, 1977)

Haward, W.I., 'Economic Aspects of the Wars of the Roses in East Anglia', *EHR*, xli (1926), 170–89

——, 'Gilbert Debenham: A Medieval Rascal in Real Life', *History*, xiii (1928–9), 300–14

Hayward, M., *Rich Apparel. Clothing and the Law in Henry VIII's England* (Farnham, 2009)

Head, C., 'Pius II and the Wars of the Roses', *Archivum Historiae Pontificiae*, viii (1970), 139–78

Hicks, M.A., 'Dynastic Change and Northern Society: The Career of the Fourth Earl of Northumberland, 1470–89', *Northern History*, xiv (1978), 78–107

——, 'The Yorkshire Rising of 1489', *Northern History*, xxii (1986), 39–62

——, 'The Last Days of Elizabeth, Countess of Oxford', in idem, *Richard III and his Rivals* (London, 1991), 297–316

——, 'Lord Hastings' Indentured Retainers', in idem, *Richard III and his Rivals* (London, 1991), 229–46

——, *False, Fleeting, Perjur'd Clarence* (Gloucester, 1980)

——, *Bastard Feudalism* (Harlow, 1995)

——, *Warwick the Kingmaker* (Oxford, 1998)

Holmes, G.A., *The Estates of the Higher Nobility in Fourteenth Century England* (Cambridge, 1957)

Hooker, J.R., 'Notes on the Organisation and Supply of the Tudor Military under Henry VII', *Huntington Library Quarterly*, xxiii (1959–60), 19–31

James, M.E., *A Tudor Magnate and the Tudor State. Henry Fifth Earl of Northumberland* (Borthwick Papers, xxx, York, 1966)

Johnson, P.A., *Duke Richard of York* (Oxford, 1988)

Jones, M. and Walker, S., 'Private Indentures for Life Service in Peace and War, 1278–1476', *Camden Miscellany*, xxxii (Camden Society, fifth series, iii, 1994), 1–191

Jones, M.K., 'Henry VII, Lady Margaret Beaufort and the Orleans Ransom', in *Kings and Nobles in the Later Middle Ages. A Tribute to Charles Ross*, ed. R.A. Griffiths and J. Sherborne (Gloucester, 1986), 254–73

——, 'The Myth of 1485; Did France Really Put Henry Tudor on the English Throne?', in *The English Experience in France, c. 1450–1558*, ed. D. Grummitt (London, 2002), 85–105

——, *Bosworth, 1485. Psychology of a Battle* (Stroud, 2002)

Jones, M.K and Underwood, M.G., *The King's Mother. Lady Margaret Beaufort, Countess of Richmond and Derby* (Cambridge, 1992)

Keen, M.H., 'Treason Trials under the Law of Arms', *TRHS*, fifth series, xii (1962), 85–103

——, 'The Jurisdiction and Origins of the Constable's Court', in *War and Government in the Middle Ages. Essays in Honour of J.O. Prestwich*, ed. J. Gillingham and J.C. Holt (Woodbridge, 1984), 159–69

Kingsford, C.L., *English Historical Literature in the Fifteenth Century* (Oxford, 1913)

Kleineke, H.W., '"Morton's Fork"? – Henry VII's "Forced Loan" of 1496', *The Ricardian*, xiii (2003), 315–27

——, 'Why the West was Wild: Law and Disorder in Fifteenth-Century Cornwall and Devon', in *The Fifteenth Century III*, ed. L. Clark (Woodbridge, 2003), 75–94

——, 'Gerhard von Wesel's Newsletter from England', *The Ricardian*, xvi (2006), 66–83

——, *Edward IV* (London, 2009)

Lander, J.R., 'Council, Administration and Councillors, 1461–85', *BIHR*, xxxii (1959), 138–80

——, *Crown and Nobility, 1450–1509* (London, 1976)

——, *English Justices of the Peace, 1461–1509* (Gloucester, 1989)

Luckett, D.A., 'Crown Office and Licensed Retinues in the Reign of Henry VII', in *Rulers and Ruled in Late Medieval England*, ed. R.E. Archer and S. Walker (London, 1995), 223–38

——, 'Crown Patronage and Political Morality in Early Tudor England: The Case of Giles, Lord Daubeney', *EHR*, xc (1995), 578–95

——, 'The Thames Valley Conspiracies against Henry VII', *Historical Research*, lxviii (1995), 164–72

——, 'The Rise and Fall of a Noble Dynasty: Henry VII and the Lords Willoughby de Broke', *Historical Research*, lxix (1996), 254–65

MacCulloch, D., *Suffolk and the Tudors: Politics and Religion in an English County, 1500–1600* (Oxford, 1986)

Madden, F., 'Documents Relating to Perkin Warbeck, with Remarks on his History', *Archaeologia*, xxvii (1838), 153–210

Maddern, P., *Violence and Social Order. East Anglia, 1422–42* (Oxford, 1992)

Maddicott, J.R., 'Follower, Leader, Pilgrim, Saint: Robert de Vere, Earl of Oxford, at the Shrine of Simon de Montfort, 1273', *EHR*, cix (1994), 641–53

McFarlane, K.B., *The Nobility of Later Medieval England* (Oxford, 1973)

——, *Fifteenth Century England* (London, 1981)

McGill, P., *The Battle of Barnet* (Lincoln, 1996)

Mertes, K., *English Noble Households from 1250–1600* (Oxford, 1988)

Miller, H., 'Subsidy Assessments of the Peerage in the Sixteenth Century', *BIHR*, xxviii (1955), 15–34

——, *Henry VIII and the English Nobility* (Oxford, 1986)

Mitchell, R.J., *John Tiptoft* (London, 1938)

Morant, P., *The History and Antiquities of Essex* (2 vols, 1768)

Morgan, D.A.L., 'The King's Affinity in the Polity of Yorkist England', *TRHS*, fifth series, xxiii (1973), 1–25

——, 'Hearne's "Fragment" and the Long Prehistory of English Memoirs', *EHR*, cxxiv (2009), 811–32

Morley, C., 'Catalogue of the Beneficed Clergy of Suffolk, 1086–1550', *Proceedings of the Suffolk Institute of Archaeology*, xxii (1934–6), 29–85

Payling, S.J., 'The Waning of Noble Lordship in Late Fifteenth Century England?', *Parliamentary History*, xiii (1994), 322–32

——, 'The Economics of Marriage in Late Medieval England: The Marriage of Heiresses', *Econ HR*, liv (2001), 413–29

——, *Political Society in Lancastrian England. The Greater Gentry of Nottinghamshire* (Oxford, 1991)

Pollard, A.F., 'Council, Star Chamber and Privy Council under the Tudors', *EHR*, xxxvii (1922), 516–39

Pollard, A.J., *John Talbot and the War in France* (London, 1983)

——, *North-Eastern England During the Wars of the Roses. Lay Society, War and Politics, 1450–1500* (Oxford, 1990)

——, *Warwick the Kingmaker: Politics, Power and Fame* (London, 2007)

Poos, L.R., *A Rural Society after the Black Death: Essex, 1350–1525* (Cambridge, 1991)

Powell, J.E, 'The Riddle of Bures', *TEAS*, third series, vi (1974), 90–8

Powell, J. E. and Wells, K., *The House of Lords in the Middle Ages* (London, 1968)

Probert, G., 'The Riddle of Bures Unravelled', *TEAS*, third series, xvi (1984–5), 53–64

Pugh, T.B., 'Henry VII and the English Nobility', in *The Tudor Nobility*, ed. G.W. Bernard (Manchester, 1992), 49–110

——, 'The Magnates, Knights and Gentry', in *Fifteenth Century England*, ed. S.B Chrimes, C.D. Ross and R.A. Griffiths (Manchester, 1972), 86–128

——, *Henry V and the Southampton Plot* (Southampton, 1988)

Rawcliffe, C., 'Baronial Councils in the Later Middle Ages', in *Patronage, Pedigree and Power*, ed. C.D. Ross (Stroud, 1979), 87–108

——, 'The Great Lord as Peacekeeper: Arbitration by English Noblemen and their Councils in the Later Middle Ages', in *Law and Social Change in British History*.

Papers Presented to the Bristol Legal History Conference 14–17 July 1981, ed. J.A. Guy and H.G. Beale (London, 1984), 34–54

——, *The Staffords, Earls of Stafford and Dukes of Buckingham* (Cambridge, 1978)

Rawcliffe C. and Flower, S., 'English Noblemen and their Advisors: Consultation and Collaboration in the Later Middle Ages', *Journal of British Studies*, xxv (1986), 157–77

Richmond, C.F., 'The Nobility and the Wars of the Roses, 1459–61', *Nottingham Medieval Studies*, xxi (1977), 71–85

——, 'After McFarlane', *History*, lxvi (1983), 46–60

——, 'The Murder of Thomas Dennis', *Common Knowledge*, ii (1993), 85–98

——, 'The Nobility and the Wars of the Roses: The Parliamentary Session of January 1461', *Parliamentary History*, xviii (1999), 261–9

——, 'East Anglian Politics and Society in the Fifteenth Century', in *Medieval East Anglia*, ed. C. Harper-Bill (Woodbridge, 2005), 183–208

——, *The Paston Family in the Fifteenth Century. The First Phase* (Cambridge, 1990)

——, *The Paston Family in the Fifteenth Century. Fastolf's Will* (Cambridge, 1996)

——, *The Paston Family in the Fifteenth Century: Endings* (Manchester, 2000)

Roskell, J.S., Clark, L. and Rawcliffe, C., ed., *History of Parliament: The House of Commons, 1386–1421* (Stroud, 1992)

Ross, C.D., *Edward IV* (London, 1974)

——, *The Wars of the Roses* (London, 1976)

——, *Richard III* (London, 1981)

Ross, C.D. and Pugh T.B., 'The English Baronage and the Income Tax of 1436', *Historical Research*, xxvi (1953), 1–28

——, 'Materials for the Study of Baronial Incomes in Fifteenth Century England', *Econ HR*, vi (1953), 185–94

Ross, J., 'Seditious Activities? The Conspiracy of Maud de Vere, Countess of Oxford, 1403–4', in *The Fifteenth Century III: Authority and Subversion*, ed. L. Clark (Woodbridge, 2003), 25–41

—— 'Richard Duke of Gloucester and the de Vere Estates', *The Ricardian*, xv (2005), 20–32

——, 'Essex County Society and the French War in the Fifteenth Century', in *The Fifteenth Century VII: Conflicts, Consequences and the Crown in the Late Middle Ages*, ed. L. Clark (Woodbridge, 2007), 53–80

Round, J.H., 'Two Great Vere Documents', *TEAS*, n.s., xiv (1918), 298–302

——, *The King's Serjeants and Officers of State with their Coronation Services* (London, 1911)

Rowling, M.A., 'New Evidence on the Disseisin of the Pastons from their Norfolk Manor of Gresham, 1448–1451', *Norfolk Archaeology*, xl (1989), 302–8

Rowse, A.L., 'The Turbulent Career of Sir Henry Bodrugan', *History*, xxix (1944), 17–26.

Sayer, M., 'Norfolk Involvement in Dynastic Conflict, 1467–71 and 1483–7', *Norfolk Archaeology*, xxxvi (1977), 305–26

Scofield, C.L., 'The Early Life of John de Vere, Earl of Oxford', *EHR*, xxxix (1914), 228–45

——, *The Life and Reign of Edward IV* (2 vols, London, 1923)

Smith, G., *The Coronation of Elizabeth Woodville* (London, 1935)

Somerville, R., *History of the Duchy of Lancaster* (2 vols, London, 1953–1970)

Squib, G.O., *The High Court of Chivalry* (Oxford, 1981)

Starkey, D., *Henry: Virtuous Prince* (London, 2008)

Storey, R.L., *The End of the House of Lancaster* (London, 1966)

Stourton, C.B.J, ed., *The History of the Noble House of Stourton* (2 vols, London, 1899)

Taylor, T., *St. Michael's Mount* (Cambridge, 1932)

Thomson, J.A.F., '"The Arrival of Edward IV" – the Development of the Text', *Speculum*, xlvi (1971), 84–93

——, 'John de la Pole, Duke of Suffolk', *Speculum*, liv (1979), 528–42

Townsend, G.J., *History of the Great Chamberlainship of England* (London, 1934)

Tucker, M.J., 'Household Accounts, 1490–1, of John de Vere, Earl of Oxford', *EHR*, lxxv (1960), 468–74

——, *The Life of Thomas Howard, Earl of Surrey and Second Duke of Norfolk, 1443–1524* (The Hague, 1964)

Tucker, P., 'The Early History of the Court of Chancery', *EHR*, cxv (2000), 791–811

Vernon-Harcourt, L.W., *His Grace the Steward and the Trial of Peers* (London, 1907)

Victoria County History: Berkshire (4 vols, London, 1906–1924)

Victoria County History: Buckinghamshire (4 vols, London, 1902–1927)

Victoria County History: Cambridgeshire (10 vols, London, 1938–2002)

Victoria County History: Essex (10 vols, London, 1903–2001)

Victoria County History: Hampshire and the Isle of Wight (5 vols, London, 1900–1912)

Victoria County History: Northamptonshire (4 vols, London, 1902–1937)

Victoria County History: Oxfordshire (15 vols, London, 1907–2006)

Victoria County History: Rutland (2 vols, London, 1908–1935)

Virgoe, R., 'A New Fragment of the Lord's Journal of 1461', *BIHR*, xxxii (1959), 83–7

——, 'Three Suffolk Parliamentary Elections of the Mid Fifteenth Century', *BIHR*, xxxix (1966), 185–96

——, 'The Composition of the King's Council, 1437–61', *BIHR*, xliii (1970), 134–60

——, 'The Recovery of the Howards in East Anglia, 1485–1529', in *Wealth and Power in Tudor England*, ed. E.W. Ives, R.J. Knecht and J.J. Scarisbrick (London, 1978), 1–20

——, 'Crown, Magnates and Local Government in Fifteenth Century East Anglia', in *The Crown and Local Communities in England and France in the Fifteenth Century*, ed. J.R.L. Highfield and R.M. Jeffs (Gloucester, 1981), 72–87

——, 'Sir John Risley (1443–1512), Courtier and Councillor', *Norfolk Archaeology*, 140–8.

——, 'An Election Dispute of 1483', *Historical Research*, lx (1987), 24–44

Ward, J., 'Elizabeth Beaumont, Countess of Oxford (d. 1537): Her Life and Connections', *Transactions of the Monumental Brass Society*, xvii (2003), 2–13

Watts, J.L., '"A New Ffundacion of is Crowne": Monarchy in the Age of Henry VII', in *The Reign of Henry VII*, ed. B. Thomson (Stamford, 1995), 31–53

——, *Henry VI and the Politics of Kingship* (Cambridge, 1996)

Wedgwood, J.C., *The History of Parliament 1439–1509* (2 vols, London, 1936–8)

Westervelt, T., 'The Changing Nature of Politics in the Localities in the Later Fifteenth Century: William Lord Hastings and his Indentured Retainers', *Midland History*, xxvi (2001), 96–106

Westfall, S.R., *Patrons and Performance. Early Tudor Household Revels* (Oxford, 1990)

Williams, C.H., 'The Rebellion of Humphrey Stafford in 1486', *EHR*, xliii (1928), 181–9

Wolffe, B.P., *Henry VI* (London, 1981)

Woolgar, C.M., *The Great Household in Late Medieval England* (London, 1999)

Unpublished Theses

Archer, R.E., 'The Mowbrays, Earls of Nottingham and Dukes of Norfolk, to 1432' (D.Phil thesis, Oxford University, 1984)

Bernard, G.W., 'The Fourth and Fifth Earls of Shrewsbury: A Study in the Power of the Early Tudor Nobility' (D.Phil thesis, Oxford University, 1978)

Cavill, P., 'Henry VII and Parliament' (D.Phil thesis, Oxford University, 2005)

Cunningham, S, 'The Establishment of the Tudor Regime: Henry VII, Rebellion, and the Financial Control of the Aristocracy, 1485–1509' (PhD thesis, Lancaster University, 1995)

Harrison, W.E.C., 'Maritime Activity under Henry VII' (MA dissertation, University of London, 1931)

Jones, M.K., 'The Beaufort Family and the Wars in France, 1421–1450' (PhD thesis, Bristol University, 1982)

Moye, L.E., 'The Estates and Finances of the Mowbray family, Earls Marshal and Dukes of Norfolk, 1401–76' (PhD thesis, Duke University, 1985)

Pollard, A.J., 'The Family of Talbot, Lords Talbot and Earls of Shrewsbury in the Fifteenth Century' (PhD thesis, Bristol University, 1968)

Richmond, C.F., 'Royal Administration and the Keeping of the Seas, 1422–85' (D.Phil, Oxford University, 1962)

Ross, C.D., 'The Yorkshire Baronage, 1399–1435' (D.Phil thesis, Oxford University, 1951)

Ross, J., 'The De Vere Earls of Oxford, 1400–1513' (D.Phil thesis, Oxford University, 2005)

Stansfield, M.M.N., 'The Holland Family, Dukes of Exeter, Earls of Kent and Huntingdon, 1352–1475' (D.Phil thesis, Oxford University, 1987)

Starr, C., 'The Essex Gentry, 1381–1450' (PhD thesis, University of Leicester, 1999)

Thomas, R.S., 'The Political Career, Estates and "Connection" of Jasper Tudor, Earl of Pembroke and Duke of Bedford (d. 1495)' (D.Phil thesis, University of Wales, Swansea, 1971)

Woodger, L.S., 'Henry Bourgchier, Earl of Essex and his Family, 1408–1483' (D.Phil thesis, Oxford University, 1974)

Index

Members of royal families are indexed under their Christian name and peers under their family name. People and places appearing in both the text and footnote on the same page are indexed only under the page reference, with no separate reference to the footnote.

Lightning Source UK Ltd.
Milton Keynes UK
UKOW06f0746270916

283835UK00006B/282/P